Innocents of the West

INNOCENTS
OF
THE WEST

Travels Through the Sixties

JOAN COLEBROOK

Basic Books, Inc., Publishers

NEW YORK

Library of Congress Cataloging in Publication Data

Colebrook, Joan.
　Innocents of the West.

　1.　Social history—1960–1970　I.　Title.
HN16.C64　　　309.1'046　　　78-54504
ISBN 0–465–03295–8

Will the democracies consent to their own survival?

William Stevenson
(from the introduction to *A Man Called Intrepid*)

Foreword

This journal owes its existence to the reading of a *Diary of a Man in Despair*—remnant of a record written and hidden during the rise of Nazi power. Buried in the ground in the woods near the author's home, dug up often, and re-hidden again so that they were never long in one place—the pages of this diary present a painful image of one individual's preoccupation with the oppressive future. They record the unpleasant, unimportant, even laughable impression Hitler created as he visited Austrian villages before he became chancellor. They describe—as the Nazi movement grew in strength—the darkening of a civilization.

It was the "immediacy" of Count Percyval Reck-Malleczewen's diary, and not its doomlike mood, which prompted me to start recording my own rather different observations, experiences, reading, conversations, and interviews. Yet if no close similarity existed, if here in "fortunate" America in 1964, no vast internal terror loomed (as it did in Germany thirty years before), some wider global threat seemed to exist; and this "asking" to be recorded developed and became clearer from day to day. One might say that this "threat" was just the threat of history, that all ages are clouded with catastrophic possibilities, yet all ages are not alike. Our age is a nuclear age, in which—war being too expensive—the natural tool of deceit comes into its own, and subversion becomes a "growth industry." It is an age of total power, in which the democracies lose their confidence and the individual voice has little resonance. It is also an age when slaughter is carried out, not only without pity but with technological exactitude—unfortunately it is in our own twentieth century that we must expect ever more ingenious experiments in human control.

Acknowledgments

The author gratefully acknowledges permission to reprint the following:

Portions of "Cario Journal," by Joan Colebrook, which appeared in *Commentary*, October 1970. Copyright © 1970 by the American Jewish Committee.

Some of the material on pp. 149–151 and pp. 181–186 appeared originally in *The New Yorker* in slightly different form. © 1970 The New Yorker Magazine, Inc.

1964

THE WEST COAST

November 17, 1964

Night. The last flight from Boston to Los Angeles, via Baltimore, Chicago, Kansas City, St. Louis. The enormous unwieldy plane, moving slowly across what is seen as a field of blue illuminated flowers, splashed here and there with a glow of poppy red. As the long monster, in whose entrails we sit, lifts into the air, it rises above an urban vision of craglike piles of lumber and dull water to which cling palpitating adherences of light.

Inside the plane everything is on a flatter level. The hostesses with their polished nails, high heels, and stiff little uniforms wear tricorns of greenish-yellow and sway along the aisle in tune to tinkling piano music. They look like pages in some faintly dated comedy; serving dinner in paper wraps, offering coffee to men with hair like fur, and to women who are already discarding their shoes and leaning untidy coiffures against tiny white pillows.

Later, long insulated from the mystery of the night, we sink through levels of darkness to the tarmac of some strange city. ("Is this Mississippi?" a child asks fretfully.) Here the plane is wheeled effortlessly past great hangars lit up like theaters and branded with scarlet letters, past enormous domes cut by white pillars and marked in depthless gold, Transworld.

November 18

5 A.M. Arrival in Los Angeles. Descent to what Ginsberg calls "the metal-faced terminal."

The Foundation has low, white buildings and is built in a deep

3

fenced-in canyon on the coastal side of the city. At this early hour the involutions of the earth—carpeted with eucalyptus, acacia, agave, tamarisk, sagebush—enfold the Community house, the pool, the studios, barn, and sheds. From one particular studio, and into a landscape framed by a huge glass window (enclosing a scene of rocks, and smooth eucalypt trunks, all of it still dimmed and made unreal by white drifting fragments of mist), there is seen delicately a huge deer with spread antlers, followed by a doe and a fawn, moving rapidly and almost soundlessly. The procession disappears down a tunnel of brown leaves.

12 A.M.

I have come to California to write in peace for a few months, and the leisure is precious after work in the Boston slums, and day by day encounters with pathology, crime, and racial maladjustment. Now I have escaped to the fresh, warmish canyon air, filled with the resin of pine and eucalyptus: a perfume bringing back with nostalgia, a long-ago early life spent in Australia. Other escapees are scattered up and down the canyon on this, which seems to be an average working day. Certain writers stand thoughtfully knee-deep in dried grass, or perch on sun-bleached stumps. A devotee of art nouveau paints with shades drawn (portraits of ladies in pink velvet with hair like serpents, young men with greenish skin leaning against scrolled woodwork). Another artist prefers to sketch outside, using vast sheets of paper and Japanese felt pens. The sound of notes struck again and again echoes faintly from a composer's studio perched high above the coast road.

On the hillside which is parched from an unusually long dry season, the roots come helplessly from the soil. Pieces of earth slide. A pebble falls to the empty river bed, making a high metallic music.

The Foundation station wagon transports us to nearby Santa Monica, where a pale sun gleams on an almost empty beach, and ladies in elaborate hats parade along straight streets lined with palms. Inland, a network of avenues mounts the low elevations of Beverly Hills, where simple wooden California houses are glossed over with luxury (private decks jutting from bedrooms, Greek pillars uselessly festooning entryways, swimming pools transforming backyards, and outside lighting effects turning mere plants into tropical gardens).

Along the coast and to the south, crowded picturesque structures cling to piers and encircle socially-sacred stretches of sand (to these centers came the antimaterialistic beats, the flower children, the dreamers, the hippies). Now the whole long strip of coastline, which stretches from southern San Francisco to southern Los Angeles, has become politically productive; the extended summer and the crowded beach enclaves foster intimate cults and groups; the loud vociferous conversations nourish and sharpen dissatisfactions.

Watching the procession of cars skimming over the white boulevards which enter and leave Santa Monica, it is easy to remember the restless motion which influenced followers of Kerouac and Ginsberg, who "ate the lamb's stew of imagination"; those poets with "pacifist eyes," those "saintly motor-cyclists," those "human seraphim" who sat quietly and smoked on the roofs.

But ephemeral memories are soon lost in a solid, anonymous matrix which spreads out into endless humbler avenues (glimpsed only on a trip to a far-off parcel depot near the railway station). Here a world takes over which is less articulate and less aware of despair. Over the heads of these inhabitants have rolled all the liberation movements of the America of the early sixties—the rallies, the demonstrations, the sexual freeing, the scientology, the warlockry, the subliminal motivation (for them something more fundamental and closer to home: the fist, the pill, the hypodermic). Here are the true activists, kin of the teddy boys of England, the *blousons noir* of France, the *raggare* of Sweden, the thunder boys of Japan, the *stilyagi* of Russia. More importantly, these outsiders (with little understanding and almost against their will) are helping to usher in a political drama. They follow the students of Istanbul who managed to topple the government of Menderes; they swell the 76,000 crowd of students rioting outside the Diet building in Tokyo which forced Eisenhower to cancel his visit; they learn the methods of civil disobedience in India from the students of Pathumwan Technical Institute.

Yet it is among the discontented middle class, in the enclaves of students and intellectuals, that another movement takes place—a vague neo-Communist gathering of forces, colored emotionally by an urge for change. In this the fume of old memories is important (for instance, Ginsberg: "America, when I was seven Mama took me to Communist cell meetings . . . Mother Bloor made me cry," etc.). A fresh political outreaching is asked for. Drug-food is not forbidden. The guru-poet recommends "alcohol, cock, and endless balls." Even the sexual outsider is beckoned to the Revolution. ("America, I'm putting my queer shoulder to the wheel.")

November 20

The poet who inhabits a nearby studio is rather handsome in a raffish way; tall with a small, beaked nose and dark eyes. He writes competent and non-nourishing poetry; there is a distinctly ideological cast to all his conversations. (In fact it is possible to gather from it a blueprint of current political fashions—that it is *de rigueur*, for instance, to dislike the Establishment, to hate the Vietnam war, to accept the counterculture, to be interested in the perception-extending power of drugs, and to be what is loosely called "committed." (According to this blueprint it is also necessary to read the works of such gurus as Marcuse, C. Wright Mills, Régis Debray, and Ché Guevara.) B—'s conversation employs certain clichés which are generally used to establish ascendancy. A discussion will begin with the preface "For those who are *obsessed* with law and order. . . ."or "If you feel it possible to even *consider* our participation in an unjust war. . . ." or "Like most of the older generation, he is *afraid* of LSD. . . ." The use of these key words suggests that individuals who dare to differ are obsessed, unjust, and afraid; that it takes an extreme rightist to be concerned with lawlessness, a paranoid to mention that Ho Chi Minh is an old-time Stalinist, a timorous oldster to question little-known drugs. They also suggest that Communism is after all no longer "taboo," that Stalin may be criticized, but that other worthy Communist leaders remain—Trotsky, Mao, Fidel, Ché—leaders much to be preferred to the Western "servants of Capitalism and Imperialism."

No longer do the young sit at the feet of the old, to hear those tales of the past customarily handed down from generation to generation. Now youth often meets age with a headlong lack of grace. Stewart, a short broad man with an affable, rosy face, is seventy-four years old; an extrovert with a long history of allegiance to the political Left. Once admiring of and hopeful for the United States Communist party—and like most of the intelligentsia of the thirties rounded up to support it— he later became disillusioned, and because of this took his share of vilification. His current political view is one of irascible anger. He remembers long-vanished confusions and deceptions. He loses some of his self-control and is apt to launch into bitter monologic musings.

Tonight at the dinner table, as he recounts conflicts with Stalinists who continued to believe in the fake trials of the thirties, he clashes with B—.

B—, who was probably scarcely alive during the thirties, lapses into stony silence; it is obvious that he can't compete with the historical view. (What is at issue, i.e., the need to join forces against the drive for total control of the human being, is buried under the immediacy of current events, under the polarization caused by the Vietnam War, the striving of the Civil Rights movement, and the riots in the cities.) But B— as in former discussions, seems to have no fear of that coarse folk hero, the *Tyrannosaurus Rex*, who might rise again from the mud of a revolutionary age, this time with a whole army of well-trained technicians beside him. It is easy for B— to show his scorn for Stewart (who has recently begun to press slightly worn-looking manuscripts onto reluctant readers and to bring sonorous poems with nineteenth-century meters to be read during the coffee hour).

Two days later—Stewart, in one of his more exuberant and irrational moods, announces that he is one of the greatest living American poets! His face, which is sometimes beautifully calm and rosy, is today congested with the reflection of his own decline, as leaves are reddened with the approach of the end of their lives. He pauses to demand the attention of those at the coffee table. "I've written more poetry than Robinson Jeffers and more prose than James T. Farrell!" His wife W— seems rather embarrassed. Stewart looks around with a challenging expression and concentrates upon his rival B—. But B— refuses to be engaged and takes the first opportunity to leave the room. Later when someone accuses B— of unnecessary rudeness, he replies that Stewart can't teach *him* anything, a statement which is certainly in line with the times. To sharpen the point, B— mutters that listening to Stewart is an effort: "It makes me feel that I'm shut up in an old people's home."

November 22

Today is the anniversary of the John F. Kennedy assassination—that event from which seems to date a certain American failure of nerve. The Warren Report (released on September 28) has been supplemented by twenty-six volumes of hearings, enough to fill a whole bookshelf. What is noticeable (and the more noticeable considering the controversies already surrounding the release of the material) is that the report not only concludes that Oswald acted alone but states that he had "no political motivation." (This in spite of his defection to the USSR; his telling the United States consular authorities that he had offered to deliver to the Soviet Union the secrets he had been exposed to as a radar specialist; his later attempts to join the Socialist Workers Party— SWP—a Trotskyist group; his support of the Fair Play for Cuba Committee—FPCC; and a well-traced antagonism to the enemies of Cuba—JFK, General Edwin Walker, Nixon.) This conclusion on the part of the commission may have something to do with the tendency of a functioning democracy to hew to the stable line and lean religiously away from all suggestion of political conspiracy.

In any case, this strange solitary devotee of Marxism—who was so far from the subversive life in his own country that he only knew the words of the "Internationale" in Russian; the grown-up fourteen-year-old who told Aline Mosby of the UPI in Moscow that when he discovered a copy of *Das Kapital* on a dusty shelf in the New Orleans library, he felt like a "very religious man opening the Bible for the first time"; the captured assassin who admitted under interrogation that it was Karl Marx he was religious about—may go down in the history which he so exalts as a non-political!

Stewart says that it is uncomfortable to watch Moscow and Havana blending their propaganda with Mark Lane's! B—, on the other hand, delights in dwelling on the certainty that Mark Lane is right and that the CIA is "deeply" involved.

It seems a new departure in the face of a national tragedy of such magnitude that Russian and Cuban experts in psychological warfare demonstrate so macabre a confidence. It is bad enough that they have the confidence to attack from without. It is much worse, and stimulates a sense of restlessness and unease, to see them concerting their attacks with the help of those within (not to mention the chorus from Western Europe). Even the aging Bertrand Russell in England (who had attacked Kennedy's "aggression" during the missile crisis and had sent him a preemptory cable: "Your action desperate. No conceivable justification") quarreled immediately with the verdict of the report and called it a "disgrace." When asked how he had managed to read it less than twenty-four hours after its publication in the United States, Russell admitted that he had not read it but that his opinion came from a transatlantic phone call from Mark Lane. So the big lie was carefully transported across the Atlantic.

November 30

First encounter with practical, California student politics, a visit from a student from Berkeley, who had taken part in the picketing of the Sheraton-Palace Hotel in San Francisco (this led by a Negro girl of eighteen called Tracey Sims). The student has long black shining hair and a pretty, even thoughtful, face. "Yes, the hotel was charged with discrimination, although as it turned out," her voice grows doubtful, "it was all somewhat controversial. The hotel claimed that it hired 7 percent of its personnel from minority groups, and the committee which ran our demonstration (the Ad Hoc Committee to End Racial Discrimination) maintained that they hired only 2 percent of Negroes in a city where Negroes made up 11 percent of the population."

And had she herself gone to the demonstration out of enthusiasm for the cause?

"Well . . . of course I'm for equal hiring . . . but I must admit that I went out of boredom, and because of the pressure of militant friends. Some of the group had been in the civil rights movement in the South.

That influenced the rest of us; there we were, chanting 'Jim Crow must go' and 'Freedom now.' "

And what happened?

"Well we walked around for hours. The committee monitors told us 'Take off all earrings and bracelets. . . . All those under eighteen please leave the lines. When they arrest you, lock arms and go limp.' At 11:00 P.M. about 1,500 of us went into the hotel, and of course the TV cameras came. It was a question as to whether to be arrested or to sleep-in. A vote was taken and showed that a large majority preferred sleep-in to arrest. Ten minutes later, however, the announcement came. 'A vote was taken—we're going to be arrested.' A cry went up: 'What vote?'

"The vote it turned out had been a three-to-two vote of the Ad Hoc Committee. Finally it was the police who arrested us. One by one the picketers were lifted and carried out by four policemen each to the paddy wagon. One girl screamed 'Facist! Beast!,' but she certainly wasn't being hurt! . . . I noticed that Tracy was talking to a variety of people, but all of them were within the same radical group."

And you were arrested?

"No . . . finally after 167 demonstrators had been carted off, the rest of us were told we could leave. . . . I couldn't help wondering what the arrestees would think. They had expected to be followed by hundreds of others loyal to the cause!"

And in the end what was your own verdict?

She hesitates. Obviously she has some doubt about the spontaneity of the whole thing—not only some sense of having been manipulated by the Ad Hoc Committee, but reservations about the actuality of racial discrimination on the part of the hotel.

"Well I don't know how I feel." She appears to have vague premonitions which don't please her. "What I am afraid of is that it's going to become harder and harder to remain neutral."

December 1

It is the Christmas month. Blue birds frequent a certain tree on the canyon's side. They have azure wings, their breasts are striped with grey, their shoulders are greenish brown. When their wings suddenly open in flight, an ineffable light cuts across the sky.

See for the first time the Christmas cholla, with its long thin jointed stem, its ripening red fruits. It is still hot enough to smell the eucalyptus and the sage; there is always that sense of extended leisure, of a hiatus of reflection in the middle of the whirlwind. Somewhere far ahead on one of the paths, a fellow colonist walks slowly, wearing a blue skirt and a red sweatshirt, her figure passing in and out of the trees as if through a pillared temple.

December 2

Politics of the past increasingly confront those of the present; as if all across the board some reassessment were under way. Stewart, trying to resist the baiting of the younger supporters of the New Left, recalls a time when certain figures—Max Eastman for instance—were pilloried for dissent by the fashionable Left. "Don't you know that even today in certain circles, Max remains a traitor, a pariah? Yet all he did was to supply very necessary political information to his former comrades. This was considered a sin. Mike Gold wrote about it in the *Daily Worker*. He said something like 'Max Eastman—former friend—you are a filthy and deliberate liar!' "

A few of those present began to laugh. Some, too young to be occupied with a Stalinist period long gone by, simply look puzzled.

Talk continues into the night. From one corner a quiet little anthropologist remarks that in a country new enough to be uncertain of its moral condition, the "Club" would tend to be to the Left. "You see that if the old world has to be down-graded, then *all* conservatism tends to be 'bad.' " The anthropologist is listened to with respect, partly because she often uses scientific terms which lend objectivity to her conversation. She notes that the current political scene differs from that of the thirties. B— asks what she means. "One gets the feeling now that the laboratory findings of Soviet behavioral scientists are being applied to the indoctrination process. The idea of inevitablity is suggested, then driven home by certain Marxist successes. Obviously, the present sequence of arrests and confrontations with the police is reinforced by hostile bodily contact; the idea of the political martyr is also used. This encourages emotional escalation. With such a blending of suggestive experiences the whole idea of struggle soon becomes obsessive."

Somewhat ostentatiously, B—has left the room.

December 4

More West Coast politics. Apparently eight students have been suspended at Berkeley and given punishments by the Board of Regents. The result has been a sit-in of 800 sympathizers at Sproul Hall, led by Joan Baez and Mario Savio. (Just as they call the radical house in Madison "Kremlin-West," so the area in front of Sproul Hall is named "Red Square.")

Now it is seen that Mario Savio is using a lot of physical images. Apparently he wants those sympathizers to *feel* the coercion of the law. He calls out: "You have to put your body on the levers of the machine."

1964 / The West Coast

(Mario Savio is distinguished for having bitten a policeman on the hip but also for being known as a "Trotskyist"—which since the Trotskyists should be the bitter enemies of the Communists, poses the question as to whether there is now a gentlemen's agreement among radicals. Today, at all events, the radical scene has spread, and the Marxist message, or what passes for it, stretches beyond Moscow and Peking and Eastern Europe, to Algiers, Hanoi, Pyongyang, Havana. Moreover the point seems to be that this multiplication of radical centers, if creating problems for the Soviets from the point of view of the international Communist movement, also acts as a stimulus; so that the United States and the West in general, instead of being faced by one simple monolith, may be faced instead with a universal situation of revolution.)

The seemingly unimportant fact that Mario Savio is a Trotskyist rouses a current interest in Trotsky himself; in fact, that here in Berkeley a Trotskyist can play so prominent a role is only one small indication of the importance of the Marxist legend on the campuses of the world.

As his biographer Isaac Deutscher points out, Trotsky was in disagreement with Lenin for five years and in bitter opposition to Stalin for more than twenty, during which time the KGB hunted him down with a monumental patience, at last gaining entrance to his Mexico City study, where an agent buried an alpine pick in that great and active brain.

However useless it may be to theorize about what would have happened had Trotsky held power instead of Stalin, it is clear that while he had come to grips with important issues—"bureaucratic degeneration," the "infallibility of the party," "repression of free debate"—he too undertook reprisals, he too was hypnotized by the stern authoritarianism of the "possessed" intellectual. Ideologically it might be said that Trotsky was the victim of certain predictions and "necessary" ideas (that the working class *must* be the chief actor in social revolution, that the revolution *must* be global, that society *must* keep developing through social collisions—in other words that the revolution *must* be permanent). But he at least entertained, as Isaac Deutscher, his biographer, records, the possibility that the "system of the USSR could be the precursor of a new and universal system of exploitation." He realized that during the worldwide campaign against the Trotskyist heresy—that time of horror when, as Ciliga says, "The workers were hungry and cried for bread but the government threw them human flesh"—the question of Stalinism was not solved. Nor was it solved in the Far East where Trotskyism had been brought to Shanghai and Wuhan in 1927, and where some leaders were later to acknowledge that the opposition criticisms of Stalin were well-founded. But the situation in which Mao found himself—attempting to carry on the struggle in a remote rural area—made such an ideology sectarian and negative. Trotsky could not have known that soon after his death the greatest revolutionary advances were to be played out in the East (and not in the developed countries of the West as he had hoped). Nor could he have known that the Stalinism he abhorred should have flowered again there, and would with all its fantastic regimentation be here linked with his name. In these ideological struggles the truth seems to be glimpsed rather than exposed. The Russian experiment had an inbuilt stripping process. At the core of the Stalin-Trotsky rivalry there lay the problem of free debate inside the party; and automatically one goes back to that day when at a session of the Central Committee, Trotsky was shouted down by Stalin's followers, and inkpots, books, a glass—not to speak of threats and curses— were thrown at his head, to the cry of "Go—Go—Get out!" And at once there comes a flashback to an earlier day, when Trotsky himself, watching Martov lead the Mensheviks in their exodus from the Soviets, had shouted in the same way (in this case, "Go—Go—to the dustbin of history!").

December 6

Into the heart of Los Angeles by public transportation. What seems like an interminable bus ride under a heavy fog of pollution, creating a gloom more oppressive than any created by nature.

Nor is the day's experience enlivening, devoted as it is to research into Marxist influences among the students—and all the boring ramifications which this involves. One professor says that the "messianic avenger type" seems at work on the campuses. He says that the 1959 convention of the United States Communist party decided that the time had come for a new youth drive. "Perhaps this was because it was obvious that many of the old timers were getting tired and somewhat out of it. The present generation was not hostile to Communism; it knew little about the stealing of the United States nuclear secrets in the forties, or about the aggression involved in the Korean War—or even about the taking over of Eastern Europe. You will find they are extremely vague about political action. At all events, the Politburo must have felt that American youth could be pushed in what they call a progressive direction.

"It is all laid out in the 1960 Communist Party journal *Political Affairs*. Attention is drawn to the disorganization which has resulted from the baby boom. As you know, we got more than a million extra students last year. Naturally each generation is born with new confidence and innocence. I myself have been in a position to see some of the young leaders who got into organizing."

And which leaders were those?

"Well, Douglas Wachter (whose parents were in the party) was one of them. He's been playing a key role in organizing mass student disorder and rioting; and he had gone to the 1959 Communist party conference as a Berkeley delegate." The Professor gives a resigned sigh. "It seems to have been decided what slogans would best succeed. Madison Avenue has been the educator to those who theoretically want to do it in!"

And the slogans?

"Well, there was Civil Rights. . . . And Peace. And the special favorite, Jim Crow Must Go. And of course Get out of Vietnam and Hands Off Cuba."

How many of the young activists, like Wachter for instance, inherited radical tendencies from their parents?

The Professor smiles. "It's interesting that while the student mass, that is, the rank and file, are being asked not to trust anyone over thirty (that is, their parents), the student *leaders* are certainly not liberated from *their* parents—in fact many of them have been indoctrinated since they were infants!

"By the way, Tom Hayden of Students for a Democratic Society (SDS) also spent a summer here in 1960. He was an understudy or observer of Wachter, and also of Wachter's older Communist party comrade, Archie Brown, who was hardly a student, since he was a veteran of the Stalinist brigade of the Spanish war!" (Another leader of the present activities meets the requirements of Professor K—Bettina Aptheker— daughter of an old-time Communist party national committeeman— who left home in 1962 to enter Berkeley, where she organized the first chapter of the Communist party's new youth front, the W. E. B. DuBois clubs. (She also led the Hands Off Cuba picket line during the missile crisis not to mention her role now as one of the chief organizers of the Free Speech Movement Steering Committee.)

On leaving the Professor's study we pause in the street. "I don't want you to think that I give too much credit to the CPUSA, or that I don't allow weight to the multiplicity of radical parties and their diffuse influence. It is rather that the essential structure of Marxism, and the body of knowledge that Marxist experience has accumulated, is of great importance now. Students have stoutly defended their leaders against accusations of Communism, saying that their fathers are Communists, but *they* are not. They also claim to have abandoned all rigid ideologies themselves. And in a very narrow sense they may be right. These students have been subjected to diverse influences—to the Cold War, to Fidel's guerrilla-style victory, to the romantic cult of Mao's peasant warriors, to Frantz Fanon, Ché Guevara, and so on. But what the students don't talk of is the tremendous global spread of Marxist and neo-Marxist works. It is estimated, by the way, that there are millions of party members in 106 different countries; and the works of Marx are certainly translated more often than the Bible. As to how many terrorists are trained and graduated from the new revolutionary academies, I don't know, but certainly enough to make effective what is being called a state of 'revolutionary pluralism.' " (At this moment, the Professor's insights and his use of that phrase put new coherence into my own scattered thinking about curent radical forces. The recrudescence of Trotskyism for instance, and the popularity of Mao and Fidel with the young—these could obviously help to form a powerful new, united front on a global scale.)

The amorphous nature of the New Left, now daily publicized, doesn't seem as harmless as the enthusiasts in the canyon insist it is. The Progressive Labor Party (PLP, the pro-Peking group) is said to be involved in pushing drugs, and there is talk of Red China making these available. (San Francisco, gateway to the Pacific and Southeast Asia, is supposed to harbor a large share of the 4000 Chinese who illegally enter the United States each year; and one of the newspapers has brought up the old case of November in 1952 when a large quantity of heroin characteristic of China's Yunnan province was confiscated from a smuggler on the deck of the *S.S. President Wilson*. Likewise in the fifties there was the offer of 430 tons of opium from Communist China in exchange for U.S. cotton, and a further offer of 500 tons to the British Imperial Chemical Industries, Ltd. in Prince's Building, Hong Kong—the last resulting in an expostulatory letter from the British government to the United Nations Narcotics Commission. The theory now is that these astounding quantities of opium from Communist China slowly found their way into the illegal drug market, some of it to the "beat" market of San Francisco. It is besides only a few years since Japan's bitter complaints about the trade in heroin which was inaugurated during the Korean War, and passed from Canton to North Korea via Kobe.) [Later this year a Soviet journalist, W. Ovchinnikov, charged in *Pravda* that the Chinese ran a narcotics trade worth 80 million dollars a year. The poison, he said, was being passed on to the West in return for "capitalist dollars which were being used for anti-Soviet propaganda." Ovchinnikov said sarcastically that this opium production was the only successful part of the Great Leap Forward!]

This morning a girl knocks at the studio door before breakfast. She is pale, and the flesh of her bare arms is blue and puckered. She admits that she had spent the previous evening "getting high" with a small group in one of the other studios; and afterwards had wandered about restlessly—in fact she had been up all night. "I was just walking," she insists. "It really got to me. God, I've been everywhere since I started." She ends up by sobbing violently. For the first time I hear the revival of an old word: "stoned."

Rather suitably, yesterday the papers headlined an incident in Santa Monica where several children between the ages of eleven and fourteen were rushed to the hospital after a party. A twenty-seven-year-old student had given wine and beer to all present; the children had added to this effect by sniffing glue. The result was damage to the lungs, unconsciousness, paralysis and, in one case, death. It is all very reminiscent of Boston and New York City.

Afterwards it is a relief to go outside, to see a bird with a bright orange beak with brilliant black and white wings, swaying on some bush loaded with hard black berries. Disturbed, it throws itself upwards, seems for a moment suspended in the air, then streaks across a canyon wall, made dull by its spectacular flight.

A little later, like some unsuspectedly sad counterpoint, the sound of mourning doves at the bottom of the valley . . .

December 20

A professor of philosophy and social sciences at Berkeley, Lewis Feuer, has published a fascinating article in the *New Leader* about the student rebellion—pointing out that his university has "carried out the largest quantity of original and successful scientific research of any institution in the world," and that English Laborite publications have hailed it as a "model of socialism in action." Yet this kind of overcrowded, research-heavy university—the "multiversity" as it is called, steadily growing in bureaucracy, with researchers at the top with their large salaries, and grants, and royalties, and the student "untouchables" below—illustrates a cruel paradox. This is that "a superior faculty means inferior teaching." Feuer explains that the recent radical assault of September 29, with its roster of non-students—Maoists, Stalinists, Trotskyists, and varied Leftists—all making a plaintive demand for freedom in this "the freest of all major U.S. universities"—had a combined membership of not more than 170 persons. (The total student body numbers 27,000.) Also that generational solidarity is a factor in student activity, that music plays a part (Joan Baez and "We Shall Overcome"), and that there is emotional pressure (Thus Mario Savio, "I went to Mississippi where I could be killed. My reasons were selfish. I wasn't really alive.").

But why labor, Feuer asks, to gather together twenty-seven thousand students on a single campus, when in such vast university areas "lumpen-agitators will . . . advocate a mélange of narcotics, sexual perversion, collegiate Castroism, and campus Maoism. . . . when every year [will] see its own quota of horrible murders and rapes on the university's grounds . . . [when] the expenditure on police . . . to be adequate. . . . would have to increase geometrically . . . ?"

A discussion at dinner about the political directions of America.

1964 / The West Coast

Considerable enthusiasm about the radicalization of youth ("Kennedy having given a new task to the young," etc.).

The anthropologist asks innocently whether the young are really concerned with changing society for the better; "Or are they after some greater excitements? It would be natural if they were. The idea that Utopia is just around the corner is very old and very attractive." Her voice is low. "Rousseau, Buonarotti, Bakunin . . . they all thought that one had only to destroy the ruling government, and that then a perfect society would result. . . . Perhaps we should not ask whether activists want a better society, but rather what element is going to bring this society into being?"

"What about Cuba?" someone asks aggressively: "Fidel is *young* . . . ."

"What about Cuba?" the anthropologist asks gently.

"Well there's such a thing as participatory democracy," the speaker begins eagerly. "Fidel's revolution is an active one . . . it wants to make the revolution, to form *focos* amongst the students, the peasants, the blacks . . . ."

Someone else interjects: "Cuba jails and kills her dissidents."

"Fidel can teach us something," urges (even pleads) the first speaker. Our society needs radicalizing . . . ."

Again the obstinate anthropologist comes into the conversation. "Don't you think that we might make a comparison between the young supporters of Fidel Castro and some of our own violence-prone activists? In Cuba those supporters became known as *los resentidos*—'the resentful ones.' We too have our resentful ones. . . . But tell me, can personal resentment truly be called a *political* attitude . . . ?"

At this point a young male visitor (a writer of detective stories; also reputed to be a Maoist and a member of the Progressive Labor Party— i.e., the PLP strongholds in the Bay area) claims that it is no use trying to change society. He has been rather late to dinner and tends to concentrate on eating (stretching without inhibition across the table to get salt, pepper, butter, bread).

"If we can't change society then what is the answer?" asks someone rather anxiously.

"Blow it all up," answers the young writer. He finishes his food, pushes away his plate and gets up to refill his coffee cup. Over his shoulder he adds: "It's insane anyway . . . all this discussion. The only way for the future is to organize the poor, the dispossessed; we have to go out to the lumpen proletariat. We have plenty of Indians, Negroes, Puerto Ricans, Chicanos around . . ." (He speaks as though these were commodities on the shelves of a warehouse.) "As for capitalism itself" (his tone takes on an edge of profound satisfaction), "let it explode!"

Outside near the swimming pool, W—, wife of Stewart, expresses indignation at this attitude. "Why it's pure Nechayev . . ." she keeps saying.

Someone else describes how the last time the PLP visitor had been invited, he had used Castro's phrase about "making the new man," and had said quite blandly that "to make the 'new' man, it may be necessary to shoot a lot of the 'old' ones."

"Why how horrible that is!" It seems that tonight W— takes on the spirit of her absent husband. "There you have Nechayev again!"

Attempts to find out what the PLP represents, end in B— (the friend of the PLP member) describing him as a "great guy with tremendous idealism," but, according to the student he rooms with, unable to make his own bed. "He wants a quite new—a *pure* society." (B— does not go into the contradictions involved in this expectation by imperfect citizens, of "perfection" from the impersonal state. It is the sort of divorce from reality which Karl Marx experienced at the age of eighteen; and like Marx this PLP member is disturbed by the conflict between what is and what ought to be. He is dreaming like Tom Hayden of the "new" man.)

On further inquiry it seems that the PLP on the West Coast is pro-Peking, pro-Cuba, pro-struggle, supposedly Havana-financed. Its talk is generally "Mao" talk: "to set up strategic hamlets," "let the country encircle the city," "defeat bourgeois ideology," "die on the streets," "defy the paper tiger" and so on. Technically the group started in 1961 when four young Communist party members in the East were thrown out of the CPUSA—supposedly for party insubordination. B— says that in spite of the violence of their come-on, the easy talk of frame-ups, assaults, assassinations and sloganeering, the PLP considers itself a "vanguard" party and subjects its members to a strong inner party discipline. "You know, on the surface it's all 'Hate City Hall,' 'Land-lords are Ratlords,' 'Killer Police.' They're known as the 'Mao crowd,' referred to often as 'Mao Now'; and they are supposed to be very much in the swing—sexually, politically, racially.... Oh yes, they bear down heavily on the coloreds." He adds, "They're getting the blacks and Chicanos radicalized. The home party is already about one-quarter Negro and Puerto Rican."

Later considerations

How does a party go about "getting blacks and Chicanos radicalized?" (Hitler explains in *Mein Kampf* how he studied the mass demonstrations and character assassinations of the radicals in Vienna. *"Book after book ... pamphlet after pamphlet ... my daily reading of the Social democratic press enabled me to understand the inner nature of these thought pro-*

cesses...." It was this kind of reading which illuminated for him the vast possibilities of the technological diffusion of ideas and the manipulation of followers by skillful use of psychology, sloganeering, repetition and theater.) Whatever know-how the PLP has, is likely to have come from Mao. The Chinese Communist party certainly looks forward to the time when the whole colored world—the masses of Asia not yet brought into the Socialist paradise, the tribes of Africa, the world of the islands, the Indians of Latin America—all will be available for socialism. And already in Africa an aggressive campaign is being waged to make Arabs and black Africans aware that they share a darker skin color, not with the Russians, but with the Chinese. Brandishing the color weapon, the Chinese have ranged themselves alongside the United States Negroes since last year. Mao has made approving statements, such as "They [the Negroes] have found the correct path of struggle," and "This is a revolutionary opportunity." Naturally the Russians, in the face of the widening Sino-Soviet split, have been discomforted. On one occasion Mao said in a slightly menacing manner: "We are the majority and they [the whites] are in the minority. At most they make up less than 10 percent of the 3000 million people of the world." This resulted in the Russians having to face the fact that *they* were "white."

Out here on the West Coast the aggressive rivalry between Russia and China seems to be overshadowed by activism per se. Regular Communist party members are effectively combining with Maoists and anarchists as well as with Trotskyists. Pragmatic experience is apparently considered a primary need. In fact at this very moment some of the young leaders may be setting out on well-rounded careers as lecturers, politicians, psychologists, street fighters. (Obviously all the radical parties will need trained and trusted activists; so that one of the uses of radical activities—demonstrations, confrontations with authority, brief prison terms—is to give experience and confidence to their younger cadres, and to build a permanent nucleus of force around which expansion can be launched.) This is the quasi-military approach which easygoing Western liberals tend to ignore.

In a phone call Professor K— confirms the fact that the PLP had been deeply involved in Harlem. "Well you know that area up there is a tinder box. PLP was clandestinely financed, and disowned by the Communist party proper; yet the key dissidents were products of thorough Moscow training in social demolotion. You know Jesse Gray. He was the official Communist party organizer in Harlem from 1950 to 1958, and he was involved in the organization of the Harlem riots in more ways than one. He was the one responsible for calling for guerrilla warfare at a church rally, and then saying that he needed 'one hundred skilled black revolutionaries ready to die, and to recruit platoons of one hundred men apiece.' Soon after Malcolm X split with the Muslims, Gray moved in on the Organization of Afro-American Unity, Malcolm X's new organization. He became general helper and propagandist. As well, some of Malcolm's young men began getting together black street kids under the name of the Blood Brothers. (Later a group of youths were seized for the stabbing of a Harlem storekeeper and his wife, and were identified as having connections with the movement. One newspaper announced: "The little shop, the Eve and Pete Clothing Store at 3 West 125th St. was a blood-spattered mess. Blood dripped from a raincoat-covered clothing dummy. Crowds heard the screams and commotion and no one went inside to help.") The professor goes on to talk of the *Crusader*, edited in Havana by exile Robert Williams, a black ex-Marine who took over the NAACP chapter in Monroe, North Carolina, and armed a number of Negroes and encouraged them to shoot back at the Klan outriders. Williams finally fled to Cuba.

It was at this time that copies of the *Crusader* began to be picked up on the Harlem streets. The pages of its June issue were filled with useful hints on how to upset a sensitive urban center. (Sporadic rioting, massive sniping, all-night warfare and so on. Gasoline fire bombs, bazookas, light mortars, rocket launchers, lye and acid bombs were also suggested. These last are made by injecting lye or acid into the metal end of light bulbs. The *Crusader* noted that kitchen matches placed in air conditioning systems will cause delayed explosions; it confided that "flame throwers can be manufactured at home.")

In July, William Epton of PLP said that he could claim thirty black communities to his credit; and declared that although he was a Communist, he intended to coordinate with any group in Harlem on these issues. Soon there came a campaign against the police. Pictures of aggressive policemen were rushed out onto the street, along with bulletins suggesting various kinds of sabotage. Rioting spread from block to block, from city to city.

December 24

Malcolm X has spoken in Harlem at the first Organization of Afro-American Unity rally held after his visit to Africa. His words suggest appreciation of the political rule ("When weak, find a suitable ally").

"We have always thought that we were struggling by ourselves." He warned, "You waste your time involving yourself with any organization that is not directly connected with our brothers and sisters on the African continent ... You and I will never be respected because we have nothing behind us ... We must have a strong Africa ... when you and I link our struggle up with [our brothers] struggle ... you'll find that this man over here will pay a little more attention ..." He declared enthusiastically that there were numerous organizations in Cairo which were involved in liberation movements for Africans and Asians and spoke of how "beautiful" this was, and how exhilarating to see "the brothers getting together." "... it is necessary to link up with our own people, our people in Paris, and our people in London ... We've got to link up with our people who are in the Caribbean, in Trinidad, in Jamaica, in all the islands, and we've got to link up with our people who are in Central America and South America ... we've got to get together. And once we get together, brothers, we can get us some action. . . ."

December 31

A brilliant day for the last day of the year. Sage is crushed underfoot as we struggle up the summit road; a golden hawk wheels and circles above us. Yet we walk too, hearing the drone of planes along the coast and an occasional police siren far away, faint and complaining. It seems inevitable to think of coming confrontations in 1965, to hear those sounds which now never cease in our cities; to be aware of the fragility of the peace we enjoy in the canyon.

The new year comes in with dancing and gaiety. Brilliant paper birds flutter from the ceiling. Supper is served at midnight. Everybody sings "Auld Lang Syne" and a Mexican-American girl with long, shiny black hair sings "Fruta Verde," a song which seems popular at the moment.

> Sabor de fruta verde
> De fruta que se muerde
> Y deja un agridulce
> De perversidad

1965

January 7

Malcolm X is speaking again, this time before the Militant Labor Forum in New York City (a Trotskyite organization with which he has had contact, and which—along with CORE (Congress of Racial Equality) and SNCC (Student Non-violent Coordinating Committee)—is vying for his attention). Malcolm accuses the United States of subsidizing Tshombe and Tshombe's mercenaries, and of murdering Lumumba.

Although the terms used are nationalistic, his speech, following the recent one in Harlem, indicates allegiance to an "international" viewpoint. Particularly relevant to his potential leadership is the fact that he is gaining followers at the same time that the Chinese have set themselves apart from the Russians, in calling for militant action throughout the "Revolutionary Third World," and stressing the fact that the Chinese are yellow and their adoptive Third World groups are also "colored"—yellow, black, brown, as the case might be.

(The Communist tradition of using minorities is an old one in America. Louis Budenz, long-time member of the Communist party USA and editor of the *Daily Worker*, stated in his book *Men Without Faces:* "When I joined the party in 1935 the Reds were still clamoring for the creation of a Negro Republic, to be separated from the United States, by force if necessary. Many leading Negroes rightly denounced the proposal as putting them in a false and dangerous position . . . . In the next twelve years there was to be utter subservience to Moscow, with the exception of short periods . . . and whenever opposition to the U.S. was strong, as during the period of the Hitler-Stalin Pact, the Communist cry for 'Negro Rights' reached shrill heights . . .")

In any case to ask the Leninist question *Kto Kgo* (who does what to whom) it seems that both Russia and China, in their different ways, and whatever their publicized views, are interested in the revolutionary intensification of racial and religious situations. In other words both have found that extreme nationalism is a good route to Marxist "internationalism"!

A year ago (in April) Malcolm X—soon after his break with the Black Muslims—had spoken in Manhattan under the sponsorship of the Militant Labor Forum. James Wechsler (editor of the New York *Post*) was present and described the forum as a unit of the SWP—the continuing "modern manifestation of what old radicals define as Trotskyism." Wechsler added that it was hard to believe that "Trotsky had ever anticipated such an alliance . . . ." (As George Breitman, a latter day Trotskyist points out, this opinion of Wechsler's springs from ignorance of Trotsky's prophetic concern with the struggle of the American Negro, since even from exile he had warned his American sympathizers to "find the road to the most deprived, to the darkest strata of the proletariat, beginning with the Negro, whom capitalist society has converted into a pariah, and who must learn to see in us his revolutionary brothers." Again in Mexico, in Cayoacan, in 1939 Trotsky was visited by J. R. Johnson, a revolutionary black intellectual who pointed out that the Negro remained "profoundly suspicious of whites." Johnson suggested that they must be "won for socialism" on the basis of their own experience and activity, and that an all-black organization should be formed, open to all black militants, including SWP members. Trotsky's reaction was approving. The organization he said should be oriented towards the masses and not the intellectuals who "always (have) the desire to take on the Anglo-Saxon culture. . . ." He pointed out that the Negroes were "the most dynamic . . . of the American working class"—that "the American Negro would develop leaders for Africa"—and that "we do not need today to break our heads over a possibility that sometime whites will be suppressed by the Negro." To read this is to see that Trotsky foresaw the possibilities for Mao's marshalling of the "Colored International."

February 4

Identifying plants in the canyon: golden crownbeard, a common yellow desert daisy; different kinds of pine cones—the huge ones are the *Pinus Nelsoni* and measure as much as five and a half inches across!

Afternoon. Raining. In the canyon the bark of fallen trees turns grey and dull like the skin of elephants.

Back in Colony Hall the women are talking about sexual freedom. For some reason they look like portraits by Picasso. One is sprawled in a chair, muscled legs thrown outwards, feet in cheap patent leather shoes, tight skirt, large breasts under an Indian red sweater. Her figure seems indolent, but as thought struggles, her actual expression is startled, almost agonized. The other woman is round and plump and her shoulder makes a comfortable curve; but as with Picasso's brilliant schizophrenic technique, her face is caught *in medias res*—one enlarged eye, one enlarged nostril expressing anguished emotion, the other eye, the other nostril waiting in profound quiet. In both women the breasts seem to be offered objectively, startlingly separate appendages. But the faces try desperately to move and communicate.

February 22

Malcolm X was assassinated yesterday as he spoke at a rally in the Audubon Ballroom at 166th Street in Harlem. Just as he had begun his speech, "Brothers and Sisters . . ." there was a diversion at the back of the hall, and three of the killers raced down the aisle and began to pump bullets into Malcolm's chest—with his wife Betty screaming "They're killing him . . . they're killing him!"

February 24

The body is still on display at the United Funeral Home at Eighth Avenue and 126th. Elijah Muhammed indicated that Malcolm had urged blacks to arm themselves, and so he "got what he preached." He spoke like this as he stood surrounded by his own elite troop of karate-trained men, the FOI or Fruit of Islam.

(With his defection from and criticism of the Nation of Islam; with his call for militant international action, Malcolm X had become a threat to Elijah Muhammed and to the "National Establishment." The general consensus is that there had been orders to "get" him. Moreover, the week before, fire bombs had been thrown at his house; he and his family had had to escape in the middle of the night. "It doesn't frighten me, it doesn't quiet me down," Malcolm had stated.)

But James Farmer of CORE called the killing "political", and said that the case should be taken out of the hands of the New York City police and dealt with by Washington. He even spoke guardedly about the Red Chinese. Apparently he was drawing attention to the fact that in order to speed the "Black Revolution," Peking may possibly have encouraged the assassination through penetration of the Black Muslim party.

Moscow's reaction to the killing was restrained; but Peking organized massive protests and used the occasion to stress how right Negroes were in their militant stand, and that they should "meet violence with violence." In the meantime Norman X. Butler, a "hit" man for the Nation (already arrested once for taking a shot at another defector from the ranks) was accused of acting in concert with Talmadge Hayer.

More evidence of the struggle for power and influence in the "Black" movement. Shades of the Sherry Biltmore Hotel in Boston—that narrow red brick structure which rises out of the flatlands of the South End with its seedy dollared clientele and the bar where so many odd ladies sit patiently, waiting for the night's business to begin. Here a black man called Leon Ameer (describing himself as a follower of Malcolm X and now suggested as his possible successor) was found dead in his room. Apparently on Christmas day last year, Ameer, in the lobby of this same hotel, had been beaten up so badly that he had to be hospitalized. The four assailants were later identified as Black Muslims.

March 12

Dinner at a phony Hawaiian-style eating place at the end of a pier (the front of the restaurant is built up in the form of a war-canoe, and the meat we eat is dressed up with canned pineapple and coconut!)

1964 / The West Coast

The discussion, however, is about what has come to be a common subject—the Vietnam war (stimulated in this case by President Johnson having ordered air strikes on North Vietnam). A Mr. Peng, apparently from Malaysia, and an assistant tutor at one of the smaller universities, has joined us as the guest of a blonde girl from Kansas. He challenges anyone at the table to prove that the South Vietnamese wouldn't have been better left alone. "After all, before that they were simply slaves of the French." The anthropologist protests that the South Vietnamese are not being "left alone;" they are making an effort to withstand the Communist takeover; surely this should be supported by someone, if not the United States then by whom—the U.N. Security Council? Mr. Peng seems to suggest that the whole battle against the Communists is unnecessary, that it (the battle) is a "civil war," and that Ho Chi Minh is a nationalist and a patriot. "He refuses to kow-tow to the Americans."

The anthropologist maintains that to see North Vietnam as a gallant David before a United States Goliath is inaccurate. "It was never a 'civil war.' Ho Chi Minh was trained in Moscow and was Stalin's top agent in Indonesia. He carried out the usual deception when he created a secret Communist front in 1946, and that party worked underground until 1950 when it was resurrected again in 1951 under the name of Dang Lao Dong Viet Nam, that is, the Workers party. In fact you will find that between 1946 and 1950 when there wasn't supposed to be a Communist party in North Vietnam, the actual party membership increased from 20,000 to 500,000. Of course, it remains debatable to what extent the United States should have intervened in this unresponsive war, but for some reason the campus Left thinks that the North Vietnamese regime is infinitely preferable to the regime in the South. Why? The truth is that the North Vietnamese regime is known all over Southeast Asia for its tremendous human repressions."

Mr. Peng breaks in in a tone of suppressed emotion: "This tiny little country standing up against the largest military force in the *world*."

The anthropologist sticks to her point. "What has the size of the country to do with it? Sparta was the terror of the then civilized world. There was a brutal land reform in North Vietnam. There were denunciations, extortions, executions. At least 100,000 were killed. The intellectuals tried to revolt and were suppressed. . . ." (She refers to Oxford's Patrick Honey whose books she says, are "authoritative on the subject.")

Some of those listening at the table join in rather tentatively to support Mr. Peng. One suggests that perhaps it is better for the Vietnamese to work out their problems without interference from the West. America should keep out of it. "Let the peoples of Southeast Asia be Communists if they want to!"

The young blonde girl turns her attention to her date, Mr. Peng.

Ignoring everyone else at the table, she confides that she has been reading Ho Chi Minh's poetry. "It is *beautiful*," she breathes.

What is so unsatisfactory about such conversations is that they are completely divorced from history. The blonde girl's beautiful brow is not furrowed by the thought of the Calcutta Conference of 1948 (prepared by Prague, and with its 900 delegates including some from Vietnam, Indonesia, Soviet Central Asia and even Australia; and bent upon deciding the "correct line of revolutionary guerrilla warfare" and the "arena of struggle"—which as Palme Dutt of the British C.P stressed "must be the whole region of Southeast Asia"). In 1948 this girl would have been about four years old. Neither does Mr. Peng, mature enough to have been her father, play a proper father role. He avoids the core of the matter which is the steady Vietcong attack on the villages by terror, and subsequently the setting up within them of hostile infrastructures. He blandly refers to the sacredness of "local government" and to the "neo-Colonial mentality of Americans" imposing upon them all the shortcomings of the undeveloped countries.

This does not mean that the situation is clear-cut. An unpleasant possibility is part of the emotional burden of United States observers and military men, who realize that their very presence may turn to entrap them. The North Vietnamese Truong Chinh had talked of guerrilla war: "The enemy attacks deep behind our lines, we launch attacks deep behind him. The war has the characteristic of two combs whose teeth are interlocked." In this tragedy of entrapment, crypto-Communists and their allies attempt to weaken the will of the West as they play upon every generous gesture of the politically uninformed. (Lenin had seen politics essentially as a form of warfare; and Stalin had spoken of the colonial possessions as "the Capitalist rear." Now Peking stresses the fact that warfare against the West must be waged through the underdeveloped countries, by exploiting their real tensions, and by—if necessary—turning their territories into "one vast battlefield.")

March 16

As multitudes of Americans have been influenced to believe it possible that the FBI, the Dallas police, and/or President Johnson himself had Kennedy murdered, so the majority of the people around the table last night seem to have been easily persuaded that Ho Chi Minh is a "nationalist" and an "agrarian reformer," and that the war in Vietnam is a "civil war." How does such opinion making operate?

In a piece by C. L. Sulzberger in the New York *Times* about the murder of Diem, it is claimed that the Vietcong directives captured last year reveal that cadres in Saigon had been ordered to sever their Communist party links and to join the Buddhist organizations, with a view to stimulating anti-government and anti-American demonstrations.

The story is remarkably somber, and has been dealt with by objective observers, including the intelligent Father Christian Simonnet (student and admirer of Father Pierre Dourisboure). Some of the blame for Diem's assassination must be put upon the shoulders of those journalists who, lacking easy entrance to North Vietnam, spent an inordinate amount of their time tracking down and exaggerating Diem's villainy. A typical article of that time, clipped from the *Saturday Evening Post* ("The Edge of Chaos," by Stanley Karnow) reads like a macabre preview of the assassination. It is full of emotion-provoking accusations which are hard to prove or disprove. Madame Nhu is "arrogant," the Ngo Dinhs resemble "a cross between the Borgias and the Bourbons . . . narrow, devious, obstinate and imperious." Ngo Dinh Nhu is a "voluble shifty-eyed man," and so on. Simonnet notes that Diem's regime was almost liberal compared to that pitiless one in the North; that Diem was honest and courageous if mediocre politically; that Madame Nhu was insulted even for being beautiful; and that the ruthless policeman Ngo Dinh Nhu was after all no more than an Oriental despot. Karnow's article finally suggests that military elements were spontaneously plotting to kill Diem; the actual truth seems to have been that it was the United States government (half persuaded by the subversion of the Communist underground, half horrified by the immolations) which gave implicit permission, via Lodge, the new Ambassador, to "do away" with him. What—apart from this sordid encouragement—really happened? One religious historian (Piero Gheddo) notes that there had been between 1930 and 1940 a widespread Buddhist revival, during which period many intellectuals were attracted to the movement with resultant political ramifications. The Buddhist opposition was an upcoming group, historically subject to frustration, that now found itself confronted by an already successful Catholic group. There had been a largely Catholic exodus of more than a million people from the Northern state, but in spite of this Catholics and Buddhists lived on good enough terms together. As Simonnet points out—while Diem and his ministers, the majority of whom were *not* Catholics, were tactless in their handling of certain issues concerned with Buddhist demonstrations and festivals, the famous "persecution" was nothing more than a fabrication. Authoritative publications of the Society of Buddhist Study in Saigon, and also the material of Mao Tho Truyen, attest that under Diem's rule Buddhism enjoyed full religious freedom and that Buddhism in Vietnam, a combination of Buddhism, Taoism, and Confucianism, was accepted by the masses without prejudice and became the chosen faith of the farming poor.

(An earnest letter supporting Diem and sent to a "liberal" Catholic priest protests: "You do not remember that Diem sent thousands of students abroad . . .? That he opened the country's doors to newspapermen from every country . . .? That he respected basic liberties like those of the trade unions and the freedom to strike, as well as religious liberty . . .?")

Under the orders which Sulzberger now notes, Simonnet explains that the Vietcong agents infiltrated certain chapters of the Buddhist movement and tried to convert them into political groups—systematically stimulating religious fanaticism. It was Vietcong agents who saw that foreign newsmen were told discreetly on June 11 of 1963 to go to the Cambodian Embassy at a certain time, where they saw bonzes supporting a colleague who seemed almost unconscious. (Later films taken of the scene show the aged monk Thich-Quang Duc, arriving in a little Austin, appearing to be heavily drugged, being helped out, being placed in a squatting position, being sprinkled with gasoline; and, since he was unable to ignite himself, being set afire with a cigarette lighter by one of his supporters.) The picture of this event—that vision of a small dark human silhouette enveloped in fierce orange flames, was to scorch the pages of thousands of newspapers and magazines, to be flashed on a thousand screens. (The outcome of the Vietnam war had been all but decided. A preliminary death blow had been dealt to Diem.)

In the United States full page ads of the picture were appearing under the signature of scores of clergymen. "We, Too, Protest!" and "Mr. President, in the Name of God, Stop It!" A copy of that first picture was to remain for a long time on President Kennedy's desk.

But it was not enough to assassinate Diem; all other governments in South Vietnam had to be discredited. More bonzes were burned until the spectacle seemed banal. A young woman from Pan Thiet, drunk with opium, was brought to the public square to be burned; and this too was publicized. What was not reported was that later her mother and father came to the place and wept, and cursed the bonzes, and lamented with piercing voices. Three days before the killing of Diem a bonze had been arrested with a plastic container of gasoline under his saffron robes, a knife to pierce it with, and some pink pills which he told police were given him as a poison to take in order to escape the pain. He was found near the site where a number of selected journalists were waiting with a UN fact-finding commission to attend a celebration. The monk, whose name was Thich Minh Tuyen, explained how a clandestine "suicide promotion" group came and told him that Diem was burning down all the pagodas in Saigon and torturing hundreds of bonzes to death. They showed him pictures of this (apparently they were documentation of Chinese Communist massacres of bonzes in Tibet) and promised him that if he died in defense of the faith, he would be reincarnated as a Buddha. They then took him to Saigon and showed him how to take a special route to the Cathedral; but due to the crowds that day he had had to deviate from the route, and had suddenly found himself in front of an "undamaged pagoda." It was here that the police, alerted to rumors of another immolation, found him staring in surprise at the pagoda.

The exploitation of these unworldly bonzes was evident. (As a scholar, M. Pecheron, wrote in *La Croix* in 1963, it is totally alien to Buddhism to have "a public, a spectacular suicide with self-immolation in flames of a protesting bonze, since the respect for life extends to one's own." He adds that in no other country of the Orient where there are religious conflicts with the government—for instance, Burma or Ceylon—did such things happen. Only in Vietnam alone, where the political stakes were high and the Communists organized for psychological warfare.)

In the case of Thich Minh Tuyen, the exploiters went to the extent of supplying him with fake pills which would not in the slightest lessen his pain. Such plots have an unbelievable twentieth-century quality. In the case of Tuyen, the conspirators were caught, but it was too late to subdue the publicity.

Individual commissioners in the U.N. Report, however, declared that they were satisfied that the allegations of persecution were largely invalid. The Mission did report the testimony of one nineteen-year-old bonze who had been recruited for immolation and asked to sign propaganda letters to the Mission. He was saved by a friend who informed the police; he broke down and wept as he told his story to the U.N. Ambassadors. The whole affair was a prelude to the final confusion in Saigon. When the news of the "coup" came, the Australian journalist Wilfred Burchett happened to be with the Vietcong. Burchett (famous or "infamous" for carrying out on behalf of North Korea the brainwashing of allied prisoners during the Korean War) described the joy of the Communists, who were incredulous when they heard that the Americans had actually been "inspired" to get rid of the one man capable of holding Vietnam together!

In this way freedom of religion—and that potential for the *very imperfect* government which Diem represented—went down together.

March 19

The wattle has gone from the canyon's sides; in its place a small yellow bell has sprung up from a low cloverlike plant. Along with the change of flowers, there comes also a change of colonists. Stewart, who has been ill, has gone back to the east with W—, his wife. B— has taken a house at the beach and plunged into campus politics. And today a wide-faced young Korean called K— arrives (first glimpsed as he walks around the living room touching the furniture and murmuring to himself the names of West Coast cities: "Seattle . . . San Francisco . . . Los Angeles. . . . ") There is also a painter from Pakistan, whose face has a gloomy and rather distrustful look: "My name is E—, yes, I am a painter and have come here to be present at my one-man show this month in the city."

With his smooth golden skin K— looks much younger than he is. But in a mournful voice he insists that he is more than thirty years old. "I am divorced and I have three children. I have published several books of stories . . . and yet," he sighs, "I don't like to live with a family; I like to be apart from other lives." He doesn't like critical people because if people criticize *others*, then they will criticize him. "If I hear them say X— has done so and so, then I know that they will also say, look at poor K— how he does so and so!"

With the new guests a certain culture clash becomes noticeable. E—, the Pakistani, resplendent in a dinner coat with dark navy satin lapels, is indignant with K— because he innocently remarks one evening over a late cup of coffee, that he himself and E—are the only ones not at work in their studios. E—'s eyes smolder angrily and he replies stiffly: "I don't have to carry on public relations with my work! I've got two one-man shows coming up in Los Angeles this month, and not in small insignificant galleries, but in *top-flight* galleries. I'm not like those amateurs who pretend to be busy all day. I spend *one* hour a day and that's enough for me. . . . "

K—, on the other hand, is very clear about *his* opinions. "Why have a car? You Americans have to have cars. I never *think* of a car . . . " He lapses into silence until someone else makes a chance remark about her sister being the least gentle, the least feminine in a whole family of women. At this K— wakes up and says: "Gentle and feminine! That's a contradiction in terms . . . Women often scratch!"

March 21

K— is stretched out on the padded bench in the dining room. He has apparently been having drinks before dinner, and the slightest flush appears on his flat cheekbones. He has the feeling that China has been insulted. "Why did they say that in the newspaper about China? China has a wonderful culture. The Russians are people from the North, a very harsh people."

(According to the paper the Soviets have persuaded eighteen parties to attend a consultation meeting in Moscow, with a view to getting the

world Communist parties to counter China's growing success in wean-
ing individual parties away from her by means of money and propaganda. Not very many parties made it to Moscow.)

It seems that K— has already taken sides on the Soviet split. He is
soon stating that only China "means what she says about revolution."

Stretched out on the bench he goes on to defend his choice from
nonexistent "revisionists." Then, curiously combining pro-Chinese
and anti-American feeling, he adds that the Chinese are kind to those
who drink too much and nods vigorously as someone sits down beside
him. "Yes, they are never nasty to drunk men. . . . In America they
don't *like* a drunk man."

March 25

The controversy about the Warren Report hasn't died down: Dwight
Macdonald, in one of the only intelligent articles about the whole
question, explains (March issue of *Esquire*) that "most of the critics have
a large left-handed political ax to grind. . . . "

This is not all; the left-induced hue and cry is extremely successful;
thousands of horrified observers in Europe, Latin America, the Middle
East accept uncritically the macabre and muddled versions of those
who have come to be called "assassination ghouls."

This is having its effect upon Americans, whose uneasiness about the
killing itself is compounded by uneasiness about their institutions—
the law, the police, their government representatives, and (if they are
to believe Mr. Joesten and Mr. Lane) even their President. The situation is made worse by the wilder fringes in the magazine world. (M. S.
Arnoni, for instance, in *Minority of One* speaks knowingly of "the
junta" and says that it's hard to tell whether JFK was "felled by this
junta" or merely on "the say-so of a supporting fringe group.")

The point about 90 percent of the accusations is that they only give
the impression of trying to distract attention. As Charles Roberts (a
Newsweek correspondent who was seated in the first press bus in the
Kennedy motorcade) stressed, "Those for the 'Rightist conspiracy' are
like hunters who want to be sure of killing *something*. They fired with
large shots and with both barrels."

Yet there is a much better case to be built up for a conspiracy from
the Left. Oswald did after all defect to Russia, spend time there,
married the niece of a KGB colonel, and apparently offered valuable
information to the Soviets.

Gary Powers wrote in his book, *Operation Overflight:*

> When the U-2s altitude is referred to as "secret," that term is qualified. In
> addition to those personally involved in U-2 flights, a number of others

... have access to this information. These include air-traffic controllers and at least some of the radar personnel at the bases where U-2s were stationed.

In 1957 the U-2s were based in a new location, Atsugi, Japan. In September of that year a seventeen-year-old Marine Corps private was assigned to Marine Air Control Squadron 1 (MACS-1) based at Atsugi. MACS-1 was a radar unit whose duties included scouting for incoming foreign aircraft. Its equipment included height-finding radar. The private, a trained operator, had access to this equipment. ... He remained in Japan until November 1958 at which time he was returned to the United States and assigned to ... El Toro, California. El Toro was not a U-2 base, but U-2s frequently flew over this portion of Southern California. At El Toro he had access not only to radar and radio codes but also to the new MPS 16 height-finding radar gear. ... In September 1959, he obtained a hardship discharge from the U.S. Marine Corps. The following month he defected to the Soviet Union. ... His name was Lee Harvey Oswald. ... Six months later my U-2 was shot down."

A trip to Santa Barbara, where the sea stretches along the car-ridden highway, where the architecture is unanimously Spanish-inspired, where the geraniums grow like trees, where the surf-riders try to avoid the sewage. The little house is surrounded by a hedge of silvery-grey olive trees. Behind it stark mountains are just showing green again after last year's fire. In the garden dwarf orange trees are laden with fruit—for dinner: lobster, steak, artichokes.

April 1

In a few days I leave for Mexico. The fate of the traveler is that he is always being thrust into new situations; so that the last dinner is with "acquaintances" rather than with friends, in a house skillfully built on the lip of a hillside, with a continual descent of floors towards a final platform with a view of the sea. The host collects orchids; perhaps as a symbol of "privatism" (the general impression is that he and his wife operate in an affluence far removed from the imperfect world around us).

There is a broad stairway, where huge blooms are illuminated behind glass—some blonde as cream, some intensely startlingly pink, others purplish-black like a tropic night. They flank the staggered descent, and it is all exactly what might have been expected of lavish West Coast life. Finally everyone is seated for dinner at a teakwood table glittering with glass. And the table itself seems suspended over dark masses of plants and shares in the sky and the far glimmering ocean.

Late night reflections

Until recently an optimistic hope for the continual evolution of free societies has seemed natural enough. (Sociologists have pronounced the thesis that societies are free if values are widely rather than narrowly shared; if the society continues to be mobile rather than restricted by caste; if an open society exists rather than a police state. Liberal sociologists, like other liberals, depend upon the hope of evolution; Marxists on the other hand predict that only social revolution will lead the way to freedom.)

Perhaps the hopes of liberals may not be borne out after all; perhaps those varied, tumultuous and often manipulative forces encouraged by the Marxists and neo-Marxists are now in the ascendancy; perhaps evolution may work in a negative fashion (just as the cancer of misinformation may eat away at United States faith in its own institutions). In other words, the assumption that even relative freedom is secure may be erroneous.

In packing suitcases and books, it is impossible to avoid packing as well a certain amount of depressing intellectual baggage!

April 3

Inside the bus, the seated passengers are humbler and less assured than those writers and artists encountered during the last months—a salesman going over his accounts, a woman with three children, two nuns, a couple of workmen in overalls and small cocky blue hats. It is a pleasant descent to ordinary life.

Rain beats against the bus windows, washing away the past, drenching the last remnants of the city, clouding life as it was in the canyon's protective enclosure. We roll along to the tune of endless radio commentaries, to the smell of cigarettes, the crackle of sandwich paper, the flipping of magazine pages.

IN TRANSIT

April 2

There is a symbolic quality to border crossing which keeps travelers awake at night and provides that clash of values inevitable when the worst aspects of two countries confront each other.

In fact as an early morning bus crosses the border into Tijuana, it passes also into a world faintly Mexican, but with an iron disregard for that country's family values. Here muddy tracks and gutters converted into drains take the place of streets. Bedraggled shacks of tin and odd lumber crowd the outskirts of the town. The bus driver gives advice: "Don't sleep in Tijuana; it's absolutely unsafe. There's no law and order . . . . Women are raped in the hotels . . . the place is one big whorehouse, that's what it is . . . . The girls get 24 dollars a week, and they can make about fifteen dollars a day. If you buy vodka it costs one dollar; fifty cents goes to the girl, and fifty cents to the house . . . . But the girls are better than you'd think in a town like this. . . . a lot of Spanish-Americans and many Mexicans, but they come from all over, and most of them have children to keep." He turns a plump super-serious face. "But I'm warning you, don't you stay there at night. Look around and go further south."

Soon the small clustering sandy hills are dramatically covered with greyish wooden houses, all close together and managing to convey a sense of barren and stripped earth. The main streets themselves have been converted into corridors for amusements of all kinds—bars, games, bowling alleys, "French" movies. There are large placards announcing RACES and JAI ALAI; the other signs are in English and Spanish. The bus driver also seems to undergo a metamorphosis; he becomes more familiar, speaks in Spanish, says *"Buenas Días"* to passengers who get on at street corners, and adds politely *"Quieres sentarse?"*

In Transit

Walking along one of the bigger streets it seems too early for business, but early as it is, arms extend from the darkened doorways of bars, stretching like the appendages of octopi to make contact with unwary tourists: "Come in . . . come in . . . *Ven, ven.* . . . Nice movie, *muy interessante.* . . ." A girl wearing small black panties and a black lace brassiere from which burst large pale breasts, leans from a hole in a wooden wall and pleads in a bored way for money to buy a drink. Her black fringe is glued to her sweaty forehead. And painted above her head there is the suitable legend: LOS BANDIDOS.

Further on shops sell every imaginable kind of cheap curio: carved boxes, fake ebony statues, brass ashtrays held up by nude figures in plastic, gilded dragons, bronze buddhas, pictures painted on black velvet, knives with bone handles. Another whole area is given over to pornography: prints, books, records, films, mechanical toys, and postcards neatly packaged in little wooden boxes with sliding tops chastely painted with violets.

"*Las flores . . .*" pleads a skinny little man. "*Mire Senora, las flores mas bonitas.* . . ." He slides back the lid and gives a grin of toothless triumph as the lewd pictures leap into view.

In actuality the whole ugly sketchy little town with its few fake luxury hotels, can be seen as turned over to the exploitation of one single experience. So that beginning now, even before noon, and going on until dawn comes over the hillocks on the outskirts (somewhere or other in these packed quarters, behind doors or curtains, on stages or in cribs) men and women, women and women, men and men, and all the foregoing with a variety of animals, are to be found—to the tune of rustling dollar bills—going through various gymnastic exercises. Money having replaced sexuality, the practicality of the commerce is so overwhelming that it palls even in a day. Soon, it seems ordinary to glimpse little girls in the streets where the shacks are, dressed in shabby but sexy finery, and being corralled by an older woman from the seas of mud and told to put their shoes on like sober, older whores (many of whom come out to lean in open doorways—*El Changito, La Fê, El Capicho, Rancho de Flores, Angeles de Hollywood*—to sit at linoleum-covered tables, to eat fried eggs for a late breakfast, to drink beer lazily while the early afternoon crowds wander curiously by).

At the airport the crime climate is less perceptible but equally effective. The booking clerk pretends that I have no seat reserved on the afternoon plane. An opaque expression appears in his eyes, he waves aside the proferred ticket, shows a chart of the inside of the plane with crosses on each seat, and claims that I must travel tomorrow.

"But here is the ticket . . . I have a proper ticket."

"The ticket is good, but there is no seat."

"But the ticket has today's date. . . ."

"I am sorry, Senora, but without a seat you cannot travel. . . ." He shrugs his shoulders and gazes into the distance. But the ticket could not be sold without a seat? It is only permissible to sell as many tickets as there were seats? The booking clerk reverses his stand. "Well it is true that there are one or two seats on the afternoon plane, but these are more expensive. In other words a thirty-six dollar ticket to Muleje costs fifty-two dollars . . . If the *Senora* will pay another sixteen dollars? The *Senora* protests. That is bribery. The manager of the airport refuses to discuss the matter.

A red-headed boy with a guitar, also mysteriously stranded, says that everyone in this town is "shitty."

"Perhaps you should pay him off. . . ."

"I refuse. . . . I absolutely refuse."

He offers Chiclets as a consolation.

In the taxi back to town the driver sympathizes, too, and speaks of the *mordecita* (little bite). "Is bad here, but no worse than San Fran . . . or Shig-ā-go." He adds: "I will take you the only possible, The Caesar Hotel. *Peor is nada*. . . ."

Afternoon is advancing in Tijuana's streets. Pink lights have appeared, and cars are slowly passing the checkpoint. Hucksters are energetically corralling customers for the shows. One small boy insists that he can find something special.

"Such as?"

He looks wise and pushes a lock of black hair out of rather beautiful eyes. *"Especial,"* he remarks laconically.

"I don't like 'special' sights."

He accepts this, in fact gives the impression that instead of such a guide job, he himself would prefer to explore the country on a bicycle.

"Drinks?" He tilts his head.

"No thanks."

"Coffee?"

"All right."

We walk along companionably.

"Lots of people come here?"

He nods. "They turn back the kids." He pauses. "They can't turn me back. I live here." (Tijuana is legally out of bounds to anyone under eighteen, although it is said that many manage to enter by means of fake identity papers. The checkpoint is the only one of its kind along the 1400-mile Mexican border and is considered to serve a valuable purpose—not only by protecting American minors from drugs, liquor, cabarets, and brothels—but by identifying and sending back to their parents, hundreds of runaways.)

In Transit

"So, where do you live?"

He points to one of the cribs nearby and gallantly gestures to a seat under the open arch.

The smell of hot fat floats in the air, and a large woman comes out from behind a screen and without greeting me, takes the boy by the arm and propels him into the makeshift kitchen. She mutters something about *"Coma tus papas fritas."* Immediately a girl appears and offers a menu. Her hair is done up on top of her head, and she has a rather pleasant if swarthy face with a small dark mole on one cheek. The linoleum is wiped swiftly with a very dirty cloth; a bottle filled with blue and orange, orchid-like Bird of Paradise flowers is seized and plunked in the middle of the table. Beer appears in thick dark Mexican bottles.

"Would you like one?"

"Gracias." She sinks into a seat.

"Why do people come to this place?"

"To get their hair done," she answers unexpectedly, *"tambien para perfumes.* And some for *fronton."* Neither of us goes on about the more obvious reason for the town's popularity. The girl says that her name is Carmen. She used to live in the south near Monterrey. She remarks: "Then my father had a lot of debts and he sold me." We sit and look at the expanse of mud which makes up the street.

"He *sold* you?"

She looks embarrassed. "He had many many debts."

"When was that?"

"Long while. I was fourteen."

We go on talking politely.

"And do you like the life?"

"It is not a *good* life." She bites her lip nervously. An oldish man appears from nowhere, asks "Photograph?," levels a Polaroid at us, and soon a rather faint colored photograph is unpeeled from the back of the camera. Just as it is paid for, three other men appear from behind the screen, dressed in shabby Mariachi costumes. Lining up behind us they burst into song about beautiful Mexico. *"Mejico . . . lindo y queri-i-ido . . . Quando soy lejos de . . . t-i-i-i . . ."* One of them is scraping at a small scratchy fiddle. This too is paid for. Finally a rather aggressive young man appears behind Carmen's chair and plays with her piled-up hair, so that suddenly it unrolls and pours down her back like coppery-colored silk. (It is said that all women have one special beauty; with this girl it is certainly her hair.) The young man looks us both over.

"Want to see a show girls?"

Carmen appears angry and turns away. The young man disappears. Carmen volunteers the information that his name is Eduardo, that he'd been raised on a ranch and is rather *bruto. "Pero el no le gusta el trabajo de aqui . . . Pues!"* (But then he doesn't like the work here either.) Once long ago she had had a brother called Eduardo. *"Me siento muy solita,"* she says suddenly, *"muy solita."*

In the large perfectly clean but transient-seeming hotel, practically no guests are visible. Similarly in the vast dining room where a Germanic-looking *maitre d'hotel* in a tuxedo stands staring at an array of sparkling glasses. "No one is here yet." His blond hair, his straight and rather immovable features, his flashing blue eyes give him an impeccably Nordic air. "This place doesn't wake up until around eleven . . ."

"The dining room is very large."

"You'd be surprised. At midnight there won't be a free seat in the place." He serves a drink, and we talk about "the crime business."

"Yes, there are 7,000 women here, and the entire economy of the place rests on this trade. Each girl has to give a dollar-fifty a day to the Governor's representative. The girl must go to the doctor each week— that costs her one dollar. Half of the dollar goes to the Governor and half to the doctor. There are a lot of big houses and a lot of hot shows. There are about 250 people putting on shows each night—from that alone 2,000 dollars a week goes to the Governor. Abortionists also pay to the Governor."

"The governor seems to do well."

"He does well," admits the Nordic statue (now perched on a bar stool and being addressed as "Commodore" by the other waiters). He pauses and looks up and down the room with its sea of empty tables.

"Then there are the narcotics."

He gives a short braying laugh. "Yes, it was ordered from the United States to get rid of our narcotics trade. They trained some men specially in the U.S.; and with their help, Mexico City closed a lot of places up. Then three men were sent up here."

"What happened?"

"They killed one of them. They caught up with him in Monter-ey. . . . Then they killed another. That one was half German. He came to me late one night and asked me to help him. I told him to get away fast. And he did . . ." His voice lowers. "But it was too late . . . they got him on the way."

"And the third man?"

"He is still here. Now he knows better. Nothing happens to *him*."

"Here in the town—is there much addiction?"

"Yes, the sickness is very strong here. And there is reason. The hills to the south, at certain times they are red with the poppy flowers. The governor says: 'We grow it—they use it.'" There is another silence. After a while the "Commodore" says: "They will never win over the crime. We need a Hitler here." In the big half-empty room there is a feeling of loneliness; an alien spirit. As if the shell of living were here, but the matrix missing.

In Transit

"And *you?* How do you fit in?"

"Ah!" He gives the same short abrupt laugh. "They can't touch me. My wife is cousin to the Governor!"

Late that night the hotel comes to life—Footsteps hasten up and down the corridors. Telephones ring. Water runs. Doors open and shut. Cars start and stop in the parking lot below. Later still, when dim light is penetrating the screen of palm leaves at the window, there is the sound of drunken singing.

MEXICO

To Mexico! To Mexico! Down the dovegrey
highway, past Atomic City police,
Past the firey border to dream cantinas!

Allen Ginsberg
from "Ready to Roll"

April 14

Leave by train from Guaymas (the port on the Gulf of California settled by Spaniards in 1769, depot for the gold and silver of Sonora, and home of pirate raiders).

No time to explore Serpent Bay or the Mission, to see the old Spanish-Moorish houses or the brilliant parakeets which flash in and out of the trees in the nearby forest. The long train, due to leave in a few minutes, already waits in the heat at the station, and a cooperative taxi driver pushes me onto it with my bags and gallantly rushes back to find coffee and a magazine. He returns soon with a copy of the lurid but fascinating *Magazine de Policia*, plus an enormous plate of the famous prawns from Bacochibampo Bay; extending this gallantry still further by refusing money and patting my shoulder with the comment *"Guardelo para tus gastos"* (Keep it for your expenses).

At once the journey takes on a sensual southern quality, for the train apartment is shared with two young lovers, who spend most of the journey in each others arms, where they murmur to each other and exchange interminable glances. The girl has pearl earrings dangling against her dusky cheeks, a pearl rosary with which her little hands are often busy (unless they are, as now, stretching through the window to caress her mother whose plump neck is also festooned with pearls, and whose tears are soothed by cries of: *"Oh Mamacita . . . Mamacita!"*). The thin, big-eyed young man (husband or fiance) seems more detached; simply kisses the hand of the Mama quite formally and, after watching the helpful taxi driver who brought the prawns, comments cryptically: *"El FBI de Guaymas!"*

As the train gathers speed, a boy outside, his hair, his face, his

Mexico

tattered clothes black with what looks like coal-dust, runs too—white teeth gleaming with delight.

Night. The train making curves in the darkness. The *Magazine de Policia* has failed to please, occupied as it is by the petty details of the arrest of someone who is called *El General,* and the career of Maria Hernandez— large, fat, smiling—who has been selling bottles of gasoline mixed with ether to boys who, like those in Santa Monica, enjoy sniffing fumes. This humdrum list is scarcely representative of Mexican crime, which so often has a wild and exaggerated flavor of rural passion. (As Alfonso Quarez Cuaron, a criminal psychologist in Mexico, suggests: "The difference between crime in one area and another is interesting . . . each country gets the crime that it deserves.") The ordinary people of this area are still talking of a *fantasia* up near the lonely border of Guanajuato, discussing it in hushed voices—as they are now in this train compartment—shaking their heads, and calling the protagonists by their bestowed names, i.e., in the case of the two sisters, Maria and Delfina Jésus Gonzalez—*las diabolicas.*

The two ran a white slave ring and, with seven male accomplices, were charged with kidnapping, homicide, clandestine burying, rape, corruption of minors, and prostitution. They had surrounded themselves with armed bodyguards, chauffeurs, killers, and talent scouts, one of whom, army Captain Hermengildo Zuniga Maldonado, so far forgot his real role as to use members of his platoon to help with the fortification of a series of convenient caves to be used as cells, and to subdue reluctant teenage girls abducted from nearby villages, or lured from Mexico City. The sisters operated a private cemetery, and curiously adopted the children of their victims. (The children were often given nothing to eat but chili, along with cigarettes to dull their hunger.)

An important point is that if Mexico is noted for its homicides, it is also noted for its births. And this last, with an informal marriage system, has led to a disregard for female security, and so to an increase of informal prostitution.

Holy Thursday, April 16

Early morning. The train moves through better watered country. Fields of cane. Open sheds in which golden leaves of tobacco hang to dry. Little mountains cut to show their red flesh-like soil. Tepic (hard stone) capital of Nayarit, at the foot of an extinct volcano (Sananguey). Here women move beside the train holding up, with gentle hospitable gestures, *petate* baskets of fried chicken. The waiter in the car where coffee is served, borrows a pencil, and hints gracefully that he would accept a bottle of beer. ("Since you earn more than I do," he adds with a polite bow.)

Arrival in Guadalajara (Arabic for "rocky river"). It is *Semana Santa*. The holy hours approach! The sunset lingers on the splashing fountains in the main plaza and on the half-grown but perfectly formed poinciana trees in full bloom and stretching like scarlet umbrellas. Under these branches and against the background of the great golden-domed Byzantine cathedral with its Gothic-inspired towers, its medieval glass, its Arabic enamel, a whole population seems to be gathered—rich and poor, respectful and abandoned, frivolous and *mocho*. All of them smiling joyously and fingering their rosaries. Men in respectable dark suits, women with *rebozos*, a host of older ladies in black, many young girls in spotless dresses with white starched aprons, their hair plaited and shining—all of these pouring out of side streets, and struggling into the flower-filled churches in which the carved prostrate figure of Christ lies, wrapped in black or purple.

Good Friday, April 17

Memories of other Easters. A rustic broken village church outside of San Cristóbal de las Casas in Chiapas—a realistic statue of a suffering Christ being detached from the cross by Indian volunteers in their rough white hand-woven *chamarras*, and carried tenderly to burial. In this hushed moment, against a background of green palms, a little brown woman wrapped around with her *rebozo* suddenly pushes through the watching crowd, with tears rolling down her cheeks, and flings herself onto the burden in the arms of the Indians. *"O Cristo!"* she sobs, *"O Cristo . . . Cristo mio!"*

The night in a private home in one of the *colonias*, where a picturesque blond woman with a massive hairdo (*"Dos hijos y cuatro hijas Señora"*— Two sons and four daughters Señora) serves delicious *empanadas* (pies) and a flat basket of sweet pineapple, during the serving of which she becomes very annoyed with the little kitchen girl for forgetting the *servilletas*.

In Guadalajara it seems automatic to think of politics again, not only because political change is the theme of the sixties, but because the political vehicle here is José Clemente Orozco, one of the great Mexican muralists (whose art is associated with that group of painters identified with the Revolution of 1910 and with the rise of peasant leaders like Pancho Villa and Emiliano Zapata), and who was born here in Jalisco.

Mexico

It is hard to evaluate our debt to those we admire: and it had been Bertram Wolfe and his wife Ella who had first introduced me to Mexico, and afterwards to certain aspects of the country's political life. Now it is Bertram Wolfe's book, *Diego Rivera, His Life and Times,* which acts as a guide to the city. Orozco's work is fascinating because he seems the most effective portrayer of the complexities which plagued this country, and the leader of those who—with paint as a medium—carried out something close to a national psychoanalysis, and spread upon all suitable walls an anguished display of man's need for redemption. In spite of the cult of "art for the masses," Orozco is less simplistic in his views than Diego Rivera or David Alfaro Siqueiros—more aloof, never subject to rigid ideology, yet as much an evangelist as either of them. He seemed in reality an upholder of a "heretical Christianity," its "satiric recorder," the self-appointed scourge of the Mexican Sodom and Gomorrah. As Bertram Wolfe says, while the others painted the Revolution with faith, Orozco saw its demagoguery, its betrayal: "his revolutionary soldier is not inspired by its red flag, but blinded by its folds." In 1926 three dominant super-exuberant artists were attached to the *Sindicato Revolucionario de Obreros Técnicos y Plásticos*—Diego Rivera, David Alfaro Siqueiros, and Xavier Guerrero. According to Wolfe the drift towards Communism in Mexico among officials and government-controlled labor unions had declined by 1922; but a year later the famous trio of painters was elected to the Communist party's executive committee. "From a party of Revolutionary politics, it was converted into a party of Revolutionary painters!" Diego Rivera with his quaint frog-like features and his six-foot, 300-pound figure saw the "party" romantically; he had had a vision of the great star "which shines red and is five-pointed" and "fixed . . . on the slate of the Mexican sky." For Siqueiros even more than for Rivera, Communism had been a formative influence. This aggressive green-eyed man, trained as a union organizer, was for ideological reasons never completely at the service of his talent. (It was Siqueiros for instance who had been involved in the first attempt on Mexican soil to kill Trotsky; the broad implications of which murder are so far-reaching. Siqueiros had gone off to Spain in 1937 to fight with the Loyalists after a farewell from Cardenas during which he was presented with a pistol! Apparently he had joined the NKVD as early as 1928, and in Barcelona he is reputed to have spent a good deal of time at the Union of Revolutionary Artists when he may have known the Mercaders, who were to play a key role in the second and successful Trotsky murder attempt. One can guess how much he, i.e. Siqueiros, became changed and hardened during his submission to NKVD training.)

There is no time to see all of Orozco's work. His frescoes with their love of iron-grey, their use of fire, blood, smoke dominate the long empty neo-Roman chapel of the *Hospicio Cabañas* (in strange contrast to the luscious gardens outside and the merry faces of children peeping through the doors). But by mid-morning it is imperative to go out and into the streets; to watch the old Easter rite of penitence and resurrection with choristers parading, dressed in black gowns and white surplices, wearing crown-like mitres with blue dobbins. Soon, under the high roof of the Cathedral, there swells and grows the melancholy chanting of the "Stations of the Cross."

Holy Saturday, April 17

By bus to Pátzcuaro, sitting beside a girl holding an enormous bunch of artificial flowers. Through the tinted glass of the bus windows, Lake Chapala appears to be pink—the earth, the little adobe houses, a white house—all take on a pink glow. Along the lakefront fish weirs are accented by nets hanging up to dry. Trucks of melons mixed with enormous bunches of red carnations stand in the fields. Behind on a hillside a charming model village is dominated by a pink cross; and this faint pink irradiates a whole scene, so that with the help of the brown girl and her flowers, hours of travel appear as nothing. Again in true Mexican fashion, reality is allowed to intrude. (The bus stops for lunch at a restaurant filled with flies, and a dirty old man with a squawking hen takes the girl's place.)

April 18, EASTER Sunday

In Pátzcuaro (place of delights) a sedate procession with candles and chants is winding from one plaza to another and up the cold cobbled streets. Heavy laurel trees give a certain classic solemnity; female marchers are wrapped in *rebozos,* and the *serapes* of the taller men show only their eyes and hang dark and straight, covering their whole bodies. It all seems immensely far away from the political and sociological thread of the century; and indeed the male marchers in their long straight blanketlike coverings might have stepped from the niches of a medieval cathedral.

April 19

In the daylight the houses appear particularly solid and compact—squarish with projecting rooves. Women walking to the ancient wells with *ollas* for water. The market selling pottery with a dark green glaze.

Mexico

There is as well a certain eccentricity in many of the local characters. An intense old German philosophizes about the meaning of death and walks slowly along with his great friend Dr. Mendez from the *farmacia*.

En route to Mexico City

Past streets lined with jacaranda trees, violet against golden stone. Wheat fields. The pink city of Morelia. The inevitable drunk man, his face lost in his sombrero, swaying gently. The ascent into the wooded mountains, past lonely greyish plains decorated with a pattern of maguey which might have been cut out of dark metal. The bus moves out of the circle of large towns (where for the first time newspapers and magazines from the capital are on display) and mounts for 7,000 to 8,000 feet to the Mexican plateau, with its one city to end them all (often simply called Mexico, which means in Aztec "the navel of the moon"). This city is said to have a population of 5½ million; although no one really knows; because shortages of work in the villages have caused such an inundation of human beings—who conjure up fragile shacks on vacant land—that the peripheries expand every night, creating satellite communities which lack water and electricity and ring the capital around like a cordon *pas sanitaire*. The situation is similar to that of the *favelas* of Brazil, the *matsu* of Japan, the shanty towns of Africa. Mexico City's maternal Catholic embrace encircles a people whose true heritage is still the *pueblo* (the village as opposed to the town); and in times of crisis those villagers move as they have always done. In their simple clothes, sandalled or barefoot, with strings of children, and sleeping babies on their backs—with hope in their eyes, they climb the mountains and trek along the entrance roads, to gaze in wonder on the "navel of the moon."

Here where the bus travels over an austere and rocky landscape which borders the city—enlivened every so often by some disrupting spot of color, a small shining Byzantine church, or a barefoot woman in a long blue skirt and a blouse of shocking pink—it is easy to admit that the traveler escapes with pleasure from that society to the north, so top-heavy with technology.

But immediately political interest is stimulated by the magazines bought at the bus stop. This is election time; and five celebrated leftist intellectuals, among them Carlos Fuentes, have abandoned their campaign to oppose the candidacy of Diaz Ordaz for the presidency. Apparently Castro's arrival on the Latin American scene has been forcing intellectuals to put their ideological cards on the table. Many have declared themselves closer to Mao and to Fidel than to their own IRP (Institutional Revolutionary Party) which is accused, so to speak, of ceasing to progress after the solidification of the 1910 Revolution. (Coming from Los Angeles—at present in the throes of demonstrations and riots—I might have thought that a Mexican election would be the very time for new demands to be placed before the electorate; but in Mexico this is not necessarily so. It is an underdeveloped country, profoundly influenced by its Revolution in that this Revolution still represents Mexico's most important values—but also occupied with trying to evolve a system of politics in which most local groups can make their claims effective. Mexico is in fact—according to one historian—attempting to make that definitive transition towards the acceptance of change, without which a society cannot become "Westernized.") In the meantime whatever the declarations of dissidents, it is clear that Diaz Ordaz is going to lead the country. The five former supporters of *Politica*, therefore, are crossing to the "other side" (that is the "successful left," where all the benefits and favors are given out). As the commentator says, *"Eso es todo."* (That is all.)

Apart from election activities, Mexicans (according to the *News*) are also involved in a dramatic "putting down" of the United States. This has become known as the "Sanchez case." *The Children of Sanchez* is a study of poverty in Mexico by the anthropologist Oscar Lewis which has been a recent publishing success. (I am already half-way through it.) It deals with the struggles of a family which tries to exist in the slums of the capital; and it is hard to believe that the material, ordinary to anyone who knows Mexico, could have so abraded the sensitivity of certain citizens that they are calling it obscene and slanderous.

Typical extracts from the book:

JÉSUS SANCHEZ

I can say that I had no childhood. I was born in a poor little village in the state of Veracruz. Very lonely and sad is what it was. . . . My father didn't allow us to play with anybody, he never bought toys, we were always alone. I went to school for one year only, when I was about eight or nine years old.

We always lived in one room . . . just one room. We slept there, each on his little bed made of boards and boxes. In the morning I would get up and make the sign of the cross. I washed my face and mouth and went to haul in water. . . . Usually I would take a machete and rope and would go into the countryside to look for dry wood. I came back carrying a huge bundle on my back. . . . I worked since I was very small. I knew nothing of games. . . .

We were living in a poor little house. It had a roof only on one side of it; the other side was uncovered. We borrowed corn because we really had nothing to eat. . . . There were no medicines of any kind for my mother, no doctors, no anything, and she went to my father's house to die . . ."

And so on. Here are the dramatic extremes of a country still emerging from feudalism; the deprivation of those who approach the city unprepared—from the pueblo, from the isolated mountains, from the desert—who are thrust into the raw dramatic life of city streets, who carry with them outmoded ideas, respect for the powerful, a mystical belief in the church, the acceptance of the female as a creature born for the use of the male.

We enter Mexico City to this theme of poverty and faith and *machismo*. But in spite of it, the gross national product has been rising here by a steady 6 percent a year, and land reform with all its shortcomings has brought the country from a state of near famine to the edge of a glut in production. Education has become available to about 80 percent of the children in the larger cities—and this is a nation which has been involved in transforming a semi-feudal society and emancipating its Indians. Since the poverty is only too evident, spread out against the sober yet grandiose architecture of the cities, the interested newcomer cannot fail to be impressed by it and to expatiate about its injustices; but also to sense hope in it, as if the humble citizen (off-spring of two strains, Spanish and Indian, both God-oppressed, both accustomed to frugality and lack of comfort) is at last beginning to look up from a sleep of resignation.

The bus moves slowly up the wide rather chilly but still crowded streets, where people stand in doorways wrapped around with coverings. Over everything is spread a curious golden-tinted dye; over markets, factories, *pulquerias*, warehouses, faces—over the great city a romantic gloss of anonymity.

April 20

Am now a guest in the Pedregal on the outskirts of San Angel. Here some enterprising architects have developed, among those dark outcrops of volcanic rock which characterize the area, a rather striking array of living areas which the architect muralist Juan O'Gorman, has sourly called "processed gardens" ("a clump of daisies here, a stand of *colorín* trees there.")

It is true that on the suburbanized edge of the valley, the familiar Mexican feeling is diluted. But there are still the high walls, the vines of bougainvillea and Capa de Oro—still the peepholes in the big heavy gates, the neat brown-skinned servants coming to answer the clang of the bell in their full dresses and white aprons, still the smell of wood fires, the barking of dogs; the distant cry of the cock.

April 23

Meet Alfredo for lunch. He is an anthropologist and one of those who has been involved in the Sanchez controversy. He stands outside the restaurant, a short rather stocky figure, his suit a little loose, his straight dark to silver-grey hair which he brushes back with his hand, his unmistakable Indian air (yet with the features and expression of a Spanish intellectual). Behind him, though far away, the buildings of the University rising from their lava plain, the red and metallic-colored tower of the Administration building; the horizontal Siqueiros mural with the outstretched arms of its student figures giving an extended effect; and further back still glittering in the sun, what can be seen of the O'Gorman mural—which seems squat and solid like the squared-off abstraction of an ancient Mexican god. We eat *enchilladas,* drink coffee, talk of the past. (Remembering a visit to a lonely village in Oaxaca where we spent endless long hours sitting on rather rocky ground, while Alfredo tried with infinite patience to persuade the village *mayores* to consider using the government clinics.)

Afterwards we discuss crime and poverty. Alfredo suggests that one of the most interesting groups to write about in Mexico would be that of the *pepenadores.* (These are the rubbish collectors of Mexico City, of whom there are supposed to be at least 6,000. The word *pepenador* is derived from the Nahautl *pepenaditla* and means "he who gathers up what is spread on the ground, particularly if it is done rapidly." Sometimes in Nahautl-speaking villages it will be said of a pecking chicken that it is *pepenando,* and one can see how the word *pepenador* came to refer to those who make their living by gathering up, sorting, and selling to the factories, old rags, glass, discarded paper, bones, and pieces of worn leather. In the city proper, trash is called *basura,* and those official workers paid to dispose of it—drivers, helpers, street and park cleaners—are called *basureros.* The *pepenadores,* however, are part of private enterprise. They are the humble parasites clinging to the fringes of an industry worth more than 10,000 dollars a day, and accepting the tiny profits which remain after everybody else has had his cut.

"They too gradually lose their traditions," Alfredo maintains. "Like so many Mexicans, they disappear into the anonymous mass." As he admits dryly and without pleasure that he himself is "too successful," it seems real for the first time that he carries within himself that conflicted, double personality of the *mestizo.*

"There's more and more administrative work," he says. "I like to be in the field, and to ride and walk and talk to the people. What do I do instead? Go to meetings and conferences; conferences and meetings."

We walk in the sunshine beside a canal planted with casuarina trees. Alfredo is interested in the riots in Harlem, the protests against the Vietnam war, the struggle for civil rights. Speaking only Spanish and never having been out of Mexico, his provincial naïvete is such that he cannot imagine the American situation where a constant battle goes on in the open arena of public opinion. In fact, confused by the attrition of a tested democracy, he is convinced that a "revolution" might at any moment break out across the border! (Similarly with his faith in the

Mexico

"idea," he feels that his opinion as to the necessity of armed insurrection in Mexico is not only correct but a vital contribution to the future.)

It is of course true that the political scene here is so bound up with nationalism and the myth of the *caudillo* that the dominant effect is more that of a socialist myth than of a socialist achievement. But for Alfredo, who thinks of himself as a radical, the only way to deal with this is a battle to the death. Once in answer to a direct question he said: *"Si—soy Communista"* (Yes, I am a Communist). The conversation had stopped there. Now we talk about whether the aspirations of Mexicans are properly expressed by the Marxist philosophy, to which so many professionals, writers, artists give lip service. Is this lining up with the left only representative of the will and drive of the articulate sector, or is it something more profound, and closer to the sympathy of the masses? "We hope for the future," Alfredo says.

That element of the macabre so native to this country—that fascinating intermingling of what is Indian, Spanish, continental; that dark mystery of Mexico's plateau—has been made more understandable to the outsider by Bertram Wolfe (not only in his writing but in his "personal" understanding of the international Marxist movement, and its catalytic influence). Here is a culture where only four hundred years ago hearts were offered to the sun, and death was considered so beautiful that it was woven as a flower into tapestries and rugs. It is therefore a culture which, opening wide its capacious embrace to all who required it, still stolidly accepts. After the Spanish Civil War in 1936 the Russians preserved their Spanish *apparat* of spies, executioners, propagandists by setting up a secret Spanish headquarters in Moscow; but also by dispatching a concentration of veteran killers to Mexico itself (to which country the Spanish government-in-exile had moved). The aim of the killer-clique was to liquidate Trotsky, who in spite of the official clamor of the Mexican party had arrived in Tampico in January of 1937. Preparations to assassinate him had been so thorough that they included the purging of the local party and the discrediting of the current leader, a romantic pistol-packing poet called Herman Laborde.

After that first unsuccessful attempt in which Siqueiros was involved, the famous old revolutionary knew that it could only be a matter of time. "What another day to live!" he would exclaim to his wife in the morning.

So soon after Kennedy's assassination it is natural to reflect now that Ramon de Mercader, Trotsky's eventual killer, acted as did Oswald, the assassin of JFK, under "ideological" demand; and that in the century in which we live, such killings are to be expected. As far as Trotsky was concerned, the long arm of the KGB (reaching boldly into the "new" world) at last grasped its prey.

April 25

In the Calle Viena the gardens are dark with tropical plants, and the house in which Trotsky lived still has its high brick wall and the square guard towers which suggest a prison. ("This is not a house," Trotsky joked, "it is a medieval fortress.")

The first assassination attempt took place on May 24, 1940. Telephone lines were cut, Communist party women seduced some of the guards; others were immobilized by gunfire. A young American, Robert Sheldon Harte, serving as house guard that night, opened the gates and was himself abducted. The room where Trotsky and his wife Natalya were sleeping was raked by a withering fire, some of which was deflected by steel shutters. The Trotskys only saved themselves by rolling under the bed. Only one of the three bombs used went off. Altogether the affair was a fiasco.

General Leandro Sanchez Salazar, Police Chief put in charge of the investigation, arriving at the house, found Trotsky's grandson, the twelve-year-old Esteban, was playing tranquilly in the garden, but limping because of a bandage on his left foot. Salazar listened to the nightmare of Trotsky's wife, Natalya, who had wakened during the attack to see, illuminated by the flare of an incendiary bomb, the silhouette of a myth-like man of war, "the curve of a helmet, the shine of buttons, an elongated face." While the sound of her grandson calling chilled her to the marrow, she saw "amongst the flames a thin trail of blood leading out into the patio." Fortunately the child was only slightly wounded.

Salazar was convinced at last that he faced no ordinary criminals, but the vast power of the Russian Secret Service; and in his book written later, *Asi Asesinaron a Trotski*, he included a declaration which Trotsky added to clarify the attack for the Mexican government.

> During the last years Stalin has killed thousands of my supposed or real followers. He has exterminated all my family except me, my wife and one of my grandsons . . . he has assassinated one of the Chiefs of the G.P.U., Ignace Reiss. Those very agents of the G.P.U. who killed Ignace Reiss hounded my son in Paris. On the night of the 7th of November of 1936 the agents of the G.P.U. broke into the Instituto Cientifico de Paris and stole part of my archives. Two of my ex-secretaries Erwin Wolff and Rudolf Klement were killed by agents of the G.P.U.; the first in Spain and the second in Paris. . . . All the Moscow Trials during the years 1936-37 had as their aim to turn me over to the G.P.U.

Salazar was discouraged by this extravagance of political crime. By mere chance he went into a bar where five tramway workers were sitting, and an oldish heavy man with a grey moustache was declaring, "The *sopolones* are not sticking to their investigation. Hypocrites! The other night I ran into a group of comrades at this very place. Close to us was the big Chief of Tacubaya, good and drunk. He was telling his friends that he had lent two police uniforms to the attackers. And they want to make us believe that the police stick to their jobs? I say tell that to Juan Diego!"

Salazar immediately followed up this clue, only to find that the trail led to none other than to Siqueiros, today's showman for tourists! Along with Siqueiros were implicated his two brothers-in-law, Luis and Leopoldo Arenal, and another painter Antonio Pujol.

The house in which I am staying in the Pedregal is not far from the San Angel Inn (an attractive restaurant), and the San Angel Inn is not far from a humble little *jacal* on the *carretera* leading to Santa Rosa which had been chosen for the hiding place of Sheldon Harte. When Salazar and his men hastened to inspect this small house, they not only found signs of habitation, but suspected that the earth floor of the basement kitchen had been recently disturbed.

> "... the earth gave way easily ... at a depth of thirty centimetres it was mixed with lime. . . . We began to sweat, but we could not stop for a moment, nor did we think of doing so. Such was our anxiety! The blows of the hoe resounded through the house. . . . About thirty centimetres more and a terrible odour arose . . . we looked at each other. . . . It was clear that it was a body."

Salazar placed men on guard and went off to get a judicial authority to serve as a witness. It was now raining heavily.

> "We . . . had come on foot, and had to return this way from the scene of the crime, because we had left our cars on the highway. . . . Stumbling and falling . . . we arrived back at last, tired and covered with mud. . . . As the spades of the *campesinos* unearthed the body, it was seen that it had acquired an impressive bronze color . . . by the . . . bluish glare of the lanterns the red hair seemed to spread out like melted metal . . . the lime had further whitened the face and hands."

A somber little caravan started out towards San Angel, the Judicial authority, the body, the agents, Salazar himself, some diligent reporters. Day was just dawning when there came cries of "Trotski! Trotski!" And it was seen that Trotsky himself had come to meet the party.

> The old Russian exile . . . was depressed, sad. He looked for a long time at his ex-secretary, his eyes filled with tears. This man who had directed a great revolution . . . who had had to direct bloody battles, who had seen disappear one after the other, his family and friends, cried now in silence.

The atmosphere in the Avendia Pedregal is darkened by the thought of that house in Santa Rosa, where a young American had been yet another victim in the worldwide victim-filled hunt. The blatantly "foreign" character of the attack was of course evident, since the exposé showed that the core group had been Mexican Stalinists (most of them active in the Spanish Civil War). It was not until September of

1940 that Siqueiros was finally discovered in Jalisco in a mountain hideout, dressed as a miner, with clothes and boots thick with mud. The Mexican Communist party was careful to disown him as an "uncontrollable element, considered half-mad." At the same time another purge of the Mexican party leadership was carried out. Pedro Checa, who had served in Spain, was transported to nearby Cuernavaca where he was kept incommunicado, and then died under mysterious circumstances.

One of the most extraordinary features of the whole case is that the cultural and legal situation in Mexico combined curiously to shield the front-man Siqueiros. Countless sympathizers rallied to his cause. Independent artists and intellectuals urged the President to be lenient. There was a chorus of "artists and men of science . . . are . . . bulwarks of culture and progress." With extravagant perversity, these intellectuals applauded an attempted murder which might at some time be a prevision of their own! Siqueiros was indicted with his accomplices on nine counts and charged with organizing the massive assault, and with the responsibility for Harte's death. At this point *amparos* (legal devices to protect individuals against unjust persecution) were brought forward to concentrate on the lesser charges. He was absolved of homicide charges, criminal conspiracy and the use of firearms; the only charges left were those of robbery, damage to property, etc. Out on bail, he immediately escaped to Chile to paint a mural. (It was later discovered that this had been arranged by the pro-Communist poet Pablo Neruda.)

Today the first sight of a *pepenador*. It is in the Paseo de la Reforma where the golden Angel of the Independence stands poised—holding out a wreath as if to drop it squarely onto the marble head of Hidalgo. She trudges along, a small bowed woman in bright voluminous skirts, a tight dirty jacket, and a flat straw hat, oblivious of the stream of traffic, the exclusive shops, and the airline offices which sell tickets to far places. Before her she pushes a wheeled cart, laden with cardboard, milk cartons, old newspapers, and pieces of flattened tin; and against the backdrop of the sophisticated buildings and the tall monument with its glittering *Angelito*, she seems to represent all those who live obscurely and are cut off from the aspiring mainstream of the country's life. Perhaps she belongs to one of the *colonias proletarias,* or in any of those corners in the center where a few dilapidated crowded courts are wedged between solid shops and churches—or, possibly, as do so many of the city's *pepenadores,* in a *barrio bajo* (low area) such as Tepito, site of the thieves' market, or the Candelaria de los Patos, home of the capital's murderers, dope sellers, and thieves.

She is probably on her way to one of the depots, where she could sell her paper and tin. (Later Alfredo tells me that if a *pepenador* like this woman is working alone, she might have fifteen pesos by nightfall, which she would tie up in a corner of her skirt; and possibly also some valuable item to dispose of, for instance a pair of old shoes, a piece of rope, an article of still wearable clothing.)

Conversations with Alfredo are long, but linguistically limited. Although the tumult about the Sanchez affair is dying down, he still seems involved with it. Lewis has been examined from every angle, even to the extent of having his mother insulted and his tapes discredited. Yet it is a symptom of Mexico's growing political and psychological maturity that numbers of intellectuals—even those noted for anti-American attitudes—jumped to the book's defense and agreed with the novelist Carlos Fuentes, who dismissed the tempest as "neo-patriotic chauvinism."

Ironically, the endless discussion has so turned the spotlight on poverty, that it becomes clear that here is one of the few problems which Mexico shares with the United States—namely that the poor are getting poorer.

"In many parts of Mexico the Indians suffer greatly," Alfredo explains. "In some areas they live close to the starvation level."

And this is the reason for criticizing Lewis? Surely Lewis himself is making a contribution to Mexican understanding of the problem simply by showing how the economy is rejecting its most underprivileged members . . . ? Again wasn't he himself pressured by the Left to take the point of view that he did? Hadn't the whole affair had an artificial quality?

Now Alfredo looks a little embarrassed. He finally admits that he thought quite highly of the *Children of Sanchez*; that it has been policy on the part of a certain section of the far Left to condemn the book.

Then the exploiter is neither Lewis, nor the middle-class Mexican, but the "Chief Azteca de Moscú."

Alfredo is murmuring: *"Porqué? Porqué?"*

"Because he—they—are serving up Lewis on the anti-American altar!"

He laughs.

And did he himself believe in what he was doing? Alfredo shakes his head.

"Lo hizo en mala fé" (I did it in bad faith).

But why? He shrugs his shoulders.

"It was ordered?"

He smiles. "Suggested."

Alfredo's admission is a vivid example of how Western Communists and fellow travelers do violence to their own values; but it brings us back to a corruption greater than that lack of intellectual integrity to which Alfredo admits. It is a reminder of the fact that not so long ago as history counts time, in the very late thirties to be exact, GPU plans for Trotsky's assassination necessitated the direct or indirect involvement of numerous North Americans (Americans whose acceptance of "comradely discipline" did not condone, after all, the silencing of dissent with Alpine picks, and who did not live in an underdeveloped country like Mexico—where intellectuals had limited informational sources at their disposal.)

April 28

The refuse trucks, the *camiones collectores* as they are called, roll along the highway under the vast skies of the plains of Ixtapalapa, while there hover in these same skies the black *zopilotes*, vultures of Mexico. Alfredo is driving in his little car and long before we reach the brick fence of the *tiradero* itself, we are conscious of the flavor of the trade which goes on there, a trade which has marked the entire countryside. Herds of sheep, horses, and black and white cattle wander in the far distance, along with the solitary figures of shepherds, odd children, and occasional women bowed by burdens. The joyless shacks blossom from the earth like flowers indigenous to the earth of Ixtapalapa; apart from these and the wandering searching human beings, the country grows only the sad casuarina tree and that tree which human beings plant—the telephone pole.

The dump here, like a prolific mother, is the source of all life! A young man with a round unformed face tells us that he is a *pepenador* and is waiting for his brother-in-law. He shows a card made out to Antonio Velasquez Rodriguez, and then with a shy hopeful smile asks the inevitable question: "Don't you want to take us to the United States? I am a good carpenter." He leads the way to his sister's house, with its pink tank on the roof. Inside a young woman (Remedios Velasquez) obviously pregnant, holds a baby in her arms while two healthy-looking boys cling to her skirts. The baby has a fever, its round, solemn sweating face is crowned by a scarlet knitted cap. Behind Remedios stands an improvised altar holding several holy pictures, decorated by a dusty wreath of wax flowers and a tiny candle; these she tells me, are her *santitos* (saints).

Not only is Antonio a *pepenador*, but also Remedios herself. "My father died and then my mother worked in the *tiraderos*—first one *tiradero* and then another; from the beginning I remember picking up paper or bottles and carrying them to the weighing machines.

"I went to school for one year," she goes on, "because my mother wanted me to get out of the *tiradero*, but then I married my husband Tomas, and he had no work; so we came back to the *tiradero* again." Antonio explains that he too remembers little but life in the dump, that from six- or eight-years old he had "worked like a man," that he had

Mexico

had to help his mother and sister because his big brother had been *perdido* (lost), and there had been no one else to help. At fourteen he had been married, and after that he had had three children. He would like to introduce his wife to me, he said, but at the present moment they were "annoyed with each other."

Antonio confirms the fact that prices paid in the *tiraderos* are lower than those paid in the open market, saying that in the *tiradero* you get five *centavos* a *kilo* for glass, but in the center you get fifty *centavos*— that the present price of paper in the city is fifty to sixty *centavos* per *kilo*, and that here they give you only twenty *centavos*. He mutters vaguely about *mal gente* (bad people), about threats from the bosses and about mysterious deaths, and adds that the scales are fixed, and that if you have a load of forty or fifty *kilos*, they would weigh it in at thirty *kilos*, and so on. As if it were a prison or a concentration camp, he talks about "inside," which means inside the fence of the *tiradero*. At this point, Maria Rodriguez Camacho, mother of Antonio and Remedios, and so grandmother to the Remedios' children, comes in. She is a tiny, wiry, brown woman, with a parched monkey-like face and two sparse plaits. She comes barefoot into the room, and when Remedios introduces her, she bends over and places her hand on my left shoulder and bows her head in an attitude of old-fashioned submission. "Yes, I suffered a great deal," she says, but then she says, with a little laugh, *"Ya—estoy acostumbrada"* (Now I am accustomed to it). She has been forty-eight years in the *basura*. Folding her wrinkled hands about the child she holds, she tells the story of the death of her husband (who had previously abandoned her and his five children but who had come back to die), and of how she had sent for all the children (knowing how sick he was) and how they had knelt down and she had put his hand on each of their heads in turn. The next day he had died. She reproves Antonio, who has somehow got hold of a small bottle of *pulque*, "You made your promise not to drink in front of the Virgin. Better to pay the rent than to drink."

The white hen wanders about her feet, and the old lady, clasping the other grandchild with one hand, scatters corn on the floor with the other. Antonio, who has bent his head as if in shame, suddenly lifts it and states logically: "I have been drinking since I was twelve years old."

April 30

At a small cocktail party someone uses the phrase "social dissolution." (This charge is equivalent to "subversion" and is frequently employed here to accuse potential or actual Communists. For some time now the extreme Left has been stressing that the charge of "social dissolution" is not only unconstitutional, but a politically dangerous tool in the hands of the demagogues. Apparently some conservative Mexican lawyers agree with this view.)

The truth is that the bitter international intrigue which centered around the dissident Trotsky has not vanished. Siqueiros is still in the news and since his arrest in 1960 there have been frequent "free the prisoners" campaigns. Clippings which had arrived in California reported that last year Gustave Diaz Ordaz was being pressured to modify his stand on prisoners held in the federal penitentiary—the rationale being that these particular inmates were political prisoners and not criminals. They included such well-known activists as Demetrio Vallejo Martinez—former head of the railway union; Valentin Campa—head of the pro-Communist Mexican party of Workers and Farm Laborers; and Dionisio Encena Rodriguez—head of the Mexican Communist party. In 1960 Siqueiros for involvement in similar activities had been sent to join them; and mug shots appeared in the American press, showing a pained look on his strong-featured face, and what seemed to read as No. 46-788-600 stamped on the card placed across his chest.

Listening to the indignation of a handsome woman at the party— who talks first of the necessity of freeing the "great Siqueiros" and then of the arrogance of the investigative police—my first thought is that something else should be stressed first. Why was Siqueiros—who along with accomplices had been indicted in September of 1940 on the grounds of organizing the attempt on Trotsky's life, and of responsibility for the murder of the young American Sheldon Harte, free at all? In other words, since all the evidence had pointed to his leadership in an early stage of what turned out to be one of the most dramatic and horrible of all political assassinations—why was he (Siqueiros) not in prison long before 1960? Why had Mexican justice allowed him to go free, to escape to Chile in 1940, and later to reenter the country?

As a postscript to the cocktail party at which Siqueiros is so lauded, the morgue of a local newspaper is visited to research relevant events. One article claims that Mexico is and will be an important target for the USSR—not only because of its material resources but because of its proximity to the United States; and that the aim of the representatives from the Russian embassy is less to collect information than to influence Mexican policies, and to create disorder; that the Russians do very little trade with Mexico; that Russian ships seldom come to Mexican ports; that the Embassy offices are open for short hours, leaving the officers free time for influence peddling.

Another mentions that of the men now in prison for attempting to paralyze the national railway system with wildcat strikes, the labor leader Demetrio Vallejo is the first, and that his sentence is for "social dissolution." Caught with KGB officers Nikolai M. Remizov and Niko-

Mexico

lai V. Akensov from the Soviet Embassy, Vallejo admitted to accepting from them a million pesos (eighty thousand dollars) to initiate strikes. (This is written up in the *Chicago Daily Tribune,* the *Baltimore Sun,* the *New York Herald Tribune,* and *Newsweek.*)

May 4

Discussion about Communism with Alfredo. We wander over the waste lands behind the houses of the Pedregal, where the dark rocks seem darker than ever under a rather violent sky. Every so often there are small delicate trees with red flowers, which Alfredo says feed upon the rich volcanic earth. Under a volcanic overhang a bone-thin woman is washing at a tub (a puzzling fact since there seems no house nearby, and no water).

The question is whether the Russian establishment cares anything about Mexico and its problems. Did the Russian party, for instance, care that it was paying Vallejo to stir up strikes at a time when the Mexican economy was making gains?

Alfredo, whose attention is always fixed upon the Indians, speaks of radicalizing *los de abajo* (the most underprivileged) and teaching them to reply to exploitation.

Would the Indians, or the *mestizo* for that matter, have a better life if the Communists did gain the upper hand? Surely Russia, whose people still labor under terrible disadvantages, is trying to solve her *own* problems by exporting revolution? Why do Alfredo and his colleagues wish to impose upon Mexico, still struggling with its underdeveloped state and its feudal and religious past, the strangling grip of Communism? Mexico, if lacking certain democratic structures, still has Christian values; she has moreover in many ways a freer society than has Russia. The creative solution for her problems is certainly not subordination to so alien an ideology. Nor can the United States be expected to remain passive under certain circumstances.

Alfredo's hooded Indian eyes do not light up as we stumble through this analysis, for his strong point is not rationality. It is hard to explain that the theme of sacrifice which runs through the art, literature, history of Meso-America is akin both to early pagan beliefs and to that ideology which developed out of Karl Marx's labors in the British Museum; and was then spread through the world by his ideological heirs. As Isaac Deutscher said in his *Prophet Unarmed,* "Many in their ambivalence felt that . . . the victim must die, if they . . . the others . . . were to live. . . . "

While we sit for a while on the sun-warmed rocks, lizards scuttle to and fro in front of us. What can one say of a regime which encourages one of Mexico's best artists to machine-gun one of Russia's best brains?

Again that flicker of negation and question on Alfredo's face. Whatever he believes about the Trotsky case, he has evidently put it behind him. It is not even clear that he has not accepted the rationalization of Siqueiros himself, who had claimed that the machine-gunning of Trotsky's bedroom was done for "psychological" purposes. And perhaps it is important to understand and accept that intellectuals are as much at the mercy of rationalization as other human beings. In Selden Rodman's *Mexican Journal* he records that even a man as *simpatica* as Miguel Covarrubbias could blame the whole Hungarian uprising on United States propaganda, saying that pictures in *Life* magazine had clearly shown the Hungarians themselves to be the aggressors!

To the *tiradero* with Josefina, a tall willowy Mexican girl. It has been raining, and we sit in the semi-darkness with Maria who has lit a single candle in front of the saints. The white hen, fluffing its wet feathers, wanders as usual around our feet. The door opens, and Antonio comes tumbling into the room, his trousers wet to the knees. He wears no hat, and his hair hangs over his eyes as he lurches to and fro, obviously very drunk. Maria asks how he could shame her by coming in this condition. *"Me cayi"* (I fell over), Antonio answers.

"You're drunk," scolds the mother in her soft voice: "Aren't you ashamed in front of the Señoras? Didn't you swear before the Virgin not to drink?" Antonio asks his mother for a sombrero.

"Where is the one I gave you yesterday?"

"Lo perdio" (I lost it), says Antonio in the voice of a child. His mother gives him the towel she is wearing over her own head. Seated in the half dark, with the towel over his head like an Arab, Antonio is drunk enough to speak with poetic freedom. "I was born—born—born in the *tiradero*," he says slowly. "I am poor—a poor man." He mentions that his wife has left home again, and he begins to cry a little. *"Hablo en plata,"* he keeps saying (which means literally, "I speak in silver. I am sincere"). He goes into his mother's bedroom, brings out the colored photograph of his wife (who according to Maria is independent and *muy hombrera,* very fond of men), and begins to kiss it.

Maria talks about the deaths of her children. "After Juan Cruz there was Juanita—she got an illness and there was no money for the doctor."

And then?

"Then came Ana," the old lady says. "She died in the street. I felt her little body stretch out and stiffen, and I ran, ran to the house of the doctor, holding her in my arms. But it was too late. Ah Señora but God is good! Remedios came and I named her for the Virgin."

And who next?

Maria thought a moment. "Antonio—*el borrachincito*" (Antonio—the

Mexico

little drunkard). "When my first child was born I didn't know enough to put its mouth to my breast. But the baby didn't die all the same, although it had something wrong with its spine, and its skull was elongated—we put a little gourd on its head. It died later when it got wet in the rain. Afterwards in the *tiradero* I had children with the help of the midwives. Some say that the midwives study and some say not. . . . Sometimes I cried so much that you'd have thought I expected the baby to be born through the mouth. All my children were born in the *tiradero*. I would be afraid to go to the hospital where men look after you."

"As for me," the pregnant Remedios interjected, with her voice of the new generation, "I would be afraid to *stay* in the *tiradero*."

And the other children, what happened to them?

Maria is tired now. She makes a deprecatory gesture. "Ah, *Señora*," she murmurs, "what of it? They only lived one day, two days. . . ."

In front of the University coffee shop the students linger for a moment to smoke cigarettes in the sunshine; and with the end of this trip to Mexico in sight, it seems important to try here to follow through with campus themes encountered in Los Angeles.

We all sit down and talk of Latin America and its place in the new revolutionary movement. "In the States *radicalismo* is very strong— no?" one of the students says with a delighted smile. He has long black moustachios which dangle almost to the neck of his blue sweater. A second student is dark-skinned with intense eyes and a stubble beard, and is addressed by the others as *El Barbudo*.

A tall younger boy tilts his head toward *El Barbudo*. "*Amigo de Guillén*." (Friend of Guillén.)

"You mean the 'Revolutionary'?"

"Yes—*El Barbudo* comes from Argentina where Guillén was. This is a great thing to be friend to Guillén." (Abraham Guillén is a Spanish neo-Marxist with Trotskyist leanings, famous for his prowess in the Civil War, and for his writings on guerrilla theory.)

El Barbudo explains that he (Guillén) has written a book called *The Agony of Imperialism* which all this generation tried to get hold of and read. "Not always easy," he says in halting English, "it was *prohibido* . . . but very worthwhile. He is a believer in *Retorno*. *Retorno* is—(there is a whispered consultation). "*Retorno* is in English 'Retaliation.' An important part of his theory. To pay back the police if they punish the guerrilla . . . *Otra cosa* (another thing) is firepower. In a demonstration it is good to have fire power."

The boy in the blue sweater begins to talk of Cuba, and to say that Ché and Guillén had quarreled about strategy, but were in agreement along general lines. *Guillénismo* does not see fighting with the peasants as does Ché. It sees an abandonment of frontiers in Latin America, and continuing war in the cities for a common purpose.

Soon no English is being spoken, and the Spanish is almost too rapid to follow. Hands are waved in the air and expressions grow intense. The empty coffee cups and the empty *refresco* bottles spread out over the table. A vague shape of Latin America materializes in the smoke-filled air. Dotted with names of towns, guerrilla groups, *sierras*, revolutionary leaders, engagements with police units—all linked together by the solemn reiterative incantations of names like Fidel, Che, Mao, Ho Chi Minh, Kim Il Sung, General Giap, Guillén, Marighella—and with key phrases such as "strategy of confrontation," "common front," "Yanqui Imperialism," "historical exception," "last stages of Capitalism," "Indigenismo."

At the same time a sense of unreality hovers over it all; for it seems that these four young Latin Americans, one from Argentina, one from Costa Rica, and two from Mexico, talk without controls, as robots might when programming has gone wild. The tall thin boy mentions a certain Roberto who has abruptly left his studies and gone to train in the *sierras* of Cuba. *El Barbudo* says in the most natural way in the world, and as if it were a foregone conclusion, that soon a broad coalition of forces in Latin America, including Christians and anarchists, stretching from one spectrum to the other, will be lining up for the "Second Latin American War of Independence against the Yanquis."

"Todo el continente (all the continent)," he proclaims with grim satisfaction. *"El Sur contra el Norte Imperialista* (the South against the Imperialist North)."

Here in this grandiose vision of pitting one half of the continent against another, is that same wild wish to destroy, encountered across the border on the West Coast; where the young member of the PLP had said when referring with such satisfaction to Western society, "Blow it all up! Let it explode!"

Inside the great *tiradero* itself. We walk (Antonio and I) through the neat streets of the housing development towards the dump. As we walk our footsteps are dogged by others who make their way there also: men with *costales* (bags), an old woman leading a burro, a boy with two little pigs (these last, Antonio explains, to be tethered as in any feeding grounds). Again there is this sense of the *tiradero* as a fertile mother—repulsive, steaming in the hot sun, giving life to her less fortunate children.

Beyond the fence we find ourselves in a desolate world of some 100 square miles. It seems to stretch forever, and we walk a broad, freshly tarred road, with expanses of low ground on each side of us, bearing here and there miniature towers of trash—piles of abandoned mattresses, little collections of tin and iron. One old man, crooked and bent, leads his burro towards a heap of feverish green. Occasionally women in long dresses with brightly colored aprons or turbans move slowly in the distance, bending to pick up precious pieces of refuse—a tin, a bottle, discarded food for themselves or their children. These workers are the lone pickers who have to live on what little they can salvage by gleaning. Others younger and more energetic, dig and search feverishly, toiling like ants over the hills of fresh garbage. One or two men, dark against the sky, hack with machetes at a tower of sodden paper, cutting it into bundles suitable for handling. Others tie up bottles into straw bales. Further on the gold and silver towers of tin flash like beacons.

Since the agitation about living conditions brought about by a group of charitable ladies and social workers and some resultant newspaper publicity, it has been against the law for anyone to live in the *tiradero*. But although the government ordered ploughed under the wretched huts in which families like the Velasquezs had been living and transported the owners to the development at Santa Cruz Meyehualco, this had no sooner been achieved, and the dump cleared, than, from Mexico's inexhaustible supply of poor, new squatters had moved in. At the *tiradero's* edge there are many little shacks to be seen, made of wood, tin, and *petate,* and from the doors of these makeshift houses, the arms and legs of numerous children protrude as they creep in and out of the trash. On the roofs made of sheets of tin there are pots of plants; smoke rises from the fires being lit under casseroles; and in all probability the food being cooked in those pots has also been taken from the dump. Unimaginable as it might be to the more privileged, these houses burrowed into the *basura* mean "home" to some dispossessed Mexican families. Even at the brink of one of the dark-watered canals, a small girl scrubs clothes, with all the faith in civilization and cleanliness that this implies.

Do they really live here?

"Only illegally," Antonio says, "It's allowed to put up shelters—from the rain and the sun. Sometimes they live there all the same."

"How many?"

"*Hay muchos,*" (there are plenty) he says philosophically.

A boy about eight—his hair long as a girl's, tangled and dirty but wonderfully curly, his eyes suspicious, turns away from us to burrow into a pile of tumbled papers and settle down to sleep.

May 6

It has seemed inappropriate to leave the country without visiting Vera Cruz, that port through which the mother of the man who was to kill Trotsky entered the country.

Mexico

The car is small. The single golden flame of a banana tree is lit up by the sunrise against a dark mass of pines. Past a brickmaster's colony; past the well-known Ixtapalapa where the *pepeñadores* labor under *costales* of paper. A feeling of descent. (The usual Mexican panorama—mules, barefoot women wearing flat hats and guiding burros and goats with their switches, skeleton-bare country showing its white rocky bones and decorated by tiny brilliant churches, anonymous towns with large empty plazas.) But always the descent, with lop-sided trucks swinging around hairpin curves; with thick white mist curdling up from rocky crevices.

The second and successful attempt on Trotsky's life took place in 1940, when a young man passing himself off as a Trotskyist entered the Cayoacan house and buried an alpine pick in his victim's brain. The American papers gave a good deal of space to the event, the weekly *New Masses*, with quaint reserve, avoided real mention of it, in the end referring to Trotsky's murder as if his trouble had been pneumonia or old age. (Perhaps the *New Masses* was taking its cue from *Pravda* which on August 24 headlined a short article "Death of an International Spy!" In actuality Communist papers in the West carried further an earlier line. Joseph Freeman in the *New Masses* had already reproved Cardenas for admitting Trotsky to Mexico, and denounced the hounded exile as if it had been Trotsky pursuing Stalin rather than the other way around.)

In the crowded town of Orizaba ("Rejoicing of the waters") which stands about 4,000 feet above sea level, it has begun to drizzle, and a huge Ferris wheel turns and turns in the main plaza, bringing to view again and again, animated wet brown faces.

Lunch at a big table where a young man called Gerardo shares the grilled fish and *papaya con limon* and talks of his *novia* (sweetheart) who is jealous and gives him a "hard time" (*muchas molestias*). After the brawny woman with the big arms and brow beaded with sweat carries in two steaming kettles, one with coffee, one with hot milk, and fills our cups at the table, Gerardo complains about the poverty of the student in his country, about the long hours of study, the delay in recognition, the loneliness. In his voice as he berates the stupidity of officials in the *tierra caliente*, where hookworm and leprosy are still known, there is the resentment and alienation of the would-be intellectual.

On the road again. (This road is one of the more dangerous ways to reach Vera Cruz.) Soon the tiny car seems a beetle racing along the lip of the plunging gorge. The trucks roar by with their loads leaning askew. The mist thickens. There is the passing image of three women, dark kneeling figures wrapped in rebozos, praying before the Virgin, in a tiny chapel perched above the abyss. At last the *tierra caliente*.

Mexico

Zopilotes wheeling against vivid green, against trees covered with pink blossoms, against the pastel walls of houses. A white cemetery flamboyant with *capillas,* domes, plaster doves, carved wooden birds. Chile spread in the sun on sheets of tin. The smell of coffee as a truck passes, and a passing smile like a sunrise on a brown face.

Finally the outskirts of Vera Cruz itself. The odor of bad gasoline mingling with the smell of the sea, and the perfume of hedges of lilies.

It was on January 9 of 1937 that the tanker Ruth, with Trotsky, his wife, and a police escort on board, entered Tampico harbor a little further up the coast of the Gulf. Here two North American Trotskyists, Max Shachtman and George Novak, waited on the wharves along with Rivera's wife (the tall exotic-browed Frida Kahlo). President Cardenas had sent his own special train to meet the boat; there was the dramatic scenery of the new refuge, the sunshine, the warm welcome. Nobody was aware—least of all the victim—that before his arrival, there had docked in Vera Cruz on November 6, 1936, another ship, the *Manuel Arnuz* from Barcelona carrying some of the organizers of his forthcoming murder, in particular a striking-looking woman called Caridad de Mercader. This woman born in Cuba and brought up in Spain, was educated at a convent where she had fantasies of being a nun; eventually she developed into a NKVD agent able to kill with gun or knife at thirty feet. Forty days after the arrival of the Caridad entourage, the Mexican consul in Barcelona alerted the Mexican government that this group had entered the country on false papers; but it was already too late. The Mercader-tour had made possible first-hand knowledge of the terrain and of local forces available for "Operation Trotsky."

By comparing dates it is clear that even while Trotsky was spending his first months in Cayoacan, Caridad's son—Ramon de Mercader (with the subsequent name of Jacques Mornard in France, and Frank Jacson in Mexico) was getting guerrilla training in Spain directed by his mother's lover, also a GPU agent, a stocky man with piercing eyes under bushy brows, known as Leonid Eitingdon. Ramon brought up in the radical atmosphere of Barcelona, where anarchist disciples of Bakunin, and Syndicalist followers of Sorel mingled for years with the more orderly and controlled Marxists—and scheduled to play the leading role in the future assassination—was handsome, dark-eyed, and tense.

Here, where the brilliant sunshine illuminates the town, long hours are spent in the plaza, which is paved with white and greyish stone, offset by the stained off-white of the *Catedral de la Asuncion,* and decorated by a fountain surrounded by orange trees, oleanders, and the tall sage-like *habanera.* Along the sea front a vendor sells crab-meat pies, and *zopilotes* wheel over the weather-beaten buildings.

Mexico

Down by the wharves no one seems to have heard of how the *Manuel Arnuz* sailed into this port long ago, carrying a handsome woman who wore the overalls of a Spanish *militante,* and who lectured about "defeating fascism." "Ah no, Señora," the old sailor says, "we must ask Roberto, *el viejo,* he will know."

But *el viejo,* who is supposed to live in one of the fish-smelling huts down at the beach, has gone to Yucatan." "*Aqui solamente su perro* (only his dog is here)," explains a boy sitting under a palm tree and tapping at a wooden drum.

Back in Mexico City at the Avenida Viena. In front of the house (with its walls pockmarked with bullets and its heavy gate, to this day opened with caution), a memorial to that time when sympathizers in the United States were convinced of the reality of the GPU danger, and subscribed large sums for a military engineer to build the walls up until they were twenty feet thick; to plant barbed-wire entanglements; to put in a redoubt with bomb-proof ceilings and floors; and to install doors of double steel controlled by electric switches. (How vulnerable even this fortress was is established by Eudokia and Vladimir Petrov, the two Russians who defected in Australia in 1954 and explained that the Trotsky dossier in Moscow contained a complete photographic documentation of Trotsky's life, from his first days in Russia to those last days in Cayoacan. Many of the later pictures had been taken *inside* the fortified walls, and provided shots of guards, fences, and court-yards, as well as intimate scenes of Trotsky having tea with friends and talking to his dog).

But material protection was only part of what was necessary to protect the old man. Nothing demonstrates better the split in the political personality than Trotsky's hope for the recruitment of his would-be murderer. Ramon (i.e., Jacson) had gained access to the house through a social worker from Brooklyn, a follower of Trotsky, who had been deceived as to his purposes. Jacson (personable as he was) had courted her, followed her back to New York, eventually became her lover, and lived with her in Mexico City at the Hotel Montejo. All this at the order of the GPU!

The GPU had probably also instructed Ramon to exploit the master-disciple relationship; and Trotsky had told his suspicious guards that "in order to change society we must have confidence that people can be changed." While he could ferret out a Siqueiros—the logic of whose political process was familiar to him—he could only too easily subdue his animal-like revulsion to the husky ashen-faced Ramon. It was this optimistic intellectuality which finally betrayed Trotsky's physical intuition.

Mexico

May 10

Alfredo arrives to say goodbye with an enormous yellow sunflower made of paper. The huge flower, with its brilliant curving petals, waves in the air, making us part of the little park where children play with balloons and animals. Alfredo says: "You can take with you the Mexican sun!"

Soon we are talking about students and their "reality." "If kidnappings, assaults, bombings, and organization for revolution are going on in Latin America, where is the 'reality' for the students? Aren't the students all middle-class after all, and in the struggle for their own identity aren't they transferring their frustrations onto the peasant or the worker? They all speak of blood as though it were nothing. The methods of violent change they advocate are manipulative and outmoded. While they work in libraries and deal with theory, they get pleasure from advocating holocausts!"

Alfredo is silent; then he confesses in a low voice that he has been to Red China.

To *China?* But I thought you had never been out of Mexico.

"*Solamente a China,*" he says, "*China Roja! China linda*" (Only to China—Red China—China the beautiful).

How long ago?

"*Un año*" (one year). He looks serious again, and there is that familiar contrast between his slightly sleepy-looking Indian eyes with their full lids, and the narrow scholastic features.

Was this a secretly arranged trip, or had he gone openly? He seemed to have flown first to Geneva, and then by stages to China; moreover, the party had been met in Geneva by a Chinese interpreter and manager, who had stayed with them all through the flight and throughout the two weeks in China itself. What had he seen? The answer seemed to be the usual ones: the great Hall of the People, the Great Wall, factories, communes, villages, housing, schools. And does he side with China in the quarrel which is developing with Russia?

I gather that he feels sympathy for the Chinese point of view, and believes that the Indians in Mexico with their peasant society are closer to the Chinese than they are to the white half-Europeanized Russians. It makes political sense that China should try to influence professionals and intellectuals like Alfredo, and try to build up a revolutionary infrastructure in Mexico along with a skeleton liberation movement— as they had in Cameroun, Tanzania, Ghana and Congo-Brazzaville. Or support and train local communists (as in the Philippines, Sarawak, sections of the PKI, Thailand, Laos, Burma, India, and Ceylon). In fact it has been rumored here that special Red Chinese agents enter Mexico illegally through the Pacific ports. Some are said to have been caught mingling with isolated Mexican tribes and encouraging them to protest government edicts.

More threateningly, there are also the same rumors which were encountered in California—namely, that the Chinese Communists are involved in the drug trade and paying for the support given to the various Maoist underground activities, and for the boosting of their own gold reserves, by the sale of heroin. The elusive morality of "class struggle" (as proclaimed by Lenin, "Anything that serves to destroy the old . . . society . . . is moral.") hangs over us as we stand in the little park, both of us smaller than the big paper sunflower!

My mind has been going back to those isolated villages in the sierras above Oaxaca, and in the highlands of Chiapas. I see the Indians seated on the ground in that ancient and endless repose, their dark eyes staring for hours at a time into their prescribed world. Here is that element of Asia in Mexico, spoken of by historians and anthropologists. Here are those whose fathers and mothers accepted feudal servitude with resignation, and are now ripe to come under the influence of leaders who profess to combat "barbarism"—but who to do it advocate "barbarous" methods.

"There is a difference between being the friend of the Indians," I protest to Alfredo, "and being what the Chinese would like you to be. You're white and Spanish. And moreover you'll never be able to be a racist for political reasons."

Alfredo has been laughing, but his face turns serious again. His confession, and the previous conversations with the students, increase an uneasy sense that under the conservative pro-United States surface of Gustav Diaz Ordaz's reign a certain amount of ferment is building up: not only in the alienated mass of the student body at the university, much influenced by professionals like Alfredo, but also among the Indians and peasants in the mountains and coastal areas where a perfect terrain exists to provide the setting for a "People's War." (As Mao has indicated, the tools at first must be humble—propaganda against guns, subversion against airpower, space against mechanization.)

"Surely, hope for the *pepeñadores* and the more deprived Indians rests ultimately in what the Mexicans themselves do? Money, arms, agents, sent by Communist countries to subvert the present imperfect government, will serve the Chinese or the Russian cause, but not help the Mexicans."

Alfredo, who always seems to listen intently and with a certain kind of emotion and gratitude, sighs a little. We walk along the paths in San Angel towards the taxi stands.

As if he did not quite approve of his own actions and direction, a direction after all not known to me in detail; and as if he senses some sort of moral appeal; he allows himself a moment of weakness and fatigue. He says in a heavy voice, *"Quizas me voy a la carcel* (Perhaps I'll end up in prison)."

1965

These men not only hopin' for a wind when there's a fire. They *set* the fire. They bring the matches honey, . . . *an'* the kerosene.

Jasmin

September 20, 1965—Boston

Now Mexico with its tropical fevers seems far away, and in its place the dome of Boston's State House gleams between the cold blue sky and the Commons, where the grass stays stubbornly unhealthily green. There is that general tone of New England as the season turns— withdrawn, reflective, restrained. Old men sit on the green benches. Couples walk with their heads bent to the wind. Only the children are demonstrative, following each other like birds in flight, their short coats streaming behind them.

Living temporarily in this "citadel" on Beacon Hill, looking over narrow streets lined with replicas of antique street lamps, it is easy to project change. The existence suggested by these nineteenth century houses, with their harmonious fanlights (through which light falls like golden silk onto protected hallways, cherrywood tables, and stocked bookshelves) is a pale image of that which is trying to come to life on the radical campus and in the hostile slum. The atmosphere of an earlier time—the general sense of culture and reflection, suggestive of some ideal community in which money and knowledge, taste and restraint, were skillfully combined, and from which the aim had been to exclude all that was "excessive and indecent"—is now fantastically out of date. Technology has outmoded those graceful doorways and hand-finished furniture; so too time has taken certain social aims and made them unrealizable. A new kind of life pushes its claims to the future.

September 21

All the same in the South End no change seems to stir the static streets. Here the air is still redolent of crime and pathology. Here a dark pattern is superimposed upon ordinary living. Looking from the

1965

Hill over the Dome and the Commons, past the Combat zone and across the sunken line of the old railroad track, it is almost possible to glimpse and quite easy to imagine the familiar areas—lower Tremont and the streets which run off it towards Washington (which lies under the Elevated). The heavy trees there are dropping their leaves, the backyards are fertilized by garbage, the bow-fronted houses are tinged with the color of the rose-red brick for which Boston was once noted. Lives lie open with a certain poetic abandon, with the minimum of shame.

The area has always seemed subject to the rise and fall of a tide. Parents get up, send their children to school, go off to work themselves. Mothers meet for coffee. Housewives market. Legitimate businesses operate. Social workers, clergymen, real estate dealers, urban renewal officials gather to discuss the "strategy of change" and expatiate upon strengthening the community. But towards the end of the day legitimate life ebbs away, locks its doors, retires into neighborhood meetings, or goes home to other parts of the city. And then the bars and dens come alive. Cars cruising the dark streets are surprisingly elegant. Prostitutes emerge from rooms and apartments to find, along with Lesbians, homosexuals, and pimps, their way to favorite bars. In their train, like rats fascinated by a Pied Piper, follow a thousand attendant professionals—con men, salesmen with horrendous catalogues, B and E men (i.e., breaking and entering), loan sharks, "dip broads" (i.e., female pickpockets), crooked lawyers, pushers.

The area is not a racial ghetto (in 1960 it was about 38 percent Negro), but in spite of efforts at urban renewal, it is still a crime-sealed capsule that works around the clock. And its evils: a broad extension of criminal values seems to be spreading across the nation. Juveniles are murdering, rape figures are mounting, women are getting into serious crime. The gangs of the past are consolidating and hiring media men and front lawyers to camouflage their activities.

September 22

In the houses of the Negroes there are always older people; an infinitely old man with a seamed face, an ancient woman, nut-brown, honed-down, rocking and nodding. "We's all from Africa. That's our homeland . . . That's the truth." (This present mania for Africa is like the resurrection of an old song suddenly fashionable again.)

The interiors of the rooms are filled with social clues. There are shiny typically-American school photographs, the old reprints of Southern towns, the newspaper clippings of Garvey and his Cadillac—these giving place to current posters of Malcolm X and Martin Luther King Jr. (The cult of identification with Africa suggests that a violent internal struggle is going on, as its members search for security. So says Vittorio Lanternari, an Italian anthropologist [*The Religions of the Oppressed*]. He explains that such projections, part of West Indian and American Negro black liberation cults, are also common in Africa itself—not to mention among the races of Oceania, New Zealand, Brazil—in fact wherever there are cultural clashes between populations in various stages of development.)

A visit to a Georgia woman called Jenny who has eight children and no visible man, and who came up to Boston two years ago. She is long and lean and stalklike. Her hair is tied up in a handkerchief, and her dress flaps around her ankles. In the summer of 1964 she used to pad around the house in bare feet. Now she wears stockings and tattered sneakers. Her eyes are bright, and ambition burns in her somewhere like a small, sullen flame. She explains why she left Georgia, "I does no work there now," she says, "the work is all done by machinery." She shakes her head and sweeps the air with long narrow-fingered pink-palmed hands. "They can use no *peoples*," she protests softly. Jenny was born of a large sharecropper family and is a victim of what is being called the "tractor revolution." Between 1940 and 1960 almost 164,000 people had flooded up from Georgia, Mississippi, Alabama. Cities in the north which had been 70 to 80 percent white suddenly reversed their composition, so that within four or five years the population trends had changed.

Back in the street the child of a Puerto Rican family leads the way to an apartment house which leans to one side and is scarred by the demolition of the buildings next-door. Upstairs, her mother, a thin wiry little woman from the slums of San Juan, is sitting on cushions with two female relatives and a swarm of children. An oversize color TV set corrects—like some swollen parasite—the absence of other furniture in the apartment and commands the fascinated attention of adults and children alike. The shy smiling mother hurries to the kitchen; soon we are all sitting in a circle, eating limp saltines, drinking Coca Cola, and watching a soap opera about a housewife who leaves her job as a factory worker to elope with a successful and insincere song-writer in a large shiny car.

Further up the street a dark-skinned Syrian girl called Hannah shouts a greeting; together we go to her aunt's house where she has been to carry home a dessert her aunt bakes each week, made out of flaky pastry, honey, and sesame seeds. The aunt, Mrs. Say'ed, is only half the height of her tall American niece. On her walls large photographs of her brothers and sisters, and of their children and their children's children bridge the gap between Syria and North America. I am addressed as "darling," and the short rounded Mrs. Say'ed weeps as she explains that she is soon to be "located" (relocated). "What am I to do, darling?" Her hand clutches at my sleeve. "Where am I to go after the *years!*"

1965

Hannah is less worried about her aunt's distress than she is about her own maladjustments. Out in the street she complains about the "old style." Her aunt is "old style;" her father is "old style." She tosses her dark head willfully. "The girls" (she refers to her contemporaries) "wouldn't stand for it! It's only the Syrians who are so 'old style.' " Moreover her brothers knock her down if she goes out with a boy they don't approve of. And there are eight brothers. "If one of them knocks me, then the others imitate him . . . all of them think they have the *right*. They keep saying 'Mind yourself—or you'll be a *whore . . .*' "

The old people of this area are like hermit crabs being wrenched painfully out of their familiar shells. They are wounded by this forceful evacuating. Yet they know that thousands of oldsters like themselves have already been relocated, that their pleas could never stand up against the 225 million dollars in public funds earmarked for urban renewal. In fact demolition had been taking place long before that trip to the West coast. The houses had been in dreadful shape: sagging doorways; desolate halls redolent of dirt and urine; cracked plaster; rotten window sashes; inadequate heat! In spite of the grief, there has been a kind of joy as the great exposure has taken place. The housing traumas of individuals have become the public property of all!

And this too is not local. Major urban areas all over the United States have worsening slums, and while the middle-class flock from the cities to what Paul Goodman calls "deadly dormitories," Southern negroes, Puerto Ricans, poor whites, and unemployed take their place.

Coming home to the Hill at night. Relief: The quiet streets well paved, the house fronts exquisite, the street lights marching down the river in a reassuring procession. The next door neighbor, a slim handsome man with curly hair (who, whatever the weather, always seems *a l'anglaise* to lean slightly on a folded umbrella) talking to a pretty woman who is a leader of the local "Preservation Society."

But they too are concerned with crime. "People have simply re-moved themselves," the man says to the woman. "They have opted out of the battle." Apparently he is referring to the people who have migrated to the nearby suburbs of Milton, Wellesley, Newton. He adds that nobody knows now who their neighbors are. "Last night," he points towards the next street, "a friend of mine went to that letter box down there and was mugged." The woman nods her head briefly.

Returning to Boston has meant the picking up again of my old work in the South End; and therefore of the threads of South End lives. . . . A telephone call comes from Cleopatra's mother. (Cleopatra is a particularly pretty Latin-looking girl, part negro and part Portuguese. She has been a heroin addict since the age of sixteen.) "We live here," her mother says, sitting in the tiny living-room of a little wooden house, her chair surrounded by photographs of Cleopatra (as if in a shrine). "We live here like this, not rich, not poor."

Cleopatra's children, product of her trade as a prostitute, gather around their grandmother's knee and stare at the visitor. "The father of this one was at M.I.T. . . . Cleo saw a lot of him . . . and this one," (a dark-skinned sturdy sulky little boy) "he's the child of Jacob, the sax in the Knight's Club band. No, no, I keep them here, but Cleo pays for them; that one never takes a piece of bread from home without she pays for it. As long as I draw breath, I'm here for her and the children. She knows I'm here."

The mother is fat, swarthy, and resigned; a little dark moustache lines her sweaty upper lip. "Yes, Cleo was beautiful. They wanted her bad and they put something in her drink. She was only sixteen. She was quiet, always quiet. I would say, 'Why are you so *quiet*, daughter?' How could I know? Then she was in the hospital, and she had bad jaundice and I said, 'Doctor, what is it, what does she have?' (Through this litany she is rocking, rocking) And the doctor said, 'She's using drugs'. My Cleopatra! I couldn't believe my Cleopatra would be mixed up in that! I had her on a pedestal!" The mother suddenly drops into the present tense. "So, she is home again. . . . Sometimes she feels bad and I wash her back, and sometimes she is quiet, very quiet. Then one day she says, 'Ma, I'm going to the store,' and I don't see her for months. And then she comes home and she says, 'Ma, I'm pregnant,' and I say, 'You're not the first, and you won't be the last.' "

The story goes on and on. Dark, densely living, coiling on and on like a snake which settles itself into hibernation.

Two days later. Another call: this one from Jasmin, a friend of Cleopatra's (but younger, darker-skinned, with a history, as characterized by one social worker, of "cohabitation with both her father and her young cousin").

A year ago Jasmin produced a resume of her career (in the form of a letter written to a local religious institution). "Since the age of twelve," she had written, "I have been in and out of correctional institutions. I have been a drug addict for the past three years. I have something in my favor and that is my faith. The Lord has promised to deliver me. He has promised my mother that I will be saved to work for Him. I have been saved and called to preach but I have chose to ignore my calling and live the life of the streets. I have been baptized by the Holy Ghost several times, but I am still a backslider. My church is the Pentacostal church. I have been in this church all my life and at times did very well, other times extenuating circumstances forced me to the left. I was moved by the book, because I know the ways of the Lord and how he moves. I know he is married to the backslider, so I know there is hope for me."

Now temporarily out of prison she explains that a horrible thing has happened. The cousin who had been so close to her, has killed a friend with a knife. It happened in Malden down near the Boston and Maine Railroad tracks; and Jasmin feels that it wasn't her cousin's fault ("because he was all wired-up and high at the time"). She has been asked to go to the Police Station and wants me to go with her. "You see," she explains rather primly, "this has upset the family."

October

Walking today in that section of the South End where the streets approach the black area of Lennox and Dudley Street. A few years ago an encounter here with one of those salvation cults, which tend to center around a "guide in human form" and to pay allegiance to the idea of a "promised land" (in this case to the home country of the Black Muslims). The spokesmen were young black men from sixteen to twenty-two who gathered at a settlement house every week. The doors would swing open downstairs. There would be the sound of feet on the steps, the swift dramatic entry of David and Willie. David wore a red waistcoat, tight tapering pants, and a small round hard black hat on the back of his head. He came in drumming and doing a swift, agile step. Willie followed behind smiling rather sheepishly. Both, when the time came to discuss Elijah Muhammed, the leader of the Black Muslims, were serious and eloquent. (Elijah Muhammed talks about the "Home Country," a "Negro" place where Islam rules, where the white man is a despised mutant, and where the black man owns wealth and dresses in silks. Elijah Muhammed is known as the Messenger of Allah, and he preaches that the white man—monster, snake, devil—is responsible for all the ills of the Negro. The Negro, he says, must save his energy for the Battle of Armageddon, a battle which is to be the final struggle between the black and white races, when Allah will give you [the Negroes] "your own blood to drink like water." Fortunately, Muhammed also preaches the giving up of drink and dope, and the practical virtues of hard work, and the owning of property. "Separate yourself from the slave-master," he urges, "stop forcing yourself into places where you are not wanted. Rid yourself of the lust for wine. Learn self-love," etc.)

David and Willie have both spent terms in prison, and both were converted there and brought to "Allah." What is pleasing about this conversion is that they have not dropped their gaiety or their love of music; they have only become more serious about their roles. They are in the process of solving the dilemma of identity, of learning "self love."

October 2

Two white and one Negro workmen, all of them wearing denim overalls and heavy sweaters and blue knitted caps, are swinging along the icy streets. The Negro has swollen lips and is angry with the driver of a car with whom he seems to have had an argument. He clenches his fist and shakes it against the chilly sky: "I should throw a brick at him!"

Does he remember Marcus Garvey?

"Go to the library," he replies; then pauses for a second thought and adds thickly through his swollen lips: "Garvey were too clever for them. He scared them. They put him outa the States, and sent him to Africa." As he passes on he looks over his shoulder. "Peace be in your heart." (In areas like this, Garvey is part of a collective black emotion. Carrying on Martin Delaney's interest in "Africa for the Africans," Garvey in the twenties could persuade thousands of deprived blacks that he—this fattish man in a musical comedy uniform, wearing a feathered helmet, and riding in an open Cadillac—was their one and only representative.)

E—(ivory-skinned and plump-faced) who is an American Negro graduate studying at MIT, has been keeping up to date on movements such as the Black Muslims. He explains that the Garvey meetings were crowded.

Was this only because Garvey was glorifying the African homeland, and calling for the expulsion of the white man and the establishment of a truly Negro religion?

"No, Garvey was also stressing conscious pride and black economic freedom. Once in North Carolina, in 1922 I think it was, Garvey spoke just as you hear Elijah speak: 'When I came down here I had to get on a white man's train . . . on a white man's railroad . . . I landed in a white man's town, and am now speaking from a white man's platform . . . where do you Negroes come in?' "

It is good to hear this almost white scholar, explaining the myths which grew in the hearts of black exiles. We walk up and down the South End streets. He talks about the relationship between the Negro in Harlem and the Negro in the Caribbean. He says that Garvey's evangelism can be linked with the current Black Muslim movement, not to mention the *Ras Tafari* cult in Jamaica. (The followers of *Ras*

1965

Tafari also have an imaginary homeland, in this case Ethiopia. The cult says that Marcus Garvey was sent by *Ras Tafari* to "cut and clear," i.e., to perform magical psychological clearance. It also claims that the black man is superior to the white man; and that in the near future the white man will be compelled to be the black man's servant.) According to Lanternari the Sunday services of the *Ras Tafarians* include a dialogue like this:

> *Speaker:* How did you get here?
> *People:* Slavery.
> *Speaker:* Who brought us from Ethopia?
> *People:* The white man.
> *Speaker:* The white man tells us that we are inferior, but we are not inferior. We are superior and he is inferior . . . the white man says we are no good, yet Solomon, David, and the Queen of Sheba were black. The English are criminal, and . . . Ras Tafari started Mau Mau . . . Ras Tafari says "Death to the Whites."

Just a few years ago such manifestations of the frank desire on the part of subjected Negroes to get rid of the whites and take their places, would have seemed only sparks from the smoldering fires of discontent; sparks to be easily quenched in the active life of North America. But now those with colored skins are being asked to do more than speak. They are being organized to act.

In the university enclaves a different kind of black (that is, non-white) politics is proliferating. Black fans are discovering Frantz Fanon, for instance. (Fanon thinks that the black man must be liberated from himself, and proposes a therapeutic violence and conflict, a cleansing immersion against the power of psychological enslavement. He rejects assimilation, speaks of the Third World, urges the non-white to re-create himself by whatever means necessary, and above all warns him not to withdraw into the twilight of a "tribal" past.) The image put forward is rather like that of Aimé Césaire, poet from Martinique, who mourns the *"lost quality of exiled black men,"* who celebrates the "word" which makes the scattered black man function (*". . . words . . . fresh-blooded words, words that are tidal-waves, erisipelas and malaria and lava and brush fires and flaming cities. . . ."*). It is this Césaire who projects himself as having risen from a "plank bed in a tiny hut built of flattened gasoline tins, old boards, straw and gray mud redolent of decay"—that plank bed from which his race has risen—*"to start something. To start what? . . . The only thing in the world that's worth the effort of starting; the end of the world, by God!"*

So the politics of violence enters the picture of the Black Renaissance. One can see that in Boston's areas of "color," the battle is less that of "slum clearance" than it is of "psychological clearance."

Coming from the West Coast where PLP members were talking about "organizing" blacks, Puerto Ricans and Chicanos—and from

Mexico where there is a renewed attempt to politicize the dispossessed poor and the Indians of the Highlands—there is the fear that the "moral" question may be taken up by extremists before it is solved by humanists. A wedge has been inserted to open up the ghettos of the world, to urge the inhabitants to act for themselves (and incidentally to place them more fully at the mercy of demagogues). "Instead of moralizing over such horrible cruelties as the press does," Engels wrote long ago, "it would be better to realize that we are dealing with a 'people's war.'"

Weekdays are spent with the slum-dwellers but weekends in different company; although due to the upheavals taking place in American life, the disturbances of the one echo the disturbances of the other.

At a cocktail party on an elevated terrace, someone talks of an article in last year's *Atlantic* dealing with Nasser's buildup of nuclear missiles on the Nile. Twenty-five German scientists dating from the Nazi period are supposed to be engaged in operations directed against Israel. (Operation Cleopatra, for instance, i.e., production of a large Hiroshima-type bomb; and Operation Ibis, the making of small radioactive rubbish bombs of strontium 90, which if exploded would poison Israeli territory and water sources.) The British government is concerned that in view of the Egyptian government's obvious desire to "blot out Israel," and Nasser's remark that Israel is "a burning cancerous growth" in the Middle East, such weapons of genocide might actually be used. A city planner admits that there are ex-Nazis working in Egypt; and he simply hopes that "the pro-Israel lobby won't go getting into high gear in Washington—that would do more harm than good." He adds that he thinks "Israel will have to go anyway, because she will never be accepted by the Arabs." When asked whether he thinks this would be desirable, he answers that it would *not* be desirable. "But we just have to look facts in the face."

Tonight a dinner party is disturbed by the arrival of little W—, who comes home (unannounced) to visit his long-suffering middle-class parents. (He is peripatetic rather than in any way violent; another of those young Americans, drawn by the longing for an idyllic community, who joined the great trek which has been fanning out across the country—from Portland, Oregon to San Diego, California; from South Orange, New Jersey to Wichita, Kansas; from Greenwich Village to Bangor, Maine—trekkers who drove in patched-up cars, hitched with bed-rolls, hopped the Greyhound, hiked with back-packs—wore headbands and jewelry of the Indians, deerskin from the vanishing frontier, the long skirts of pioneer women, the sneakers of the A&P.)

1965

Through the evening there are half-glimpsed scenes; a conversation beside the telephone, a confrontation in the kitchen, a pleading at the back door. W— wishes that his girlfriend would hate him, for this would make it easier for him to leave her. He wishes that his friend would come and get a job and support her, while he went out to "find himself" (so that he could return again filled with hope). He wishes he did not have to "leave" everything because all he can find in every place is misery. Again there is the question. "Who am I? What am I? Am I a genius or a fool? Why do I want two things at once—to go and to stay, to work and to play, to sing and to cry . . . if only I knew what I was, then I could really dig myself."

W— seems like a weak attenuated by-product of the political crisis, someone disturbed in his natural growth by unnecessary stimulation and then left rootless. At the dinner table a visiting cousin takes over and serves the course which had been interrupted by the sudden arrival of the wayward son; but he can still be heard in the kitchen complaining to his mother that her friends only think about food and drink! He stands against the telephone table in the hall as if in the act of a perpetual long-distance call, trying to explain why his best friend Jerry got back into prison, and why Jerry's girl tried to kill her father with a golf club and had to be admitted to a state hospital. "These are the most *beautiful* people," he insists, "you've no idea how *beautiful* they are . . . They are just feeling pain and hurt and trying to do too much living."

Later at the doorway, while the chill winter air blows towards the guests, his father is asking him what he wants. "What in God's name do you want?" The son is tapping his guitar with the back of his knuckle. "I want to play this piece of wood, and drink wine, and fuck everyone, and shout at people to dance. . . . I want to travel without deciding where to go!" He brushes the long hair out of his eyes and hunches his shoulders made thin by a diet of grains and lack of exercise. Then after a long silence filled with nervous conversation around the coffee table, his voice comes again; "I don't know . . . I dig myself." The voice turns into a lost wail. "And I don't come up with an answer. . . ."

Four years ago Toole was in a Massachusetts prison. She had been an exceedingly thin girl, her stomach sinking inwards, her long legs exposed, her hair cropped closely around a wistful long-chinned Irish face. (Her real name happened to be Kathleen O'Toole, but in the prison, partly in deference to her skill with locks, they had shortened it to "Toole".)

Now she has written to me to ask me to visit her. The streetcar goes up a long hill to an apartment house. There is a peephole in the door of the apartment itself, with a small curtain over it. The door opens and Toole stands there smiling, showing that her two front teeth are still missing. In spite of the fine, even tender, line of her lips, and the now large breasts under the navy sweat shirt; she seems suddenly taller, heavier, coarser; she has turned from a slim slouching girl into a fleshy man-woman with a man's haircut and unashamedly masculine gestures and expressions. And she no longer hides her sexual preferences. "There is Primrose, who's living with me, and there's Marybelle, who's living with Pat" (Pat is a light-colored Negro girl).

"She's gay," Toole says with emphasis. Then she jerks her head towards an inside door. "Don't say too much in front of Primrose. *She's* square."

In the next room Pat, Marybelle, and Primrose sit around a big table with the omnipresent icebox in the background. Marybelle is handsome, with blonde hair streaming over her shirt and jeans. Primrose seems to be Italian, a little pallid, but with a slightness and air of delicacy.

There is gossip about who is living with whom. (Lesbianism, however, is discussed with a certain evasiveness. The subtlety of the situation which exists between Toole and Primrose overrules certain comments. Pat and Toole think of themselves as the "men of the house," and as such entitled to a certain reserve in front of the "little women" who, even if they are living upon the gains of the sex trade and being asked to so some of the dirty work, must not be exposed to the brutal truth.)

When the doorbell rings, Pat says "That must be the baby!" Toole informs me that Pat had gotten pregnant from a "trick" two years ago and it had been decided to keep the baby. This baby is generally looked after by Pat's mother. Today, however, she has been out for the afternoon with Kim Wan, the baby's father. "He's Korean," hisses Toole across the table. "For God's sake don't let on that Pat's gay. He thinks she just lives with Marybelle so as to have company."

Pat returns holding a large, eleven-month-old, golden-skinned baby girl, stuffed into a yellow snow-suit and wearing a bonnet which almost obscures its serious black eyes. Behind her a slender Korean man, whom Pat introduces as "my friend," stands hesitating and watching the ensuing scene of baby-worship during which Marybelle holds the child on her lap to remove its outdoor clothing, Pat prepares its supper, Primrose looks remote and wistful, and Toole makes complimentary chucking sounds. The *real* father, who judging from Pat's caution, helps to support his offspring (and probably claims some portion of Pat's services as well) stands behind the table as if uncomfortable in this household of women. He finally departs after a couple of deep bows. The girls seem cemented together by the baby's presence, accepting the part she plays in linking them to the society they have rejected; in fact they gather rather sadly around this child-goddess who regards them with inscrutable black-button eyes.

In the sunny chill Hill streets, the policemen unburden themselves of their present resentments: one of them complains with a certain grim bewilderment that fantastic technical advances have been put at the service of the underworld. (Crime takes are assessed in terms of billions of dollars. In Boston the recent Commission pegged the total flow of cash into the illegal gambling rackets alone, at 2 billion dollars a year. As an example of the octopus-like reaching out of illegal money, efforts were made eighteen months ago to get concessions at the airport; efforts which exerted so much pressure on the Massachusetts Port Authority that even the Attorney General's office in Washington was drawn into the struggle.)

Walking along Charles St. with the policeman, past the antique shops, the little bars, the drug stores, the dress shops—the conversation covers dope, and crime, and fatigue, and overwork, and indifference, and lack of understanding on the part of the public. "Everyone's against us—we're a down-trodden group. . . . Who are we but a minority in blue?" He stops and points to two boys who lounge against a sunny wall, cigarettes in their mouths. "See that—once we could ask them why they weren't in school. Now if you're not careful you're in trouble for molesting a minor." (In Boston juveniles have been marking up a dramatic share of the recent crime rise. Those under eighteen have been responsible for most of the auto thefts, 20 to 25 percent of the rape, half of the burglaries, and 8 percent of the murders.) The policeman strolls along with a grim detachment; his anger is felt as something controlled and long-term. Then for a moment his face darkens. "The other day—in Oakland—those *punks*—were *spitting* at policemen!"

The feelings of the policemen are rather like those of the Negroes. Like the Negroes they feel oppressed. Like the Negroes they depend upon the uncertain esteem of their opponents. Today a brief talk with Professor Harold Isaacs, a short vigorous man who is making various political studies at MIT. He analyzes the idea of organizing the Third World. (A distinction must be made here since the "undeveloped" that is the Third World was non-Europeon and poor. But naturally it had no real political entity. What did Nigeria have to do with Burma, or Yemen with Thailand? Yet the phrase has now come to mean something fairly complex; referring not only to those countries which are uncommitted, not industrialized and without financial resources—but also to those which were former colonies, or which had been in some way exploited, and are therefore politically vulnerable, and to be bargained for or influenced.) Professor Isaacs notes that the Chinese, like the Russians, play heavily upon racist themes, although theoretically racism is anathema in Communist ideology. "Peking's efforts to whip up support for herself in Africa and the Third World (through the movements associated with Bandung, Cairo, and Algeria) is supported by racist arguments. In fact in Peking's open propaganda, the Third World formula becomes a code name for the 'colored world,' and the Third World in conjunction with China is counterpoised to the white world of the West and the Soviet Union."

The Soviet Union then has not used racism in this same context?

"Perhaps not in the same context," he admits, "She could hardly speak of the Colored International, being largely white herself, and being conscious of the divisive effect this would have upon her own Asiatic subjects. But in other areas and by using other methods she has been adept at using race and religion. For instance not only has she used anti-Semitism against Israel, but she has encouraged Marxist penetration of Islamic institutions." He goes on to stress that after World War II—with the rapid Japanese military thrust down the Peninsula of Malaysia, the victorious sweep through the islands, the landing in New Guinea, the threat to Australia—the consciousness of race received a special impetus. "All this has left an indelible mark on the colored people of the world."

His words recreate a disturbing vision of the white men of the East; no longer lords and masters, but weak with hunger and thirst, driven, prodded by bayonets on marches from which many of them were never to return. "This world of the sixties," Professor Isaacs adds, "is a world in which the system which supported white dominance has crumbled; native inhabitants have seen the white man humbled."

October 3

Dinner with Waldo Frank. Twenty-five years ago he had been a fairly robust energetic man, small but stocky, ruddy-faced, with dark thoughtful sad eyes. Older now, and ill, he is distressed by his inability to manage those small tasks which make up ordinary living. "I can't make my own bed. I can't even use the step ladder to get at books on the top shelves." Recently, knowing that his health is not likely to improve, he has even thought of suicide; but has been deterred by the thought of his children.

"Why shake your head?" he asks in a low voice (explaining patiently that in some nations, in Japan for instance, suicide is considered the only honorable course).

We walk slowly down the street under the bright winter stars. He talks of early radical days, of his time at Yale, of his espousal of various causes. (As Mencken says, "to be an American is to be burdened by an ethical predisposition, to lean towards causes and remedies.") "I had a propensity for being chosen to head Committees and groups. I was for instance considered a non-Party writer, a symbolic figure . . . . I was Chairman of the League of American Writers; in those days of course the Left was generally acceptable."

Had the criticism of the Russian Trials in the thirties affected him?

"Yes, it affected me to the extent that I wrote an open letter to the *New Republic* and asked that an international commission of socialists and communists be appointed to study the evidence; this had the effect of making me a renegade!" (When the next American Writers Congress met, Waldo was conspicuously absent.) Walking towards the square we speak of how he had tried to help Cuba, in which (because of his earlier relationship with the country and with Castro) he had a special interest. He had allowed his name to be used to head the Fair Play for Cuba Committee (the FPCC), but now he admits that he had soon withdrawn his support.

Why exactly did he withdraw his support?

"I didn't like what was going on. I saw that there was a certain manipulation, a certain use of well-meaning liberals, a certain covering-up . . . . Then the finances were not absolutely clear; I began to be unsure of my own role."

Further thoughts of Waldo Frank (a tremendously educated man in spite of certain ignorances; a humble man in spite of certain vanities; a man of courage).

Once he had commented that Castro and his group of young military followers were simply *"barbudos"*—as he put it "bearded boys." Affected by the romantic aspects of the Cuban Revolution, he had apparently discounted or failed to understand the international structure into which Cuba had been integrated. For some reason I remember a photograph of himself that used to hang in his study. Taken by Steiglitz in the early twenties, it shows a shock-haired, eager-looking young man with eyes that were even then a little sad, and a mouth which was full and sulky. Was it some constitutional innocence which had hidden from him the actual nature of Soviet manipulation? As far back as 1937 when the American Society for Technical Aid to Spanish Democracy was formed, he had served as Chairman (of what was ostensibly organized to raise funds to send skilled American workers to Spain; but which in actuality had been planned so that OGPU operations in the United States could be facilitated). Yet some of the same optimism which had caused him in the thirties to give his name to that committee, still lingered on in the early sixties when he agreed to head the Fair Play for Cuba Committee, and later to support the Communist-sponsored Youth Festival held in Helsinki.

As death approached him, Lenin, according to Deutscher, experienced doubts for the future of the Party which no longer conformed to his dreams. If Lenin himself was haunted by such doubts (Marxists in trying to be consistent must necessarily be caught up in the conflict of those who attempt to adapt an intellectualized consistency to the inconsistency of life itself), there is no reason for latter-day followers to be immune from them. Like his contemporaries Waldo Frank has been much influenced by the Marxist climate. His idealism, his gullibility are also a reminder of the physicist and crystallographer John Desmond Bernal (whom I'd come to know in England when he was already a much-revered figure and used to be met at intellectual gatherings, invariably wearing a jacket too short for his arms and with his shock of pale hair standing on end above an extremely pliable, good-natured but alert face). If not actually a card-carrying Communist, Bernal was known for his support of the Party, which he tended to look at long-range (as at one of his experiments). He had told me at the time that he blamed the Hitler-Stalin pact on delays contrived by the British government, and that during the Munich emergency he had tried to get firmer action from Whitehall by waking up one Minister in the middle of the night.

His (Bernal's) apologias for Stalin had not seemed convincing then; but his enthusiasm for the great scientific experiment in Russia which was to improve the lot of the "workers of the world," was understandable. In his imagination the whole of the Soviet scene had a classic importance far beyond day-to-day error; and he talked of the dialectic as religious leaders talk of the catechism.

How much imagination had gone into making sacrosanct the intellectual processes by which he had reached his conclusions it is hard to know; but Koestler, in his own confessions of political exaltation, suggests that the "political libido is basically as irrational as the sexual drive, and patterned, like the latter, by early, partly unconscious experiences; by traumatic shocks, complexes, repressions, and the rest." When it became clear that in spite of Desmond Bernal's trips to Russia and his role on many occasions as spokesman, liaison man, or frontman for the Communist party, he had never learned to speak Russian well enough to do without an interpreter, it was natural to wonder whether his beliefs, or for that matter those of Waldo Frank, were as much a matter of intellectual integrity as they were of emotional prejudice.

In considering a curious blending of power needs with moral pretensions, and in asking what relationship there is between history as it is being made around us and the political libido of the makers, the more important question seems to be whether a large segment of the

Western "liberal establishment" does not actually tend (at this moment) to lend support to the strengthening of a totalitarian actuality.

One intellectual certainly not guilty of this tendency is Karl Wittfogel, who is an expert on China, and suitably also an expert on "despotism." He is a tall distinguished-looking man with a craggy face. ("My father," he says, "was a village schoolteacher and looked rather like a rustic edition of Tolstoy—*his* forefathers seem to have been peasants.")

We talk about the bizarreries of the political libido. "I am sure that you include in this not only the will to power, but also the readiness to submit to power; and this I can relate to my book *Oriental Despotism.*" He often refers to this book (which was published in 1957, and has gone into nine American editions and into many languages) simply as "O.D." We agree that the readiness to "submit to power" depends a great deal upon the institutions involved; institutions which both in China and Russia itself had been shaped by a despotic past. "In the book I explore the Asian mode of production as conceived of by Marx. According to Montesquieu the Asiatic-style states were not restrained by the 'intermediate' forces which characterized the states of Europe, and so prevented the Western states—in spite of thrusts towards despotism—from matching the power of 'the state' to the east. The Eastern agro-managerial state accomplished an atomization of society which made such absolutism incomparably stronger than European absolutism. Then came the Bolsheviks, the heirs of a despotic power system with semi-managerial functions, and the Communist ruling class were able to exercise a qualitatively new type of power, a power which verged upon totality—to paraphrase Lenin: 'Oriental despotism plus electrification.' "

This discussion of limitless power leads to another discussion about the horrendous death toll in Communist China. [According to Richard L. Walker of the Institute of International Studies at the University of North Carolina, this toll could be between thirty and sixty million, what with purges, aggressions, executions and forced labor—not to mention the despotic forcing of more than 120 million families into 26,000 communes during the Great Leap Forward—or the advance into India, or the taking over of Tibet (with thousands killed, thousands more in camps for ideological cleansing and 200,000 forced into labor on the roads—50,000 of them dying of hunger, exhaustion and freezing).] Wittfogel mentions that he himself had quoted similar figures.

We walk up the canyons of the city streets. The chill wind beats up from the river as if to strike down those who struggle against it. There is the familiar nervous stimulation, the familiar crescendo of noise.

"We of the West," Wittfogel says, "would do well to view Marxism not only as a powerful analytic tool, but also as an effective device for arousing political passions."

Isn't it possible that the satisfaction derived from these passions could be greater than any fear of future global harm? He nods. "Of course. Marxist-Leninists have done their best to hide Lenin's unease that should the Russian Revolution 'go wrong,' it might lead to a restoration of Russia's old order—that is, to an 'Asiatic restoration.' Marx himself had been under attack from anarchists, who warned that the Marxist state might turn into a slave state practiced in the name of the masses."

These Marxist-Leninists then refused to recognize their fears, because many of them must in their own societies have experienced a certain alienation. (Marx himself had described "alienation" as an inevitable companion of the lowest level of Oriental despotism, with the peasants literally atomized by their poverty and slavery, and barred from a natural human existence.) Wittfogel suggests that alienation and human loneliness are to be found in all human societies. "I speak more of larger groups, when the whole social structure is set up so as to make it quite impossible to establish the essential conditions of human confidence and love. To the observations of Marx I would reply that if in Oriental despotism the citizen was atomized by the state, the Communist regimes went further still, and subjected their peoples to a complete 'pulverization'. . . . In my book *O.D.* I refer to it as 'total terror, total submission, total loneliness.' "

Back in Boston the question of mainland China intrudes in a more concrete manner. The historian George H— (well-informed upon a number of subjects) mentions that there is a macabre link between this country and the situation of young Americans. "Your Jasmin, for instance, may be imbibing Chinese heroin along with Chinese propaganda!"

In this there surfaces again the story which had been afloat in 1964 on the West Coast, and I ask whether the evidence seems to him convincing.

"I realize that there are vehement denials," he says. "It's true that mainland China permits no addiction. Thousands of pushers and addicts have been publicly executed. In Canton as many as 275 in one day! Because of this puritanical 'internal' attitude, many find it hard to believe that 'externally' China has developed into one of the largest dealers in the world."

And how does one document the existence of the trade?

"By scientific analysis it is generally possible to tell where the heroin was processed. Moreover, some of the seizures have been of opium stored in the stems of a bamboo grown *only* in China; and of drugs put up in bags made of material processed *only* on the mainland. Then there are such matters as evidence that opium seized entering Japan was found to be of Cantonese origin. Reports came from responsible governments all over the world as well as from the supreme command of Tokyo, and from Communist defectors. Traffickers were seized who stated that opium was being grown in Jehol and manufactured in Tientsin, and that poppies were being grown in huge quantities in Yunnan, where long battles raged on the border over drug control between the exiled forces of Chiang Kai-shek and Red Chinese border patrols." (His analysis suggests obvious questions. If Red China is engaged in such a gigantic trade, why is it not more publicized? Why does the U.S. government not accuse China openly? Is it possible that because of the American presence in Vietnam, the United States hesitates to take official notice of what might be seized upon for protest material by anti-war groups?)

While their contemporaries, those lost offspring of the underworld (Jasmin, Cleopatra, Toole), try to mitigate the harsh reality of their lives with make-believe, students in Harvard Square—in their fatigues and combat boots, indulging in passionate rhetoric about sitting-in and having the police carry them off to jail—conjure up for themselves a make-believe world of "action" so as to divert themselves from their dream-smooth academic existences!

According to Feuer, Bakunin exerted a tremendous influence over the revolutionary movement; he spoke of the "instinctive passion of the masses for equality" and characterized the Revolution as an "uprising of the unencumbered." The popular instinct of revolt, he understood, was enfeebled in civilized people, although often found in the disinherited and wretched. And unlike Marx, who shut himself up in the British Museum and didn't get around among the workers and students, he (Bakunin) sensed the themes which Freud was to make popular—that, for instance, the young loved to revolt against their parents—that the aroused masses had a passion for destruction. Lenin, recognizing something of this, was anxious to utilize it, and acted as Feuer pointed out, as an intermediary in importing this ingredient of "neo-Barbarism" to Marxism.

The point seems to be that one section of the alienated *lumpenproletariat* (the lower strain of propertyless and unemployed and crime-prone minorities—elements of the Negro, Puerto Rican, Chicano populations—by color alone fulfilling the necessity of Mao's "colored international") are for *quite other reasons* than the serious solving of problems, ripe to be motivated by Bakunin's passion for revolt! How easy it is in the South End for instance to imagine these *resentidos* suitably bemused by a few Marxist slogans, being used as shock troops for the uprising of the legendary Marxist Phoenix.

In her small room, decorated with the trophies of a "Black" experience,

Jasmin describes her first introduction to heroin: "I was in Washington D.C., and at that time I'd run from Robert (Robert was the man I married, and he was a sailor, very dark and handsome. Oh baby, he was just like Peter Ustinov). Yet, I'd run from him, although I used to meet him every week to pick up his pay check. . . . Well I was in this house and across the hall from me there was a fellow used to leave his door open. So I noticed he had books, and one day I asked to borrow some. He had Plato's *Republic,* and Homer as well. When he saw I by-passed the baloney, he said to me; 'You're sure you don't want *True Confessions?* How old are you?' I said 'Nineteen' and he said 'Well, you're the first young broad I've ever met wanting to read anything worthwhile.' "

Jasmin, who by now has come to enjoy telling her story, lapses into the present tense: "One day he knocks on my door, and he's wild-eyed and the sweat is running down his face, and he begs me to come help him. I go over to his room, and he has these capsules and a spoon, and a little bottle top, and a spike. He is trying to inject himself; it dawns on me, 'This man is a drug addict.' He begins to scream at me because I am clumsy helping him. 'You stupid bitch, you can't do anything' he keeps saying. He'd got his arm tied up, and he couldn't hit the vein. He is crying 'Baby, you *got* to do this for me.' I manage to hit, and the blood shoots up in the air, and I press the plunger, and in no more than three seconds he sits up and his voice is all quiet, and he says 'Baby, hand me a kleenex.'

"Afterwards he says to me 'Baby, I'm sorry for hollerin'. But from that time on I dig he's a junkie, and I'm looking at him harder. He's a creep thief, and he'll take anything that's not tied down. He'll slip out something of value when the proprietor's in the back. He'll walk among squares, in art galleries and in Grand Central and ease them of their wallets. Yes, I'd sit and watch him when he hit himself, and one day I told him 'I wanta try some' and he says, 'Baby you don't want none of *this!*' But I keep asking, and he shoots me up with a cap. I remember that first shot. I'm waiting, and he says 'You feel it?' All of a sudden this warm feeling like deep heat. It just killed me!"

Jasmin closes her eyes, leans back and allows her voice to fade into that old and powerful memory. "It is a hot summer day and I sit there on the stoop and nod for four hours. I don't throw up till those four hours are over. I want to drink cold cold liquids. Finally I throw up and then I get higher—very very lethargic it is, very very far away and dreamlike. It was three years before I had another shot. But when I did, then that was the end. I was hooked!"

Cleopatra talks about her "habit" too, but with her it is bound to a certain cautious refinement. "To be a whore you have to have no feeling," she explains. "I mostly hustle in the daytime, because in the daytime I feel less conspicuous. Nine o'clock is very late for me. I dress very restrained. Although I'm a whore I don't like squares to know and to say 'There goes a whore!' When I was pregnant the first time I looked terrible . . . Herbie saw me and took me to have a coke. Addicts don't like to drink—and this seems a little thing, but it's very significant if you're holding onto your self-respect.

"My mother found out when I went to have the baby. The doctor came in very excited, and he saw my eyes were yellow and my finger nails, and the doctor said 'You have hepatitis . . . could you have used anything, any instrument that could have transferred this to you?' And my mother is sitting there crying, and asking 'Where did I fail? Where did I fail?'"

In a low expressionless voice Cleopatra speaks of the pains and embarrassments of her life; of hustling for her "habit," of fear on dark nights in strange streets, of being attacked as she was once by a man in an alley, who tried to cut her breasts with a penknife.

But where Cleo draws superficially upon middle-class values and cloaks her shame, Jasmin turns hers towards religious glorification.

"Why am I doing this? I'm doing it because it's part of the pattern that's been created for me. Some people want to be whores, but I don't want to be a whore. I have to *see* this side so that I can do what I have to do in this world. I had a dream, and a voice told me to pick up a bible. 'Go ye therefore into the highways and byways and bring them all unto the Lord.' Yes, I had to go this way to be dynamic enough to do better. I got *labor* to do in His vineyards. He said to me 'If you do not follow my words I will turn you over to a retrobate mind and you will become all manner of lascivious woman. You will lay with man, woman, and beast. . . .' I keep turning my back on Him, although I know that *man does not live by bread alone.* Now I must trust Jesus. Anything I need he'll give me, just like I trusted Robert I must trust the Lord and what matter if I go to prison? Where than there would I find a better group of souls?"

At this point Jasmin strikes a posture which is like that of the many preachers she has seen. She raises her arms above her head and stretches out her fingers. Then she turns and gives a mournful look from her glowing eyes; "I tell you honey, every time I put a spike in my arm, I cry out to God."

Again she speaks, often in the voice of fantasy. "I'm goin' to New York City to cop. I'm slippin' off the plane and I'm so fly I'm takin' a cab and I think we should run all the red lights . . . . I'm on 118th and Lenox lookin' for the right face . . . you ain't goin' on *no* corner there where you won't find a junky! . . . So I'm asking who's got the best, who's straight, where to find the best shag . . . an' they say to me, 'You lookin' baby?'" She bursts out in a scornful laugh "I approach *no* whitey about *no* dope!

"So they tell me 'California Bobby got good stuff,' or 'Henry King got the best' and I say 'I'm trying to get a coupla loaves in half, (That's meaning I'm buying fifteen three dollar bags for twenty-five dollars; that's in volume). So someone say if you straighten me baby I'll take you . . . an we gets us a cab and he say 'You know it goin' cost you fifty cents to use the works?' an' I say 'alright;' and we get there and reach a doorway and go down in the basement and knock the door and a voice say 'Who there? You by yourself man?' 'No—I got company.' Well the door opens a crack and you slide in, and this is where your eyes is peeled, because they can bag up some milk sugar for you real fast. (The janitor he gets free fixes and he gets the fifty cent pieces, that his hustle.) An' you make your deal, an' you shoot up." She gives a profound sigh. But standing there in the skimpy wrapper she wears, all it is really possible to see in the dusky light are the long white tracks against the dark skin of her forearms.

In this by now familiar sense of counterpoint, another visit to Toole. The meal is made of cold cuts, potato salad, and beer—all delivered from the deli in the "combat zone."

Toole whispers that Primrose is mad at her because of her drinking, and going out at night. "I done all that painting and put up all the shelves, an' fixed the lights." She jerks her head in the old way. "She's just not reasonable. D'you see she wouldn't eat hardly any supper? And here am I trying hard to get off the booze." There follows a brief discussion about life in general and about "what you can expect from people." Toole does not consider herself a revolutionary as do Jasmin and her friends; nor does she have yearnings for respectability as does Cleopatra. But she wants security of a clear-cut sort. She identifies with the "Right Wing of her world" (that is the Mafia) and remarks that she knows some of the women who have friendships with the "big men" in the North End. "Those Italians," she says approvingly, "they're square about their women."

(As an ironic follow-up to this remark the phone rings and there are consultations between Pat and Toole. "He wants . . ." "She wants . . ." "No, he's not her husband, she's some sort of girl friend . . ." "No, they don't want . . . only to watch . . . ."

Primrose is listening uneasily. Finally when Toole approaches to say that she is "going to town" for a few hours, Primrose swings around and slaps her face—Toole's reaction is strangely feminine. She doesn't retaliate, but only winces and holds her jaw. Finally, recovering, she pushes Primrose angrily into one of the bedrooms and shuts the door. As I walk downstairs I can hear Primrose sobbing.)

. . . And as in a theater, Toole appears on the landing above, ready for the street. She is dressed in a man's suit with a stiff white collarless shirt. The shirt has a stud at the neck, but no tie. And she wears a rather rakish brown felt hat pulled down over her eyes.

1965

October 31

That fierce irrationality so characteristic of many of Jasmin's male friends and relatives is especially characteristic of one of her closest companions, a male prisoner who is serving a term for trying to kill his brother's rival. He is an extra-tall, extra-strong, extra-black young man, who moves lightly on the balls of his feet when he comes into the Walpole reception room. His hands are almost as nervous as his feet, and he has a mobile and blank face, with eyes which glare a little, although occasionally they soften into something close to good nature. His name? "Junior."

As is generally the case the visit has been prefaced by a letter.

> Everything I tell you through the pen is my real true self . . . I am doing hard time. . . . But around me I see men with twenty to forty, forty to fifty, thirty to sixty years, and believe me these are years, not days or weeks. . . . cold-blooded years. . . . I am digging myself. I have just read the *Color Curtain* by Richard Wright. It is about the Bandung Conference. Just think here is just a few of the twenty-nine nations of Asia and Africa that met at the Bandung. (He lists them.) I have to stop and pull myself together to realize that these nations were ex-colonial subjects, some of them have been ruled for 350 years. The undeveloped of the human race were meeting at Bandung. I couldn't lay the book down for one second.

This is the kind of book that American Negroes are now reading!

Afterwards the prison social worker admits that a number of black prisoners (blacks make up a large proportion of the inmates) are interested in politics. "Oh the Black Muslims were always trying to convert the addicts; and they did a good job too. But it doesn't end there."

In what way doesn't it end?

"We-ell there's a sort of attitude—nothing you can put your finger on. But being white I feel it. They're waiting, that's it." His brow is furrowed.

Is it that the white officers fear attack?

"We-ell—a lot of meetings go on. And then there's talk about 'self-defense.' And about violence being 'necessary.' It's not that you expect a knife in your back exactly; but things are not comfortable, and under certain circumstances that knife might even eventuate. I think I'm talking about one race against another."

We sit there silently in the impersonal green-painted room. It has probably not occurred to him to think of these inmates as particularly suitable troops for the new political war—as were once the criminals recruited to the French or Russian revolutions, or the *dacoits* taken up only a few years ago by the NLF in Burma. He is probably unaware of the recent reports of secret agreements in the South (between CORE representatives and the Deacons for Defense and Justice) to organize armed black groups for self-defense, and to keep whites out of black areas. He only knows that here in the prison these inmates may turn against their keepers.

"Well," he says uneasily, straining in a uniform a little too tight for him, "if they try to go too far they'd be mowed down." Eventually his voice relaxes. "Let's say that there are those who would *like* to see real trouble between blacks and whites."

November 3

Jasmin continues to show rapid political growth. In the cafeteria of a Girls' Sports Club, where a battered picture of Malcolm X has been stuck upon the wall, she insists that he was "as fine as May wine." Malcolm was saved by Elijah, rescued from the deep ghetto death of which she suspects she is now part. Moreover he had gone on one step further—to travel, to be listened to by "Whitey," to be received by kings and shieks!

We talk about her new political interests. What does she think of the Chinese Communists?

"I tell you I'm hip to them. I read Mao's *Little Red Book* because in the RAM papers they will always be quoting from the *Red Book* or from Lenin or Karl Marx."

And does she like Karl Marx?

"Do I like Karl Marx?" She groans. "Oh honey, his works are so *heavy*. I don't see how a human being can *understand* them. But I do feel like the *Little Red Book* is easier to grasp. Oh yeah, I read Ché's *How To Make a Revolution*, and in fact they were giving out copies of that."

What does she think of Ché?

Her small brown tight-drawn face lights up. "Oh yes, he's one of our *leaders!*"

The question of power disturbs her. "How could Mao control all those millions of people? What's amazing to me is when I first saw pictures of Mao, Ho Chi Minh and the others, they were such *little shits;* they weren't half as big as I was . . . and I thought if it wasn't the fear of God what was it? What kind of thing was they preachin' to their people to make them servile, to make them *go?*" Jasmin stands in the street and stretches out her thin arms, the fringes of her chamois coat dangle and sway. "When I read more, I found they wasn't really going on with their full program they promised the people, that maybe the army *was* in power. I read about executions, and prisoners working in mines and so on" (having been in prison herself, Jasmin is particularly sensitive to hard labor for prisoners).

And what did she feel now?

"Well, in that overcrowded land, I feel the leaders just use the people. They make them work. No work no food. I feel like if they have a war they don't think nothing of sending waves of human beings forward. Just like the Japanese, that suicide thing. It's a sort of religion, you die for the faith." But she keeps returning, as to some sort of security, to her newly found *négritude*. "What do I care about China? Why I don't know any blacks been to China, only for Robert Williams of RAM." Her voice becomes challenging as she remembers the advice of this particular black firebrand. "These men in RAM are not like those niggers that prayed for rain when Massa's house was burning down. No, these men is different. They are hopin' for a wind." Her husky voice fills with wonder. "These men not only hopin' for a wind when there's a fire. They *set* the fire. They bring the matches, honey . . . *an'* the kerosene."

November 28

Another visit to "Junior." Through the green-painted recreation room, his figure, tightly bound in prison jeans, comes lightly forward into the open well of the circular building, spangled with sun. It is easy to fantasy that Junior is one of those street blacks who make up the potential for Jesse Gray's guerrilla fighters, and that as he advances through the green-painted prison room, he really advances through a city park with his rifle in his hand. Actually today his self-esteem has been stimulated by reading up about the plot to bomb the Statue of Liberty and the Washington Monument. This plot was discovered early in the year, with several militant blacks involved, two from the United States and one from the West Indies—as also Canadians, notably, Annette le Duc, a twenty-seven-year-old blond TV interviewer who had been a member of RIN (*Rassemblement pour l'Indépendance Nationale*, a militant separatist movement).

Although this plot was easily dismissed as dealing with local separatist grievances, the international links are evident. Annette herself, child of provincial French Canada (educated in so religious an environment that she remembers being reproved by the nuns for wearing shiny shoes in case the boys should glimpse in them the reflection of her thighs), is a prototype. She appears to have progressed in a logical way from pure romantic membership in a "liberation" movement to an active militant revolutionary role. She had, for instance, lived for a while in Algeria with a young Algerian revolutionary who was in touch already with French-Canadian insurgents and who had come to Algiers for training in terrorism. She had finally, in company with

Claude Giroux, formed or been part of a more militant action-slanted movement called the *Mobilisation pour la Libération de Quebec* or the MLQ. It was Annette who obtained the dynamite, blasting caps, and primer cord for the three blacks from the United States—Dick Collins, Asa Aberrian (a member of SNCC), and Henry Bowden (a supporter of the Fair Play for Cuba Committee): all of whom also are members of a paramilitary Black Liberation Front. Collins, for instance, had spent time in Cuba and had taken orders from Ché, the great guerrilla chief himself; he had been put in touch with Annette through Thérèse Laval, a psychology instructress at the *École Normale Jacques Cartier*, who had been in Cuba with Collins the year before the *exposé*. The other American, Henry Bowden, may also have voyaged to Cuba, Land of "Revolution"—he was in any case a member of the FPCC and so linked to the island by sympathy. Naturally Junior does not involve himself with the moral issues. He expatiates in his rapid-fire, enthusiastic, but curiously flat voice about what happened. "That cat Collins is cool, he's into this revolutionary thing with all he's got. I figure that this broad from Canada was looking to use his draw to help her out with her own deal . . . that's why she got him the dynamite." The idea of Ché Guevara is exciting to him, as is the mere mention of Cuba, or Algeria. (He knows, for instance, that Robert Williams went to Cuba, and has read copies of *The Crusader*. He knows that the Algerian war was the inspiration for a film which was often shown in Roxbury.)

It is without meaning to him that Annette, the heroine of the bombing plot, was apparently in the habit of prostituting herself around the United Nations, partly for money, partly in order to influence African diplomats to the revolution, and partly so that she could be in a position to employ sexual blackmail, recruit spies, and gather information. After meeting the young U.S. blacks, she offered to introduce them to suitable Algerians, to get them false Canadian passports, and to find people who could help them to forge IBM plates (the plates used to issue government checks). Junior's eyes shine as we talk about these plates. In such territory he feels completely at home.

Does he see that the whole bomb plot was not simple cheating of the police at the Canadian border; that what is significant is that two revolutionary countries—Cuba and Algeria—both of them involved in the training of terrorists, played a role? He only looks blank. He is also not upset by the discordant finale to the "bomb" case; the grim possibilities of total commitment to a political cause escape him. Since his whole family has lived according to the laws of the street, he does not think twice of death. The fact that Claude Giroux had hung himself in his cell in Quebec is of little significance. Dressed in jeans, Junior is just a prisoner; but on one occasion he had come into the reception room wearing a black velvet dashiki decorated with orange braid. Now it seems that what impresses him most about the "bomb plot" is that

1965

Collins and Aberrian and Bowden are black men as he is. As he thinks of himself in the role of a bomber and conspirator his eyes are curiously glaring, as if unknown to himself, some tiger lived there behind his brow.

(Later it is disclosed at the trial that Collins had not only visited Cuba during August in 1964 along with other students, but had been trained in terrorist tactics there by a major in the North Vietnamese army; and Ché, as the overall organizer of a widening terroristic scene, probably saw the project as a pragmatic experiment in putting U.S. minorities into action with Third-World comrades. In a similar manner, he and his agents had been involved with young militants from Puerto Rico who needed to be made to feel that they were part of a wider organization. Claude Giroux may have been a more important figure in the plot. Annette le Duc, while in detention in the United States, seemed tremendously afraid that Claude would talk; she herself only decided to talk when news came that he, Claude, could no longer give evidence.)

No one seems to try to chart the relationship between people like Jasmin and Junior and a rapidly growing gallery of public black characters. Of these last LeRoi Jones, a New Jersey poet who runs the Revolutionary Theater, is not the least; especially since he celebrates the destruction of all "dim-witted fat-bellied white guys." [The Revolutionary Theater was given a grant of forty thousand dollars under Haryou-Act, a federal poverty agency. In March of 1966 the police discovered an arsenal hidden in the theater building: rifles, pistols, crossbows, bombs, meathooks and hashish pipes!]

It is clear that in any activity run by LeRoi Jones it will be LeRoi who will store the guns and the molotov cocktails; and it will be the duty of young men like Junior to use them. Similarly if LeRoi is not of the same material as the members of RAM or the Five-percenters, his hate (he is coming to be known as the Hate Poet) is the deadlier because of it. (The Five-percenters are quite young deep ghetto blacks who seem to be an offshoot of the Black Muslims and claim that Negroes are 85 percent cattle, 10 percent manipulated, and 5 percent leaders. They already have a reputation for causing trouble in city schools and for calling their white teachers "blue-eyed devils." So that if history is to be trusted, it is not to polite theories that cannon fodder like Junior might eventually gravitate, but rather to groups like the Five-percenters or to RAM which is supposed to have a specially trained assassination unit. In other words, to those elements whose joy is to destroy.) "Everything depends upon the value we attach to things," wrote Flaubert to M. de C— in 1857, "it is we who make morality or virtue. The cannibal who eats his brother is as innocent as the child sucking his barley sugar."

Since the revolution of the dark races is long overdue, society should deal with "cannibalistic innocence" by due process. Here in the slums, in my own "undeveloped" country, i.e. the South End, the concept of the beauty of *négritude* is necessary; nor actually are the neo-Marxist overtones of the Black Revolution "unnecessary." But it would be good to see avoided what there is every tendency to exalt—the extreme version of Aimé Césaire's "Hurrah for those who never invented everything"; and the myth that it is only in dark ghettoes, in Brazilian jungles, in archaic African villages, that pure spirit is found.

On the other hand the political element has to be subjected to scrutiny. Some Canadian professors—not aware of the contacts of Collins and Thérèse Laval with Cuba and Algeria, or of Collins's meeting with Ché Guevara, or of his training on that island known as the "Pearl of the Antilles"—fail to see that whatever the plethora of movements, cadres, sects, maqui, and rassemblements which existed in Quebec when the terrorist bombings started two years ago—or came into being later—the "separatism" of the Quebec movement does not obviate its also being surreptitiously penetrated by agents from other countries. If French Canadians have always been underdogs in a state where 77 percent of the better paid jobs go to the English, there is still no proof that much of the early emotion involved in the movement was not artificially stimulated. Two foreign-born characters, Georges Schoeters, a Belgian, and François Shirm, a Hungarian, were active in last year's terrorism, and it has been suggested that their presence in Canada is not accidental. Nor—as in Mexico south of the border—might the current re-activation of the Communist party be accidental. To rationalize hopes for political change, it is at least important to examine the sources of political behavior.

A friend called Bella, infected by the spirit of the New Left, has decided that her spare-time work will be to support the new SNCC. She talks of the early struggle in the south; of Autherine (the first black student admitted to the University of Alabama) walking quietly onto the campus to the thud of stones and vegetables and cries of "Keep 'Bama White." Bella points out that only a few years later Vivian Malone and James Hood, two dark-skinned twenty-year-olds, were met with smiles. From this she infers that from now on progress is inevitable. She seems hardly aware that the situation has changed, that the struggle has shifted onto an international plane, that would-be reformers must face a dynamic which may not be acceptable to taste or conscience, that SNCC and CORE are now working with extremists like Jesse Gray, that recently a vital change of some sort, and certainly a change towards direct action and violence, has taken place in the civil rights movement.

1965

December 24

As the year draws to its end, the counterpoint between Hill and Slum or between Cambridge and Slum becomes instead a counterpoint between "liberal and student fantasy of political action" and "Black and Third Worlder fantasy of direct action." To have experienced the primitive political outreaching of the South End and Roxbury, is not to have respect for attitudes in more sophisticated quarters. The future-oriented Marxists seem no more clairvoyant than the "by any means necessary" direct-actors. If one group is more attractive in the human sense, the other rouses more sympathy. In fact it appears that the myth-minded political amateurs who overemphasize their powers to predict are no less "angry" than the minorities of the cities. In a sense both look towards the Apocalypse.

Perhaps the point is that revolutionary activity is made by men and not by theory. Could it be for instance that human beings, whatever their protestations, act only for themselves? When the murderer and prostitute Raskolnikov and Sonia in *Crime and Punishment* are inevitably drawn together, Raskolnikov whispers in the candlelit room, as their pale and feverish faces lean, one against the other: "We are both accursed. You too have transgressed . . . your hand has had the strength to transgress." . . . "Break what must be broken," he advises, "freedom and power . . . above all power!" He admits his bondage. "I wanted to be a Napoleon," he whispers, "that is why I killed her." He records his horror of the narrow student room, and his conviction that only anyone who has "daring" and is "strong" could triumph over this narrowness. "I did the murder myself alone" he whispers.

The world of social change has come to have about it an unpleasant flavor of "race" (clearer perhaps in the world at large than here in the confinement of Boston). Already in Africa and Asia (in the name of the Third World movement and with no relationship to the needs of the life-hungry Africans or Asians themselves), tremendous floods of hate propaganda are being beamed (from Cairo south of the border to countries where illiterate and simple herdsmen and peasants gather around campfires and in village squares; from Peking across the borders of Burma and into the villages of Thailand) to tell of the "savageries" of Western leaders. From these broadcasts the listeners would learn that white men, a species known as "capitalists," are the worst villains on the face of the globe. Even as black dictators prolifer-ate, and old tribal rivalries explode into massacres, anti-white hatred is being dignified in the name of neo-Marxist systems. It may happen eventually, in Africa or even in the United States, that as Elijah Muhammed likes to prophesy, blacks and whites will "drink blood like water." It is in deference to such possibilities that advocates of rapid and ruthless social change are often taken by surprise. Over and above this, the problem remains that these men of the Third World, bemused as they are by the achievements of the West, have (if they have been able so far to take anything from the West) taken only what pleased them. They have not been able to absorb the years of discipline or the internalization of restraint. As Herzen says of the French Revolution: "At last the oppressive edifice of feudal monarchy crumbles, and slowly the walls were shattered, the locks struck off—one more blow struck, one more wall breached, the brave men advance, gates are opened and the crowd rushes in . . . but it is not the crowd that was expected. Who are these men; to what age do they belong? They are not Spartans, not the great *populus Romanus*. An irresistible wave of filth flooded everything."

December 25

And it is on the Hill of course that Christmas Eve is spent, where the customs of an earlier and securer time are followed. In Louisburg Square, under the light streaming from houses (sometimes through the prisms of ancient glass and always onto the white snow outside, where crowds of carolers gather in coats, snowboots, and gloves—their heads powdered by the fine spray blown from the slate rooves) a young woman murmurs that she feels "phony," and a smiling man in a light overcoat announces that "it's too cold for such nonsense." But still the voices rise, powerful and only slightly ambiguous; "Si-ilent night . . . Ho-oly night."

1966

They wanted to make the world clean, livable, magnificent. They fell in love so deeply with the generation of tomorrow, with the mankind to come, that there was hardly any love left for those who happened to live in today's world.

Gyorgy Paloczi-Horvath
from *A Meeting of Two Young Men*

January 5, 1966. Cambridge

City birds are flirting in the icy air. Through the apartment window
(behind which lie the abandoned relics of Christmas, the perfumed fir
tree, the lights glowing faintly on last night's coffee cups, on a sagging
crayoned sign saying "New Year's Eve—1966") the street is transformed into a glittering tableau; where a woman walks by, holding like
some sacred image of the New Year, a baby wrapped in a dark blue
parka.

In moving to this Cambridge street the weight of experience has
been changed again and that counterpoint between the slum with its
minorities and the more "elevated" life on the Hill, gives way to life on
the "city plain" to what is more balanced, more reflective, and less
surprising. As snow drifts thought becomes easier. The city is hushed.
Windows are blanketed. Faces pass half-hidden behind coat collars,
hats, hoods. In that pure white those who walk leave their footsteps
behind them. . . .

January 18

Reading *How The Poor Die* by Orwell. He describes his visits to a
hospital in Paris in 1929—the rows of beds close together, the sweetish
fecal smells, the impersonal treatments without explanation or human
comment, the waking at dawn for temperature-taking, the students
listening to the bronchial rattle of patients as they would listen to the
rattle of machines, the busy doctors walking past briskly, followed by
imploring cries. Orwell points out in his essay that there is a Nineteenth Century flavor to his hospital experience; a flavor found in

1966

Victorian novels and in the official reports of "madhouses" and "alms-houses."

Orwell's insights into the devices used to regulate human lives remind us how much these have expanded in the "technological" twentieth century. Governments which learn to excel in this direction may well control the globe! (That for the first time in history a truly interdependent community might be created does not necessarily mean that man will be liberated: in fact, the danger is that he might well be the more enslaved.) In this open situation, the attitudes of intellectuals are crucial. Djilas uses the term the New Class to describe those "who have special privileges and economic preference because of the administrative monopoly they hold"; and although he is referring to Yugoslavia, where liberty is curtailed, it is easy to see in the democratic countries also a rise to effective power of a new class who rely upon their superiority of knowledge to win special rights of speaking for others.

To be back in the academic community is to be reminded of this. America is deluged with experts, the country's complex living arrangements are being subjected to dubious social engineering. It is especially discouraging to see the student body engulfed by so great a wave of ideology, much of it of a neo-Marxist nature. When Marx produced *Das Kapital*, he misread certain social factors which were to change, and in many ways to cancel out, his theories. (The realization of prophecies such as the emerging of a proletarian dictatorship, the withering away of the state, the ever-greater impoverishment of the worker under capitalism—these proved to be elusive.) But in spite of this today's global shadow-play of Marxist symbols fascinates a whole new ideological generation. [According to Lewis Feuer's last book, the word "revolution" has become a master-symbol. He notes that the current myth must be embedded in science or philosophy—it must enlist argument and social reality; it must be linked with class or race.] One of the current gurus, for instance, is Herbert Marcuse, who condemns the language of science which "mutilates man" and claims that violent revolution is the "law of existence". Marcuse attracts the marginal intellectuals who tend to return to regressive longings, and to shed rationality. Other intellectual leaders extol primitivism and the mystic nobility of native leaders. Fanon encourages the myth of *négritude* and the catharsis of Césaire's "end of the world." The ideologist, profoundly influenced by his own internal myth, can rapidly lose sight of reality; and it is this which now creates a sense of unease. We are living through a period when political life tends to be irrationalized.

A fascinating little news sheet put out in Hong Kong (*China News Analyst*) covers Communist China's news in considerable detail, and points up still another myth, that of "people's democracy."

There is a current discussion going on in China during this festival time. The idea is that it is better not to invite guests for the New Year. "Better not to spend money on food, drink, or presents." "Better to sell that home-reared pig to the state." "Better to make a vow to collect more human manure." "Better to go to see a film as a negative lesson *only*" (with the purpose of increasing class consciousness). In this atmosphere emotion is absorbed into the collective of the state. And Chinese foreign policy is seen as both refined and rude—the refinement comes from the forms of an ancient culture, the rudeness from the rugged guerrilla background of the highest authorities in the country (these were men who exterminated millions of their own people without a twinge of regret).

Apparently Tibet at this point is regarded as a desert which had no culture at all until the occupation by the Red Chinese Army of Liberation. All pretense of esteem for things Tibetan has vanished. Illiterate young men who are being groomed in Peking are fostered as cadres and future leaders. It is obvious at the same time that the real importance of Tibet is not ideological, but rather that it represents political and military security to the Chinese government. In the name of such security and in the best brainwashing tradition, the young Panchen Lama is confessing publicly to his past sins.

January 22

As a sign that alienation is not only found in Communist China, various souls in the South End remain caught in the same profound inertia as before; in fact Jasmin has now developed so heavy a heroin habit that, according to Cleopatra, she has gone to New York City to be "closer to cop" (nearer to the source of supply). Cleo herself is also on the move, and has time to talk for a short while only as she packs to catch a plane to Chicago. (Her mother tells me in a fearful but respectful whisper that her daughter is now "teamed up with a very big man!") In trying to explain to me what Beetle (this "very big man") is like, Cleo throws off several vivid descriptions. "He come into the bar and tells me I'm fly. . . . He says he'd like to see me in pretty things. ('Pretty things for pretty things. Ah Momma, you dress up the best!' he says.) I say if I had a man he'd be like *him*—outsize. That's wot he is, big and dark, a big 'Blue' from the Georgia backwoods. He got scars and he's pockmarked." She is moving rapidly about the room, putting piles of clothes into the suitcase, stopping to throw out her little hand in demonstration, holding up a wine-colored silk Shantung suit faced with black satin, and explaining that Beetle bought it for her.

"He give me this, and tell me he's tryin' to tighten up the noose." She pauses, kicks off her shoes, and puts them into the suitcase as well.

1966

"He's a big man in coke." Then she adds dramatically, "He got a collar!"

What is a collar?

"So you can lead him aroun'. I tell you that when Beetle wants box, he *wants* it!"

There is another pause. Some sadness crosses her excited face, and her voice lingers slowly. "He got scars on his ankles—scars from the chain gang of Joliet!"

Another friend of Jasmin's calls to claim psychological support; this results in a trip to the far end of Dudley Street where the girl (Corinne) is to be at home "because my ma is giving a dance. . . ."

In the kitchen a muscular rather tough-looking brown-faced girl, half-Negro and half-Indian, dressed in a mini-skirt and a dhoti-like shirt of heavy beige cotton shot with gold, is standing against walls covered with fake brick paper. The nearby parlor has been emptied of furniture and is filled with sweating teen-agers, clinging together and swaying in a half light provided by bulbs formed in the shape of red roses.

"This," says Corinne, introducing her mother who has just come in, "is the hostess with the mostest." The mother offers "beer or Burgundy wine," adding that she hears I know Jasmin, and that is "one girl she is worried about."

"She's gone down something terrible. She was never much for size and now she's thin as a pencil. Almost all her hair is gone; her cheeks is sunken and I tell *you* she's just white—*dirty*-white. Why, I wouldn't let *myself* get down like that." She smooths her plump brown body under its black silk. "Not for me either," Corinne affirms, "I keep myself way up, take iron, go to the doctor! I got a *long* life to live!" She adds that Junior is out of prison, too, and he's strung out. "All dirty and wore out!" This conversation is interrupted by the entry of "Vic," Corinne's twelve-year-old brother, who is tall for his age, and handsome with a full mouth and black eyes fringed with especially long lashes. He leans up against his sister and pleads for a taste of rum. "That's only for those that can handle it," explains Corinne, pushing him away, "you goin' to live *fast!*" She indicates another brother who is circling the room inside, holding a tiny girl hungrily against him. "That's Dicky; he just back from 'Nam."

Apparently Corinne makes her living by putting other, more amenable women on the street. Now she tells me that Marguerite, the girl she is living with, is "pregnant from a trick," and that like Toole and her friend, they plan to keep the baby. "Yes, we goin' to keep it," she declares in her harsh low voice, "she'll go to Mass General; the City's real up on babies. Look, Ma's makin' clo'es." (The mother has brought out a pile of crochet and has settled down to work in a chair.)

In the meantime Corinne organizes the party in the parlor, keeping the extra boys out going onto the dance floor with a flashlight ("Turn that light out!" she yells. "Keep your voices down.") providing more jellies, more pickles, more Kool-aid. In the kitchen she produces a bottle of rum, and turns to arbitrate between two young men ("He's messin' with my girl!") and with the girl herself, who wears an aquamarine dress edged with black, and has her hair shaved on one side and the rest teased straight out, and the bangs greased to her forehead. The boys who drift in and out of the kitchen are also "sharply" dressed. They wear tan suede jackets, sweaters with stripes, and straight creased pants rather short at the ankle.

Later the mother's friends arrive, a woman and two very black men with bloodshot eyes. One of the men claims that he works seventy-nine hours putting snaps on in a factory. His eyelids flutter angrily.

Isn't that a very long work-week?

"Seventy-nine hours" he repeats.

"He don't have to," the wife comments. She is dressed in a red blouse with frilled sleeves, a white skirt tight over her stomach, and black lace stockings which end under the knee. The third man makes some over-familiar gesture towards her and she admonishes him. "Don't handle the merchandise!" Then adds in heavy good humor, "You alright, Ernie! You alright!" She finally dances with him, displaying curious elephantine grace.

Corinne takes me into the back room where there is a big double bed with brass knobs. On the table lies an album containing photographs of Marguerite wearing a blonde wig and lying around, always showing her brown shiny breasts and her long shapely legs.

Saying goodbye, I have one last glimpse of the parlor where the dancing is going on in the pitch dark, except for the red lights. Little Vic is dancing alone in the middle of the floor, doing the "Charlie Jones," the latest hit; speeding over the linoleum, dancing, it seems, on the threshold of that world where vicious ready-made values wait to claim him.

In facile condemnation of Communist societies it is easy to forget the ills of the world of Jasmin and Toole, of Cleopatra and Corinne; but these "arrangements" seem not only more natural but certainly more human than the sadistic remedy dictated by Ho Chi Minh as he decreed after taking power in the north: "Streetwalkers? . . . We shall arrange that they walk the streets all the nights of their lives!" (And so last year Dennis Bloodworth, the English journalist, saw them in the dark streets of Hanoi, cohorts of grim faded women, advancing down the pavements, no longer pushing sex or drugs, but heavy village brooms.)

1966

Corinne and Marguerite have journeyed to Cambridge, arriving at least two hours late. "I know we late," Corinne remarks, paying the taxi and marching up the path, brilliant in a suit of post-box red, her legs shining in pale polished boots. "But I don't like to be on time."

"What you got in the way of liquor?" she demands afterwards, fingering her purse as if (should the supply prove unsatisfactory) she might go out to buy some. Marguerite stands by, a pale coffee-colored girl at once pliable and feminine, giving sad disillusioned little laughs and appearing, in her well-cut black dress which swells out over her stomach, like some ancient portrait of "pregnancy."

"Corinne were born under the sign of Venus," she murmurs.

What does that mean?

"It means she seeks for and finds beauty," Marguerite responds seriously. Her eyes under the somewhat dull blonde wig are round and believing. "She's a Leo. Leos are funny people, they like to be dramatic, to attract notice. They are very unsure of theirselves."

Corinne is tired of being discussed. "That's all crap," she decides.

"There must be *something* to account for the differences in people, Corinne," Marguerite protests in a soft hurt voice. As the two girls talk together their interest in their hair, their faces, their bodies, is intense, because it centers around the sex trade; yet their talk often appears high-minded and respectable. "I am very tactful," Marguerite announces. "I'm not afraid to live like I do, because I am very respectable about everything. People come in and out. The children from next door. Of course people will talk." In her sad wise little voice she questions me, "Isn't that what we have to expect with friends?"

Finally Corinne challenges: "Marguerite, so you didn't go to the doctor? So you told me a lie?"

"So I told you a lie," admits Marguerite. (Last night Corinne had talked as if Marguerite were already being well cared for, but now it seems that she has not once been to the doctor.)

"I want the baby!" Corinne announces aggressively.

"Who wants it?"

"I want it" Corinne says.

There is a silence. Then Marguerite replies in her dark fatalistic voice, "I'll go when the time comes."

After all, isn't it true that they are good to each other?

Corinne thinks about this, her heavy black brows knitted above her stubborn brown face. After Marguerite has gone to the bathroom she turns to me, "Yes, but it's not like it was at first. Now we talk to each other; but we don't talk deep."

Various cocktail parties. Walking along the back streets of Cambridge, past the pleasant houses with their winter gardens, their pines and their bare maples, their gnarled vines and berried bushes. The pleasant feeling of coming in from the cold through halls with shining fanlights, to rooms with shaded lamps, to fires and bookcases, to low laughter and the cries and murmur of conversation—The clink of ice in glasses, the discussions about people, about the latest play, the latest academic scandal, the latest "confrontation." A girl in a long purple wool dress showing her hipbones and the scantiness of her breasts; but all in all the lines make for elegance; and her eyelids shine with a dull but daring violet. A number of fine-featured scholastic-looking men; a few "thinkers" busy working out everything by "first principles." Another party where there are a number of sociologists ("I counted ten," whispers S—, whom I had taken with me). A third party where everyone is an authority on French literature, French history, or the French nation. But at all these gatherings an expressed dissatisfaction with U.S. life and the U.S. role in the world. This dismay and discontent overwhelm us—conversation tends to concern itself with the Vietnam war, with crime, with the difficulties of day-to-day living, and with the polarization of society.

February 15

What is happening in the American world seems to herald a turnabout of national opinion, as if a consensus formerly cut along a firm and clear line had suddenly doubled back upon itself and gone off in another direction. This does not seem possible. The values of a nation do not change overnight. Yet all the same, the pendulum of opinion appears to be swinging loose far away from the center. The question is whether the change is authentic.

Again opponents meet in a pervasive atmosphere of question, attempting to test the reality of their own opinions. Ernest is an old friend whose name expresses his nature. He is dark, rather short-sighted, and curiously gentle-voiced; in face-to-face encounters and in his work (he is a novelist) he is almost always tolerant. As he advances along the Boston street in his shabby dark coat and his thin scarf inexpertly knitted by his daughter (and in spite of his "reputation" and a certain financial success) he looks rather like the modest owner of an out-of-the-way bookshop in which the books are "interesting" rather than saleable. At one time Ernest was a member of the Communist party, and he has retained that flavor in his thinking, not because no new facts have been presented to him (the trials of the thirties, the purges of Stalin, the slavecamps of Siberia, the takeover of Eastern Europe, the Berlin Wall) but because for some psychological reason the "aura of the believer" still clings to him; so that now when he talks about Cuba in 1966 he uses the same sympathetic terms which party members used about the Soviet Union in the thirties, terms which are hardly suitable to a totalitarian state, but suggest a family-centered concern ("the Party has been very patient. . . . You can't blame the Party for protecting itself against fascists"). Now Ernest says that he is sure that if the state of political prisoners in Cuba were "only brought to the attention of Castro and other top figures," it would produce an investigation. "Some objective group outside of Cuba should try to get to the truth," he says.

But since few non-Communists are allowed into Cuba, except for propaganda purposes, or for special requirements, how are these investigations to take place? The prisons are closed, and isn't Cuba a police state?

Ernest's face mirrors a curious closed obstinacy. He does not believe that Cuba is a police state. Finally he asks, but in a rather joking way, "Am I being idealistic?"

J—, another old friend, is more aggressive, in fact a completely different type—verbal, witty, genial, gregarious. He is a journalist who was once briefly a Trotskyist and still thinks of himself as a socialist. But unlike Ernest, he has so adopted the pleasant pattern of American life, and so dipped into its financial nectar, that he has been somewhat removed from the sordid realities of political manipulation—in spite of the fact that his talents could have produced excellent analyses of the tumults of the sixties. Again the argument is about Cuba. He has just announced that "Fidel" is his "favorite Communist leader."

Doesn't the concept of having a "favorite" leader suggest frivolity— unless at least the regime of that so-called "favorite leader" was found to contain some new elements of freedom which could give the statement real meaning? How can Fidel be a "favorite" when his regime includes all the usual Communist horrors?

J— gets angry and talks about "paranoid" reactions to Communism in general.

Is it "paranoid" to question the reality of China and Cuba? Why then in the old days was it not paranoid to question the reality of Russia? In any case, isn't it logical that the tradition of purges, prisons, executions, which the Russian experiment fostered should be handed down to the new regimes?

J— begins to use his charm to get the conversation onto a more affable footing. At the same time he does not like specific questions, such as why does Fidel allow Czech doctors to experiment in Cuban prisons?

One reason for the fact that neither J— nor those like him—seem able to approach the later Communist regimes (China for instance, and Cuba) with the inquiring spirit they were forced into utilizing in the case of Russia, may be that they take at face value the strident disagreements between Communists, Maoists, Fidelistas, Trotskyists. They seem not aware of the firm allegiance of self-interest which exists between these factions—all of them automatically against the democratic West. Embracing a delusion, therefore, they hope, consciously or unconsciously, that competition between tyrants, what is called "revolutionary pluralism," will be to the West's advantage.

Again the question of intellectuals.

Re-reading letters and an essay from John Desmond Bernal (who explains how he felt about war in the past, and tells why he is now "marching for peace").

He refers to political conversations. "I would like to spend long evenings talking . . . but although I understand these things much better, I have not changed politically . . . . I realize and I think so do all conscious scientists that we have been working all our lives against every kind of obstruction and diversion in the service of profit and war." (But had Bernal for instance, with his political activity—and long ago he had admitted to me that he gave what concrete scientific help he could to the Soviets—really been able to do anything to prevent nuclear war? In fact, isn't it possible on the other hand that he had aided the fantastic development in these last two decades of the Soviet arms buildup, and thereby perhaps made war more feasible—a point of view of course with which he would not agree.)

His essay is still a moving account of political development. "We are part of all the events of our time. For each of us experience . . . is unique . . . when I was asked to write this essay I felt that there is some use in looking back to the course of my own life, to see . . . what it was that made me think and feel and act as I did." Bernal had been born in the south of Ireland in that land divided between the conquering English gentry and the dispossessed Irish Catholic workers. He saw the destruction of Dublin after the rebellion of 1916, and the burning of the country houses in reprisal. "It was only through violence," he writes, "when people cared enough about liberty and were prepared to die . . . that they won in the end." Later at Cambridge he became converted to socialism, although it was then "outside the experience of the respectable." His real faith, however, was and is science per se, the new science of relativity, the quantum theory, the question of the structure of matter. His "religion" lies in the hope that science (and of course he views Marxism as science) will liberate man. In fact "a philosophy must correspond not only to the picture of the world as it is, but as one may reasonably hope by collective action to change it."

(We live in a quandary, when a man as generous and humane as this one not only passes the Cold War off as a deliberate "tactic" of the West, and as having nothing to do with the relentless postwar pressures of the Soviet regime, but claims that the Russians were not the aggressors in the Korean War; and that North Vietnam now has no designs on South Vietnam. He also renounces, in the name of "obedience" and "discipline," that intellectual liberty which is the most essential part of his own Western heritage. By failing to examine the exactitude of "Marxism," he fails to explain—for instance—those vast developments of slave labor, which have come into existence in both Russia and China. We see, therefore, the great scientist Bernal indirectly aiding Stalinist repression; and during the Lysenko controversy— the dismissal of scientists, the shutting down of excellent laboratories, and the very disappearance of dissidents to an unknown fate.)

The disturbing aspect of absolutism is that it is often linked with idealism. In an oblique way Bernal seemed to know that his idealism could be used. Ilya Ehrenberg, writing about him in *Postwar Years*, records how he had a letter from Moscow in 1954 (where B. had been given a good room in a "far too luxurious hotel"). "My apartments are richly decorated in good academic taste," the latter says, "with pictures painted in real oil-colors. A program has been worked out for the few days I can spend in Moscow, a ride in the metro, Gorky St., and on Sunday to see the architecture of the agricultural exhibition. This is my eighth visit to Moscow; I know a dozen clever interesting people . . . but instead of giving me the opportunity to talk to them . . . I am treated like a sacred cow." Bernal here is aware of the strait-jacket; but perhaps is too modest to see himself as so valuable a propaganda asset. (The important "cow" mustn't be allowed out of its pasture.)

Ehrenberg describes him as a true scholar, and it is a description which fits him. It is this man who, when he went to Moscow in the thirties with a group of English scientists and stood in the Central airport under an awning while it was raining, conceived the idea of the structure of water. It is this man, who sitting with friends in a restaurant once, made beautiful diagrams in abstract mathematical terms, of human relationships, on the paper napkins. And this same man is described by Ehrenberg during a walk when he picked up some stones, and after it was suggested that they were meant for paving the road, guiltily threw the stones away; then suddenly bent over, picked up one or two and put them into his pocket. Later he broke them open to show Ehrenberg the fossil imprint of a sea shell.

Two years after the long letter about his political development, he wrote to say that he had had a stroke: "I thought it was the end, but luckily not for the time being . . . I could not write and hardly talk . . . I could think and feel as ever, but could not communicate. It was especially hard because I wanted to write."

As Koestler suggests, the origin of emotionally-tinged beliefs evidently lies in early childhood, when enthusiasms and experiences overcome reason. As J. D. B— never forgot the poverty of the Irish peasants and the burning of Dublin, so political emotions are absorbed before the age of true reason and are afterwards transformed into concepts. Totalitarian states have exploited this truism. In reading John Hevi's *An African Student in China* it is interesting to see that toddlers between two and three are taught revolutionary songs, and to adulate Father Mao Tse-tung. "I had a big surprise the day I heard a little girl shout the slogan: Dǎ dǎo měi dì guó zhǔ yì (*Down with American Imperialism*) and this mind you from a little child who had hardly learned to speak coherently."

A book by Meir Kulhane also describes the procedure of emotional indoctrination in China, as written up in an article in *Chungkuo Funu (Women of China)*. First the children are shown knives and bloodstained clothes said to be those of peasants killed by reactionaries. They are then taught to raise their hands and shout at the sight of Mao on the screen. When they see ugly pictures of landlords, they are taught to make gestures of anger: "I'll beat you to death you big bad man!" ... One child drew a picture of an American minus a leg and said, "That leg has been broken by Vietnamese uncles." A child also saw a picture of the head of President Johnson, and said that he "wanted to pull out his eyes."

February 14

Plans are already being made for a trip to Australia next year—but in spite of this the current pursuit of political events is stimulating enough to push away the thought of the future. It is rather like sitting in a theatre and waiting for the final act!

In fact Australia too, because of its geographical position, can be considered a suitable political target, and is important beyond its size or intrinsic significance. There in that outsize island with its small and in some ways provincial population, the structure of psychological warfare is already obvious.

According to Geoffrey Fairbairn, an especially astute Australian journalist and scholar, the 325th division of the Democratic Republic of Vietnam (DRV) entered the south two years ago. Last year Denis Warner, Robert Shaplen, and other reputable journalists recorded the infiltration of arms and men from the north, but the escalation of the northern struggle, beginning on a small scale in 1957, was well established by the time the United States intervened, with the toll of terrorism rising in those areas where the Vietcong were driving for control. At the end of last year 20,000 minor officials had already been murdered in the southern countryside—chiefs, school teachers, nurses etc. ("The front is everywhere," as Maoist doctrine goes.) What is not enough stressed by United States observers is that General Giap and his teachers foresaw the American reaction to the camouflaged attack on South Vietnam, and prophesied that the enemy would "pass slowly from the offensive to the defensive." He foresaw the difficulties a democracy would have in such a war and how much they might overplay their hand. "The blitzkrieg will transform itself into a war of long duration," he said. It is especially part of Chinese Communist doctrine that the political battle is as important as the military battle; that parallel to attacks there runs the long ceaseless battle of terror and propaganda, and that the victory inevitably goes to the patient. Westerners, who are by nature *impatient*, try to cope with the surface phenomenon, unaware that they are really watching the actual "engendering" of warfare; the beginnings of insurgence being difficult to detect. (A comment from Fairbairn: ". . . future revolutionary insurgencies may be expected to get off the ground before international public opinion has taken much interest in them, by which time the nature of their origins will have become so beclouded by sedulously infiltrated fellow-travelling propaganda and wish-dreams propagated by guilt-laden progressives, that purposeful counter action . . . becomes less likely . . .")

February 23

Walking past Central Square towards MIT. Sun stretching across the pavements. A black man in a shabby coat picking up pieces of paper from the gutter with a long sharp tool; the sun catching his dark polished cheek. That sense of joy in the morning; that recurrent awareness of the pleasures of American life. The anticipation of coffee and hot rolls at the familiar drugstore around the corner. The waitress early at work, with her hair done up on top of her head, curls escaping down her neck. Her broad country-attractive face. (She says that she comes from New Hampshire. At once there is an image of green fields, big barns, fences made of stones). The steam from the coffee urn mingles with the fresh inky smell of the morning papers.

Sometimes in this calm academic life—or when returning from now rare expeditions into the ghetto or prison world—the memory of tropical Australia returns with nostalgic force: low wooden houses under the shade of tropical trees, gullies filled with poinciana, the red and yellow blossoms breaking, the cradle of the monsoons, the screech of jungle fowl, goannas rustling through the leaves searching for water, the green Torres Straits pigeons in the mango trees. Four months ago my sister wrote of the fierce sun. "Now in November the summer is at its height."

But Australia does not escape the scourge which assaults the rest of the West. An international drug ring has been operating in Sydney. Stories of long-distance truck drivers taking LSD (and there are few countries where the roads are longer and lonelier) are common—the drivers finding themselves suffering from fantastic hallucinations on the road: ocean liners on the horizon; imaginary gates which they get out to open; and most characteristic of all, flocks of woolly sheep moving impressively across the landscape. (Other parts of the Empire complain of floods of drugs—in Britain teen-agers are the target, and basement drug-clubs rented by West Indian pushers are in operation.)

In New England the alarm about narcotics in general, and heroin in particular, is complicated by the claims of Timothy Leary for "expanding consciousness" and the "ritual of rebirth." It is to be the "year of the cube." Supplies are flooding the campuses and the suburbs. Many newspapers show pictures of teen-agers, girls with bent heads hiding behind long streaming hair, boys leaning back with their mouths open. The word "rampant" is used; the other day a girl from the School of Music and Art fell down in the street, and during the investigation it was stated that the use of LSD was "rampant" in the school. Cases end up in Bellevue. It even seems that the euphoria of "political liberation" is, in some cases, being displaced by the euphoria of "taking off" or "tripping."

March 4

Recently William S. Burroughs, the great experimenter and author of *Naked Lunch*, flew to London and committed himself to a pink-papered bedroom in a building in Cromwell Road, where he went through a course of apomorphine.

"To say it country simple," he writes in the *New Statesman*, "most people enjoy junk. Having once experienced this pleasure, the human organism will tend to repeat it and repeat it and repeat it. I was on junk for almost fifteen years. In that time I took ten cures. I have taken abrupt withdrawal treatments and prolonged withdrawal treatments, cortisone, tranquilizers, antihistamines, and prolonged sleep cures. In every case I relapsed at the first opportunity."

Timothy Leary's various houses have already been raided. The mansion in Millbrook, which was described by some journalists as

1966

"musty" and "smelling of cats", was entered by the police, and films were confiscated as they were being shown to a group of followers who were lying around on mattresses.

The specter of drugs poisoning and weakening the sons and daughters of the great American middle class has frightened a number of observers. [In 1971 a current anarchist leaflet *Agit 883* exalted the fact that the opium war has been turned against its original perpetrators. "It no longer serves the capitalists. The poison has now been directed against the bourgeoisie."]

What can be said to those who not only want the Americans out of Vietnam, but also want the North Vietnamese to win the war? Some of these innocents are of so transparent and stubborn a quality that they express this desire without inhibition, as if no excuse were necessary for so strange a desire.

A fair-headed boy of seventeen or eighteen says that he supports Ho Chi Minh. He adds that the U.S. is at fault in the first place in Vietnam because it did not support the holding of elections in 1956.

But since the Communists had hoped to gain control of the South regardless of the Geneva agreements, and since the North had three million more people than the South, and since a completely controlled vote would be turned in, in the North, the North would have been assured of a clear majority in a National Parliament—why was he surprised that this option was turned down? Again, didn't the South refuse to sign the Geneva agreement?

A slow flush is beginning to spread over the young man's face. He protests that he hadn't known about these qualifications. The South refused to countenance elections unless they were free and supervised. Why isn't this logical? The gentle insistence on pressing the subject home throws him into a state of panic. Is it that he automatically saw his own country at fault, simply because someone else had *said* that it was at fault? In 1956, for instance, the British complained that guerrillas were descending into the south, bombing bridges, attacking schools, killing teachers and nurses, forcibly impressing southerners into the Vietcong. Wasn't this aggression?

The beautiful young blond American begins to protest. "In 1956 . . . in 1956. . . ." He is red-faced and stuttering. He makes a strong and only too logical a defense: "I . . . ? Why in 1956 I was only seven years old!"

Another conversation about Vietnam. In the Wursthaus in Cambridge a student announces that he blames President Johnson for ending the bombing pause.

"If he was sincere, why did he pretend to stop the bombing?"

(Apparently between 10,000 and 40,000 Chinese coolies have been moved into Hanoi during these weeks to repair the network of damaged roads; while further south interconnecting roads are being marked out to serve as alternative routes. According to *News Weekly* ten times more war material is being sent south than before the pause.)

"Well, Johnson was disturbed because the SAM missile sites have doubled, most of them equipped with modern radar systems and manned by Russians. The VC in the South also now have 21 and 37 AA guns for the first time."

"And what do *we* have?" asks the student aggressively. (Johnson's actual words were: "I'm not going to have our troops return to the coast and let the marines go fishing—while the VC ravage the countryside. . . . I'm not going to hunker up and take it like a mule in a hailstorm!")

On the tattered edge of Asia's shawl, on that ragged fringe embroidered with mangrove and palm, a wider battle has been joined than that at present recognized. And in this battle Americans cannot be detached. Therefore, whether informed or not informed, whether for or against the war, no one speaks in a light tone, and as with discussions centering upon religion, all mention of the war takes on an air of moral censure.

Sometimes it is only possible to be silent in front of an expected onslaught. The suggestion that America is not really responsible for the great weight of evil and guilt being heaped upon her triggers so strong an emotional reaction that it is impossible to deal with it. The moralistic view is that only those opposed to war, only those opposed to *this* war, only those opposed to *this* war in a certain *total* manner, can be tolerated. Sometimes the discussion is primitive. "He's nice," a student says, referring to his professor, "but he's *for* the Vietnam war."

Is he a militarist?

"Well he's not exactly a militarist. In fact, I think he used to be a pacifist. But now he's gung ho for ROTC."

Would he like us to bomb China?

"Oh no!" In a shocked voice. "He's not *that* bad. He just wants us to go in there and *win*. Personally I think we deserve to *lose*."

At other times, however, it is the university spokesmen (the most articulate group in the country) who assert the primacy of the "conventional wisdom" of the age. [In 1977 a book was published, *Vietnam* by Gunther Lewy, which utilizes the classified information now open to scholars and which attempts to bring more light and less heat to this undiscussable subject. Lewy not only indicates the special and little understood difficulties of fighting the Vietnam war, but exposes the veritable "industry" of accusations, many of them made on the flimsiest evidence, or even purposely manufactured, against the United States. A brief section of this book was published in the February 1978 issue of *Commentary*.]

Polarization casts an eerie light upon these partisan conversations, conversations easier to come across than those which are more informative. The Tri-Continental Conference which took place last January in Cuba, for instance, had passed by without my own realization of its importance, and it is only today that an ardent Zionist stresses that this gathering took place because the Soviets wanted to push the "global revolution" and to re-establish a Comintern-like Secretariat for this purpose. The Zionist, super-sensitive to the threat of danger, pointed out that Israel—ostensibly a Third-World country—was not represented at this eighty-two-delegate conference; not even by a *Communist* delegate. (The delegates were of three types: those from Communist countries, those from more zenophobic anti-Western nations, and those who represented guerrilla and revolutionary or Communist-dominated groups from the democratic countries—many of these last were to be wined, dined and influenced.) "Then," the Zionist explains, "the head of the top 'political' committee was Khalid Muhieddin, who was a member of the original Free Officers Executive in Egypt and a close friend of Nasser's. He was supposed to influence Nasser's thinking. The relationship of this man to Nasser, in fact, seems not unlike that of Raul Castro and Ché Guevara to Fidel. You can guess where this leaves the Israelis!"

(As might be expected the Conference called for a drive to undermine the West, and statements made urged the three continents to "join the popular insurrection." To collect contributions, a helmet—and naturally that of a dead American pilot shot down over North Vietnam—was used. A rather barbaric note among the rhetoric!)

Tonight talking with Moshe, a Jewish friend who *unlike* the Zionists is loath to believe not only that Cuba has been transformed into a police state but that the fate of Israel can in any way be linked to Vietnam. Moshe is ruddy, with mobile Semitic features. "It is very hard for me to accept," he keeps saying, "Israel is one thing and Vietnam is another." But didn't the Soviet delegate at the Tri-Continental Conference keep saying that Tel Aviv and Saigon were one; and wasn't Israel abused in speech after speech?

"I didn't read all the speeches."

And does he imagine that the Arabs think Israel is not linked in any way to Vietnam? The Arabs surely feel that the North Vietnamese are guerrillas like the Palestinians?

"But Israel," Moshe insists, "doesn't threaten North Vietnam. Israel has no troops in Asia!"

The U.S. doesn't threaten North Vietnam in the sense of invading her territory either; but it threatens the "takeover" of South Vietnam. And doesn't the U.S. also threaten the Arab takeover of Israel? If it is true that the real target of the Conference is the United States, isn't it also true that Israel is the intermediate target?

Moshe is trying hard to exonerate Cuba and China, with whom—as is so typical of many liberals at the moment—he feels vague sympathies. I ask him whether he hasn't heard Mao's remark to Ahmed Shukairy, "If you Arabs are 40 million and the Jews only 2 million . . . what are you waiting for?"

"Surely this is a misquotation!" he protests in a shocked voice.

As usual such disturbingly vague conversations are dissipated by a more realistic analysis. A laconic character called Donald McF—who has been introduced to me by a sailing companion, expounds on the role of the U.S. Negro at the Tri-Continental. "Not only is the black militant getting aid and comfort *here*, but he was being wooed seriously in Havana by the Russians and the Chinese. After the original meeting the Latin American delegates even included black representatives, Puerto Ricans, and Caribbeans, in discussions with Castro and the Cuban Chiefs of Staff; links had to be forged between Cubans, Latin Americans, and colored U.S. militants. Other input from Africa was equally natural. There was the rather engaging "Babu" (that is Abdul Rahman Muhammed of Zanzibar) who's been back and forth to secret meetings in Harlem. He's part of what is by now a long line of African, Arab, Chinese, and Algerian activists who've been cultivating blacks. We're facing a new kind of warfare; it's a war without a war." (It is the first time I have heard this phrase). He begins to talk about terrorism.

"Moscow, Havana, Peking as well as some of the Eastern satellites have their functioning academies of revolution. Cadres trained by Peking vie with cadres trained by Moscow. Algerians were trained in the Sierra Madre for action against the French. Zanzibarians were joined by agents trained in Russia and China to overthrow the pro-western government; native Cubans combined revolutionary activities in Puerto Rico with Chinese-trained students; and according to the *New York Times*—in June three years ago I think—a Belgian operated along with members of the Quebec Liberation Front in Canada." He pauses; "The point is that the Tri-Continental did make concrete decisions. There was a *key transfer of support* from the Latin American Communist parties to the guerilla leaders. The decision has been made. 'Anti-U.S. storms are rising everywhere,' Peking announced. The idea seems to be that revolutionary war is to be brought to the shores of the North American continent. . . ."

Donald McF—'s world is certainly rather different from the world of Barbara Deming who is a devotee of nonviolence. She is a tall graceful-ly-awkward youngish woman with straight brown hair cut in a bell-like fashion, and a fine-featured face which appears sometimes pixyish, sometimes anxiously strained. Three years ago in May she had been in the Albang jail in Georgia, her crime being that she had broken a city ordinance by taking part in an intergrated march in the streets. In jail she underwent a hunger strike described in her luminous little book *Prison Notes.*

It is clear that B.D. is one of those creatures for whom world events show an immediate opportunity for moral action. She wants to be "part of her time"; because of this she has been active against the Vietnam War, been involved in demonstrations and strikes, and been to Cuba as a "Pacifist" observer. But what isn't clear, and what is of great interest is whether this idealism also means (in BD.'s case) some sacrifice of "reality"?

She asks; "Aren't you yourself against the war?"

I answer that I am against the extent and method of the American involvement; that a slower and more educated and modest approach might have been made. In spite of this some sort of stand had to be made against the Communist advance. The analysis of the war in most of the press, and on most of the campuses, and at hundreds of liberal gatherings is often inaccurate. If this is so, then won't the West and even more the East pay dearly for the inaccuracy?

She wants to know what is meant by inaccuracy.

Aren't there three issues upon the truth or falsity of which hang arguments already made so familiar? Does she, for instance, like so many journalists, insist that the war is a *civil* war?

"Yes, I certainly think that it is a civil war. The National Liberation Front is to some extent politically representative of the South, and of those in the South who want liberation from a reactionary govern-ment."

But surely the NLF represents the communists?

It seems that she is not familiar with this makeup of the NLF. When asked what support the organization has in the South, and why it has been denounced by so many political and religious organizations, she simply says that it does *not* represent the communists, even if it has been influenced by communists, even if there are those in the leader-ship sympathetic to Communism.

But the International Control Commission itself reported that the NLF was under the control of the Lao-Dong, the Labor Party of the

North Vietnamese Communist Party. Surely this *alone* makes the war one of conquest?

She hesitates. "I don't think that the ICC is to be trusted particularly, and in any case if the Vietnamese want freedom from foreign interference, as U Thant pointed out, that in itself is enough. It is enough reason for the United States not to be there with its 16,000 advisors and its massive arms and chemical warfare techniques and now . . . *troops*." But it wasn't always like this. Didn't the North break the Geneva agreement in the sense that it constantly prevented the Northerners from leaving to go to the South? Not officially, by denying passports—they didn't want to appear to do that—but indirectly, by terror, endless red tape, and physical prevention?

As with those who have long ago determined to meet their opponents with love, she listens earnestly and even humbly. (We talk about Tom Dooley, who was in Haiphong in 1955 when a series of laws, high exit fees, and long delays prevented the peasants from travelling legally; and as a result many tried to escape. The roads and swamps were sown with mines. Dr. Dooley treated boys whose ears had been amputated, and whose eardrums were broken for listening to the "evil" words of the Lord's Prayer. These victims were among numerous others who had been tortured or mistreated. He set the broken shoulders of a woman who had been "punished" by border guards because she "tried to leave her land." All this was before the escalation of the war.)

Ho Chi Minh is also an issue. Just as Barbara contends that the NLF is indigenous to the South, and that the war is a civil war, she describes Ho Chi Minh as a "nationalist." She quotes as an authority Jean Lacouture, the leftist French journalist who is a correspondent for *Le Monde* (and whose biography of Ho Chi Minh came out recently).

Doesn't even this book at least make clear that Ho is more than a nationalist?

"Perhaps he *is* more than a nationalist," Barbara admits, "but surely his overriding desire was for independence for his country." (The conversation is a reminder of that one two years ago on the West Coast, where as fake torches lit up the waters near the pier at Santa Monica, a Mr. Peng maintained that Ho Chi Minh's only error was to "fail to kow-tow to the Americans.")

Because Ho is a very frail, thin, unostentatious man, often dressed in a frayed robe and cheap sandals; because he is subtle, intelligent ("with guile and subtlety" according to his friend Jean Sainteny*); because he learned from both the Chinese and the Russians; and because he so often used the tactics of the United Front—some observers try to deny that he is a true Communist. When this is put to Barbara, she maintains that all of Ho's activities are those of a patriot.

"But as a pacifist how can you condone the violent disdain for

1966

human life shown by Ho's obedience to Stalinist precepts?—for instance his liquidation of the Trotskyists as recounted by Daniel Guérin in his book *Au Service des Colonisés?*"

She answers that she does not condone violence, and with so truthful an air that it is impossible not to believe her.

As savages lessen their fears of the unknown by making images and setting them up and then falling prostrate before them, an author may only wish to place some control over what is felt to be historical truth, to exorcise, to make less terrible. But it is difficult, as Bertram Wolfe has suggested, to "stare straight and steadily at the head of the Medusa."

In view of the Tri-Continental, and because of Cuba's key role in current history, there is an impulse to go to New York City to try to clothe with flesh and blood (since the proof of history lies in the direct knowledge of those who have lived through it) the experiences of the Cuban refugees. Already many reports have been smuggled out of the island in unorthodox ways; including early photographs made by a tiny Minox camera which penetrated the Cabana fortress inside a tin of guava marmalade, and which showed male prisoners, including starved-looking teen-age boys, in the *galerias* overlooking the courtyards where victims were being "sent to the wall" each week. The report explained that medieval facilities in this ancient fortress allowed stagnant seawater to carry excrement into the special punishment dungeons to rot the flesh of unlucky prisoners; while up above the other prisoners lived on scanty rations of rice and beans and scantier rations of water. The report of the American Commission on Human Rights three years ago stressed "that in the underground arched tunnel-like wards of *La Cabana* and in its dungeons known as *bartolinas*, prisoners of the regime were kept for months at a time without sun, light, ventilation. It also spoke of pitch-black earth-floored cells in the lowest depths of all—called *chinchorros*—from which unfortunate prisoners came out completely broken in health. . . ." This, then, a reactivation of medieval dungeons, is part of what the revolution brought to twentieth century Cuba!

From the hotel tonight at Fifty-eighth Street, to Elizabeth, New Jersey, with a young Cuban, Rojelio Matos, who is twenty-four years old and the son of Major Huber Matos (that earliest hero of the Revolution, whose column liberated Santiago de Cuba and consolidated Castro's victory, and who was later imprisoned by his old comrade for the crime of having questioned the appointment of Communists to the new government).

His wife lives at this moment in a little frame house in Elizabeth with her sixteen-year-old daughter Carmen (if she had been a boy Carmen was to have been called Fidel!) and earns her living by making wedding dresses.

"We lived close to the sierra" Rojelio says, "in Oriente near Manzanillo, on a small rice farm. My father was a teacher and passionately interested in the restoration of the Constitution. When Castro and his group landed on the coast and took to the Sierra, our farm became a key supply post; we helped to get men, money, weapons up into the mountains. It was a bad situation for the revolutionaries then; in fact, my father was responsible for ferrying a whole plane-load of weapons from Costa Rica. This was a turning-point in the battle. Fidel actually cried for joy when he saw them. . . ."

Mrs. Matos is an impressive woman with dark eyes and a soft voice. She stresses that her husband felt Fidel could never betray him. "He would have protected Fidel with his own body. After the big success he could see Communists being put into positions of power, and he brought this up with Fidel. Fidel said, 'Well, keep your eye on them, we need people like you;' then the next time Huber protested Fidel promised to talk to Raul and Ché, and Ché was actually sent for a while to Holland to get some data on tulip culture. Huber was pleased when Fidel said, 'I authorize you to kick out any Communists you see in important positions.' "

"All this time," Rojelio broke in, "my mother could see the intense dislike Castro was developing for my father, who was immensely popular with the army."

"Yes," Maria Matos goes on, "Castro was planning our destruction. On October 21st we were sleeping. It was three in the morning when an officer called to tell us to listen to Fidel's denunciation; and on the radio there were professional agitators accusing Huber of having 'stabbed the Revolution in the back' " (Rojelio remembers the radio playing loudly and Camilo Cienfuegos coming with his red beard and his cowboy hat). "That night they took Huber to the Military prison, and the soldiers because they recognized me, let me in to see him." She adds: "After that he was kept almost incommunicado." Her voice grows slower and more toneless; ". . . after that I didn't see him again."

According to petitions presented to the Inter-American Commission on Human Rights of the O.A.S., there were from 15,000 to 20,000 Cubans put to death by public execution in those early days. An escapee, Manuel Alvarez says, "It was in the Cabana that the first mass shootings were held after popular trials which were accompanied by the cry '*Al paredón . . . Al paredón*' " (literally "To the wall"—a cry so reminiscent of that of the French Revolution "To the guillotine"). "The executions were in ditches and against three walls, and these came to be known severally as the ditch of the Laureles, where the shooting was done up to March of 1961, the ditch or ditches of the Morro,

1966

presumably at the Morro Castle not far away, and the ditch at the back of the Cabana cellblocks, from which so many political prisoners distinctly heard the commands of officers, the shouts of the condemned, and the final shots."

Among the prisoners interviewed, all of those who served time in the Cabana testified to the shootings. In the four years in the Cabana, Manuel Alvarez says, "I saw (that is heard) 400 men shot . . . It happened just about seventeen yards away from us, across the passage on the other side of the wall."

What did he hear on such occasions?

"Oh you could hear the voices shouting far away 'Get ready . . . fire.' Sometimes you could see the smoke drift up from the guns." Pedro Monte also testifies, "I remember at least 270 men shot in the Cabana. This was before the Missile Crisis in 1962. The first time I heard a man being killed I was half asleep. I jumped up my heart beating. . . . After I got used to it, it was never the same again."

As a relief from these oppressive stories it is pleasant to go to a party on E. 80th Street. An old brownstone house. Enormous sofas with sinking pillows of apricot plush; curtains in what are called "decorator" shades. Several good paintings, one little piece of erotica by Egon Schiele. The hostess looking delicious dressed in biscuit-colored silk, with her mop of slightly red hair, and with some sort of amber-colored chain around her waist. A girl floating in white, her bosom very high. Yet even here the possessed intellectual who is in love with the revolutionary milieu. A conversation near the bar about the vitality and *élan* of Cuba. . . . At one point I open the wrong door to find an empty library; books to the ceiling, many of them bound in leather with gold lettering; also gold-colored velvet sofas, gold-colored red-shaded lamps—the whole thing definitely *doré*.

Although peace-minded people have their own kind of courage—another kind of bravery now seems important.

Along Fifth Avenue towards downtown, past the big shops with their alluring windows, across town to Grand Central, a short cut through the lobby of the Commodore. The late winter light scarcely noticed above the buildings; a tree suddenly realized as fragile and mortal; a florist's shop with its poignant scent of carnations, water, leaves—like some expensive oasis of nature in this crowding stone. Down Madison where the crowds press at this late hour like a tumultuous human sea through which one has to beat one's way. Finally towards the river; and a few hours with James T. Farrell in his high-up apartment looking down to the light which by now flows like gold into the East River. (Memories of first seeing the figure of this honest, intelligent, and prodigiously productive writer on a Cape Cod beach, when he had come over the dunes and joined a group of us in drinking wine around a fire. Dark tousled hair, gray eyes, rather masculine tough-cut Irish face, and long arms hanging from broad chest and shoulders.) Today nearly ten years later, he seems as vital as ever, and soon attempts to prove it by executing a high football kick which nearly dislodges some of the array of manuscripts in gray folders stacked on the surrounding shelves! At the same time there appears something out of place in finding this writer—whose work, like Zola's, was banned, and whose Lonigan trilogy was the center of a trial in which Vanguard Press sued the city of Philadelphia for interfering with sales—living in this one room, working in the afternoon and for most of the night at the cluttered desk from which it is only one or two steps to a small single bed in the corner.

At once and without disguise he begins to speak of what he describes as his unpopularity. "It is partly because of my position on the Vietnam War. I think that we should go in and win. I think that it is a necessity. For the sake of the precarious world balance we should win. . . . But if it is because of this position I take that I am unpopular, it is not the first time. I don't want to enter into the positions of a hundred intellectuals such as we both know. I want to make one comment only. They are all insensible to the explosive danger of a power vacuum in a world of deadly power, deadly danger, where victory is the ultimate means to controlling the destiny of mankind."

Later Barbara Deming seemed vaguely disturbed that I was interviewing refugees. "How 'objective' can refugees be?"

Are refugees a special class?

"No, of course not; but the feeling that they have no stake in the country now might tend to prejudice them."

Is this true of all refugees? Of Russians? Germans? Poles? By this classification an enormous number of Americans are prejudiced?

In troubled acceptance of this, Barbara nods her head.

One wonders to what extent her implicit approval of Castro's regime is simply a lack of fear? An article for *Liberation* (April 1963) had answered this question. She states in it that she is not afraid of Communism, either in or out of Cuba. She refers to an organization she works with—Women's Strike for Peace—which had allowed Communists to join it. "No one in the Peace movement, I hope, shares HUAC's (House UnAmerican Activities Committee) view of the threats Communists among us would pose—that the simple-minded view of the few would lead the foolish rest of us astray down reckless paths."

A colleague, Caroline Urner, expresses herself more clearly still: "We who have grown up in a democratic society, and who function in democratic families . . . don't worry about being 'taken over' by other people's ideas."

What is striking about the above is its truth. Isn't this very innocence, this very refusal to fear, important in the wrong way? Is it possible that by moving so easily from nonviolent resistance against racisim and war to the political support of a regime with which she is little familiar, she may, as a peace-lover (who rejects the power of the state over the human being, who places her dependence upon nonviolent love) give credence to the state in its most total form? A state in which the political terror has everywhere escalated, in which there are no *habeas corpus*, no elections, no free newspapers, no free unions, in which thousands have been shot at the *paredón*, thousands are in exile, and thousands, even by Castro's own admission, are in jail for their political beliefs.

At this implication her eyes widen and glow with disbelief. Her faith seems to wish to resent intrusions. Her face turns pale. Here is much more than the inevitable American "lack of guile." Just as "envy and resentment" edge black revolutionary thinking in areas like the South End, here is a preference edged with "pity for the underdog." For Barbara, Cuba has become a mythical kingdom.

Later.

A letter from James T. Farrell.

"There are things you don't understand. I had to fight for my survival at the risk of life. . . . I closed out a whole crowd of people. They were not worth seeing. I had to set myself a huge task in order to survive. I did, and it absorbs my time.

"You should not tell me I am losing anything—that I should go out and see people. People of the *Times,* the *New York Review,* the *New Republic,* the *New Yorker* brand? . . . I should go out where I am not invited . . . ? You do not understand. Only now, after twenty years, am I getting cleared away. Today I lock myself in and don't go out."

May 1—New Hampshire

Birds in the lilac bushes. Earth worms crawling out of the leaf mould onto the roads.

Voyages from a paradise of woods in the spring and down into the village show that the social mix there repeats the national pattern. As is usual, the generations are polarized. In one house near the post office, a group has moved in—with their children, their dogs, their guitars, their pipes, their bedrolls, their cheap wine and their herb teas. It is reported that they cut each other's hair, support themselves by selling their blood to the local hospital (and that recently several of them went into carbohydrate shock because they had been living solely on potatoes and oatmeal!).

To watch this group is to be reminded of a thousand little processions, on the streets of towns or on the big roads of America—the same bearded men, the same packs, the same women and children, the same thin dogs, or kittens carried inside shirt fronts, the same air of having a long long way to travel yet. . . .

It is also to be reminded of the evening last year when little W— came home, and the dinner with his parents turned into a forum for his psychological difficulties. In this situation in which a whole generation has separated itself from its parent generation, the question of "reality" rises again. If the oncoming generation has cut out of its life the usual "reality testing" period—when and how will "reality" be tested?

July

The illusion that going to Australia will mean an escape from the political marathon is dispelled by letters which suggest that Australia is considered legitimate ground for political contest. Danny—the Irish-Australian journalist, who was formerly a Labor supporter, writes that he is now aggressively against ('bloody well fed up with') the activities of the Seamen's Union which refuses to allow Australian ships to take supplies to Vietnam. "Of course seamen are free not to offer for this work," he writes "but that a union should boycott ships supplying Australians in the field is a different matter!" (Shades of the Korean war, when in 1950 an Australian battalion joined the United Nations force and the Federal Executive of the Seamen's Unions under E. V. Elliott, a member of the Australian Communist Party Central Committee, got a resolution passed pledging Australian Merchant Seamen to refuse to handle supplies for Korea.)

July 8

This time it is British institutions. Prime Minister Wilson has just openly accused the British Communist party of organizing and encouraging the strike which is cutting the country's lifeline. Wilson was never very anti-Communist and cannot be accused of McCarthyism so that what he says is of special importance, which is that the strike is under the control of the Executive of the National Union of Seamen—and that a tightly knit group of politically motivated extremists has the upper hand.

Wilson's implications were met with indignant denials; whereupon he replied in the House that the intent was to direct the unions along the Soviet Union "line" and to smash the economic policy of the British government. He also spoke of a campaign of telephone intimidation, of brutal slogans, of harassment. (Specifically he named Bert Ramelson, the BCP organizer for industry—a barrister and a Canadian—and Gordon Norris, an Australian member of the Seamen's Negotiating Committee; also Jack Coward and Roger Woods, Communist members of the Strike Committee in London and Liverpool.)

Summer on Cape Cod. The hot clear beach days are here. Those who are so privileged stretch out their cooled and reddened bodies . . . at six o'clock laughter and the clink of ice in glasses—on lawns, under trees, on wooden decks beside lakes. Cleaving through the human flesh at parties, scraps of conversation, blurred by the slow relaxation of liquor.

An urgent letter from Jasmin.

To leave this clean sea-washed scene, to fly to New York City, and to plunge straight into the Harlem streets is to remember the reality of another kind of summer—that "long hot" one promised by the new SNCC, during which the cry of Black Power will be no more attractive than the cry of Get Whitey. (Stokeley Carmichael and Rap Brown are guiding the fortunes of SNCC after the displacement of John Lewis last spring—and, as Stokeley announced with satisfaction, "White blood will flow.")

Up Amsterdam Avenue in the heat, past the rows of apartment houses which date from better times. The growing skin darkness; bars outside which lounge patrons whose white shirts form the only contrast. Neon signs against grimy housefronts. In the late afternoon the falling sun edges a cluster of faces—one angular girl's face crowned with a wreath of pink curlers, a lugubrious chocolate-colored woman's face wrapped around in a black turban. Two thin trees. A church front. Jesus Saves in electric light bulbs.

The taxi driver warns that he won't wait. "Not in *that* street!"

Is the street as bad as that?

"They'll do anything to you there—slit your tires, mug you for two bucks!"

A big sign The Ebony is glowing in neon letters, marking a door where jazz belches forth. In what passes for a lobby inside the hotel, a long thin man with a pale cigar-colored face sits motionless at the desk. The walls around him, and mounting up the well of the stairs, are a bright electric blue. His face doesn't change when he hears Jasmin's name. He simply mentions a number and jerks his thumb to the stairs. Another man sits in the darkened phone booth; as I start up he comes rapidly behind, almost soundless in his sneakers and says in a low urging voice when I hesitate on the second floor, "Further up, baby." A moment later he looks down from the floor above and directs with a gap-toothed flirtatious smile, "Keep *going*, dear."

At the knock on Number 44 someone calls, "Come in." The door opens to a disordered bedroom with an iron bed, where a big blonde lies; pale flesh, pale hair, heavy eyelids, stomach bursting from small black panties, breasts from a black lace brassiere. On one breast "W.T." is tattooed; "Dokie" is tattooed on a knee. When she gets up to open the window, "Jacky" appears on her back.

"I thought Jasmin . . ."

"No honey, Jasmin's out . . . Don' worry. I'm her frien'." She stretches out on the bed in an even more abandoned position. I sit in the only chair. A towel and a coke bottle are on the window sill.

"My name's Dokie: Will you have something?"

"No, thank you. Not now."

"Jasmin's told me about you. She thinks a lot of you." After a while: "I'm on drugs, too. I run from my boyfriend three days ago. I don't like anything to disadvantage me—you see, I'm not in love with my man." Languidly she stretches over and picks up a snapshot and hands it to me (a small grinning colored man wearing a ginger jacket, and sitting on a fence).

Finally Jasmin arrives. In the intervening months she seems to have shrunk. Her little frame fits tightly into blue jeans and matching jacket, so that she looks like an odd boy. The effect is intensified by the way her hair is cut and slicked down, one lock tinted a strange orange color falling over her forehead. Her usually sweet smile is bottomlessly indifferent.

Just up the hall in her own room she takes off her jacket revealing a small thin T-shirt damp with sweat; her forehead is shining and tiny rivulets run down the sides of her hollow cheeks. At once she opens the door and tries to use it to fan herself. Then she flings herself down on the bed on her back and hangs her head towards the floor, making restless movements with her shoulders as if in pain. In this position she asks for money to pay for her room. Although suspecting that it is for drugs, I give her the money. She leaps up, to disappear without a word.

Half an hour later, restored to an extraordinary normality, she leads the way to the corner shop to buy two Ripples (small bottles of cold white wine, which she calls the "poor man's champagne"). We walk the street to talk about the recent riot in Cleveland (where the ousting of an unruly Negro patron from a bar ended in a riot which raged for six days). During the enquiries which followed, members of a teen-age gang described how the arson had been systematic, the sniping and window-smashing planned. Adults belonging to RAM and the "Deacons For Defense" had taught them not only how to make Molotov cocktails, but how to focus their hatreds. Jasmin boasts in a wondering way, "It gone on *six* days. No, don't tell me it were rehearsed. . . You don't believe that we got tired of all this patience shit? I tell you, baby, *all* the ghettoes is goin' to explode."

The warm evening streets. "I'm mostly on cocaine," she lies, "I don't dig it too tough. Yes, I left Junior and went to my mother's house. But he thought I turned him in, and I woke to find him standing over me when I was asleep on a sofa." She pauses. Her small face twists into an angry grimace. "He goin' to bug me, I goin' to put him away, getting me back on dope and everything. . . ."

On 116th Street, as we join the slow evening procession which moves up and down the pavement, she points out with pride that this is "the dope center of the world." The minor characters of the Harlem underworld parade under the lights and signs and prophecies: pushers, pimps, prostitutes, con men. Two girls in white dresses with broad black stripes. A boy with a peeled head and gleaming shoes, wearing an orange and yellow sweater open to the waist to show his bare brown chest decorated with a fake diamond pendant. Women gleaming from the doorways; one has hair piled up and crowned with a splendid tiara; another wears an African batik in purple and green and has smeared mauve paste over her broad lips. Two men in stiff white tunics and flat African caps. "Soul brothers," Jasmin says. A moment later she exclaims, "Heavy!" and we talk with a man, whom she describes as her "partner." He is a conservative-looking Negro with a coarse but competent face, who listens without interest to Jasmin's tale of not being able to pay for her room, of needing to get back to Boston. "Man to man, Heavy . . . ." she pleads (at which he looks down sardonically at this thin little addict). Later near the hotel at dusk there is an altercation going on. Under the red glow from a shaded bar, a broad and belligerent woman in a green suit with an enormous white hat (rather like a Bishop's miter) flourishes a knife and yells at some invisible victim to "Come out of that bar!" A policeman whirling his baton watches her speculatively from a distance. "You mother-fucker," she yells into the bar, "I'm waitin' for you mother-fuckin' bastard!" Her voice cracks with fury, the knife gleams, she is almost in tears. "Be a man! Be a *man!*" she pleads. The policeman watches, his face impassive.

"Just a poor lost nigger," Jasmin comments. For a moment her voice, which since last year has changed almost as much as her person, loses its hoarse weak note. "So that's why we need Black Power, so we can get back our manhood—thats why." She quotes Rap Brown and adds:

"You see *The Liberator* magazine? You know what Dan Watts said? That there'll be a long hot summer, and its comin' true! He says that the Jewish shopkeepers going to get it this time. I know what you're thinkin'. Well, I don't hold for no prejudice against any race or creed; but it's time these shops in the ghettoes got wise."

We walk on, discussing crime. She interrupts to castigate the whites for their fear. "You palefaces think we're all savages! Don't think on *that!*" Apparently feeling that I shrink from Harlem's streets, she draws her small thin frame up to its full height. "Anyone put a hand on you, I'll *kill* them!"

An unsuccessful attempt to avoid going up to Harlem again. ("I got no one to depend upon but you," Jasmin says on the phone.) At six o'clock she is in the hall talking to a man in a bright emerald suit and a black hat with a cocky little feather. They are arranging some deal. "Just you wait for a few hours," she suggests with dignity. "Heavy have his business associates in town."

Upstairs in the room there is no light, and a small curly-headed Spanish-looking man is nodding in a chair in the dusk. Jasmin goes to a corner and begins to make a little structure with a hairpin, some waxy substance and cotton wool. "It's a *bambita*, we call it a *bam*." (It seems to be made of raw opium. Alonzo, as she calls him, is buying it from her.)

Eventually we start off for the Apollo Theatre, talking about China on the way. Primed by her Harlem world (and by reading the Black Power press) Jasmin believes that China is firmly on the side of the blacks; It worries her that her people, at last being appreciated abroad should lose any of their social gains. It is hard to explain that in the world of totalitarian power, where people are forced through coercion and terror into any desired shape, advocates of Black Power—welcomed as they might be to the international political arena—are also pawns in a very long and tiring chess game.

At the Apollo, a group of Gospel Singers from Ohio are already out on the stage in suits of sky blue silk; and the audience is already rising in its seats and clapping to the beat. (My own face is the only white spot to be seen.) By the third number, (The Mighty Clouds of Glory), a little woman downstairs near the stage has dashed into the aisle to dance; and one of the performers has leapt off the boards to pursue her with a mike. Immediately she chimes in with a solo rendition of the current number. Jasmin comments in a matter-of-fact way, "She got the spirit."

And in the street at midnight it is the hour of vulnerability. Jasmin, caught up in her myth of protection, hurls herself onto the pavement to try to get a taxi, but one by one they pass her by, and she has to

1966

admit to her helplessness, and to her odd, if not unimpressive appearance. She can only remark bitterly of the rare speeding cabs: "They don't even come up here now; they downtown kissing whitey's ass!"

A quick trip to Washington, to talk with a defector from the Chinese Communist Embassy in Beirut who has personal knowledge of earlier purges, as well as Peking's exploitation of religious figureheads in the Middle East.

Sin Pa (this is an alias) sits in a white-painted chair in a pleasant walled garden in Georgetown, his face sympathetic, but rather sad and ironic, his slim hands wrapped around his knees.

"I defected for psychological reasons." His voice is low. "The Chinese Communist way of life is strict and very very narrow. It is an invisible prison. There seem to be no bars, but it is stronger than prison." He sighs and shifts in his chair. "In Peking we had to spend hours engaging in political discussions every day. Even when I was abroad there would be discussions. Sometimes it would be eight hours! Americans think of political discussions as arguing. With us it was not arguing. All of it is self-criticism, that is facing the bourgeois feelings inside you. One must always confess to the party what is in one's mind."

Doesn't this become automatic?

"No, it has to be very well done." He smiles a little as if at many memories of imperfection. "It must be very delicate. You have to search and search to find the best words; they can't be just copied from the book. They must be Mao's own words, utilized and applied very delicately to Mao-thought. The process makes everybody nervous."

During this conversation which covers a good deal of his personal history, Sin Pa uses the word "nervous" a number of times. He says that he is nervous and uneasy even in America. He is still not sure that it is alright to 'discuss'. In the past I tried very hard to be an activist, and to be an elected "hero". When I became unhappy, I couldn't show it because the party members would think I wasn't loyal. So this training still operates. I still have the feeling that I cannot speak as I feel, that I am being watched." He glances over his shoulder at the flowering trees, the blue sky. He gives a shrug, followed by another small uneasy smile.

Early morning in New York City. Thoughts of Chairman Mao, who uses the seasons of nature to express his revolutionary fervor and his apocalyptic desires, who speaks of the time when the seas rise high, the waters rage, the "five continents tremble"—who loves especially to depict his enemies as insects which must be ruthlessly squashed.

In the comfortable small coffee shop in the hotel light glints on the silver-plated muffin dish, and the silver-plated teapot, and on the forks and spoons set beside the snow-white damask napkin. The morning papers present the usual interesting, but often slightly off-center facts. There is an ingenuous reference to a book soon-to-be-published, *Why the Vietcong is Winning*, written by Wilfred Burchett, that plumpish ruddy Australian, sometimes known as the "Australian Lord Haw Haw" because of the role he played during the Korean war, when he helped to set up the show trials of that period. Apparently the writer of this note on Burchett has no idea that he is so well-known an agent. (It was Burchett's dispatches which first gave birth to the germ warfare lie in Korea. He described how he had spoken to a North Korean soldier who claimed he had seen "a long brown stream" emerging from an American plane, and that afterwards an epidemic had followed. When it became clear that there was no epidemic, Burchett and five other Communist journalists issued a statement that there was "no epidemic because of efficient Chinese and North Korean precautions." In 1953 the British Minister of Defense formally accused Burchett, in a paper called *Treatment of British Prisoners of War*, of actively engaging in brainwashing British prisoners; and evidence was given by returned Australian soldiers that Burchett had personally questioned and punished them. Apparently this followed a long history of partisan activity. He had been in charge of *Soviet Intourist* in London in the thirties. In 1940 he was the sole Western journalist given a visa by the Hungarian government to cover the trial of Cardinal Mindszenty, whom he called a "miserable intriguer," and also the trial of Laszlo Rajk, who was executed by the Communists outside his wife's cell and whom Burchett described as "cheap police spy." How is it that with such a career behind him this journalist is still being taken seriously as a source of information?

August 11

Leaving New York City with a slight hangover; the hot damp air; the sensation of not being able to get enough oxygen. After a week of frenzied activity, a general disillusionment with the city's noise and dirt. Seen from a taxi, a headline about some horrible murder. The taxi-driver's opinion that "the more they talk about crime the worse it gets." In spite of the heat, his head is covered with a thick grey woolen cap.

Tonight beside the sea again. Immediately to a party where the guests present the fresh rested air of vacationers, where the cool salty air blows through glass doors, where everyone seems to have pure, guileless, "liberal" thoughts.

1966

August 16

China again. Apparently on the 16th of last month a man was found lying and moaning on the sidewalk of a street in the Hague, only ten minutes from the center of the city. The house at this site was rented by the Third Secretary of the Communist Chinese Diplomatic Mission. The man Hsu Tsu-tsai, was a member of a team of eight Chinese delegates visiting Holland for the nineteenth Annual Assembly of the International Institute of Welding. He seemed to have tried to defect, or to climb from a third floor window onto the roof, in the course of which he had fallen and been seriously hurt. With the help of the police he was taken to a local hospital, from which he was actually abducted by a group of Chinese security men and returned to the Chinese Embassy, which was of course privileged territory. Two days later, it was reported to the Dutch government that he was dead.

September 2

And again China. A few days ago eight nuns were expelled from the Mainland and crossed the border into Hong Kong. Sister Eamon, aged sixty, originally of Cork, lay on a luggage cart where Chinese border guards threw her when she collapsed; she died in a hospital next day. Mother Mary of the Cross, seventy-six years old, with shadows under her haunted eyes, weak after days of the Peking ordeal, came slowly across the border supported by Mother Provincial of the Hong-Kong - Macao Franciscan Mission of Mary.

In his history of China, C. P. Fitzgerald reports that "Even the memory of the past must be stamped out." But abolishing history is not easy—as is evidenced by the fact that while these humble nuns are expelled from the Mainland paradise, other citizens leave without permission. Generally they come from the mountains of South Kwangtung and find their way into Macao, but the road is too difficult for the old and weak. Most travel is by night. One group of eight boys and girls walked all night through rain, hid by day, lived on roots and fruits after their rations gave out, managed in darkness, and under the guns of the Red Chinese patrol boats, the four to five hour swim which separated them from Macao.

Three hundred and three refugees made it during this August.

1967

THE VOYAGE

January, 1967

Plans to sail the Blue Pacific, to escape to Australia, appear as superficial as any tourist's dream. Yet the syndrome of escape, even if conflicted, is a real one—as much a need to escape real knowledge and real thought (according to an old Japanese poem, "To try to avoid thought, is of itself to think") as a dislike of trying to do so.

January 17

In New York City snow once white has turned black underfoot. Even behind the barriers of walls and fences its bloom is darkened by the breath of steam vents and automobile exhausts and city smokestacks.

Before packing, a brief talk with Jimmie Farrell stimulates a new confidence in the overall purposes of the trip. His eyes drift to an article which he holds in his hand and which was written in 1956 when he went to Australia and found the Labor Party involved in a bitter factional struggle. "There was then" he says now "and there still are, thousands of miles separating Australia from her potential allies. I prophesied then, and I prophecy now, that Australia will tend to think in neutralist terms. I think that you will find this to be happening."

1967 / The Voyage

February 18

Today the boat sails. There has been a last exchange with a wise-cracking taxi-driver, unloading suitcases and boxes of books from his trunk, expatiating about the lunch-hour, philosophical about the delay caused by some Pier official. "So you gonta study on that boat? Say you a stoodent or something?" He unloads more boxes of books. "Say, I know some big words too—like delicatessen!"

A friend has taken me to the freighter, which leans its shabby bulk against the pilings of Pier 2. In his dark overcoat he suggests all the concerns of the city; and his is the last friendly face, as he stands waving with a folded newspaper. Soon the smell of varnish and paint in the warm passages under the decks, that faint exciting rock caused by the swell of water; the sound of the foghorn.

February 19

The lemon-yellow curtains at the cabin window are bellying in the sea breeze. Breakfast brings a dilemma of German-speaking officers and two fellow passengers (a rather capacious couple with blank faces—the male in real life is an official at a prison in Vermont). While munching good German bread, he talks about Roosevelt and his traditions ("The state's taking everything over . . . a man can't have any pleasure in his own home").

The ship's officers, very healthy-looking and clean-cut, appear in-scrutable. Outside the portholes, the grey water flows by.

February 24

Savannah! The early pearly light on the wide brown swampy river. The drowned grass, the low trees. Ashore the formal beauty of the town, with its dense ancient live-oaks, its Regency houses supported by pink Greek Revival pillars.

On the boat another passenger has joined us, a Mr. L—(first glimpsed slinking into his cabin with a liquor bottle tucked under one arm). He is no more interesting than the prison official from Vermont, or the prison official's wife; his face is plain, crooked, and a little congested. Within minutes he has declared himself in favor of what he thinks is Australia's policy towards the dark-skinned races. "Your country certainly knows how to treat Niggers!"

140

After dinner the Captain also speaks about race. He is a smallish rosy man with a pleasant but pig-like profile, and a slight roll to his walk. He seems to be interested in the "white Australia" policy; and in a grave voice he congratulates me on my native land having had the foresight to avoid the pitfalls of marriage between black and white.

But since miscegenation has already taken place, perhaps interbreeding is not so perilous after all? His face closes up, and we part with mutual politeness.

Walking the scanty space of the freighter's deck, where there is only room for one short turn around, it is important to try—as a protection against the fantasies of temporary companions—to clarify the actual Australian situation. This is done to some extent by recapitulating the recent letters sent by Australians, especially one from Danny K—, journalist in Townsville. "You must remember that things have changed. At the time you left, the Australian Governor-General was still an Englishman, and the Archbishop was still chosen by the English Church. English values, English manners, English cricket, English literature. We all stood up to recite in a springless country 'Oh to be in England, now that April's there.' While England talks of pulling out of Suez and tries to join the Common Market, we're getting gradually detached over here. We think of our own defense, and of how to sell goods to Japan to make up for the inroads in the British trade, and of how to get investment money from Americans because they're more aggressive in business than the "Brits".

If, as Danny writes, so much is outdated, so also is the Captain's view of the white Australia policy; even the hard-liners would be ashamed to support it publicly in Australia today. In fact whether they want it or not, Australians are part of the Pacific world, their logical friends, allies, companions in trade lie in that magic circle which may be drawn with its center in the rising sun and its peripheries stretching to Guadalcanal in the east, Broome in the west, Northern Japan to the north, and to the south the Tropic of Capricorn, which actually and psychologically separates Northern Australia (the "hot country") from the Southern part—where development first started, where the big cities now cluster, and where occasional Antarctic winds and rare drifts of snow mark the link with the Southern pole.

February 28

Today we are supposed to have passed the Bahamas. The week is dominated by the question of race. Mr. L—is ever ready with his stories of "Niggers" and "Jews." He is apparently some sort of dealer in real-estate, and describes himself as having "a finger here and a finger there." His crooked little face wrinkles as he boasts that his son-in-law made 200,000 dollars out of deserts in Arizona. He can't understand, in fact constantly ponders about the non material. (Errol Flynn is his *bête-noir*. "There's your Errol Flynn, always in torn sneakers, but *still* they want his autograph!")

One of the officers, neat in his dark uniform nods as Mr. L—speaks. Since English is not his natural language it is hard to know whether he really follows all the conversation. The other officer who is the Chief Engineer is almost silent and gives no indication of agreement or disagreement. Quite the best-looking of the four officers on board, his black curly hair shadows deep blue eyes fringed with thick dark lashes. (Beauty seems to be its own justification.) After a five-course "Welcome Dinner" for the (four) passengers on board, the officers and the Captain sing vigorous marching songs in the small bar outside the dining room. Even this innocent diversion has faint overtones of a time when such sounds struck terror into the hearts of German Jews.

March 1

The Isthmus of Panama, lying at the wharf in Cristóbal Colón— desolate and grim as such areas often are—under a pale warm smothering sky. Very hot. The slightest exertion brings sweat to the skin. A walk to town along a flat road where huge grey iguanas with orange-tinted throats crawl slowly. Past big houses with ill-cared-for tropical gardens.

Returning to the boat under the shadow of a long colonnade where the shadows of pillars stripe the pale gold tiles worn by thousands of feet. A little Indian woman from San Blas is leaning against an arch. Her neck is circled by numerous copper bands; her blouse is an intricate patchwork of colored cloth appliqued into tiny animals and birds; her skirt is handwoven and wraps her narrow hips. She seems to be the only glimpse we are to have of that life hidden away on the islands and mountains to the east. Tonight the canal. All through the hours of darkness the red and green lights flash across the walls of the cabin. The noise of the tugs, the electric cables, the remote shouts of men. Slowly inch by inch we are lifted up and lowered into lock after lock.

Rather than try to sleep, it is a time to read the mail and newspapers which have caught up with us here: facts and figures about Australia are striped and blended with the stain of the canal lights; the realization that the country (Australia) has been pushed into the modern world is stressed to the far-off whine of the cables outside (machine tools, optical goods, aeroplanes, cars, irrigation schemes, hydro-electric schemes). There is an article about Menzies, leader of the Liberal Party and sometimes known as the Australian Churchill. His sonorous mocking rallentando can almost be heard in the cabin—rolling in the best British tradition through the Chamber in Canberra. ("The conducted *tour* of the Honorable member's *mind* would have been more *instructive* if it had *not* taken place in gathering *darkness.*") Menzies retired last year after being twice as long in office as any other Australian Minister. He was succeeded by another Liberal, Harold Holt. Why after so long a time out of office was the Labor Party not able to gain office? Apparently because in Australia the Federal Conference is the supreme body of the Australian Labor Party—and this Conference is broadly speaking, run by the extreme left. In other words Labor has not been returned to power because its policy has represented a particularized Labor ideology rather than a consensus of party opinion. The Federal Conference was against Vietnam, and the country in general was for it. It was against the American base at North-West Cape, and the country saw the American alliance as its only protection now that Britain was losing its military position. In spite of what this ruling body of the ALP insisted upon, the ordinary people in Australia tended to be pro-American.

So at dawn, following the Panama shore to the North-West, the boat slips into the hot still Pacific . . . the sea like oil. Everyone sunbaking.

March 5

We cross the equator. The sky is faintly pink and holds a sickle moon which hangs over the honey-smooth grey satin sea. Under the surface a dark wave spreads and swells without disturbing the perfect finish—leaving only the faint agitation of its presence.

The whole day a sense of the Pacific, its vastness, its ability to swallow continents, so deep that it is a task to fathom it. The endless movement of the waves, tiring the eye and filling the soul with thoughts of eternity. (The Captain says that the Pacific is 60 percent of the earth's circumference, and holds a similarly vast and unknown sea floor, cut by huge trenches—the Kuril, the Tonga, the Mariana—which eat deep into the earth's center.) So much that is human has disappeared into the Pacific: the first sacrifices to the water gods; the elaborate carved canoes overwhelmed by storms and the tattooed warriors who paddled them; the Spanish galleons drawn by fatal reefs; the old whalers; the pearl luggers and their divers; the battle ships sunk in World War II; those lost in the graveyard of Pearl Harbor; the *kamakazi* pilots, spinning to their deaths.

1967 / The Voyage

In the bar Mr. L— is more sympathetic than usual as he talks to the prison official; "I see these islands as cemeteries. Here thousands of marines were mowed down as they approached Tarawa." He is drinking beer after beer, and there are tears in his voice as he pounds the polished wood of the bar with his fist. "On island after island . . ."

The boat is moving slowly below the equator, south-west towards Sydney, leaving the Tuamotu archipelago on the port side.

March 15

The island of Rarotonga rises out of the misty distance; tall, wooded, with jagged peaks, and of a profound deep greenish-blue. The peaks are crowned with smoke-like wreaths of cloud.

Yet this beauty does not prevent conversation at the dinner table from being hard to accept. One of the officers announces that it is a woman's job to look beautiful, to keep quiet, and to have children. As the meal progresses Mr. L— gets bolder and bolder. In speaking of a certain actress he refers to her as a "fat Jewess," at which Hilda, the wife of the prison official, asks, "But don't you think Jewesses are often pretty when they're young?" At this—to my surprise—the First Mate imitates the sound of a dog barking.

A hushed (and on some people's part, a horrified) silence follows. Mr. L— laughs appreciatively. A few moments later he refers to "New York" as "Jew York." I leave the table abruptly.

March 16

Racism is not found only in this little floating tub. Britain has been suffering recently from outbreaks against the dark-skinned invaders from the West Indies, India, Pakistan. Geraldine, English wife of the German Chief Engineer, says that the English don't like it because "there's too many of them and they don't treat women right—their men are dangerous to women."

Is it only the dark *men* that the British don't like?

She looks puzzled: "Oh no! They don't like the women either; they're not so clean, and you have to share toilets with them." She wrinkles her nose. Since Geraldine has married a German, and so far has been discreet about the question of race, it seems gratuitous to remark that whatever prejudices one finds in official Britain, they are not to be classified with the crude racism and anti-semitism of Mr. L— and his friends among the officers.

144

But aren't there people who don't even like women?

"Mr. L— ?" she asks. On the deck Mr. L— has been railing against women who wear falsies (He even claims that some women inject themselves with embalming fluid!).

Don't some men talk about women rather as they talk about Jews?

"Oh I get the message!" Enlightenment strikes her. "Negroes! Jews! Women!"

This theme of race, which has followed us all across the Pacific, and which—even on a German boat—has seemed at times highly unnatural as if gathered here as a special demonstration, is in reality close to the main stream of political events. For all its advances, the age we live in does not even pretend to recognize those qualities of brotherhood which have so often been called upon through the Christian era. It is an age in which the glory of bloodshed has been resurrected in the name of revolutionary nihilism; in which millions have been killed for their political beliefs, and millions more for their physical characteristics—and all without shame. "Let the well-bred gentry be warned," Hitler had said, "that we do with a clear conscience the things they do . . . with a guilty one."

The "impulsiveness" of the human species is not to be wondered at from the anthropological viewpoint: now as this ship moves southward it passes to the north the once desolated Tierra del Fuego where during Darwin's voyage the Indians had been seen curling up on the wet ground to sleep. It was here that Darwin wondered how far man was removed from the animals. "The main conclusion," he wrote forty years later, "(is) that man is descended from some lowly organized form. . . . There can hardly be a doubt that we are descended from barbarians . . . man still bears in his bodily frame the indelible stamp of his lowly origin." What is to be questioned, rather, are the refinements of half-civilized man, a current wonder which grows and expands as it looks at studious followers of Marx accepting anti-Semitism, and students of Confucius denouncing those with white skins. In fact at this moment there seem few countries in the world where "nationalism," "separatism" and the question of racial and ethnic minorities is not an issue. As for Australia, it would be surprising if it too (white island in a brown sea) were not vulnerable.

AUSTRALIA

The world a new leaf. . . .

D. H. Lawrence
from *Kangaroo*

Saturday, March 25

In the very early morning the Sydney Heads loom up, solid ramparts against a sky flushing slowly with dawn's red. The pilot ship alive with colored lights dances on the water, and as the sun rises the shape of the harbor with its long finger-like extensions becomes visible. White towers rise on the shore; light warms the red brick of suburbs spreading over ocher headlands; a huge liner moves majestically. This is Sydney.

And even here, in this air, once so pure and stainless, a cloud of pollution, small but ominous, hovers over the city.

Perhaps it is the long voyage, the stretches of the ocean, the endless breaking of waves against the bow of the boat—followed now by the long wait tied up in the heat at the wharves; waiting for the leisurely Australian "go slow" loading and unloading; waiting to clear customs; waiting for passport officers—which encourages a feeling less of pleasure than abeyance. Leaning over the ship's rail, staring at somnolent sheds and slow-moving cranes, caught in a paralysis of arrival, words out of that old novel written by D. H. Lawrence (*Kangaroo*) come back as curiously appropriate: "To be alive, mindless, memoryless between the sea, under the sombre wall-front of Australia. To be alone—and as absent and as present as an aboriginal dark on the sand in the sun. The strange falling-away of everything: the cabbage-palms in the sea-wind—sere like old mops. The jetty straddled motionless from the shore . . . the past all gone so frail and thin. . . . 'What have I cared about. . . . There is nothing to care about . . . .' The world is a new leaf. And on the new leaf, nothing."

Australia

March 26

The arrival in Australia is celebrated by a ceremonial swim at Coogee Beach; lolling on the baking golden sand, surrounded by athletic-looking sun-struck men and women, their torsos, their arms, their legs, all tanned to the same uniform well-turned brown; eating slices of fragrant pineapple.

The whole thing is nostalgic. The reddish suburban brick behind; to the left and right the dun headlands with their long rough grasses; blue water in front with waves curling high and breaking into brilliant arabesques of spray. Within the curve of these waves, outlined against the sun, astride on surfboards, knees bent, and in a hundred alert stances—the surf-riders. (A sense of release, a sense of being far away. To be here in the sunshine at the end of the world, to be so far from Pier 2 in New York where the stevedores were bulky in fur-lined jackets, and ragged seagulls perched upon piles of blackened snow.)

It had seemed a privilege to stay out in Coogee; even in a rather ramshackle boarding house and in the only vacant room, which has a hard bed, blue linoleum on the floor, and a rickety bureau with reluctantly opening drawers. And later, driving with W— and J— to relearn the pattern of the Sydney streets, it had roused nostalgia to follow the nautical pattern, to see how these streets converge upon the wharves where the big ships lie at anchor; and where compact ferry boats shuttle passengers across the water to the northern and western suburbs.

Australia is after all a quiet country, and Sydney is not like one of the crowded dirty industrial winter-ridden cities of the northern hemisphere. It is a large city to be sure, the biggest in Australia, a city of nearly two and a half million people, bigger than Rome, Madrid, Manchester, but still a coastal city behind which there stretches away from the populated coast a half-empty continent. And it is a city still permeated by its waterside character, marked by explorers, convict transports, whalers, traders, settlers (Anchor House, Admiralty House, Sydney Seamen's Union, Rum Hospital, The Sheer Bulk, The Ocean Wave, The Ship of Fame, the Duke of Wellington, The Hero of Waterloo, stone storehouses built by convicts, prisons like The Old Goal and the Pinchgut of the convicts, numerous figureheads—dolphins, whales, anchors, mermaids, Captain Cook holding a telescope—the Garrison where the redcoats used to pray before assembling for duties).

In fact this charming mingling of the maritime with the time of monarchs is extended to the city gardens where the sun shines through tropical palm trunks and through the primeval shapes of hairy tree ferns, not only upon formal gardens where balsams and lavender grow behind English borders—but upon a regal Queen Victoria, green with age, her scepter thrust out imperiously as if directing the first lines of "Rule Britania":

> *When Britain first at Heaven's command*
> *Arose from out the azure main,*
> *This was the burden of her song*
> *And guardian angels sang the strain*
> *Rule Britania, Rule the waves . . .*

Monday, March 27

This land which Banks, the scientist in the Endeavour, had called "the barrenest in the world" has produced one of the biggest and most vital agricultural and industrial shows in the world.

About 5,000 fellow Australians (distinguished especially by numbers of sunburnt men wearing the broad felt hats which mark them as "our people from the outback") find their way to Paddington and into the showgrounds accompanied by a good deal of loud martial band music, and past great displays of flowers, fruit, vegetables, wool, minerals and so on, all of it intermingled with milling crowds, shouting demonstrators, loud-voiced punters, and people looking for lost children.

What sets this apart from similar events in other parts of the world? Perhaps the fact that Australia for all its modernity is still in a frontier period. (Just as in the early days of the Colony, the unfurling of the British flag and drinking of the King's health and putting up a few tents didn't solve the problem of cattle straying and dying of disease, and plagues of mice devouring the seed corn, or convicts and settlers waiting half-starved for supplies from England; so today in the undeveloped part of the country there is still a fantastic hostility in the environment, and Australians are still trying to conquer it.) This yearly showing-off of riches then, this enormous expansive rural picnic, has a symbolic importance. Each year the stock breeders breed their animals in time for the Sydney Show, livestock worth more than 5 million pounds—a sum which is rivaled by the pure aesthetic spectacle—the Shetland ponies, miniature but heavy with hair, their long manes tossing and flowing—black, grey, white, shepherded by small girls wearing dusters and red club caps; marvelous shining horses mounted by the Police who wear navy blue coats, light jodhpurs and carry the gold and green pennants of the Camp Drafters; the procession of Arabs, stepping delicately; the chestnuts with plaited manes; dark greys; enormous blacks in pairs—each animal seeming shinier and more brilliantly groomed than the last. The ring becomes a great animated tapestry. The breeders enter, heavy with a kind of authority, fierce, tossing their heads. More and more cattle—the golden-hided Jerseys, the pansy-dark Guernseys, the brown and white Angus, the Dairy shorthorn—a mottled almost petunia brown. The Brahmins white almost greyish with the characteristic hump. Then the heavy Santa Gertrudis low to the ground, a lustrous mahogany color.

That night, waiting at the corner of the showgrounds, a handsome girl with a rounded chin and the kind of classic beauty which is associated with Greek statues, says that she is working with race horses.

And what is her eventual goal?

"To buy me own horse," she admits, "the first job I had was on an 82,000 acre station in the West."

Tall and feminine-looking, she leans against the side of the building, and a dimple creases her cheek as she admits that she would like to "go droving."

Isn't this generally thought of as a man's job?

"Yes, of course, but I don't care—there's somepin' about horses . . . I'd rather be with them than *people*."

At the Coogee boarding house a certain kind of aggressive egalitarianism operates. Nostalgically linked with a "remembrance of things past" (sand on the floors—an immense dining room with a gigantic cruet on each table—steak and eggs for breakfast, and a print of Queen Elizabeth wearing the Order of the Garter, hanging on the fly-specked wall) it is tremendously familiar. If the tall blond manager is casual to a fault, one gets the impression that this is because he wants his "institution," the boarding house, to play a part in that battle for "freedom" and "independence from middle-class values" which is losing ground in the growing urbanization of his country. Like an earlier generation of pioneers, he feels that he only owes to those who pay him a disdainful smile or two; and that the "Tara" (the boarding house's name) is its own justification. This hostility to "expectations" is suitable to any Irish stronghold, and hints at that old battle fought out against the Anglo-Saxons by the passionate poverty-stricken Celts who brought with them as immigrants an automatic resentment towards all Protestant institutions. (There was once an intense rivalry in Sydney, with the Irish considered "savages" and called "Micks," and the Protestants denounced by the Irish as droning creatures who looked upon religion as utilitarian.) Nor was this anti-authoritarianism only Irish; it had a deeper origin and interacted with convict dissatisfaction to shape a belligerent ethos. If Irish rebels listening to their national heroes at the historic "hill of Tara" in Meath (n.b., origin of the name of this boarding house) could be gathered up for transportation without trial or sentence, the uneducated poor of the dreadful slums of Glasgow, Edinburgh, London, Manchester could also be transported for any number of small sins (or executed for at least a hundred). It was natural that in the Colonies, all should combine against any concentration of wealth or power in the hands of the Colonial and military officers. In many ways it was fortunate that the country was so far from the civilized world that the lower classes (that is the convicts, emancipists, and poor immigrants—particularly the Irish immigrants) were able to support here the concept of equality which had been glorified by the great revolutions. (It was this emotion which helped to produce the early politicians, one of the most talented of whom could state openly "Australia belongs to the convicts!")

March 28

Reading the *Sydney Morning Herald* on the beach. In the early morning light an aboriginal boy is playing with a spear; his long-boned legs twinkle as he runs for the spear, throws it, runs again.

The papers have been full lately of discussions about the rights of aborigines. There is talk of a referendum to give the Commonwealth power to legislate on their behalf; there are opinions quoted as to what "to do" with them and reports about "digging up" their ancestors' bones; and comments about their "culture" and "art." Nervous students are hurrying off to the field to write papers on them, or to interview them for the student press. It is easy to see what will happen. The living standards of these much-discussed "subjects" will improve, but their art and innocence will deteriorate. In subduing their nomadic instincts they will become imbued with a love of possessions; and voracious political groups will try to draft them (along with Torres Straits Islanders and the natives of Papua) into various extremist political groupings.

The idea of "politicizing" the Australian aboriginal has of course been around for years. But four years ago the secret State Conference of the Victorian Communist Party, held in Melbourne, made mention of the need to pay special attention to aboriginal associations as a means of counteracting the failing Party membership! Again Charles Rowley, former Principal of the School of Pacific Administration, and now engaged in special research, makes the interesting point that the so-called "problem" is not going to fade away, that the trend towards extermination has now been reversed and that the aboriginal group is one of the fastest multiplying—not only in Australia, but in the world. Rowley also points out that since there may be as few as 45,000 fullbloods in Australia (no one really knows), there is the situation of full-bloods outgrowing the Mission psychology, and meeting standards not attractive to them; plus a parallel situation of many more mixed-bloods, completely detribalized, divorced from national values, unskilled, drifting to the towns and living on the edges of settlements. (As a footnote to politicalization in general, it is announced today that Lord Bertrand Russell, who in his old age has become a pathetic prisoner of Communist-inspired propaganda, is suddenly excessively worried about the persecution of the Australian aborigine! There is little doubt that such "black" politicking will become more frequent soon in northern Australia and its attendant islands.)

April 1

An actual "sighting" of aborigines in a pub crawl with a journalist called Les Bradey. We go from hotel to hotel; rest our elbows on the long polished bars; graduate from the rather refined wine bars where hard cider and Australian wines are sold by handsome girls with very long hair and short skirts—to pubs where the "push" crowd tend to gather. (The word "push" dates back to the *Vocabulary of the Flash Language* published by a convict James Hardy Vaux in 1812 when the *larrikins* that is "street boys", gathered in *pushes*, that is in gangs.) In some of the more interesting pubs it is possible to move about from group to group, and to listen to snatches of conversation which reflect the flavor of Sydney's rather rowdy port life. In The Fortunes of War for instance where the atmosphere is pleasantly nineteenth century, we run into crowds of working class men, holding schooners of beer in their hardened fists, and with their sleeves rolled up on hairy muscled arms. There are also sailors of all nations (garrulous and sweaty), with a fair sprinkling of American Negroes, Senegalese and Maltese. It is here in one corner that a fat crippled aboriginal male is busily pimping for three short-skirted, immature, and very plain little aboriginal girls. He sits plump and complacent on his seat against the beige tiled wall, his loosely curling hair damp on his forehead, and bargains with an occasional customer. The girls, who are bandy-legged and bony, wear little bows of blue ribbon in their hair.

Many of the white Australians are lean, scarred, burnt red and hatchet-chinned (an Australian type commemorated in a thousand nineteenth century water-colors). A huge Negro sailor from Seattle also runs true to form, with much excess energy and affection. He grasps Les, who is rather slight, and hugs him until his ribs crack. "I wanta buy you a drink," he confides, his eyes rolling in an agony of friendship. "I wanta buy you both a drink. You're nice people."

He tells us about his girl. "I love her, you understan'? I love my baby. I send her money. Every mont' I send her money . . . You understan'? . . ." As we leave he is pointing to the dark skin of his forearm and explaining it to a nearby Cocky farmer. "That color my own people," he is saying as he jabs at his skin, "my own people, my own soul people."

At the next pub (in the ladies room which is reached through a long paneled passage hung with old colored portraits of British Royalty like those once seen on chocolate boxes) a tall girl with sharp features— dark arched brows, and a hooked nose which curves so that it seems to dig into a deep curved mouth—is explaining with belligerency how much she likes her color. She is Micronesian—half-Irish, half South-Sea Islander—but whatever she is, she likes the way she is—*dark!* "Black is beautiful" has reached this part of the ocean!

And to look around the pub is to realize that the "era of Mao Tse-tung," as Robert Williams enthusiastically calls it (i.e., the era of the world revolution of colored minorities), is here also in the Pacific, in the persons of a mixture of peoples—from New Guinea, from the islands, from the archipelagoes, from Australia itself, from all the ships of the Pacific and Indian oceans—different from that in the world of the north, but every bit as colored!

The journalist I am with is not particularly aware of this political aspect of the Third World, but leaning his elbows on the bar, he says that he's not looking forward to seeing the gentle "Abos" coerced into trying to create Newarks and Detroits. "No bloody fear," he adds.

King's Cross, the center of Bohemia in Sydney, might be compared to Greenwich Village in New York (in the past it had been a rather arty section with eucalypts in the streets, a number of tea shops, and a few displays of bad bushland water colors). Now the neon lights, the profusion of espresso coffee shops, the high percentage of migrants in the crowds, the little arcades and courts—all give a cosmopolitan touch to what is after all only a block or two of animated streets. In the warm evening the crowds spill out of the bars, and at one place especially, in front of the Hotel Rex, a number of journalists and their friends drink beer on the pavement.

A little further up there is a park facing a row of rather elegant old terraced houses painted grey and decorated by a fountain which is made in the shape of a revolving sun, and glints in the light like a huge white chrysanthemum. Two old ladies, crowned with shabby but elaborate hats, sit stiffly on a bench.

Have they been long in Sydney?

"Been here orl me life," one of them answers in wonderment. After a while she adds: "Ow, there's lots 'appening dear . . ." She looks around her. "Places demolished and new 'otels built and so forth." She remains thoroughly unappreciative of the fountain. "I suppose it's pretty, but if you sit near it, you get wet!"

April 2

Afternoon drinks at the Rex have become a habit. As the journalists gather, an impromptu party develops on the pavement outside, with everyone holding a bottle of beer or a paper cup of iced white wine. Les Bradey, who has publicized this "pavement club," is making plans for a little game of "two-up" (a toss-up game, supposedly the "fairest game on earth," which is Australia's contribution to gambling, and is related to chick-farthing). The conversation around the Rex has all the affection, abuse, and invective familiar to those "down under." But the difference between 1967 and the past is that the language is a shade more self-conscious than formerly, and has been changed and glorified by contributions made by the migrants.

"How are you mate?" a big dark-haired English sailor asks a blonde young journalist.

"I'm beaut."

"You still a member of the journalist club?" inquires the sailor cautiously.

"I'm an honorable member banned for life," the journalist answers somberly.

"He's bent," commiserates the sailor to someone standing by.

"It's just 'e's never been the same since 'e fell off the bloody tractor when 'e was a kid!" contributes the bystander.

To this mixed bag of tourists, transient beatniks, workmen, sailors, and young professionals, there is added another element—a type not without charm and skill, but with a strong tendency to a drifting life. This group wear on their lapels small badges showing a pair of wings surmounted by a parachute to indicate that their hobby is free-falling and sky-diving, an incredible sport popular in Australia partly because it fulfills the national requirements of sportsmanship (as per native poet Adam Lindsay Gordon: "No game was ever yet worth a rap/For a rational man to play/Into which no accident, no mishap/Could possibly find its way").

After the drinking hour, the crowd drifts off to a party in someone's apartment. As soon as the crowd is settled in, the men tend to cluster around the two-up circle, and the women to sit in another room until the party is well on into the night (although there is one case of open heterosexual interest when a blonde in a bikini and a long skirt sits holding her partner in her arms with monotonous persistence). This separation of the sexes seems less a disregard for women than a tendency to "hold them at bay" until it's time for serious business. One sailor remarks thoughtfully, "I don't like to fight with women; I'd sooner wrestle with 'em under the shower."

Since my return to Australia two special figures have come to sum up political rivalries. One is Gough Whitlam, obviously of interest since he is the titular head of the Labor Party, that is, the leader of the Opposition, and because he might possibly become Prime Minister in the next election (and also because he represents the pragmatic and perhaps opportunist politician). The other is a man called B. A. Santamaria, a lawyer (a devout Catholic and now president of the National Civic Council) who runs a small newspaper called *News Weekly*.

Whitlam didn't come to power through the ranks. He went to the top schools and had an established lawyer's practice; but he appears to believe that a fashionable campaign will gain votes. In tune with the current dissidence he is decrying the hawkishness of Holt, the Prime Minister, and has joined in the wave of inspired protest against "scorched earth, scorched children, and scorched civilians in Vietnam." (This agile readiness to join the slogan-makers does not seem to make him the ideal man to wrest control of the ALP from the pro-Communist left; if he can't do this it seems that he will not keep the leadership for long.) At all events—in Australian terms—Whitlam will "give it a go." He has already made it clear that he hopes to orient Australia towards what he calls a "sane" China policy. Here it is that Santamaria stands as an opposing figure. In theory he too is a Labor man, but his stress is essentially on democratic procedure; and he, in the most enlightened way, is a man of the Church. (In 1937, when he was Assistant Director of the National Secretariat of Catholic Action, he was influenced by a former Communist called Lovegrove, who explained during a lecture, and in a manner which made a great impression on the young Santamaria, that the penetration of the Australian trade unions by the Communist party had created an entirely new political situation.) It was this illumination, plus the knowledge that most of the Labor leadership was in actuality anti-Communist but inert in the face of manipulation, which prompted Santamaria to organize other Catholics and anti-Communist trade unionists in a common effort to redress the balance. This organization came to be called the "movement."

Reading about the Australian Communist party on that night a month ago, as the freighter was being lifted from the Atlantic to the Pacific Ocean, had left the impression that just as the democracies in the late thirties had tried in every way possible to deny to themselves the seriousness of the growth of fascist movements, so now these same

Australia

democracies (including Australia) are refusing to believe that they are vulnerable to the growing strength of mature Communism. Their spokesmen, moreover, find "suspect" all those who document such growth.

April 3

Power struggles of the past always appear to dwarf those which are current. The present 'craze' here is for aboriginal rights.

Today a meeting with Charles Dixon, an aborigine who looks like any rather deeply-tanned Australian, except for his worried and intense eyes. We walk through those city areas where aborigines congregate, going to Chippendale, along Abercrombie Street, and into Redfern—areas which are considered substandard, and where the factories turn out shoes, plastics, paint or processed foodstuffs and provide work for unskilled laborers, not only for aborigines, but for Greeks, Italians, Maltese. There are narrow terraced houses, lacking the paint so evident in suburbs like Paddington, and seeming because of their low roofs, hunched under the blue arc of the sky. In these houses, the families may crowd into single rooms for which the rent could be 20 dollars or 25 dollars a week. The nearby shops look tattered and are plastered with faded advertisements: Bushells Tea, Bovril. (In such neighborhoods the statistics are revealing; only 8 percent of the aboriginal children go past the first year of secondary schools, as opposed to 85 percent of other Australians.) There are two hotels where the aborigines like to drink—The Regent and The Empress—which are close to the rather grubby Redfern Railway station. In spite of this, in the full southern sunlight—with so much space and air, with the citizens looking well-fed and active—it is hard to think of such areas as slums in the old-world sense.

In the Greek community the buildings change; they are painted in gay colors, azure and shining pink and with flower designs decorating doors and windows. A child swings on one of the gates here. She has the enormous dark liquid eyes of the aborigine, but her shiny dark hair is cut in a straight bang and her skin is whitish. (It is one of the aboriginal characteristics that after the first intermarriage, specific racial characteristics are hard to identify.) "I should say she is half-Maori and half-aborigine," Charles Dixon says, "perhaps one full-white grandparent . . . but who knows? Indian? Greek? Italian?"

Later, while we have coffee, Dixon talks about his childhood. "My mother was a full black and spoke no English. My father was a quarter-caste, and a longshoreman as well. There were thirteen children. I went to school but played truant almost every hot day; swimming and fishing in the creeks, bringing home my catch to help feed the family. I remember too how we gave food to all the people who passed by and came to sit around on the floor of the hut. Strangers had to be respected. It was customary to share with them what we had, and we children were not permitted to whistle or pass in front of them.

"Often as many as eight or ten strangers would be sitting there; I remember one day when I stood thoughtlessly in front of an old man, my mother hit me on the head with a stick. I married at seventeen and then I began to drink—first beer, then wine, then, as was the custom with many aborigines, methylated spirits. I had three children, and one day when I was drunk the baby was scalded to death with hot water. I drank again . . . in fact, I was never sober." He pauses. White teeth flash in a somber face.

"On April 5th of 1959, a historic day, I stopped drinking. How did it happen? . . . Well I was ragged, unshaven, dirty, driven from place to place. I went to sit on the grass outside my married sister's house. I was too dirty to go inside. I tried to shave with a shaking hand and my sister brought a mirror to see better. There on the lawn in the full light of day I saw my bloodshot eyes, my wretched face, and I vowed never to drink again, and to give my life to my people . . ." As he has been speaking there has been a frown on his face of intense self-disgust.

And had he never drunk again?

"Well, I'd get the urge to drink, I'd get it again and again . . . Then I'd go into the first bar and sit down and order lemonade and stare at the drinkers around me. I'd see how they looked, how boastfully they'd talk, how inarticulate they were. After a while I'd feel strong enough and then I'd walk out." He adds, "In those days I was always walking. Walking and thinking."

April 4

Am due to go to Canberra (the nominal capital of Australia and the site of Parliament House) and then on to Melbourne in Victoria. As part of writing commissions, there are mining men to see in the big Melbourne offices; and for my political education, Gough Whitlam is to be found in Canberra, and Santamaria in Melbourne. A liberal journalist explains that Santamaria, also called Bob or Santa (and christened Bartholomew Augustine) is perhaps the most controversial figure around.

"His detractors insist that he wants to claim the country for Rome—on the other hand his supporters glory in his mere existence and think that without him Australia would be in a bad way. Personally I find him a 'sharp' bloke, but too single-minded and intense, perhaps apt to

Australia

exaggerate . . . ." (To someone who has read Santamaria's careful analyses, the accusation of "claiming the country for Rome" seems purely diversionary. It is true that "the movement" was initiated by Catholics—and by one special Catholic—Santamaria. But it was to be a movement of laymen who were to act on their own responsibility and not through Catholic Action—although with the moral and material support of the Catholic hierarchy.)

Considering the frequent accusation of "organizing secret cells" and of "trying to take over the Labor Party," isn't it only fair to say that Santamaria's double role was far outweighed *in any case* by an indeterminate number of "double roles" on the "other" side—where Communists were pretending to be disinterested trade union members? I put this to the journalist.

He agrees that this is fair. "The Communist party has motivated a tremendous number of strikes . . . of course it is recognized that all those involved are not members of the Party. But the unions controlled are vital ones. It can be said that via the Federal Council, the Waterfront Workers are under the Communist party's thumb, and that there have been mass strikes in defense industries. In Victoria, for instance, the Engineering Union is Communist-controlled with Carmichael organizing. In New South Wales it has often been the Boilermakers Union and the Federated Engine-drivers and Firemans Association, which has held up the Naval Dock yards."

Isn't it true that the Communists are so strong in the trade unions that they don't hesitate to threaten those union leaders who don't support them?

"Yes there have certainly been instances of threats of various kinds; though this is not unusual in unions which are *not* Communist-controlled."

When we try to talk about the international scene, the journalist is less emphatic. Isn't it true that this struggle in the Australian trade-unions also involves the whole Pacific, since without control of a proportion of those unions, these first Russian penetrations into the Pacific might not be successful?

"Well there are all sorts of forces at work here, and I don't think it's gone as far as that. Of course Santamaria thinks this way, but it is one of those ways in which he exaggerates."

Only a few days before leaving for Melbourne I am in a position to hear someone who calls himself a "Communist" give his opinion of Mr. Santamaria. The man is a big bony rather attractive Irishman, of fairly advanced age (with some pretensions to being a writer) who is quite drunk, and although clinging to the articulate state, perhaps just about to pass out. He has already delivered a brief, not too clear, lecture on modern literature. "I tell you, you can bung in Steinbeck . . . you can bung in Faulkner . . . you can bung in bloody John Dos Passos the top lad of them all! For bloody scenery put down bloody Stuart" (he probably means the explorer). "For the left bank of the Seine ex-patriot condescending pseudo-intellectualism put down bloody Patrick White."

There is a dramatic pause, while all present fill up their glasses again, and two people in the corner of the room get into a more serious political discussion, "bunging in" (as the Irishman says) all the current political characters. It is apparent that those who have respect for Santamaria, are uneasy about showing it; perhaps because his (Santamaria's) comments are so clear and unequivocal, his integrity so obvious, his setting himself against destructive and powerful forces so without reproach—that he rouses fear and antagonism. The tall Irishman interjects to say that Santamaria is against Russia. "What about bloody Stalingrad?" he demands, looking around him with a baleful red eye. He then begins to rave against Santamaria, banging down his glass and saying: "I hate the bugger—there's a piece of Catholic scum!" until someone leads him away into the dining-room where he can soon be heard reciting with much feeling and in the best Empire manner:

"Nobly, nobly Cape Saint Vincent, to the North-West died away; Sunset ran, one glorious blood-red, reeking into Cadiz Bay; . . ."

To hear these small insults hurled at Santamaria is to remember how others once suffered in the United States because they extended their critical intelligence to analyze the role of Stalin in the Workers' Paradise of the thirties. James T. Farrell for instance was a favorite target. He was described as a "reactionary" who sought to "escape in a swamp." *The New Republic* published a "gang-up" letter attacking him and signed by twenty-five people. (It is interesting that Farrell, who paid in this way for his integrity, is still paying today because, right or wrong, he dares to express his support for a "good settlement" of the Vietnam war.)

April 4

Leave for Canberra by plane. From the air Sydney disappears in a flash; in no time at all the scene below shows only the winding waterways, the dark eucalypt forest and that absence of human dwellings so familiar here and so strange after the extensive megalopoli in more populated places. (In actuality this corner of Australia is where most of the population of the continent is concentrated since the Southeast triangle which includes Sydney, Melbourne, Newcastle, Canberra etc. holds about 82 percent of Australia's 11½ million people. "And" as one

Australia

serious-looking young man said, "a well-placed atomic bomb would do us in!")

Canberra itself is only 150 miles southwest of Sydney and is built in a shallow bowl-like situation, flanked by the Brindabella Range which has impressive purplish cliffs. Great wheels of streets lined with trees concentrate the two parts of the still-small city, and are linked by a lake which is spanned by arched bridges. The Government center includes a defense department (where an eagle on a long spire represents gratitude for United States help during World War II), long leafy malls, a War memorial, and an Academy of Sciences. Parliament House is a low white building, pleasant though somewhat utilitarian in design never quite forgetting its Colonial tradition, nor quite remembering its Australian ambience (in fact trying to link the two together inside the building by combining portraits of Captain Cook with those of British governor-generals, Australian politicians, and New Guinea birds!).

The Canberra night: extraordinarily quiet, a starry light rather than stars. The rustling of leaves and the sense of being in a country town rather than in a fairly-well populated capital. The sense of forests and mountains instead of that perennial sense of the sea.

April 5

A very brief meeting with Gough Whitlam at Parliament House. He turns out to be a fairly impressive figure, tall, a little solid, but moving rather lightly. His face ruddy, with that receding hairline and very slightly receding chin, that slight fullness or pucker about the lips and cheeks which suggests some forest animal (perhaps even one of Australia's own marsupials).

He seems evasive about the future relationship of Australia to China; about the Communist control of the Labor Party policy; about the long-range consequences of the West withdrawing from South-East Asia. Apparently he has ideas about reforming the Labor Party to make it less receptive to Communist control. He also suggests that his attitude towards China is only realistic—that Australia is in the Pacific and this fact has to be accepted. At one point he protests that China is not aggressive; but makes no effective reply when asked how he interprets what happened in Tibet and India.

Whitlam is an adroit man, capable of using charm to eliminate tension, strangely he also gives the impression of hiding a certain explosive force which might account for the story that he once threw a glass of water over the Minister of External Affairs!

The dual task of thinking of Whitlam's view of China, and re-reading

162

Once a Jolly Comrade by Keith McEwan. This book not only brings back an earlier political world, but all the "innocence" of Australia itself, at a time when young fellow travelers were "honored" to be considered for membership in the Communist Party. In June of 1951 McEwan was selected by the Party to go abroad to study for two to three years, and he was met at Marseilles by a courier and flown to Prague, where visas to travel to Moscow were arranged; and after that he was given a train ticket from Moscow to Peking. This latter part of the journey took ten days and ten nights. He explains that students came to the school in various ways, sneaking across borders and spending months on the way; or traveling more or less openly as he did. In Peking he lived in a building surrounded by a high wall, guarded by soldiers with rifles and sub-machine guns, and he was given a new Chinese name, a Mao-style uniform and plain unpalatable meals. He also endured a dreary expanse of study with almost no contact with the Chinese people or with the outside world. Because of security requirements there was even little talk among the comrade-students.

This continued for three years. From 6 A.M. to 10 P.M. every day he listened to dreary monotonous lectures by Soviet professors, droningly translated first into Chinese, and then into English. He allowed his "bourgeois tail" to be cut off; went through hours of self-criticism; cried with the other students in 1953 when the news came of Stalin's death; and saw one of his fellow-students, a Burmese, go insane; and another, an Indonesian suffering from excessive mental fatigue, hang himself from the balcony.

Finally in 1955 he returned to Australia, somewhat shaken in his faith; and soon to be further shocked by the revelations of Khrushchev's speech at the 20th Congress of the CPSU ("All through the night we sat up asking ourselves how this betrayal of the Revolution had come about"). The Victorian Party, to which he (McEwan) belonged, was following the Chinese line at the time (that is, against coexistence with the West, underplaying the dangers of nuclear war, stressing the inevitability of a struggle with the Imperialists). And by 1963 the Sino-Soviet clashes were so intense that, as in other parts of the world, severe splits were showing themselves in the Australian Communist party.

April 7

Today by bus from Canberra to Yass—from Yass to Melbourne by train. Occupied during the journey with notes about the early development of radicalism in Australia and about the deterioration of "sincerity" in this field of activism. The winter rains have not yet come. Beyond the windows of the carriage spreads the same sunburnt country glimpsed during the last stages of the bus ride. The pale yellow grass is silvery-white under the sun, stretching on and on without much variation, starred here and there by clumps of iron bark (a kind of eucalyptus which has particularly dark leaves of greenish-bronze, and trunks covered with papery bark which peels and hangs in long tattered forlorn-looking strands).

Since the leaves of these trees hang vertically (an evolutionary device adopted to avoid rapid transpiration in the intense heat), the clumps of trees give little shade. But under them are often gathered the sheep whose white wool looks greyish and scarcely distinguishable from the grass they feed upon. At one point the landscape is viewed under a screen of the shining silver seeds of some dry thistle which grows along the tracks; light down-like seeds which blow with the wind. Once there is a quick glimpse of a man leaning against a fence with a dog at his feet . . . All Australians have seen such scenes from the window of a train. The man is tall and wears a blue shirt and khaki pants. His wide dark felt hat is pulled down a little over his eyes. He leans against a fence post, under the sparse shade of a eucalypt, motionless, eternal in the somnolent day. Behind him there is the great cloud-piled expanse of the splendid sky.

Occasionally we pass a lonely-looking house, tin-roofed, with a horse standing in the yard outside and a neat pile of cut wood near the back steps. The names of the sidings are the familiar onomatopoeic native names—Murrumburrah, Cootamundra, Wangaratta. At one of these stations a slow goods train passes, the smell of manure and coal smoke blends with the long-drawn haunting whistle of the train while through the bars of the vans there emerge suddenly the hunched shapes of patient cattle.

At last the arrival at Melbourne. There is an immediate impression of a dignified leafy city (with a curious lack of center). But in driving from the station, the attempt to size up the city is pre-empted, so to speak, by billboards at newsstands announcing some sort of fighting on Israel's northern border. It seems that Israel has carried out a retaliatory air raid over Syria. The same paper notes that *El Fatah* guerrillas boast of carrying out more than a hundred acts of sabotage since January!

April 10

Lunch at the Melbourne University with a charming silver-haired professor. Several glasses of Australian "rough red" (the *vin ordinaire* of the country's growing wine industry). The chief subject of conversation is the recent criticism of the students of both Melbourne and

Monash Universities (these two are considered Victoria's radical strongholds). About three or four months ago a tumult had occurred in Parliament when one member had objected publicly to paying for higher education for students who "were a disgrace to the country." Another seconded this by stating that a certain group of activists were "uncouth, undesireable, unkempt and uncultured." A Mr. Mitchell alleged that these students were being manipulated by the Communists who "filled them up with beer, and urged them to demonstrate." The blame for such activities was put by someone else onto the shoulders of the left-wing academics, who comprise a large percentage of the faculties of the Victorian universities.

What did the professor feel about all this? Were the academics left-wing, and did they push the students to demonstrate?

"Well perhaps one should say that a certain percentage of the younger lecturers in the universities *have* been 'pushing' the students to support the far left." He also says that the Melbourne Student University magazine *Farrago* has recently been accused of publishing "lewd and revolting" articles, and that the editor has been asked to appear in court. "This kind of thing is always thought to come from the States," the professor notes with a small smile. "On the other hand, the impression given is that thousands of students are involved in these radical or pornographic activities; the opposite is the case. Recently a Students Representative Council survey found that 52 percent of the students were opposed to the SRC organizing political demonstrations. In spite of this the Monash University Labor Club went ahead with its protests."

Does the professor understand that it is discouraging to find here the same phony slogans heard all over the West (the universities are too large, there is too much bureaucracy, the work is too hard, the students are alienated, the students are in a state of despair, "Stop the War," "Stop Racism," and so on)?

The professor smiles doubtfully. We order some more "rough red."

April 11

A journey to the shady, tree-lined suburb of Hawthorn to see the "opposition" character in this morality play, Santamaria. He has a modest manner, harmonious, slightly rounded features, reflective dark eyes, and a subtle expression. His voice is quiet; he wastes no time on useless pleasantries; indeed, he seems to have the "weight of the world" on his shoulders.

We talk essentially of two things: of defense and of foreign policy. "To take defense first," he says, "the implicit idea used to be that Great

Australia

Britain would defend Australia. That of course is now behind us. The new idea, that the United States will defend us, implies that Australia is incapable of defending herself. The point is that to provide adequate defense Australia would have to spend ten percent of the gross national product, and not five percent, as she is doing now. There would have to be some sort of universal military training as well. The difficulties are great. If they are not overcome, however, what future can we hope for in Australia?

"The first thing we should admit is that given the internal problems of the United States—what with the war in Vietnam, the erosion of public opinion, the 'black question'—it is not clear whether in ten years' time the United States will be *able* to help anyone effectively. We can't be sure. And if we can't be sure, we must be ready to help ourselves. For the Americans, the siren song is very effective. Why take on such enormous burdens when by coming to a *modus vivendi* with China they can be averted? Of course, I myself am convinced that it *is* a siren song." Mr. Santamaria has obviously said all these things before, but they gain fresh immediacy from his grave and rather weary tone.

"As far as foreign policy is concerned, there is some possibility of a change of government at the next elections. But the DLP (the Democratic Labor party with which Santamaria is associated) refuses to help reelect Labor unless there is a change in foreign policy and defense policy; and unless the pro-Communist control in the Federal Conference and Executive is broken. You see, in Australia there is not the difference between the policies of the major parties which exists in the USA. In Australia both parties favor progressivism and radicalism. The parties can fight upon internal matters, but on defense and foreign policy we need consensus, because if we don't have it, we will see the end of the Parliamentary system. We can't afford to have a change every three years according to whether to align ourselves with the United States or with the Chinese. That's not possible.

"As for China," he adds, "the Labor party is at present wedded to the proposition that we have to accept the logic of China in Southeast Asia. To relax and to accept this is an easy and less arduous way than to deal with the problem. But by 1975 Red China will have her finger on a powerful nuclear trigger. And this may mean control of a whole area— that area in which Australia, as the Labor party points out—lies."

April 13

There is the irresistible reminder in this interview with Santamaria that moral judgment is an essential part of political judgment; that truth and justice can only be defended by those who are not ashamed

166

to invoke them. Santamaria's religious motivation links him now to the copy of a letter just sent me from the United States. The letter, which speaks for itself, is written by Bertram Wolfe to Father William J. Monihan, who teaches at the University of San Francisco.

Your letter of March 4th has plunged me into gloom, and given me a sense of the hopelessness of trying to explain why. . . . By his fruits shall ye know him, and the terrible experiences of the fulfillment of his (Marx's) call to take power in the name of the proletariat have disillusioned the intellectuals and humanitarians. . . . The latest selling device of Fromm and his friends is to make Marx acceptable to humanists and those with whom, particularly in America, psychoanalysis is so fashionable, by turning to a youthful notebook of Marx which Marx himself chose not to publish, and the very ideas of which he ridiculed so fiercely and mercilessly. . . .

One has to read and study Marx to get the feeling of *Die Geist der stets verneint*, the "annihilation by labels," the scorn for humanitarian socialism, and for the very words, justice, truth, mercy, humanity. True, Marx is vast, amorphous, ambiguous. . . . But to know what Marx really meant, one has to go not to the repackagers but to the original, difficult, but in the end clarifying writings of Marx himself.

This brings me to the subject of my gloom. Your church is now preparing to enter into a "dialogue" with the Marxists and the Communists. As men of good will, you are peculiarly eager to deceive yourselves as to those with whom you discourse and concerning what the real subject of discourse is. You . . . have not mastered their gospels, but they have mastered yours. They meet your will to be deceived with their ardent will to deceive. Hence to me it seems that the outcome of the dialogue can only be an increase in confusion and the loss of many of your best in the battle for men's spirits.

Letters like this one of Wolfe's affirm (even in the face of his own doubt) the usefulness of protest. They are supportive if for no other reason than that they express clearly the fears and therefore the warnings of intelligent men.

Here at the end of the world it seems at first uninteresting to unravel the intricacies of local politics. It is revealing to see a country as isolated as Australia, yet of great importance because of its position in the Pacific, treated in a special way by the Soviet Union (courted in some cases, bullied in others) but always with an eye to fitting the area neatly into a general policy—perhaps simply to neutralize it, or to counteract its use as a future base, or in certain contingencies to deprive the United States of an ally.

These few days in Melbourne then, illuminated by Santamaria's clarity, are also darkened by the shadow of the future.

AUSTRALIA

The Near North. . . .

Geoffrey Blainey

Men's minds are by far the most profitable and perhaps the only suitable target for the new weapons of the nuclear age. . . .

Geoffrey Fairbairn

April 15

On examination, that haunting myth of departure from old evils to a younger and better world (as felt on first arrival in Australia) does not hold up in the atmosphere of political reality.

Yet to return to Sydney is to recapture for a moment at least that original joy of arrival. The sea flows as ever into the receptive harbor, the ferries run, the big ships move majestically, the surf breaks onto the surrounding beaches. The city seems immensely attractive as it lies under the caressing sunshine; as the crowds converge towards the golden stone of the Post Office arches, through which blossom the bouquets of flower stalls. And it seems that nothing can harm this country blessed by sun and sea; while the faces and arms of the men with their shirtsleeves rolled up, the long legs of the girls in their mini-skirts, their lips and cheeks without makeup—all seem of the same deep color as is the indigenous stone.

April 16

What is lacking is an image of Australia itself. Today for instance a trip around the harbor in a motorboat. We are surrounded by hundreds of sloops of various sailing clubs, and more hundreds of small sailboats (called here Manly Juniors and captained by boys and girls in their very early teens). With the racing wind and the slap of sails there is the sensation of riding in the middle of a cloud of wild birds; with now and then a more brilliant bird—a blue or red-finned hydrofoil skimming the water at a speed of thirty-five knots. To add to this sensation

171

Australia

it is enough to realize that thousands of adults and children are swimming in public enclosures around the harbor, or fishing from the wharves, or scrambling over the rocks in the gardens and on the recreation islands. And even while this happens—while the coves in the harbor itself, and the twenty-seven beaches along the coastline are filled with sunburnt bathers—the young members of numerous pony clubs are guiding their mounts, manes streaming, along the trails under the eucalyptus trees; and climbers are tackling the castle-like turrets of the Blue Mountains; and aquaplaning is going on in Narrabeen Lagoon and the old Manly reservoir; and thousands of others are playing rugby (or tennis, or squash, or polo) and the most daring of all are the "jumpers" who from the airfields outside of Sydney, are riding up in small stripped planes, and free-falling, and skydiving, and then floating down out of the sky.

April 19

This health, this eternal thirst for earth and water is almost too good to be true. It has about it that pathos which the recruitment of soldiers has; for in the nature of the situation, this vast, half-empty island-continent may sometime demand in defense these well-trained bodies, these child-skippers, these daredevils who somersault thousands of feet as they "feel the air."

Nor is this non-populated Eden—in distance far from the older and more corrupted continents—without some of those first signs of rot and decay which begin to break down the ancient disciplines upon which were built the Anglo-Saxon civilizations. In spite of a relatively low crime rate, Australia has known horror crimes in recent years (savage killings involving youth gangs, sadistic crimes against women, the case of an old wino set on fire by three boys). The Health Commissioner says that "Sexuality has become a cult amongst the young; in certain groups it is no longer an adventure but rather a status symbol". Now the VD rate is rising. And the darker shadow of drug-addiction has begun to hang over the southern cities, so that parents, teachers, church officials are beginning to complain that thirteen and fourteen-year olds are taking heroin, that housewives in the suburbs are hooked on depressants, and that pushers constantly haunt the trucking depots to sell long-distance haulers their pep pills.

172

April 21

Have moved this week to a cabana near the water's edge where the harbor is visible at all hours of the day and night; as well as before dawn when light like old steel shines onto water faintly tinged with rose. This is not far from King's Cross where the streets are a living demonstration of rapid population growth and of Australia's "American-type" destiny (no longer molded on British lines, but representing now not only the poor, the exiled, the persecuted, the ill-adjusted; but also Greeks, Yugoslavs, Austrians, Czechs, Danes, Finns, Estonians, Swedes, Ukrainians, Hungarians, Latvians, Maltese, Dutch, Poles, Roumanians, Russians). And to differ from America's pattern a surprisingly large number of darker non-African faces are found among these Europeans; not only Asian (there has been a population of Chinese dating back to the time of indentured labor, and there are almost 13,000 overseas students studying in Australia at the moment, the majority from Southeast Asia), but Ceylonese, Indian, Burmese, Mauritian, and also men and women of purely Pacific origin—Aborigines, Maoris from New Zealand, South Sea and Pacific islanders; these last from the Cocos, Fiji, the trust territories of Nauru and New Guinea—in other words from the whole expanse of the southern ocean.

Maladjustments are inevitable. In a little German-run bar filled with blond-bearded men, a round-faced girl complains that immigrants aren't accepted. She is driving a taxi for a living, after having tried and failed to "make it" with photography. The lure of a new country seems to have driven her to search for a more "masculine" role. She feels that Australians are "rude" and even adds that they have "no conscience" (by this she apparently means that they are not alert or aware).

She is drinking from one of the inevitable pottery tankards. Her eyes are somewhat protuberant and wondering, and her skin is European skin, milky and a little ruddy. She pauses, and her tone is aggressive, "I don't think they want to accept us . . . but we're here, and we're going to stay here." (Already she has learnt the first Australian lesson.)

On the other hand, a taxi driver of several generations and of British stock, is wistful. "Oh, Sydney is all pubs and clubs now." Husky and rather handsome, wearing a white silk shirt and good-looking shorts. (Sydney taxi drivers are so democratic that they expect their customers to sit up in the front seat), he has that typical accent which is a smoothed-down version of the old London cockney. "Wa'al you gotta 'ave a good 'orse," he declares, admitting that gambling is one of his chief pleasures. "Personally, I just manage to keep me 'ead abuv water!"

Australia

We compare notes on the changes in Australian life; he voices that discontent which Australians seem aware of now, an uneasiness to see the old casual life slipping away. "There's the combies, the big fellers getting together." He shows the same unease about the immigrants. "I think we've lost the country now."

But perhaps it's only a temporary dislocation?

"Arh no," he says ruefully, "we don't 'ave the run of it we 'ad before."

May 6

Tonight a dinner at a restaurant called the *Adrias* to eat a special Czechoslovakian dish of goose and cabbage. Rudy Komon, a Czechoslovakian immigrant and the director of one of the newest and best art galleries in Sydney, is the host. Soon we are joined by several migrants from Eastern Europe, who have associated themselves with art and literature in Australia, even while earning their livings in more orthodox ways. The conversation ranges over a number of subjects, starting with Stalin's daughter Svetlana who defected from the Soviet Union last month (and who has now arrived in New York where she accuses the Central Committee and the Politburo of harboring Stalinist tendencies). Using Australianese, one of the guests comments jokingly: "Good on *her*."

To be close to these migrants is to be close to Europe for a few hours. There is even the sensation that because of those years in the United States, there is with them some kinship not now possible with Australians (because Australians, in spite of their honorable role in various wars, resolutely try to avoid identification with the sad history of the 'old world'). Most of the men present tonight are refugees. They know what it means to have been in Nazi concentration camps, to have escaped over borders with dogs at their heels.

The group sitting around the table with its white cloth and bottles of red wine are more aware of the implications of Communism than are most of their Australian hosts; but all the same an ideological split soon appears. Rudy Komon plays the role of someone who knows enough about Communism to be appropriately afraid of it; but his friend Georges Mora (who is up from Melbourne where, with the help of his wife Mirska, he runs a restaurant and gallery) is less sure that 'fear' is necessary.

"Why be afraid of what doesn't work?"

"What works?" Rudy Komon demands. "The Communist countries somehow manage to hold onto what they get. Georges, you say this doesn't *work!* Subversion and villainy are efficient, Georges."

A discussion about the recently publicized projected dialogue between the Communists and the Church, brings up the question of *Ramparts* (which began as a liberal Catholic magazine in the United States) and of the present implication that the magazine is now somehow linked with Prague. "And who is this Ramparts man?"

I explain that the reference is to Robert Scheer, the present editor of the magazine which had been running at a loss of 350,000 dollars a year. *Time* and the *National Review* had suggested that Scheer had contacts with Communist organizations in Prague and that his financial losses had been made good there.

For the first time since leaving New York City I am pinned down to give political details.

"What is the real story?"

"Well, it is only possible to repeat what has been reported. Robert Scheer was in Prague at the time, and was asked in a telephone call from the head of the USIA whether he got the money wanted for *Ramparts* in that city. To this he replied at once, 'How did you know?' "

I add that Scheer went to Cuba, a defiance of the ban that his trip to Prague was secret, that I myself feel that *Ramparts*, with its pro-Peking stand, has also tried to divert attention from Peking's world drug trade by attempting to implicate the CIA.

Later, walking along in the quiet back streets near the harbor, someone begins to sing an old Czech song. It is scarcely midnight, but our solitary steps echo as they might in some country town.

May 9

A few days in Lismore. Here most of the migrants are apolitical Italian peasants, who live in neat little houses with grape arbors and statues of the Madonna, and have built up prosperous banana plantations. They drink homemade wine. The men are handsome with dark sideburns: the women are large, comfortable, still speaking Italian: the children laugh, and show beautiful white teeth.

There seem to be few identifiable Jews in the town; and this is the time of the Jew. Every day the TV set in the kitchen shines like some threatening object, and the old anxiety about Israel surfaces as one disaster after another is reported. With the local people this global worry can be translated into terms of World War II, when Australians themselves had been in danger, so that it serves as a link to present military realities.

One man explains as he talks about the reserves during World War II. "We were just transported to Darwin, way up north, and we pitched camp and dug trenches beside the tents. There is about three feet of

Australia

bloody soil over solid rock in that Top-end country. A storm comes and the stunted trees pitch over, then the white ants come and eat the trees, and that's the end of that." (Darwin is in the Northern Territory, thousands of miles from Europe and the United States, but only 500 miles from Indonesia and 2,000 miles from Singapore, where the victorious Japanese were established at that time. When the Japanese finally bombed Darwin they met with practically no resistance, and managed in one brief raid to knock out the water supply, the wharves, the telephone service, the hospital and the communications center at the Millitary Barracks.) "We weren't too happy", this particular man goes on, "There weren't enough rifles to go around. Then there was no food. At first we had to live on buffalo meat than which nothing is worse. Then we were short of tools; it took us a year to get organized." He inspects his finger nails, and permits himself an exaggeration, "Our nails got broke from digging holes in the ground. When the Yanks moved in, everything was fixed up in a few weeks. The wharfies were causing their usual trouble, refusing to service vessels. The Yank Commander got a special order from Canberra, and his soldiers unloaded that ship in no time flat. They opened up the guts of the thing, and inside there was everything needed; roadbuilders came rolling out and bull-dozers. And here we were, sharing out a few picks and shovels." (The speech is admiring.) He slumps into his chair, a big, scarred, suntanned battler of a man. "It was a bloody miracle:"

We talk about Britain. "It's on the skids; that's what I think." He adds after a while, "It's had its day! They stop work over there because someone uses the wrong machine, to put nuts on, or because the men can't get their hair cut on company time. With things like that Britain hasn't a chance—she can only go down."

And is this how it is in Australia?

He looks somewhat self-conscious, but again truth gets the better of him. "Well, I can't say it's the same. The blighters here always had more push than they had in the old country. It's the federal level that does it here. The Coms get control of the Central Executive of the old ALP; then they run up costs with stoppages and slowdowns. They've got their corner and they use it. If a man's in the way, they'll domino him; and of course they white-ant the defense industries."

May 29

In packing to leave for the north, there comes again this sense of political isolation. Only the East Europeans in Sydney find it possible to believe that a country can be invaded and destroyed. As Nasser appears in the press and on TV to boast about a "total war" against

Israel, many of the watching Australians don't seem to accept the reality of the threat. The tension and hate in the crowded Middle Eastern cities appear far away.

The day of departure has that perfect moderate quality, that temperate but steady sunshine which is so common here. A bird in the garden swoops down with a flash of iridescent blue wings to thrust its beak into the flowering pink honeysuckle.

To go north is to turn away from the cities and to push up towards the sparsely settled northern coasts, to the outback which lies behind them. In most countries the adventurous travel southward. They get away from the cold northern areas and aim for equatorial rivers such as the Amazon, or the Congo, or islands like Tahiti or Jamaica. But in Australia where the seasons are reversed, adventurers go north—their goals being unknown beaches, the islands of the reef, or off the coast, isolated ports such as Cooktown, Darwin, Broome, the vast cattle ranches, or the new development areas such as Weipa, the Ord River, or Groote Eyelandt.

For this journal's sake the voyage north will explore Australia's future—that is what her future may be apart from her very evidently satisfactory development and standard of living. The journalist Geoffrey Fairbairn, whose work I find so impressive, has been writing about Vietnam and has done a piece for *News Weekly* about the Soviet method of unconventional warfare (a term which has become popular enough to be known by its initials U.W.). Using the term *psychostrategy*, Fairbairn points out that the aim of this kind of U.W. is to deter the West from mounting dangerous counterattacks during the prosecution of the world revolution. It is not primarily concerned with waging war, but rather with inhibiting counteraction to any situation created by the Communists. Western societies are "soft targets" because the electorate must be consulted, whereas totalitarian regimes, by controlling public opinion, can change their policies without inhibition and so keep the initiative. Fairbairn explains that the idea is to confuse the democratic adversary by using propaganda to inculcate doubts. He adds that the Soviet leaders "seem to have grasped what may be the salient strategic truth of our times—namely, that men's minds are by far the most profitable, and perhaps the only, suitable target for the new weapons of the nuclear age."

"Softening up" via psychostrategy is evident in Australia at the moment. The propaganda goes something like this: "Australia is bogged down in Vietnam"; "The guerrillas are unbeatable"; "Ho Chi Minh is a patriot"; "It is morally wrong and unjust to bomb a little country"; "It is really a U.S. war"; "An Imperialist war"; "Australia has been dragged in by the USA"; "Australia should get out."

177

Australia

At the same time, and as support for the slogans, action-provoking devices are required. Democratic societies have an inbuilt dependence upon democratic methods, and one of the methods of unnerving the West is to play upon liberal sentiment, and to accuse its societies of undemocratic procedures—cruelty, unfair practices, exploitation, etc. (An example of such a broadly-based campaign is the germ warfare campaign in Korea.) In such cases, citizens of the countries accused become fiercely indignant, suggest inquiries, send journalists to investigate, write letters to the press, and so on. The agitation reinforces the impression (among millions of TV viewers and readers of headlines) that the accusations are indeed true. By the time that they have been seen to be unsubstantiated, none of the early accusers is around to answer inquiries. The damage has been done. A proposition has become a fact. Since Australians are so sensitive to the national ethic "give a man a fair go," recent publicity about chemical warfare is playing a splendid supporting role to psychostrategy by labeling the allies in Vietnam the atrocity makers of all time; dealers in poison, gases and disease agents, with the express intention of carrying out a war of genocide against the Vietnamese people, and while pretending that they are only using a few simple weed-killers!

(According to information from researchers into Security Services, the KGB in the early fifties increased its size by a new division, Section D, that is *Dezinformatsiya* or Decomposition. This department, as opposed to the older cruder methods used against the West such as blackmail, physical threats, or primitive forms of deception, tried to cultivate certain psychological attitudes; to undermine Western faith in its own institutions; to encourage ideas among Western liberals which are conducive to defeatism; and to acerbate contradictions between Western countries.)

June 4

Arrival in Brisbane—a pleasant inchoate city built upon the winding banks of the Brisbane River. That feeling of provinciality dwarfing old memories of importance and grandeur; bringing back to consciousness landmarks once familiar: Adelaide St., Eagle St., Queen St., Lennons Hotel, the Cecil, the old convict-built Customs House, the ferry to Kangaroo Point, the long line of jacaranda trees near the Botanic Gardens, which, at a certain moment in their flowering, flood the pavements with purple.

Waiting for a friend at the bus depot, watching the passing crowd (so much less pulled-together than in Sydney)—the bare-armed women with shopping bags, the men in rather loose suits, pickled by the

178

relentless Queensland sun, the children in shorts, lanky and well-grown, their skins tending to olive rather than to rose.

The hotel on a quiet street, where once old mining-men had lounged in canvas chairs and talked the days away. Now smelling faintly of dust and worn linen, with uneven creaking floors, and a dark-painted dining room aglimmer with silver-plated cruets and pearly tablecloths. Shaded from the hot street by yellowed blinds.

Taking refuge in the hotel bar with a husky journalist—one of those men with a big frame and a quiet voice (inevitably called John): an evening which begins with politics and ends with it. Half-way up the eastern coast, as we now are, and closer to Southeast Asia than we are to Perth, the subject quite suitably is Communist China (or as one man calls it politely "Mainland China"). But whereas once China would have been a natural topic for down-under travelers, now in 1967 with the continent no longer tied to Britain, it represents a different kind of preoccupation; perhaps what might be called a preoccupation with the "Near North." Any possible uneasiness seems to be displaced by the romantic view (although it seems odd that middle-class Brisbaneites should relate to the Chinese Cultural Revolution, whose Red Guards at the moment are dressing down Tao Chu, once fourth man from the top in the Chinese hierarchy, because he made the bourgeois mistake of sending a wreath to his mother's funeral)!

Later in the evening (under the overhang of someone's house where high pilings are festooned with tropical plants) we drink a certain amount of beer. Towards midnight a noisy argument breaks out between John and another journalist. In Australianese one might say that the "beer-up" was followed by a "boil-up," and the "boil-up" was followed by a "word-up." Although only one of the men present tends to be a real admirer of Red China and his contribution is limited to an occasional phrase like "don't knock Mao" or "Chou is a pretty cluey bloke—don't wipe the bastard," a very Australian thing emerges from the torrent of words, i.e., the well-known determination to support the underdog at all costs. Later history notwithstanding, the fact that China had once been carved up by the nations of the West, forced to trade on the terms of others, and had opium sold to her at cannon-point is enough to foster sympathy for her among Australians. Everyone seems agreed that China is a "reformed society," that the land "has been given back to the peasants," and that it's high time to get "rid of the old fear that the slit-eyed hordes are going to descend and finish us off!"

Australia

June 5

The waters of the river glinting from the top floor of the hotel. Palm shadows printing their classic pattern on the pavements. Somnolent memories of the night before. (Those generous journalists can be accused of nothing other than wishing to give China "a fair go," but it is really the old reiterative deception of generations of Communist party members and fellow travellers, of statesmen and churchmen, of student leaders and would-be intellectuals. There is an irony in bored affluent free western youth trying to reform their own society by identifying with their age group in Russia, Cuba, China—this last an area where revolutionary cadres still walk from village to village, where human power is still used to drag loads through the streets, and human excrement must be religiously saved to fertilize the soil.)

In the hotel real life intervenes. The little boy who cleans shoes is going from to door to door in his old-fashioned white apron (curiously un-Australian in its implicit admission of servitude) putting down the shining shoes of the guests, and a late copy of the morning paper. The headlines flash the news that war in the Middle East has begun!

June 7

Reading the paper—Shells are raining down on Jerusalem. Last night from the back balcony of the King David Hotel, journalists watched the jets climbing beyond the Mount of Olives, but then flying in low over Jordan to try to knock out its heavy artillery. Egypt is accusing Britain and the United States of taking part in the battle; and this has been denied. The Israelis claim to have destroyed 374 Arab planes, to have captured the old city and Gaza as well, and to have sent armored columns streaking through Sinai towards the canal. The general opinion seems to be that Israel is rapidly winning the war.

Local editorials look at the world through provincial lenses. "The wisest course for Australia is strict neutrality" .... "There are other countries with more pressing interests in the Middle-East. Let them take the initiative." "Australia should avoid any military commitment .... " "Vietnam is bad enough," and so on. (Jewish citizens take a more aggressive view. Out of the 72,000 Jews in Australia, there are 16,000 here in Queensland; these are living up to the "down-under" tradition of wanting to "have a go" at the enemy, and are calling a meeting tonight for hawks only! Not to be outdone, and on the other side the Free Palestine Committee is organizing demonstrations in

180

Canberra and Melbourne. The aim: "to assist in any manner the liberation of Palestine from the hands of the Zionist usurpers.")

Leaving for the north on the slow night train to Rockhampton; sitting in a compartment panelled in dark glossy wood; Victorian-looking upholstery; big photographs of Queensland beauty spots done in sepia and set into the wood above the seats; berths made up in fresh linen stamped in blue Queensland Government Railways. The view from the window is at once monotonous and varied; a tapestry of eucalyptus trunks, dark-barked and pearly white, leaves gray-green and down-dropping, all of it characterized by an elusive delicacy derived from the intricate convolutions of trunks and branches. Early in the morning the jolting of the train on the narrow gage line, the stopping at small stations where tubs of crotons stand at intervals under wooden over-hangs, and where from the ticket office there drifts a nostalgic aroma of paper files.

Although the papers have been headlining the Arab-Israeli war, as we get farther north and as travelers spill out onto station after station, the newspapers provide less mention of that faraway crisis, and more and more about immediate problems. Rain is the main subject. "Million Dollar Rain" announces one newssheet.

June 8

Slept last night in Rockhampton at a roomy pleasant hotel, loaded with elaborate white-painted ironwork; walked up abnormally wide streets, in winds cold after the rain, past attractively pretentious buildings with domes and pillars and cupolas in the manner of the 1880s. (This lavish building style was triggered by the fabulous finds at close-by Mount Morgan, literally a mountain of gold. The ore was shipped through Rockhampton, then a sleepy port known only for its hides and wool.) The atmosphere of the town suggests this past, with its built-to-last look, its solid banks, and its crowded public bars where swinging doors allow glimpses of vociferous men, their sleeves rolled up, and huge schooners of beer in their fists.

Australia

June 9

Catching the Sunlander—the train very modern with first-class carriages upholstered in an attractive blue, and paneled with light-colored laminated plastic—the sense of being far away and out of touch increasing as the train proceeds in the general direction of the equator. At one of the stations the horizon suddenly seems wider and the air warmer, and there are reminders of Kipling—who'd said in his autobiography that memories of Australia were all mixed up with train travel—with a sense of enormous skies overhead, and with primitive refreshment rooms where he drank hot tea and ate mutton, while now and then "a hot wind like the 'loo' of the Punjab, boomed out of the emptiness." A hard land, Kipling had gone on to comment, and the inhabitants always seeming a bit on edge.

Daydreams in the train of the yellow-breasted sunbirds which had haunted Green Island farther north, of trees almost smothered with a common butterfly with muted rainbow-striped wings, of waves glittering with fish which hatch in the warm reef seas and travel southwards at certain times of the year. . . . From here the shape of Queensland stretches up to where Cape York points towards New Guinea and the equator and the islands of the Torres Straits; while down from the 'Near North', the East Indies press to meet it.

At Mackay the smell of sugar in the air, mingling with the salt blown from the sea. Some of the passengers board the train carrying suitcases tied up with rope. The figures of Aborigines and half-castes glow in the fading light, dressed in reds, oranges, purples. Two men who might have come from New Guinea stroll the platform holding cups of tea, their thick tight-curled hair making halos around strong-featured faces. A white woman descends from one of the carriages to buy a newspaper. She wears a pale blue dressing gown, and her head is covered with pink plastic curlers. . . . From the train again the shining lavender blossoms of the canefields are seen, spirit flowers receding rapidly in the fast-dropping twilight.

The indiscriminating flow of history includes the tyrannies of the past and the rebellions of the present in a single undivided stream. In an age when Black Nationalists in New York City are asking for apartheid and want to partition the United States into two separate nations, one black, one white, we are physically close here to the Black Wars of 1830, and names like Dawson, Cullin-la-Ringo, Hornetbank, Keppel Bay, Calton Hills, Maranoa, Murdering Lagoons (where in the survival style of the nineteenth century, the whites encroaching on the hunting grounds of the tribes, especially those of the warlike Kalkadoons, met with serious opposition; thus acting out the culture conflict through the years until it ended with the breakup and final decimation of the tribes).

It was a hard country anyway. "Words fail for painting the loneliness of the Australian bush," one pioneer woman writes, and another speaks of "the fierce unmitigated heat; the deathlike stillness." A third says that during the drought the sheep came around her beseeching water and that their eyes were "sending her mad." When the sacred waterholes were trampled by the white man's animals, the blacks for this and far worse tresspasses, retaliated. The dusty roads were stirred by the rapid hooves of horses bringing bearded sunburnt men to quench that insatiable pioneering thirst, to put on record the latest land taken up to the west, the latest accident, the latest reprisal on the part of the blacks. Eventually the Chinese coolies—brought in as shepherds and laborers by entrepreneurs—imported opium (panacea of earthly ills) and through the Chinese cooks on the stations, the Aboriginals developed a taste for it—as recorded by the scientist Lumholtz. "I visited a camp of 'civilized' Blacks near Rockhampton. Even before reaching the camp I smelt the opium. Around the fires sat natives pale as death itself. The opium-pipe was constantly in their mouths, and their eyes stared out bewildered from their deep hollow sockets. The man I wanted to see had lost his flesh; his skin had become yellow and sickly. It was all he could do to stammer forth a request for money to buy more opium."

(Painful visions of earlier corruptions are appropriate in 1967, because the ease with which Chinese coolies had been able to lead aborigines into opium addiction is a reminder of the present growth of such, and other forms of—addiction in Australia; and of the fact that the police in Sydney are at this moment investigating a ring which ran what was called a pioneer run from Hong Kong to Sydney to California—thus for the first time marking Australia as the focus of a large narcotics operation. Almost at the same time there comes confirmation of earlier news of an arrest of Red Chinese, posing as sailors from Hong Kong, caught at Long Beach California with 12 million dollars worth of heroin in their possession.)

Arrival in Townsville, 1,300 miles from our starting place in Brisbane, and on the edge of that area where even now the population per square mile is less than three persons. The town lies on the coastal flats, with behind it a mass of pinkish-beige sandstone conglomerate called Castle Hill (once nude and stark; now invaded by buildings which approach from all sides). Here is the *de facto* capital of North Queensland, with a population of 55,000 people, a copper refinery and a new university college. It is damp, hot, languid. Sitting on the hotel verandah, sipping lemonade with gin, we watch people slowly walking in the streets;

Australia

some of the women with paper sunshades which are sold in the Chinese shops.

And even as we sit, thousands of wounded and homeless refugees from Jordan's West Bank pour into Amman to add to the problem of the Jordanian medical and relief teams. For Israel it is almost as bad as if she had lost the war—the dead, the wounded, the prisoners, the problems. But as a recompense her people for the first time in nineteen years can worship freely at the Wailing Wall, and kiss with passionate lips that patchwork of stone and masonry which represents the remains of the Second Temple destroyed by the Romans in 70 AD

June 16

We are now in the "true" north. The train passes through coastal country which becomes steadily more fertile; ranges loom oppressively; views are spectacular. The creeks, dark with rich diluted soil, harbor crocodile and large golden-sided fresh-water fish called barrimundi. Tattered banana fronds and the glossy sheen of mango trees glorify the small stations. At Ingham raintrees spread perfect canopies. Here, a week ago, floods had been so widespread that the inhabitants had to spend the night on rooftops, until they were rescued by army ducks. At Tully (the wettest place in the world it is said) swamps reflect pale paper-barks, the ancient silhouette of pandanus, and elegant water-loving Queen of Sheba palms. It is in this area that the great Kosciusko uplift (an elevation from the Pliocene Epoch) extended like a tremendous wave from New Guinea to Tasmania, and caused the trough to the east and the resultant subsidence of the coast which forms the Great Barrier Reef.

This is home country. I leave the train at Cairns, where large islands rise abruptly from the sea and where further out the islands of the reef spread like a looped necklace. Inland the tablelands rise 2,500 to 3,000 feet, surmounted by the granitic block of Bellenden Ker Range; dense jungle clings to the inaccessible gorges of coastal rivers, heavy with the plants and trees of the rainforest, and heavy too with a perfume of water, leaf mould, ferns, which blows over the informal and attractive town, with its wooden houses and tropical gardens.

The silence here intensifies the sense of remoteness. My sister's house is built on a Trinity Beach hillside, looking over to the reef and beyond that to the Coral Sea. There is a languor in the air; the rustling of dry fronds, under the greenish-gold twilight of the palm trees, rises from the earth like sighs of exhausted pleasure. That stretch of water out beyond the reef, lying between Eastern New Guinea, the Solomons, the New Hebrides, and New Caledonia, was the site of the Battle of the Coral Sea during the last war. It was here that the Japanese were first defeated, and their advance into the Pacific halted. Port Moresby was saved; a month later at the Battle of Midway, the destruction of Japanese naval power in the Pacific was completed. (Older Australians remember well the period of fear during the first phenomenally rapid advance of the Japanese, but many have never known that Admiral Yamamoto, hero of Pearl Harbor, had wanted to land an expeditionary force on the lonely northern coast and terrorize the continent. Nor that General Yamashita—noting that however tough the Australians might be, they could scarcely be a match for disciplined troops—had seconded Yamamoto and offered to lead the expedition himself. Hirohito had vetoed the proposal.)

The war was to strip Japan of myths, as it was to strip Britain of its territorial possessions; and there is no better place to consider the fall of Empires than this stretch of empty coast. . . . Still greater changes are heralded by the retreat of British power in South-East Asia, which cannot be delayed for long. The big photographs that they like to take in London when the Commonwealth leaders get together show the darker faces predominating; but it isn't only the rise of nationalism which rules, it is what the Australian *Bulletin* calls "overstretch." As someone has put it, crudely, "Commonwealth obligations are for the birds." Britain can no longer afford to reach, even with token power, as far as Singapore and Malaysia.

What is taking place is more than the shift of power resulting from the withdrawal of the British; this in itself will take time to absorb. There is also the not yet realized rise of totalitarian powers (and if this is not grasped in the United States, how should it be grasped here, where the psychological time lag is still engaged with a slow transference of allegiance from Britain to the USA?).

In one way or another vulnerability is emphasized. We drive up into the ranges and to the Atherton Tablelands, now almost stripped (in favor of dairy farms, small tabacco plantations, and orange groves) of its original virgin rainforest. Once small lonely farmhouses—modest cottages made of timber felled in the clearings and cut in small local sawmills—had been planted in the middle of the scrubs. On such a settlement a family lived the sunrise-to-sunset life of poor families the world over. Four small rooms and a veranda; walls decorated with calendars and pictures from *The Illustrated London News*; a kitchen where an iron stove crackled with priceless woods not yet known on the southern market, where scones baked and the kettle boiled for the

Australia

traditional "tea"; a mongrel dog perhaps with a touch of dingo blood; healthy children, feet bare and tanned skins showing through torn cotton clothes, riding their ponies bareback to school, bringing in the cows for milking, going to the creeks for fish, or to hunt possum or platypus. These families listened for the lonely whistle of the train, rounding the green belt of the scrub, heard it like a call from a far-off civilization. If transport is much improved now and communications better, the sense of being among pioneers has not disappeared. In the old days there were small embattled democratic institutions—cooperative butter factories, hospitals, one-room schoolhouses ringing to the sound of spelling by rote (under tin rooves often beaten by fierce tropical storms); halls where "socials" were held, where men gathered stiffly at the door, and lavish suppers of jellies and cakes loaded with whipped dairy cream were served by tanned, rosy women. Small tight-knit communities, almost completely Anglo-Saxon, knowing only the accent, the outlook of Britain, Wales, Scotland, or Ireland. These institutions endure in essence, but some of the cohesiveness is lost. The wiry, tough, "innocent" soldiers no longer march off with their digger hats turned up with emu feathers to some symbolic Gallipoli. The communities, like so many communities in Australia, are split with "foreign" views, with questions and indifference, with taunts and doubts. Once on these tablelands the Church of England sponsored small struggling private schools founded to bring the "official" religion to the pioneers of North Queensland. More specifically, perhaps, the aim had been to combat in these bush communities the dire effect of transported Irish Catholicism. The bishop of the diocese, Bishop John Feetham—lean and dark, with burning, enthusiastic eyes—was often to be seen standing on the little railway sidings, his black gaiters stained with mud, the flat silver cross of the Anglican order swinging on his purple bib, and his few worldly possessions slung over his shoulder in a hessian sugar bag, as if to out-pioneer the pioneers. It was this man who had gone back to England to speak at the great universities, calling for young men and women to come out to Australia and brave the same excruciating journeys, the same heat, dust, floods, mosquitoes, as did other settlers; to bring not only 'God' but culture to the *tabula rasa* of North Queensland: "Men who could ride like cowboys and preach like angels."

It would have been inconceivable in those early days of untarnished faith—when men and women from Oxford and Cambridge, conscious of the obligations of their beliefs, braved the trip from England, then the "center of the universe," to serve in lonely North Queensland—that in 1967 the Lutheran pastor Richard Wurmbrand, at this moment lecturing in England, would be deploring a time when to practice "Christianity" under Communist regimes is a crime; when missionaries rather than riding with enthusiasm to pioneer communities, are subject to secular forces curiously reminiscent of the time of the Inquisition. In this mighty regression Pastor Wurmbrand was twice imprisoned in Communist Rumania (from 1948–56; 1959–64) and was held for two years in a cell 35 feet underground, was tortured and brainwashed. His wife was sent to work as a slave laborer on a canal; at one time reduced through starvation to try to eat grass. In his lectures Wurmbrand asks the inevitable question: why are these facts hidden? Why are the British churches influenced by Communists? It is not only what happens in Russia and in Eastern Europe but what happens in China. He (Wurmbrand) speaks of the deceptive role of the World Council of Churches, and explains; "When I was in prison, I was approached by the secret police and asked if I would like to be a bishop. When I asked what my duties would be, I was told that one of them would be to influence the World Council of Churches in 'our' favor."

The outer world, as seen in conjunction with the rediscovery of Australia, darkens the travel experience. Geoffrey Blainey says that "every Australian is at heart a Robinson Crusoe"; but the urge to loiter on this beach in the warm tropical days now conflicts with a need to concentrate upon that clash of ideologies which is the big battle of the century. The vision of political complications tends to obscure the pellucid sea, the islands floating on the horizon, the jungle-clad mountains. And the conviction that the West is in retreat (with even the Vatican coming to terms) is the harder to accept in a country known for nothing so much as for its fighting spirit.

The current shock story in the south for instance, is "napalm." Professor Dudley at Monash University, just returned from serving with an Australian medical team in Vietnam, asserts that "napalm" has become a political weapon ("Yet out of 1,000 casualties treated by the Australian team," he points out, "there was not one napalm burn"). Danny (the journalist from Townsville, with whom I am now travelling) admits that a group of South Australian doctors called Smith, Barker, and Cornish, were also just back from Vietnam; and that they too reported no napalm cases. What does he, Danny, think is the truth? "Well, I must say that the impression given is that they're trying to brand the United States with a special savagery—you know that U.S. troops go out looking for babies and throw napalm at them." (In spite of the testimonials of these Australian doctors, one press man here has just quoted Neil Sheehan; "I wonder when I look at children with napalm burns lying on the hospital cots whether the United States or any other nation has the right to inflict this suffering.") And in the United States Dr. Benjamin Spock, who is head of the so-called Committee of Responsibility has been on the napalm bandwagon and has helped to send an investigating team of three doctors and a

Australia

journalist to Vietnam (which visited thirty-seven out of forty government hospitals, and discovered forty burn casualties in Da Nang, with none of them identified as napalm). Disturbed by the left-liberal agitation, President Johnson sent Dr. Howard Rusk to investigate the hospitals of Vietnam; and Dr. Rusk accordingly took "private" experts to task, conceding that there were burned adults and children in Vietnam, but that in all the twenty hospitals he visited there was not a single case of burns due to napalm. ("The cost of fuel for cooking is high. As a result many Vietnamese villagers pilfer gasoline, are inexperienced with it and use it like kerosene; the results are tragic. The Allied forces are causing civilian casualties ... these are unpreventable .... they are not nearly as great as the killing and wounding of civilians by the Vietcong.")

I point out to Danny that *Ramparts* again comes into the case, that *Ramparts* had been one of the first U.S. magazines to publish pictures of children supposedly burnt by napalm, and that *Ramparts* is the same magazine accused of having contacts with Communist organizations in Prague. (This eager journal quoted and misquoted from the reports of *Terre de Hommes,* an organization in Switzerland very similar to the Red Cross. The Secretary of *Terre de Hommes,* Edmund Kaiser, wrote angrily: "A little more human intelligence and a little less political bad faith could have stood a better chance of helping us to save our children ... and because of your errors ... we will hold ... *Ramparts* personally responsible for the suffering of children whom your clumsiness will have separated from us.")

I am reminded of Fairbairn again. It may be that his fears are even more justified in Australia (where political opinion has less chance to examine itself) than in other countries. Australia is after all far away, and presents a fresh and not yet disillusioned audience.

Watching television in the hot night, with the faint tropical noises, the rustle of palms, the plop of a frog, the stir of a bird. Complaints have been coming from Britain that the TV coverage of the war over a period of twelve months reveals constant criticism of the United States ("astonishingly high quantities of explosives and napalm are being dropped"; China feels "hemmed in"; the "US draft laws are harsh"; "civilians are being killed in the North" and so on.)

An ex-pilot of World War II, a Scot, sits rather stiffly in his chair and protests that there is no program to remind viewers that the Vietcong are aggressors in the first place. "And what about the calculated mur-r-der of children, and the torture of village officials?"

He is a well-preserved man, calm-faced, tending to grip his pipe with his teeth when annoyed, rather than take it out on onlookers. Now he is especially frustrated because the Presbyterian church is getting involved with politics. "I don't know why we must listen to views on Vietnam even on Sunday."

The streets of Cairns are wide, lined with trees, almost empty, stretching to the hazy edge of the sea. Palm fronds move slowly. Men in white suits. Women half lost from sight under parasols. When someone remarks on the numbers of tourists in town, travelers from more crowded continents stare in disbelief! But the plane arrives regularly, and the newsagents display, like gestures from the outside world, crisp, brightly-coloured up-to-date magazines, such as *Time* (air-mail edition).

The news is that Newark is exploding ("It's going to be a long hot summer," had been Jasmin's prediction in a letter reaching me at the same time). A black cab driver in Newark had been taken into custody for trying to pass a police car; a rumor went out that "whitey cops" had killed him; and the riot was on: four days of looting, arson, and violence, 21 deaths, 1,600 arrested; and the National Guard called up.

The riot did not stop there. Within ten days it was echoed in cities ranging from Hartford, Connecticut, to Tampa, Florida, from Laurel, Maryland, to Kansas City, Missouri. Across the nation city streets were strewn with broken glass, flames leapt, looters staggered out of shops with suits and suitcases, with TV sets and radios, with hams and bottles of Scotch. One mother marched into a store and emerged with her entire family riding on bicycles. (The spontaneous anger of all this is much in doubt. It was evident that false rumors had been deliberately spread, that "Get Whitey" had been legitimatized. Earlier, Stokeley Carmichael had started a tumult in Prattville, Alabama, by turning to another black and saying, "Give me that gun and I'll take care of him [the Assistant Police Chief] myself." Rap Brown, Chairman of SNCC, urged young blacks in Dayton: "Honkey is your enemy. How can you be non-violent in America, the most violent country in the world? You better shoot that man to death.")

Another story hits the headlines. A group of young U.S. blacks (according to the Australian press they are "international larrikins"), is charged with plotting to murder American leaders (President Johnson, Nelson Rockefeller, and John Lindsay were on the death list); and also to get rid of moderates in the civil rights movement, men like Roy Wilkins, executive director of the NAACP, and Whitney Young of the Urban League, and to blame the killing on whites. Under-cover policemen infiltrated the organization, which operated under the cover name of Jamaica Rifle and Pistol Club, but was really a branch of RAM. During the raid, detectives fanned out to different houses in Queens, Manhattan, and Long Island, and picked up the surprisingly

Australia

respectable leaders: Herman Ferguson, assistant junior high school principal; Ursula West, a somber-faced girl who taught in Brooklyn, and Michele Kauroma, the rather attractive wife of a French Guinean student. The interesting thing is that the organization had its roots in the earlier Black Liberation Front, which had been involved in the plot to blow up the Statue of Liberty, and which had had its impetus in Cuba and Algeria.

Danny and I go further north. We travel an all-weather road to Port Douglas past the watery island-starred world of the reef, past bays where crimson-finned sweetlip can be caught, and atolls which host thousands of white sea-birds: we make a long detour to Cooktown to avoid the great jumble of mountains which here press close to the coast. The immediate aim is the annual races at Laura (an outback race meeting and carnival).

We pass the Palmer River (known as the River of Gold) where thousands of Australian and Chinese miners undertook a terrible march over the ranges where many were marooned, many died, many starved; and others were attacked by Aborigines. When, with the disappearance of easy gold, the white miners moved on, the Chinese continued to come in, thousands at a time, transported by entrepreneurs from Hong Kong and Canton at so much a head; patient blue-clad figures, plodding along the trail bent under 160 pound loads carried on bamboo poles, vulnerable without weapons to the blacks who were reputed to prefer their flesh (called "long pork") to the flesh of the white men. So it was that racial rivalry was fostered; the outnumbered whites began to protest and demonstrate. Not far from here a notice pinned up on a tree stated baldly: Any Chinaman Found Higher Up This Creek Will be Instantly Seized And Hanged Till Dead.

But in spite of such ancient savagery, the upper third of Australia (and this is the military and political point)—the tropical northeast, the Northern Territory Arnheim Land, and the northern part of Western Australia—is often known as "Colored Australia." It has always been like this; it was not only because of the Chinese and Malaysan immigration but because of the climate, the ports, the sea trade, the closeness to the Islands and to New Guinea. The aboriginal reserves were carved out here in the north; the *bèche-de-mer* fisheries were located on northern shores, and pearl shell luggers scouted these reefs; the Peninsula was a last stronghold for the Aboriginal tribes, which intermarried with the more aggressive Torres Straits Islanders.

Cooktown, reached in the late afternoon, combines pioneer charm with geographical advantages. There are rambling pastel-painted hotels;

impressive cedar-panelled banks marking the time when gold poured through the port; a pier standing over a tranquil inlet where today eight or ten people fish in the receding light. The post office, insurance company and telephone company are all in one low room. The boarding house on the hill has a tropical garden with flowers bursting out of the raw red earth. From this same hill the surrounding reefs can be seen, outlined by the white water which signals danger to the navigator; those reefs, intricate and menacing, which crippled Captain Cook's *Endeavour*, and which before World War II had been so exhaustively studied by the Japanese fishing boats.

Here we receive our last letters for some time (these are delivered by the obliging pilot who'd collected the mail in Cairns). It is odd to sit on the bare wooden steps at the boardinghouse surrounded by its raw and tropical garden and read mail from New York City—especially a letter from China expert Karl Wittfogel, who can't imagine (even as he deplores the fact of official casualty figures from one province *only* during the Cultural Revolution: "Struggled against, 1,038; persecuted to death, 61; forced to kill themselves, 6; attempts at suicide, 14; escaped, 41") that the letter will be received in remote Australia (where local "innocents" like Myra Roper have been expounding about the "great Cultural movement in Mainland China") and read in even *remoter* Australia where not so long ago Chinese coolies fell to the spears of the blacks.

"You ask why Westerners are so easily deceived about China, and about China's relation to Vietnam," Karl writes, "well events have made it clear to some critical persons, but not to the majority . . . the relationship of China to Vietnam is a broader question than pure knowledge of China itself . . . After World War I, according to Mao, Communism covered one sixth of the globe; and after World War II it had spread to cover one third. Mao boasted that after the next big war, the Communists would be able to seize the entire world . . . There's a good chance of that happening now as you can see . . . It's not just Vietnam. In terms of influence there is a lot more. Cuba for instance . . . But there's one thing you have to accept and this refers to Russia also, but especially to China, since we are talking about China and about totalitarianism and about despotism. This is that the *depotism is permanent* . . . Machiavelli said, 'You can't penetrate oriental despotism, and if you can, you can't do anything about it.' "

Along the road to Laura through the burning almost motionless air, slowed up by abrupt drops down ungraded banks into dry creekbeds (these are known as "jumpups"). A landscape that seems to shimmer with the pinks, ochres, reds of bare eroded earth; half-dead gums, their roots elongated as they grapple for the friable soil. Danny comments: "We ought to bring the Parliamentarians up here and give them a good boneshaking! Canberra's a beaut' town; it's away from all the hard realities!"

Australia

Finally we come to a low wooden bush building with an overhang and pink painted pillars. This is the Laura pub. Opposite are several tents, a merry-go-round, and three parked trucks. The hotel is somnolent; the bar is padlocked; in the kitchen two men in denim pants and white cotton singlets are holding mugs of tea and sitting near the stove. "This is Laura," one of them says as he blows at his pannikin, "five miles to the races, and three hundred miles to Coen." On the door outside there is a large hand-printed notice: Visitors Booked At This Hotel But Will Be Wanting Meals Please See The Cook Before Partaking Of Meals And Don't Go Through Kitchen To Outhouse. The store next door sells everything from rope, lanterns, picks, dynamite, horse hobbles, to canned tuna, fresh barrimundi, English saddles, U.S. riding boots, and Australian hats. The proprietor, "Bowie," maintains that the street outside is the only street in town, suitably called Terminus Street. Also that the population of the town is usually thirteen. "There's two children up for a visit," he adds thoughtfully.

Five miles through the bush to the Races. Numerous people, mostly men, all sunburnt, all with their sleeves rolled up, all with wide bush hats on their heads; women in fresh cotton under the bough shelters with their families; boys and girls, already replicas of their fathers and mothers; jockeys (gathered from the best local and station riders); gleaming horses, their hides striped with shade; a group of aboriginals in brilliant colors—scarlet, azure, green, china white—with dark impassive faces. It is all very familiar suddenly, the dust, the muted bush, the pound of hooves around the rough track, the stance of the bushmen as they lounge against fences or balance endlessly in what is called the "bushman's squat." The cries during the races: "That one's a dead bird (sure to win)," "He's a goer (trying hard)," "I got beat by an eyelash."

Two days later the caravans are beginning to move off along the solitary road. A great sea of golden beer bottles sparkles in the sun. One or two sprawling figures lie asleep face downwards in the heat.

From Laura to Lakefield in a van (with nine horses in the back): the driver, Jack, has a strong-featured face, a Wild-West moustache and a pair of bold black eyes. He sings over and over one verse of a song:

> Stir your wallaby ste-ew
> Make soup with a kangaroo ta-ail,
> I tell you things are mighty crook
> Since Dad's got put in ja-a-a-il

In spite of this song, Jack is one of those Australians with informal but erudite tastes, and keeps a copy of Villon on the back seat. He also disposes of unimaginative officials by saying candidly that he'd "knock 'em arse over head."

Australia

At Lakefield (an American-owned cattle station) the long, low homestead is shaded by lemon, orange, and custard-apple trees. Lex Bell, patient long-legged manager starts his day around six in the morning: his wife Veronica moves between the kitchen, the laundry, and the garden in her cotton dress and sunbonnet—sometimes with a child on her arm, sometimes with a basket of vegetables, sometimes talking to the Aboriginal women gathered on a patch of grass near the door. We eat station food; vegetables from the garden, beef, and *burrimundi* cooked in the leaves of wild ginger.

Leaving Lakefield in one of the Bush Pilot planes (a single engine Cessna 172) piloted by Bill Forwell, a daring still-blonde Scotsman who'd been a squadron leader in the RAF, and flown in Malaya during World War II. We drop down at station after station leaving parcels, mail, and supplies at the lonely airstrips. A woman with a small child stands by a station wagon. Her hair blows in the wind; she stands there lifting an arm in a farewell salute as the plane, curiously light and open speeds towards Jennie's Tableland. At Merina Plains two children come scampering, one calling; "He's coming...He's coming ..." while the pilot holds a handkerchief in the wind. At Lily Vale there is a small bush homestead, its garden bright with flowers, and a barefoot boy, shadowed by a big straw hat and followed by a sleepy-looking dog. The plane flies over low worn-looking saw-toothed mountains, over a sea of drab olive, over empty meandering river-beds. A moment later we plunge towards Violet Vale, where a parcel is held out to a waiting boy. "Goodo," the boy says with a grin.

As we rise into the air again, Bill Forwell confides to me that the sheep dog following the boy had been attacked by wild pigs, which had almost torn its insides out. The boy had pushed the entrails back in with a pencil and sewn his pet up. "Now it seems as rr-r-right as r-r-r-rain"!

Later at Coen (a tiny settlement with a population of 140, a school, a store, a police station where the beat is 70,000 square miles, and a hotel of corrugated iron painted shell pink with an overhang and pale blue pillars) we gather to say goodbye to Bill Forwell. None of us is to guess that we will never see again this casual, competent pilot, that in ten days his Cessna is to go down in some part of that lonely country.

A fortnight later, on the very tip of Cape York—that is at the "top" of Australia—staring across a narrow brilliantly blue channel to the nearest northern islands, and beyond that to the guitar-shaped island of New Guinea.

And it has not been easy to reach. Travel had been diverse: by Comalco (the mining company) plane across the "Terrible Archer" and the "Great Divide," to the shores of Albatross Bay on the Gulf of

Australia

Carpentaria, where the red terrain is composed of almost pure bauxite—purplish, scarlet, orange, tomato, pale salmon (red on the cliffs, red washed like blood into the sea); where the mining company has broken the isolation of the coast by building a self-sufficient town and a wharf big enough to berth 60,000 ton ships; where a community made almost entirely of males is working to bring an annual 2,500,000 tons of bauxite to world markets. After this there had been a ride in another one-engined Cessna (a Skylane 182) with His Grace the Archbishop of Carpentaria (Right Reverend John Mathew) and his pilot son Tony. The plane which flies over this superdioscese is owned by the Church of England, and in defiance of recent downplaying of Empire is painted red, white and blue.

There followed a trip by jeep to the old Mission Station and settlement at Bamaga, and then after a few days of waiting, a further day of northward travel by jeep through rough grass-tree country, over tumbled dunes, along sandy avenues lined by trees hung with thousands of wild orchids, and round the uninhabited coast of Cape York's tip, where the untrodden sands are washed by blue seas and stained pink from iron in the soil and rocks. Here at last, standing on the end of the continent (not far from that historic spot where the explorer Kennedy had paid for his efforts with hunger and thirst and the spears of the blacks) one can look out to the Prince of Wales Island, and across the Torres Strait to New Guinea where—at what later became known as Bloody Buna—the few American and Australian troops fought the first major land battle against the Japanese in World War II, and experienced through their own bodies that New Guinea terrain: those gloomy dripping stifling jungles, the icy misted peaks with their treacherous carpets of moss, and the fearsome trails smelling of corpses. Australians who remember that time remember too that the idea of the "colored international," not so labeled in those days, was one of the sharpest weapons of the Japanese, who in the course of their conquests attempted to break the rule of the white man, to degrade him publicly, to weaken his morale, to expose him as no longer omnipotent. And so it was in New Guinea. The Japanese persuaded the New Guinea tribes to build roads for them, to carry stores. They persuaded them that the white man was already defeated. Only as they ended up victors could the Allied troops prove otherwise. And they must often have doubted their capacity for victory, on those razor-sharp ridges, from which they could see at dusk the islands which lie like a barrier (or an invitation) across the northern approaches to Australia.

To be back in Townsville after this journey to the shores of the north demands a certain adjustment. The room at the hotel is tranquil, and a

194

tawny light filters through the shutters. Reading the piled-up letters and newspapers on the wide veranda gives that old deceptive sense of knowing what's going on. Long lemonades are served by a quietly-moving young man in straw-soled slippers.

It is easy enough to pick up the thread of politics. There is really nothing new—all the stories are the continuation of a serial. Through those days in the bush the black guerrilla war in the United States has scarcely ceased. Less than a week ago tanks were rumbling through the streets of Detroit, with a death toll of thirty-three and a heavy financial toll as well. Here for the first time gangs of snipers were roaming the streets and fighting it out with police. Not satisfied with this, angry-eyed Rap Brown called for more violence. "Violence is necessary. Violence is part of America's culture, and is as American as cherry pie," he told cheering crowds of supporters. At a news conference in Washington he called President Johnson a "wild dog" and "an outlaw from Texas" and threatened that the blacks would take "an eye for an eye, and a life for a life." That such groups have their international ambitions becomes clearer than ever. Stokeley Carmichael, for instance, is in England trying to stir up "black anger" in Notting Hill Gate and Brixton. Not so long ago he was in Cincinnatti, Ohio, telling audiences to stop fighting each other, and to go out and fight the police. Carmichael was born in Trinidad, and he has had a British education, with all the formality, the deference to Royalty, and the unsuitable reciting of Kipling's poetry that this implies. Although he has already had plenty of experience with "therapeutic" violence, and has been in the United States many times, it is England which should be the best place to work through that old trauma called the "return of the repressed!"

The riot in Detroit is current; what is of more interest is the information now available about the riot in Newark. In 1964 the Students for a Democratic Society (SDS) and the activist Tom Hayden had come to this potentially explosive city, at the time when SDS had voted out of their constitution the clause declaring Communists not acceptable as members. In other words, the stage was set for SDS to play a "more active" role in sedition. The national secretary, Gregory Calvert, had announced it frankly, "We are actively organizing sedition."

Hayden rented an apartment in Newark's ghetto, and he and his friends called themselves the Newark Community Union Project (the NCUP) and began to agitate about local grievances (of which there were plenty) joining up with the newly militant version of CORE to create a black network across key areas of the city. (When the War on Poverty came to Newark, Hayden and his men managed by protests, demonstrations, and skillful maneuvers to get control of a number of staff jobs, federal funds, and mimeograph machines. "Success," claimed

Australia

two activists in *Studies on the Left* (is), "to penetrate all permeable local organizations and to create or control newly developing traditional structures." And again, "at every level NCUP disrupts . . . it challenges authority.")

Even in the Australian tropics it is easy to imagine how it had all gone in Newark, as the new crop of idealistic students came in for the summer "to work with the poor and deprived." How much in tune with the Tri-Continental Conference it was that Jesse Allen, young Negro militant and man of the streets, went in April with Tom Hayden to Puerto Rico to meet members of the Movement for Independence favored by Havana? Apart from this kind of leadership training, how could emotions in Newark, escalating with the help of SDS, Hayden and his group and the inevitable LeRoi Jones (who had proclaimed that "Hiroshima and Nagasaki after the atom bomb will look like Sunday School picnics compared to Newark when we get through with it") fail to find a suitable outlet? Inflammatory pamphlets; simple instructions on how to make Molotov cocktails; hearings at city hall; picketing; violent confrontations pushed by black liberationists; prophecies (like Ché Guevara's that "blood will flow"); the fantastic exploits of a character called Hassan Ahmed, who called himself "Colonel" and had arrests for forgery and mental incompetence and was invited to the city by SNCC; Hassan's operation of a Black Liberation Center which kept in touch with SNCC and the NCUP and Area Board #3 (this last funded by poverty funds); and Hassan's dramas at city hall where he led cries of "House Nigger" and "Uncle Tom" whenever the Negro chairman tried to speak, and ripped up a stenographer's transcript! So it went. Enter Mr. John (Georgia) Smith, and the riot was on.

The point about the riots is that while a number of the cities concerned had real problems, the "riot-making" shows how well knowledge gained during both old and recent Communist takeovers has been systematized. The formal academies of revolution (in Russia, China, Czechoslovakia, Cuba, etc.) have been turning out graduates at a rapid pace. Since Emilyan Yaroslavsky wrote *The Work of the Bolsheviks in The Army Before the October Revolution*, pointing out that there is nothing spontaneous about "winning over" the masses; the techniques suggested, while they differ in detail, show no great change in aim. The older graduates of the Lenin schools, for instance, like Harry Pollit of Britain, Chou En-lai of China, Gus Hall of the United States, Ernst Thaelman of Germany (not to mention L. L. Sharkey here in Australia), differ in certain ways from the Castros, the Ché Guevaras, the Régis Debrays— and certainly the Rudi Deutschkes and Tom Haydens—but hope to destroy the power of the Western democracies is still the main idea. Courses taught in the Communist academies and institutions, whether in Patrice Lumumba Friendship University (established in 1960 to train cadres for Africa, Asia, and Latin America), in a rough somber valley in Pyongyang, in *Las Minas Frias* in the Sierra Madre, in the varied institutions of Czechoslovakia, or in modern versions of such cement boxes as that in Peking where Keith McEwen suffered for three years, all culminate in the Leninist conception of the forcible seizure of power.

A month or two later, according to the *New York Times*, Sept. 13, a full-dress week-long conference of representatives of the American Left with delegates from North Vietnam, and the South Vietnam National Liberation Front (NLF) took place in Bratislava, Czechoslovakia. According to *Ceteka*, the Czech press agency, this was the most important conference held between the American Left and Communist-led forces in Vietnam. Forty-one Americans were present, including representatives of black power and of anti-war and academic and religious groups. They included Dave Dellinger, Nick Egelson, former chairman of SDS, and Tom Hayden who had in tow among others his protege Jesse Allen, the young ghetto black he had been grooming.

In Australia when one talks about these black riots and murder plots, it is hard to relate them to the first tender beginnings of Aboriginal or New Guinean aspirations. There is no comparison—yet T. B. Millar, a specialist in defense and international relations, notes in his book *Australia's Defense* (published in 1965) that New Guinea is a special defense problem because it is a potential Afro-Asian country, and will be, as time goes on, tremendously open to Afro-Asian agitation and inducement. (The closest Australian island is only a few hundred yards from the New Guinea coast, and hostile forces in Port Moresby could endanger Australian shipping and air routes.) He adds, "The development of a China-oriented Communist Party in Papua and New Guinea is quite possible. It would be surprising indeed if the PKI and other Communist agents were not already secretly at work in the territory."

A friend who knows New Guinea well had talked one day in Brisbane about its horrible weather conditions. While he talked there were even less acceptable thoughts. In New Guinea, as in other isolated areas, the old innocence is ending. There have been growing protests against exploration and the development of land by mining companies, and there is evidence of interested "outsiders" helping to develop nationalist feelings and to force protests of a more political nature. The Australian Federal government has already provided for Aboriginals to own and develop land within the big Northern Territory reserves (there are sixteen reserves in the territory covering about 94,000 square miles) and has agreed to pay Papua-New Guinea local landowners 5 percent of the royalties from mining operations on their land—

concessions which will eventually hasten the assimilation of both aborigines and islanders into their respective communities. All the same, no one needs to be prophetic to assume that these progressive arrangements will not obviate other political developments, that there will not be deliberate attempts by various radical and so-called Third World groups to manipulate unsophisticated natives. Already in Bougainville one of the men on the island, in a motion rather like that of the Buddhists in Vietnam, threatened to cut his throat as a protest against mineral exploration.

In the meantime the inevitable has happened. About a week ago Britain decided to quit Suez. The Sahibs are really going! A friend of Danny's who has been a colonel in the army says that a vacuum has been left in the Pacific. "Moral, of course; it's a long time since we looked to Britain in a practical way." He is a tall, thin man with bright blue rather tired eyes. "We'll have to think more about defense. We'll have to put up the dukes, as they say in the Palace" (a local boxing ring). He turns his blue eyes to observe several young men who rest their brawny arms on the polished wood of the bar, and blow the froth from their schooners. In deference to Australia's tradition of rhyming cant, he says that all they care about is their Lily of Lagooners. Then he adds in a disgruntled way: "What more would they want than their sports, and their bets, and their time on the beach .... They're a lot of 'You'll be right Jacks.' "

August

Now the train is no longer the Sunlander, but the equally modern Inlander, not headed up the coast, but westward towards the center.

Once past Charters Towers the lines cut into the high pink and white clay sidings which redden in the afternoon light, giving symbolic meaning to those signs which always appear beside Australian railway lines—names like The Southern Cross and Last Lagoon—painted on wooden boards, pointing to nowhere, and emphasizing the loneliness of the horizon and the occasional desolate hut. Through the windows an escarpment appears, its sharp broken edge stretching away towards the pale sky; and flocks of brown and white goats stand in shimmering pink-seeded grass. Later as the evening wears on, rounded outcrops appear on the level plain like hard red breasts over which have been thrown silky film-like veils of tawny grass. We are approaching that long tongue of land, which belongs to the immensely old pre-Cambrian shield, and stretches, narrow rusty-red and forbidding, scoured and broken, to separate the east from the west.

Australia

Mt. Isa is a town simply placed in the bare earth, among dramatic and uncompromising ranges baked out of magenta and reddish-brown soil. The houses, in squares with tended green lawns, shining roofs and disciplined streets, lie to one side of the enormous mine open cut—one of the biggest in the world (glistening like a gigantic Colosseum of dull silver, and surrounded by mine buildings and man-made pyramids of rejected ore). The town is generally known as "The Isa" with what the linguist Sidney J. Baker calls that "relentless familiarity of an outback where everyone knew everyone else" (a familiarity now vanishing on a tide of prosperity and increasing population).

In general the country to the west is desolate. It stretches for more than 2,000 miles to the shores of the Indian Ocean on the other side of the continent; a region where the sun is fierce, where little rain falls, where the rivers are dry for the greater part of the year, where iron, cement, or creosoted posts must protect buildings from the white ant. A country of drama, fevers, back-breaking labors, marathon drinking bouts, murders and reprisals—a country which beat back successive waves of strong and determined men. But also a country which documented case histories of doggedly achieved victories over nature. (Mt. Isa, for instance, is a milestone in mining history).

In fact, to travel here is to ask a perennial question. Had it not been for the persistence and plentiful risk capital of the American entrepreneurs, would this parched red region ever have reached its present stage of development? Something more than love of gain pushed these companies to sink so much into Mt. Isa, and would any slow-deciding government have felt this same persistent interest? In such a balance there may lie, even if unpalatable to doctrinaire socialists, an important truth.

For the natural state of a large percentage of the Australian earth was scarcely adequate to maintain those nomad tribes which roamed its surface. In this particular region water had been an eternal problem. The first explorers had experienced a series of defeats. The explorer Burke had climbed nearby ranges and looked down upon the site of Mt. Isa, had named the Cloncurry River, and later filled his flask with its waters; but eventually his men had died one by one, and then he himself was dead at Cooper's Creek further south, as was Wills, his companion, with the dingoes mauling their shriveled bodies. King, sole survivor of the expedition, was rescued as he wandered with the blacks, skeleton-thin and living on roots and seeds.

In "successful" Australia—and these great new mining developments are essentially successful—there would seem to be no reason to project a future in which Third-World politics are going to cause problems. Yet the people in Mt. Isa seem half-fascinated by firebrands like Stokeley

Australia

Carmichael, who has currently been stumping London with *Burn Baby Burn* advice. If the British didn't accept "black power," Carmichael said, he would see that British homes and factories were burned down! He then went on to Prague (there is a rumor that here he picked up cash for his political voyages) and eventually caught a plane for Cuba. In Cuba, he attended (indeed, was the star attraction at) the Latin American People's Solidarity Conference of Revolutionary Forces, which is the immediate offshoot of the Tri-Continental Conference held last year. At this gathering Castro claimed an ideological victory, on the grounds that he has stalemated the United States in Vietnam, because the "theory of guerrilla warfare has been proved beyond argument." How much more invincible will it be against the weak Latin American governments, he went on to ask. (Last December the Havana Radio had reported that the Executive Secretary of the AALAPSO made a decision to set up a school to train cadres for revolutionary movements in conjunction with North Korea; and this year the representatives of Hanoi and the National Liberation Front were present, as well as one officer identified as the commander of those Vietcong forces which destroyed more than $60 million worth of U.S. planes in rocket attacks on the Da Nang base.)

As far as the black power movement in the United States is concerned, Stokeley's role at the OLAS Conference is the most important thing to happen this year. *Prensa Latina* in Cuba quoted his London speeches approvingly. ("In Newark," he had said, "we are applying the tactics of guerrilla warfare. We are preparing groups for our defense in the cities . . . This struggle is not going to be a mere street meeting. It is going to be a struggle to the death.") Two other SNCC representatives attended the Conference, Julius Lester and George Washington Ware, all taking part in a special discussion titled "Support the Negro Population of the U.S." during which Carmichael stated that "we" (U.S. Negroes) are no longer going to allow "our enemies to make us fight against you as we have done in the past. We will not fight in Vietnam, Santo Domingo, or anywhere else in the world. Our fight will be inside the U.S. . . . We are moving towards guerrilla warfare . . . when the U.S. has fifty Vietnams inside and fifty Vietnams outside that will mean the death of Imperialism."

Leaving the hotel with three visiting Americans, we run into some aboriginal boys. Bright moonlight floods the quiet street; the boys wear tight denims, high jackets, waistcoats and broad-brimmed hats. They look like mod-influenced teenagers. Although they seem too young to be drinking, the odor of beer surrounds their heads (which are so well covered with dark wavy hair that the curls escape from under the brims of their hats). Their arms around each other's shoulders, they weave to and fro beneath the wide wooden overhang of the veranda, and talk about some fellow aboriginal inside who'd become too rich and respectable to shout them more drinks. "We're bloody Myalls [wild blacks], mate," one of them says in disgust, his accent ludicrously close to Cockney. "We're bloody Myalls—that's it, mate. Isn't that it?"

"Fair dinkum," mumbles another.

"We're bloody Myalls, we share what we got."

They draw their heads closer together, and the wide-brimmed hats form a perfect barrier.

"Talk lingo, mate, talk lingo," the first one whispers, and for a moment they lapse into their own dialect. Soon, however, they are talking English again, and commenting on the extraordinary meanness of that emancipated "Abo" inside who has forgotten his tribal obligations.

It is hard to tell how long it will take to inculcate young aborigines like this with resentments as fierce as those of Carmichael's followers.

August 16

The last lap of the journey—leaving Mt. Isa by plane for Darwin in the Northern Territory. Almost at once we are flying over "red country," with only the dark of ironwood or the pale green of spinfex to relieve the monotony; or occasionally the yellow stains of poor ground marked by the veinings of waterless rivers; or the bleak dun patches where the rivers have inundated their banks during the immense flooding of "the wet."

The high land of Mt. Isa is left behind; there is a monotone of empty red plain, an ancient surface, worn and harsh.

Eventually far below the straight road to Darwin can be seen, not impressive looking from the air, but still a road. (At the time of World War II there had been no all-weather road to the south, and then, as now, the nearest rail terminals had been 1,000 miles away at Alice Springs and Mt. Isa; small 10-seater planes had been the only air connection with the south, and all supplies had had to be shipped by slow vulnerable 3,000-mile-long sea routes. Today there is not only the all-weather Stuart Highway but a far-stretching network of stock routes and the daily shuttling of big planes.)

Darwin is built on a point of land an extension of which encircles the new harbor. It is not the old wild port it once was—"last port of call before the east," home of trepang boats and pearling luggers, of adventurers and explorers, of outcasts from other cities, of half castes ("yeller fellers") and black velvet. It is a zooming, fast growing, many-

Australia

nationed town of 20,300 people, the up-and-coming port of tropical Australia. It is terribly hot. Red dust drifts in the air and settles on the smooth leaves of the frangipani trees. Many of the men go without shirts and wear only old khaki shorts and thongs on their bare feet. The public servants tend towards spotless white shirts, long shorts, knee socks, and rubber-soled shoes. They stroll towards their offices with brief cases under their arms. There is a relentless glare from the down-pressing sky. With all this something familiar and innocent in the raw, rapidly growing town.

Almost the first requirement in Darwin is to drink at the old "Vic" (a stone-built hotel until last year owned and run by a formidable Chinese family, the Fong Lims). The top floor is rather like a huge open dormitory, almost exclusively male. Downstairs there are three bars with an open-air garden attachment and numerous tin tables and chairs. Business is spectacular—a continuous stream of great schooners of iced beer is pushed along the bar, passed over heads, brought to tables, downed thirstily, and replenished. The crowd includes almost anyone who is in town, but especially workers, managers, ringers from the stations, crocodile shooters, prospectors from the mining camps and out-of-towners from Gove, Groote Eyelandt, and Frances Creek. One of the best known local journalists (a blue-eyed enthusiast called Jim Bowditch) tells how when the place changed hands everyone had come to have a last beer with the Fong brothers, their arms swathed in black crepe. "Arthur Fong was quite a gourmet, too; you'd see this board groaning with buffalo meat, *barrimundi*, goose. But he could be fast moving, when he had to throw someone out he'd vault over that bar and chuck him into the street, scolding him in Chinese all the time. There is a story that one night he chucked out a drunk three times, until at last he asked him where he was staying, and the drunk just managed to hiccup, 'At the V . . . V . . . Vic!' "

Walking with Henry Chan, Mayor of Darwin, who talks of how much of the East is here, "Japan, China, Malaysia, New Guinea, the Pacific, greater Asia. . . . Before the first part of the century there were more Chinese than Europeans; about 11,000 came out to work on the first railway line and to go to the mines. Until 1941 the Chinese completely dominated what commerce there was. Now the Chinese are here still, although there are only about 500 of us, and we are making our sons doctors and lawyers."

Time spent in adjusting to the climate, in swimming in the caressing, over-warm waters east of the town, in reading in the motel about early history. (One book, *Capricornia* by Xavier Herbert, capsules the genesis of a tropical port and has almost everything in it. The first white men, big and ruddy, men of appetite and without social restraints, who preyed on the land and the sea and the aborigines; the overlanders who came to see and remained to develop their own version of cattle kingdoms; the uneasy new bureaucrats of an infant Government Service, resplendent in white linen suits and topees; the builders of the railway line, and the drivers who drank as they drove; the race called "yeller-fellers.") The old skeletons in this community cupboard don't mean much any longer; yet they remain as reminders of the reality of passion. The habits and methods are frowned upon, but their inordinate appeal remains.

In the interest of politics, there is a conversation with an aborigine called Dexter Daniels, of the Nungaburro tribe (born at the Roper River). He is very black, has a short rounded face, rather innocent bulbous eyes and wears a blue shirt and denim pants. His brothers, he tells me, are called David, Dennis, Douglas, Dixie, Dawson, and Davis; and they all attended the mission school, where they learned to read and write. "I wen' to grade seven; then I work three years in the mechanic's garage. I did stock and mustered cattle. In one way I don't know much—but people get together, all the time they get together. I worked with whites at the hospital but I never had a chance to really know them, not side by side. To get to know people you must talk to them first, have *real* talks. It's very hard to live with white people. Sometimes on the station properties, they think I'm a trouble maker."

Apparently Dexter (following the example of his brother Davis) has become interested in politics and in unions; as he says, he has talked a lot to his fellow aborigines and has asked them about their conditions and how they live. "I want to cooperate with the white man if he gives good conditions, but I think the aborigines is used up by white people too much." Now he stands patiently by the fence, one foot resting on the other, a puzzled look, emphasized by the heavy bony ridge over his eyes, on his questioning face. In this particular political world he seems to be a bit at sea.

"Certain things I find is hard to understand. I don't know why the bosses complain. Standards are too hard. If they would give full information and tell the truth, it would be easier." He pauses. "Some of my own people, the Aborigines, are not telling the truth. I find contact very hard. Conversation is very hard, I can say *that*." Again that look of puzzlement. He adds; "I don't like it when people mix drinks."

The next morning he is resplendent in a silky orange shirt, and is a bit more explicit. He says that three aborigines had worked as contractors shooting buffalo, and now wanted to borrow money from him to get a bank book. He is taking rations down to Wave Hill to the strikers who went off the station (Wave Hill is 572 miles away southwest of Catherine and he will camp on the way). "When I am doing something I don't like to be told what to do. I have an interest in the Union, we got to organize; but there are some members of the Communist Party. My brother belongs to the Aborigine Rights Council; he's the President, but he's only a figurehead. Why can't we run our own affairs? They say, it's about time you people run your own, we'll give you every assistance; but at the same time they ask for too many things. When I went to Sydney my first trip, I didn't know much and found I was being used. I went to a meeting and met members of the CP. I talk with the Federal Secretary, that's enough for me. I can't make with any organization that tells me what to do."

Dexter's strangely garbled accounts of Communist encouragement rouse curiosity as to how deep this seeming innocence is, and how long it will be before he knows where his true interests lie. Talking to him is to remember that unless rapid assimilation takes place, "Colored Australia" will provide a political problem by forcing a split between itself and the rest of Australia. The aborigines are reproducing at a much faster rate than the whites; other colored minorities are also multiplying rapidly. As certain sections of the extreme left make a career out of influencing such groups, there will be tremendous efforts to force aboriginal leaders (as also the New Guinea leaders) under the control of the militants. There have already been such efforts.

But Australia with its *outback* and *way back* and *beyond the beyond* has its *Never-Never*, both in fact and myth. It is a country which still seems curiously unaware of its beauties and its treasures. There are those who complain about the omnipresence of Americans and other foreigners in the cattle and mining industries. But the pragmatic point is that through them at last a way has been found to open up these vast (and often difficult) areas—to provide ports, railroads, roads, air routes, services and employment. In short, bauxite and iron and uranium and cattle are doing for the north what gold once did for the south. But more threatening than foreign capital is the withdrawal of the British, the end of the Empire period. On clear days here the Russian fishing vessels can be seen close to the entrance of the Gulf of Carpentaria, and it is common knowledge that these ships are often accompanied by electronic vessels capable of surveying (for submarine purposes) the surrounding seas. And does he, Dexter, know anything about the Russians? "I don't know much." He grins, showing wide white teeth. "Some people don't know your ways, and you can't work with them."

Not far from here, on the other side of the Gulf, there had been a talk with a very different kind of aboriginal. He was introduced to me by a

Comalco mining engineer, Alan Hansel, and his name is Andrew Chevathen, one of the first of his race in Queensland to get the full-award wage. Andrew is tall, light-colored, and looks as though he might have Malay ancestry.

"I wus working on T.I. [Thursday Island]," he says, "the firm I wus working for gone broke; and I decided to see the Director of Native Affairs. He say to me 'How 'bout Weipa?' Well, I never dream of that, but I say I'll try it." He waves an expansive hand towards the impressive machinery and mine buildings. "Comalco wasn't here then. Another enterprise was here. But Comalco took over in 1960, and signed all the boys on."

And how did he like the work?

On the mobile face with the wash of paleness under the dark skin there appears a slightly self-conscious expression. "I liked it at first, Doin' all sorts of jobs." (I gather that he is on the same job every day now, getting up early each morning and working from 6 A.M. to 4 P.M.) "You finds it a bit hard—" he admits. Later at the settlement, surrounded by the vast silence of the bush, Andrew talks again. His pretty wife (whose father comes from the Solomon Islands) listens and smiles gently. There is no electric light in the house, but Andrew pumps up an acetylene lamp and hangs it above the table. One of the four black-eyed children creeps into her father's arms, and buries her face in his shirt.

"You got to do it," Andrew says, referring to the work. "You finds it hard, but you got to do it. You gets the habit. First you don't feel like it, especially going about half a mile up to catch the bus. But then you do it."

He says that the money is good and that he needs it. "Ay yes we *need* it," reiterates his wife in her soft slightly frightened way. She looks proudly around her house, which has green painted walls and a bowl of plastic fruit and flowers on the table. "We need it for the house."

And will they always stay here with Comalco?

"It all depends," Andrew answers in a low voice, "if they don't fire me." It is obvious that he is not sure he can stand the pressures. "Sometimes you gets weary . . . or sick. Or you gets toothaches. Last year I wus six weeks in bed."

And what was wrong, what illness was it?

Andrew thinks for a while and then says in his slow slightly hopeless way, "It was a stone bruise." (When the foreman of the company is asked about this stone bruise, he laughs and says that the effects of the stone bruise might have been complicated by a few hangovers.)

Further up the street there is another aborigine, tall, angular, dark but dressed in "store" clothes, wearing good leather shoes, and a gold ring on one finger. His name is Eddie John.

Australia

"In those Mission days only four or five men worked," he says, "now they can make good money." The light shines on his dark cheeks and the heavy occipital ridge over his eyes. "I love the Mission, jus like my own father and mother, but I work for Comalco and I like it. I like the money. I like the job. I'll always be here . . ."

Did he really like it, or did he just put up with it?

"I bin start workin' when the Enterprise first open the area," he says with pride. "We got all the 'quipment. In the morning I say to the boys 'get up while it cool.' I wouldn't pull sick. Some of them promise, then they fall over one after the other. Not me! Nobody going to have *my* good home." Eddie John seems to feel personally part of the excitement of the bauxite discovery, and he tries to explain what a revelation this discovery has been to him. "I bin part of when they never find bauxite in this place." He smiles expansively. "First we think it just a stone, this bauxite—then in a sudden, it's more than a stone, it's a *valuable!*" His wife in the background smiles too, and nods vigorously.

Professor C. P. Fitzgerald said long ago: "It would seem that the Pacific region is now considered by the Chinese as a part of the world in which they are acutely interested, and where they have a full right of consultation. This means Japan, Southeast Asia, Australia, and New Zealand. Probably they would not be indifferent to anything in the Indian Ocean as far as the coast of Africa. . . . If the countries concerned were brought into the general alignment of Chinese policy instead of that of the United States, it would represent a vast shifting of power in the world."

These remarks remain logical. The aim of any Communist power, either Russian or Chinese, must be to throw its weight against the United States; and if there is no reason to project a military attack on Australia by Red China, it is also obvious that in any final struggle between Western and Communist ideologies it would be essential to the Communists to "deny Australia" to the Americans, and that in any case the Sino-Soviet split does not obviate a Moscow-Peking rapprochment at some future date. Although Communism is not the essence of the military problem, a hostile power, by being Communist, would presuppose the advantage of an already arranged "fifth column" (to which due respect should be given).

Today no wind blows over the glassy water at Fanny Bay. The varicolored cliffs are stained in clays of pink and white, red and yellow ochre. There is the faint sound of a boat somewhere, chug-chugging out for a day's fishing. This is how it might have been on that peaceful morning of February 19, 1942 when Japanese Zeroes piloted by the crack bomber crews trained at the Misty Lagoon, appeared over Darwin.

206

Australia

There was no warning. The bombs fell; bullets and cannon shells cut through the little town splintering the fleet in the harbor as easily as the wooden and brick houses, sending up great clouds of black smoke into the clean blue sky and killing 250 within a matter of minutes—Australians, British, Americans, black, white, brown, half-caste. Twenty-two waterside workers were killed. Forty-five vessels were moored in the harbor as stationary targets—one U.S. destroyer, four U.S. transports, one British tanker, and four Australian freighters were sunk; 160 lives were lost. Burned sailors jumped into the water and covered with oil, crawled ashore to watch the strafing of what remained of their ships. Bombs fell onto the wharf, onto the post office, onto the hospital, Government House, and the Military Barracks. Pilots returning from an abortive mission to Java, returned just in time to be cut to pieces by the strafers.

Yet this all happened after the Japanese had taken Hong Kong, Singapore, Malaysia, and in spite of the fact that in June of 1940, eighteen months before Pearl Harbor, it had been officially accepted that Darwin would be attacked. Citizens in Darwin itself had had to push for more thorough evacuation and more suitable air raid training. Women and children were evacuated at once but those remaining were unsure of their roles. In protesting, one citizen had said, "If the sea lanes are cut by the Japanese, the town will not survive for more than two weeks."

Jim Bowditch says: "How did it happen? Because that is how human beings are, and because human beings up here are bloody well *more* like that. Some people wouldn't be evacuated because they didn't believe there was any danger. Others because they wanted to protect their property. Others because they wanted to be in on the fight, to take a poke at the Japs. There were blokes who wouldn't even dig air raid trenches. There was a shortage of food, but a lot of citizens were more worried about the shortage of beer! The Resident was a straitlaced kind of chap and didn't seem to want to make too much of a fuss. Then the command chain was all tangled up. The alert wasn't sounded till McManus went outside headquarters and saw the Japanese planes with their bomb bays open. . . ."

There are two islands immediately across the Channel from Darwin: Melville and Bathurst. I go to Melville to admire the carved Tiwi graveposts called *Pukamuni*; to visit the mission where a staff of twenty-three teach, preach, and supervise; to see the fast disappearing polygamous households.

The brief trip across the straits is easily done by plane and today almost a whole side of the airport happens to be lined by Japanese—about forty of them—young, neat, alert, smiling, intensely polite,

Australia

waiting for a plane to take them to Port Hedland to work with the iron-ore crews and to man the ships which will transport ore back to Japan. None of them speaks English, and they are represented by a Japanese "travel" man, who has them all trying out their first words. It is clear that at this moment the Japanese are not considered enemies!

Across the straits, one steps out onto a dusty airstrip where the long yellowish grasses bend to the wind and a bearded heath-like plant, a kind of myrtle, has strange ancient-looking lavender flowers. The seas spread around the island in streaks of blue and peacock green. There are the usual houses with faded paint and red tin roofs. Some of the women walk bare breasted. Dark children play under the mango trees. The men have dinghies with outboard motors and go into the creeks and bays to hunt fish and crocodile. In May and September everyone goes "bush" to look for wallaby, snake, grubs, and sugarbag from the tiny stingless bees. But these nomads and hunters are no longer innocent of the wider world. Some of them carry transistors, and at this moment are enchanted by a popular song called "Don't be a Fool," which they croon constantly.

At the hospital, airy, gay with cretonne, they try to teach the visitors a little *Tiwi*. Mary Concepta, a dark girl with a curly mop and a blue dress says that she is of the Flying Fox *totem-tauikimi* and that she is never going to marry ("Don't like 'too' much"). Everybody laughs.

Mary's mother, called Sophie, wears only a lap lap of the same bright Ricketts blue. She is enormous, Amazonian, and her breasts swing as she stands by the fire, moving her monumental arms and crooning "Don't be a fo-oo-ol."

They all accompany me on the walk back to the airstrip, past the carved Christ of the Pukamuni, rounded like an old gravepost. One of them holds my hand affectionately. "We going bush next week . . . Catch crab . . . Catch honeybag." Their dark, intent, faithful-looking faces stare upward as the plane leaves.

On the morning of the Japanese attack in 1942 the first messages had come from these islands. On Bathurst, Father McGrath was alerted by Tiwis, who saw from their houses more planes high up in the sky than they had ever seen at one time before. The Father ordered evacuation of the village and as he transmitted the news to Darwin, one of the Tiwis Paul Mangurrupurramili, said "Four squadrons, Father." This alarm should have given Darwin twenty minutes notice but, apparently, it was thought there in Darwin that the planes were those which had already taken off for Java.

So began Australia's Pearl Harbor. As the bombs crashed onto the small town (the Japanese seemed infuriated that the Australian blue ensign still flew, and tried again and again to shoot it down), patients in the hospital were placed under the beds. As soon as the attack died down, the surgeons began to operate on the wounded (148 cases came in within a few hours). When the battery operating the emergency lights failed, the operating was done by the light of torches held by volunteers. At the military base the communications system was knocked out and orders had to be dispatched on foot. This led to conflicting commands. Some airmen told to go south for half a mile to a more protected point, kept walking south ("Where is Adelaide?" one of them asked. "Twenty-five hundred miles straight down the road" was the answer.) The Governor ordered a freight train to be loaded with the wounded and the old, and this train had to be guarded by two marines to prevent panic-stricken civilians from climbing onto the roof. "There was an awful panic, a lot of men went bush," one of the officers said, "it was a horrible mess." "Inadequate emergency training was partly responsible," another officer added, "as were also rumors that the Japanese had invaded . . . in fact, when this rumor went round, dozens of men crashed through fences and began walking south." (Some got as far as Batchelor, 65 miles away; others to the Adelaide River, 72 miles; and one even reached Melbourne, 2500 miles.) According to Douglas Lockwood's *Australia's Pearl Harbor*, 5 days later, 278 men were still missing. (The commonly accepted belief is that, if the Japanese had made two assault landings at the Adelaide and Daly Rivers districts and linked up with northeast and southwest thrusts, the Darwin area might have been cut off with all its installations . . . In other words an invasion, if it had been attempted, might well have succeeded, or succeeded in the immediate limited sense. Because of this, it remains the more interesting to hear in Australia the extreme Left and its vague-thinking followers ranting against the Americans whose help was not only essential once before, but whose help in any future military crisis would probably again be decisive.)

Standing at the wharves and talking about Australia's defense, J— comments in his flat humorous voice that the "blankety-blank coast is 12,400 miles long." He then points out how extended the lines of supply are, how dependent the country still is on overseas sources, how most of the tin and rubber comes from Malaysia, how in case of war there would be a problem with military supplies, how small the Navy is, and how there are not enough bases for docking and repairs. "With the Brits going we're not at all sure how long we can use Singapore." And Timor and New Guinea? He laughs. "It would be a beaut' thing for Australia if they'd sink into the sea."

With only a few days more on the continent, it seems just as logical to dream optimistically of a future Pacific society (many-nationed, multi-racial, strong, healthy, tolerant) as it is to fear war or invasion. At

Australia

all events there is only one thing that suggests itself as certain: it is that Australia has a geographical fate, as well as that historic one which Captain Cook implied as he planted the Union Jack into the sandy soil of Botany Bay, a fate not yet known but drawing its inspiration from the Pacific, and from those wreaths of islands which adorn the Timor and Arafura and China Seas.

THE RETURN

September 1967

To be back in New York City is to feel momentary pride; pride in the tall erect buildings which pierce the September sky, a sky of that deep cold northern blue, so different from languorous and paler ones under which I have been for so long. Pride too in this hard Manhattan (built upon rock) where that relentless avalanche of traffic, spins and purrs, grinds and lurches down the long-suffering streets day after day, night after night. Streets where even the steam which gushes from vents, basements, and manholes curls around the buildings as if to suggest the insistent effort of an active people. And to be back is also to realize how far away Australia is, how clean still (though through no fault of her own!), how close to beginnings long overlaid in the polluted, choking, tired, overworked industrialized West.

At the hotel the windows don't open. Why?

"Because the whole hotel is air-conditioned." (The bellboy is curiously loveable and bears the firm stamp of Manhattan.)

"But they should at least open. There's nothing like real air!"

The bellboy nods his rounded head under the unsuitable maroon pill-box cap. He agrees, lightly, alertly, with a grin. "It's better, real air, even when it stinks!"

The return comes not long after a nine-day telephone workers' strike which had been triggered by a number of muggings and assaults, and now about 2,500 repairmen and installers are going back to work under protective escort. There are also signs around town which say The Fireman is Your Friend—Don't Fight Him.

But a colleague is reassuring. "You get used to it; besides you're all right where you are. But they say that in Wall Street some of the firms are hiring armed guards to take secretaries who work late down to the

The Return

subway, in fact, private agencies are doing a roaring business." Later walking up Forty-third Street in the broad daylight he tells about the *Times*, which had just approved extra lighting for its main entrance because of a printer who was strangled a month or so ago as he took a nap in his car opposite the building. "Well what can you expect? There are some good places around here, but also the street crawls with prowlers, muggers, perverts, addicts, drunks, and prostitutes."

And how do people manage; how do they live and function?

He adopts the tone of interested observer. "Well, many Americans are following the 'temporary' method of locking and double locking, of setting up all sorts of alarms and precautions, of living an embattled existence. The *Times*, for instance, has been giving pep-talks, warning employees not to talk to strangers, not to reply to insults, not to congregate on the streets."

To reinforce this rather grim impression of lawlessness intruding, and even taking over, areas in the center of the city, there are said to be other kinds of increases, an increase in the sale of LSD for instance. Then the struggle between the generations seems worse too, with the free-floating hostility and hatred which goes with it, and which somehow blends curiously with political struggle, and with what is called "civil disobedience."

To be in touch again with friends, with writing colleagues, to read an endless accumulation of magazines and newspapers, is to receive a flood of unpleasant information, of unwelcome feedback, to be aware of suspicions which are hard to avoid or forget. The old excitement and the old sense of being *au courant* which New York City provides (as if the electric current of the world ran right through the heart of it) is as potent as ever, but it is because of this unfailing heart-like beat that there is now such a sense of vulnerability. This is a living city. But what if it were to be fatally wounded?

At a cocktail party on Fifty-eighth Street enfeeblement almost seems possible as if through the prism of gold in a whisky glass, the tiny images of people shrank and disappeared; only their voices speaking; of the latest article on Vietnam, of Ché Guevara, of the trouble on the San Francisco State College campus, of the hurricane Beulah, of Dean Rusk's daughter marrying a Negro. As if there had been no visit to Australia, people here are still talking about Vietnam, and the talk has the same obsession that politically-oriented Americans remembered during the Spanish Civil War; or which Proust records as being shown by his contemporaries with regard to the Dreyfus case.

"It's napalm that gets me!" This from a rather aggressive woman, tall, thin, elegant, with eager snapping eyes. "Carol was trying to tell me that bombs were worse than napalm, that not many people were

214

getting 'napalmed' . . . is that what you call it? All I could say is why differentiate—children are children . . . *babies* are *babies*." But does she really think that many people, especially babies are being burned by napalm? Isn't *some* sort of effort made not to use it on villages?

"Well, it's in all the papers. Besides, napalm bombs *are* being dropped. I tell my husband that if he went into the army I'd *divorce* him"! She takes another drink with an air of defiance. Someone standing nearby says that 2 million dollars had been collected in the United States to help children burned by napalm, and that the International Red Cross had sent a team to Vietnam to bring the children back for rehabilitative surgery here, but that none of them could be found. Not a single case!

"Where did you learn *that?*" the first woman demands in a voice of shocked horror.

"I was on the Committee which met to consider it," the other woman said mildly. "I was at the meeting when the report was made."

Behind this conversation another one had started, which had to do with the essential nature of the war. A big rather solemn man is inquiring, "War has always been horrible, hasn't it? Didn't Mao say that a war isn't a dinner party?"

"A *war!*" the "napalm" woman objects. "It seems more like a lynching party of big white Americans murdering little thin Vietnamese!"

"But there are *other* Vietnamese. Aren't the South Vietnamese small and thin too?"

"The war is so . . . *dirty!*" someone says now. (Yet, in fact, and although this has been obscured by certain sections of the press, in no other modern war has so much effort been made, even at the risk of life, to avoid unneccessary civilian casualties.)

Downstairs on Fifty-seventh Street, the ribbon of asphalt seems empty of life, as if on the surface of the moon, and this in spite of the warmth a moment ago of fifty people talking, laughing, greeting friends, making plans, tilting their glasses.

Later

The interest in Ché Guevara results from the Bolivian government letting it be known that he is (or has been) in the southwest of the country with a band of sixty Cuban-trained guerrillas. During August, an army patrol discovered a hideout, which seemed to have been left in a hurry, on a 2,500 acre farm north of Camiri. A roll of film was discovered there, a diary, and twenty-one forged passports from seven Latin American countries. One of the passports showed Ché in disguise with a false fringe of grey hair over his forehead. There was also the

The Return

picture of a woman—an Argentine companion called "Tania" (who has already been killed in a skirmish with the army). The fingerprints on the passports matched. The farm had been purchased by a Castro front man. Large supplies of food and ammunition were found in nearby caves, where there was also found a small shoe factory (as per *Guerrilla Warfare*, Ché's book, "Good shoes are more important to a guerrilla than food or his rifle . . .").

Even if Ché is no longer in Bolivia, his having been there at all suggests the continuing implementation of Cuba's plans for revolution; the amount of money which Castro is willing to spend (the cost of such an action with weapons, airfares, food, etc., runs into millions); the fact that Ché can't be so much out of favor as is suggested; and above all, of course, that he isn't dead in Santo Domingo. In fact the salute to Ché in Cuba at the end of the OLAS Conference ("wherever he may be"), the concentration on Ché the guerrilla, Ché in fatigues, Ché in the jungle—the Ché who had already sent out a lyrical appeal to create "one, two, many Vietnams," all this suggests that a vast propaganda campaign is being mounted for his cause.

It is important to adjust rapidly to the American scene again because a trip half way around the world is planned for the coming year. But something about the "climate" makes this difficult, a kind of lunacy which has its humorous side but is as hard to disregard as a fever. When SNCC (whose anti-Semitic handouts are difficult to read) asks for money from the liberal community, the spontaneous reaction is to ask: "Are they *serious?*" Then coffee at the Columbia Student's Cafeteria with a group of younger friends is disturbed by two Puerto Rican radicals from Harlem circulating among the tables, and asking us to sign a Separatist petition. They seem to think the news that they are *"Independistas"* is sufficient inducement.

"But your group advocates armed struggle, and the Puerto Ricans have already voted down independence by a large majority. Are you being realistic?" As if the link between SNCC and Stokeley were quite enough to obviate the vote of an electorate, one of them answers angrily, "Mari Bras signed a protocol with Stokeley; we think *this* is realistic!"

The sense of a coherent society is not helped by a welcome back telephone conversation with Jasmin.

"I have been hospitalized almost all the time you were away. What happened? Well, I was God's chosen in an automobile accident. Went off the road at 85 miles an hour on the throughway coming from New York City. Yes, the car went out of control and turned over three times and was demolished. I got a concussion and broken nose and several chipped bones and a sprained ankle. . . ."

216

The Return

How could such a serious accident have happened since she had no license and no car? Was she alone?

"It was a rented car. Junior was waiting for me to come to pick up some stuff. Was I high? Well, I was on pills. The doctors say I am lucky to have my life, but Mama thinks I'm being kept for the uses of the Lord. I had to get back on dope to try to rid myself of anguishment and nightmares." There is a drop in her voice which heralds a plea for help. "I need a crib, because I'm kissing ass to stay with so-called friends up here. . . . If only I could lay my hands on a few hundred dollars"?

The fantasy world of the slightly more educated is also hard to deal with. A flood of letters from Samuel. Samuel is a small, big-eyed Jewish homosexual. He is lonely and touching, does pornographic sketches for his scanty living, makes dancing rituals to keep himself in touch with his traditions, and seems to drown in that "climate" which is so much part of the current U.S. scene. He also has a strange not-too-comfortable verbality.

"We are entering a new era. Radically new. New music and art. Drug use is part of the coming wave. Maryjane and LSD can both be part of civilization. A whole mannerist approach to existence, foreign to the fight-for-survival kick, a crash through program of world unity which will snowball into sophisticated hedonism. Not simply drink, eat, and so on, but sensations of *extreme* pleasure. We must have non-hysterical controls like in Czechoslovakia"(?)

He goes on about politics. "What is the connection between psychedelics and Vietnam? Well, Vietnam is only the speed freak kick for the U.S. economy."

When I see him we discuss LSD, with which he has been experimenting for a year and a half. "Has it changed me—I mean has turning-on changed me? Let's see. My teacher says not me but there has been a terrible personality disruption with his other students. He's seen *many many* problems. . . One of my friends says that LSD was good for me, that it opened me up, and that I should take it more regularly." His big round eyes widen and the light dangling above is reflected in them.

But didn't *anyone* say that LSD had harmed him?

Samuel drops his eyes as if ashamed, and nods. His fringe of which he is very proud is glued to his forehead. "Yes, my agent Sarah Slapp was worried after I'd taken it. She said that I used to be very *frightened*, that when I came to her office, I'd just *sit* there . . ." His enormous anxious eyes search *my* face. "What do *you* think?" (It seems impossible to say that he himself, his whole presence, as much his difficulty in concentrating as his inability to type letters properly, is the answer to his question.) He goes on: "I think that consciousness is expanding. It is very rapid *supra* (that is over the heads of politician's convictions),

The Return

waves of repulsion for control mechanisms leading to destruction. . . . The world is turning. And no ideology, no problem; just turning almost as if the axis is shifting." He looks at me with a delighted child-like expression. "Wow"!

As a continuation of the Australian experience I now see that the attempt to publicize America's bungling effort in Vietnam as hideously malevolent, is of definitive importance because it shapes the emotions of citizens here who will decide whether or not the Communists are to be given their way. There are all the usual signs of the old propaganda drive. An article by Sydney Hook in the *New Leader* contains questions about the use of wounded and hospitalized American prisoners for publicity purposes, and explains that it is impossible to know to what extent the prisoners were threatened, and were unable to communicate this to the rest of the world. There is another ceremony described in the *New York Times* in which some American prisoners are shown being released, with activist Tom Hayden (to whom they are being handed over) standing there with a portentous expression. (As Sydney Hook says, it is all very reminiscent of Korean-style brainwashing.) On the newsstands there is even the same *Children in Vietnam* booklet, which was branded in Australia by the External Affairs Minister Hasluck as "malicious distortion." It shows precisely the same small wounded Vietnamese girl hobbling along with a stick; which picture Hasluck points out was originally issued by the U.S. Information Service as that of a child orphaned during a Vietcong attack on the Catholic village of Dong Xai in June of 1965. Now the little girl is labeled as a victim of American action.

In the world inhabited by the victims of heroin some sense of relief operates because here no one pretends to be interested in the national destiny. Jasmin brings news that Cleo, pregnant by her "big blue from Georgia," is adrift in New York City (the "Feds" having caught up with Beetle in Chicago) and has gone back to the old trade. Cleo, she says, has been living in Beetle's carpeted wall-to-wall "stable" (apartment) in Chicago, with its glamorous two-tub bathroom and its aquamarine flood-lit basin—over which "Thievin' Annie" (a "dip-rod" named in the manner of eighteenth century London) and Jerry, known as "Worm," labored as they "shot up" under ceiling lights made in the shape of imitation tulips of black and buff-colored glass. "Thievin' Annie" is reputed to have the most lustful and diverting left hand in the world, and the most skillful and thievin' right! In her black satin dresses and with her Bela Lugosi makeup, she forms a suitable partner for a quick-footed man called Jughead (according to Jasmin, one of the "sharpest dressers" on the Avenue).

"Cleo was off the stuff then, and snorting cocaine with Beetle," Jasmin goes on. "But then she got pregnant, and Beetle he's soft for kids, and he put her in a three-room suite in a hotel on the Drive—all the walls papered in brown with a band of peach satin round the window, and big peach cushions, and a long chair in orange. It was decorated by a faggot . . . but then one day the Feds broke in while Beetle was lacin' his shoes."

What happened?

"They let theirselves in with a passkey, and they say 'Come on, Mr. Connors, the game's up . . . lets get going."

And Cleo?

"You know Cleo, always the lady. She says they were undignified with him, and she tell them, 'You don't have to *degrade* him while you *apprehend* him.' Then they turned on her [Cleo passes white] and they ask her what's she doing with this 'nigger,' and Beetle breaks in and says 'She gives me what I need, besides she's not white.' Cleo was real mad at that and called out while they was dragging him out of the apartment that he was as good as they were and not to do a snow job." Jasmin adds philosophically, "Beetle comes from the South; he always was one to clean up after himself."

October 9

The current of the revolutionary impulse flows as ever. The papers are full of the capture and death of Ché Guevara. He was taken at La Huguera in southern Bolivia, as his rifle was shot out of his hands. Later he said, "I am Ché Guevara and I have failed." He was carried wounded to a village schoolhouse and interviewed by a Colonel Zenteno (it is said a representative of the CIA was also present). During this interrogation he admitted that he had received no support from the Bolivian peasantry. Afterwards he was executed. The body was taken to the Hospital del Senor de Malta at Vallegrande where it was identified by journalists and others—the curly unkempt chestnut hair, the blue eyes, the scar on the hand . . . and the black bullet holes.

Ché and his band had been roaming over their territory (a strip of land about 75 miles wide and 200 miles long from Camiri to Samaipata, which is 60 miles southwest of Santa Cruz) all through the spring and into the summer. On July 6, when Danny and I were setting off on the journey to Cape York, Ché and his guerrillas had taken Samaipata and blockaded the main road, a victory which had demoralized the Bolivian soldiers because it had taken place to the accompaniment of a miner's strike, and to some signs of popular sympathy in urban areas. But after that the honeymoon was over. (As far back as 1963 the Bolivian government had been able to prove that two Bolivian Com-

The Return

munists were working closely with Cuban agents to push a bitter demonstration. In 1964 the UPI had reported the discovery of Castroite guerrillas on the eastern border; in August of the same year the last Cuban diplomat was expelled from Bolivia. Now Ché, inspirer of agitation, had chosen this poor and undeveloped, but geographically central country for his experiment. The adventure was "imposed" upon the country. It was a tiny foreign invasion with no base in Bolivia itself; an exercise in revolutionary vanity.

And it had not been long before things had begun to go badly for the guerrillas. "A black day," Ché had written in his diary before the hideout was discovered. "I made it by sheer guts, for I am exhausted." Without peasant support there was little chance of bringing in fresh recruits. With insecure lines of communication the small band, already decimated by sickness, accidents, ideological divisions and petty quarrels, was isolated from Cuba, the source of supply and encouragement. The leader, Ché himself, was plagued by chronic and now crippling asthma.

Tonight at dinner with friends. The teen-age son comes home from school and says with tears in his voice: "Ché is dead . . ." and he goes to his room. Almost overnight more posters begin to blossom on city walls, in bookshops, in college classrooms. The dark, sometimes soft eyes look out of the rather immature face; the young *aficionados* see in them the reflection of their own adolescence. It was the old clash between life and death. (Fidel had been described by a friend who used to see him in Mexico as "fondling" his machine gun, and Ché also admitted that he liked the "clatter" of the machine gun. With this macabre liking went a belief in the necessity of hatred, a hatred which could transform the guerrilla into an "effective, violent . . cold, killing machine." Ché seemed indeed more obsessed with violence and death than with change per se.)

[A year after his death one of his articles published in *Verde Olivo* stressed the necessity for bloodshed. "Rivers of blood will have to flow—the blood of our people is our most sacred treasure . . . it must be spilled." In fact the lengths to which this young intellectual, this self-appointed stirrer-up of liberation movements, was willing to go, is demonstrated by the added words, "We affirm that we must follow the road to liberation, even if it costs millions of atomic victims. . . ."]

It is in any case worth remembering that the Bolivians alone accuse Ché of being responsible for the deaths of fifty soldiers and civilians; and that it was Ché—sharing of course the responsibility with Castro and his brother—who led the first reign of terror against dissidents in Cuba, and who dictated the first purges—during which, according to Ed Tetlow, correspondent for the *London Daily Telegraph* in Havana, four tribunals were sitting at one time and judging up to eighty persons in each hearing.

November

The tide of opinion has turned; polls show that public opinion is increasingly against the war. For the first time it is possible to imagine that the United States will be morally (if not actually) defeated in this struggle. More and more students are taking courses on how to avoid the draft; in such cases a high moral decision has about it the aura of a lack of conviction because it chimes in with self-interest; to this there is an added bitterness. Men fight "not to fight"; and those who go to "Nam" from the ghetto are able yet again to complain of exploitation.

But it is not only a time of civil disobedience; it is also a time of palmistry, of dream interpretation, of astrology, of throwing the changes—a time when many think that "ego" and "will" are responsible for the state of the world ("You have to admit that the linear thing has got us into the mess we are in," one student confides), a time when men and women at great universities neglect famous lecturers to study the occult in little back rooms; and Ph.D.'s desert their desks for laborious building with their own white hands of little not-very-beautiful adobe houses.

These inroads into the university community, all part of the strange "homogenization" of American society, help to explain why newspaper reportage also tends to be unprofessional. William Clarke (*The Fabian Society*) notes that fifty years ago all the press writers in London could have been gathered into a single room. "Today all told they number 10,000." It seems not without reason to fear that the "soft society" as someone has called it, is being handed over to the media; that the avalanche of reporters, journalists, announcers, news analysts, writers dealing with the news can have a directive as well as a "clarifying" effect. One macabre aspect of the reporter-flood pouring through Vietnam is that only in the south are the reporters able to operate freely. (Those who are invited to the north are of course well briefed, carefully accompanied on all their expeditions, and as a general rule serve the North Vietnamese cause.) It is too much to expect anything but one-sided reporting.

At lunch Sol Sanders, who is a tall, rather cheerful, but serious-looking man, a long-time journalist and resident of Southeast Asia, philosophizes that this is a scene viewed through the eyes of those who think the country is another kind of United States. "They [the young journalists] swarm into Saigon with no previous knowledge, few speaking the language, and many of them pre-judging; in fact they are sent out to turn in work reflecting not the horrors of the war but the horrors of what the United States is doing there . . . in other words, to deliver the goods."

The Return

"Whatever the truth is," he asks, "why this attitude of hallowed respect towards Communism in Southeast Asia? The Communists, after their purges were over, had the greatest appeal to the old aristocratic elite which has formed Asian societies, in one form or another, for centuries. This elite carries with it a whole aristocratic ritual. The Minister for Education in Sukarno's regime was a member of the Javanese *Priyayi* nobility, which goes back to the seventh century; this man who was awarded the Lenin prize used to bow his way out of Sukarno's presence, and to use old forms of address reserved for the ancient court of Central Java. There is a basic elitism in these regimes decked out in Marxist slogans. No member of the North Vietnamese Lao Dong is proletarian . . . all are of the Mandarin class, linked with that which helped the French colonists to rule."

Sol pauses to add with a certain gloomy forbearance, "What are intellectuals *for* if not to know these things? All distinctions seem to go by the board. Surely it is the *Americans*—whatever their failures and blunders—who represent the 'revolutionary' force in Southeast Asia today?"

He adds, "There are other writers, Mary McCarthy for instance, who went to Vietnam already knowing what they wanted to say." (Surprisingly in view of Mary McCarthy's role in the thirties and forties, she betrays signs of being out-of-date about the current international Communist movement. Like other writers on Vietnam, for instance Frances Fitzgerald, and in spite of a crisp command to Diana Trilling "Let us drop the crocodile concern and talk about realities," she herself falls into extremely naive situations. She romanticizes the lyrical aspects of the North Vietnamese revolution.) [Later she dismisses without effort the tragic mode of departure of the refugees from the North. And she speaks mockingly of "sanguinary scenes"; she assumes that religious groups can be expected to survive as groups, despite their religious commitments "just as Catholics and priests have in the North." Not herself in danger of having to "endure under Communism," she mocks "eager beaver types who are the Communists' opponents," and makes fun of them because they expect to be hurt if the Americans leave. She says regarding this fear of the Vietcong, that "to an outsider this . . . certainly appears phobic, the product of an overworked imagination," and goes on to add that "eyewitnesses and second-hand accounts of Vietcong terror are magnified, and projected into the future." It does her little credit that she seems to be insulated from concern, even while she classifies herself as an "intellectual."]

Frances Fitzgerald, writing on a rather different level and purporting to be more thorough, is even less impressive. On the whole she is only more imbalanced. She speaks, for instance, of the origins of the NLF in an exceedingly "cloudy" manner, rather as if she could scarcely account for their existence. She either ignores or does not know the evidence (from Communist sources alone) of how Hanoi put these groups together. As one student of Southeast Asia (Dennis Duncanson) notes, she writes as if the NLF "simply evolved out of the southern revolution," fails to mention Russian or Chinese support for the war effort, and hiding behind a smokescreen of popularized history, blurs the decades-long connection between the Vietnamese Communist movement and international Communism. In speaking of the self-immolation of Thich Quang Duc she states that none of us is able to "fully understand his mysterious self-immolation." One remark is especially naive. This is when she claims that the NLF and southern Communists "never compromised their struggle by seeking the assistance of foreign powers that would come to dominate their own efforts." [In 1973 in *International Affairs,* the Oxford authority on Vietnam, Professor Patrick Honey, writes that Miss Fitzgerald repeatedly seeks to demonstrate her experience by citing Vietnamese, a language she wrongly alleges to have five tones, and that almost all of her citations are wrong. The Professor claims that he took several packed pages of notes and errors and that the author even spells the name of Saigon's international airport incorrectly.]

Again that sense of heightened danger. Reports are flooding in to show how anti-Semitism is escalating. In Poland Gomulka has publicly attacked Jews who have "applauded Israeli aggression (they even gave drinking parties to celebrate)." He went on to threaten those Jews in high places in the Party who were "wreckers of peace and for imperialism," and added ominously, "We do not want a Fifth Column to be created . . . we cannot remain indifferent. . . ." In Hungary the Jews are being forced to sign resolutions attacking Israel, and many teachers, officials, writers, scientists are threatened with dismissal if they don't demonstrate their loyalty in some way. In Czechoslovakia the same kind of thing is happening. As for Russia, considering that it was the KGB which had urged a policy of belligerency towards Israel on Nasser, and had circulated false reports that Israel was massing troops to attack Syria (which Egypt was bound to defend), in other words, considering a large part of the blame for the war rests upon Soviet shoulders, their internal repression of the Jews now seems all the more savage.

Obviously this is the natural result of the Israeli victory. According to reliable estimates, losses during the war approximated 2,000 for the Syrians, 800 for the Jordanians, 10,000 for the Egyptians, and 679 for the Israelis. The Egyptians had no resource except to make it sound as if it was not Egypt which had lost the war but the CIA which had won it. The newspaper *Al Gumhuria* came out with a suitable fantasy-laden statement: "Defeat exists only for those who admit it. . . . We do not admit it!"

The essential problem remains for the Israelis. The curses and

The Return

promises of Arab voices will continue to sound in their ears; the "mad drummer" is forever on the roads. One English woman emigrant in Haifa wrote to the *Economist* about those last days before the war when she sat listening to Arab threats: "We are coming, Jews, to exterminate you . . . to throw you into the sea, Jews . . . to cleanse Palestine. . . ."

Everyone knows that the struggle is not finished and that the Russians are pouring in fresh arms. In fact, it is likely that a problem of Soviet strategy which has been highlighted by the war is already receiving attention. Whereas the United States could have intervened on Israel's side within hours, the Soviets lacked strategic mobility. For all her huge forces posed on Western Europe's border, she was without small mobile forces to press her interests in remote areas, and needed for larger operations aircraft carriers and staging posts for airborne troops. To quote Santamaria's always astute newspaper, "The USSR— must either resist the temptation to back 'wars of liberation' in the Third World, or acquire the military capacity that supporting their regimes requires." But for *immediate* purposes the Egyptian air force is now fully restored to strength; her fleet of submarines is intact; some 20,000 seasoned troops are back from the Yemen; there are 800-odd new tanks; more Soviet advisers have arrived in Cairo; the Red fleet is calling in at Egyptian ports; Algerian and Soudanese units are stationed in Egypt; the Jordanian army has had an Iraqui division added to it; the Syrian army is getting weapons and training.

Maria speaks openly of not liking Jews. She is an Italian woman, in whom at the moment Toole seems to take a romantic interest. "Guineas don't like Jews," she explains, "not that I have anything against them myself. In fact I used to go with a Jew-boy." She speaks in a throaty rather weary voice and although she is not particularly attractive, with her unbrushed-looking hair, her slightly swarthy skin, and her sloppy white blouse and sagging black shirt, she has something feminine about her, something infinitely relaxed and sensual. Toole has just gone off to make some telephone calls and Maria stretches out her rather young figure in the booth at the Combat Zone bar, kicks off her shoes, orders gin and orange juice, and tells the story of her life without inhibition. "I was married first to a man in the rackets and then I left him for another man in the rackets. But my husband kept me off the streets, and I didn't know a thing in those days. I had five babies! . . . Well that son of a bitch my husband he had a gun fully-loaded, intending if the police came to shoot. Now here I was with five *kids!* I never knew anything about this; he kept it hidden, he had stolen stuff in my cellar . . ." her voice rises to a shrill pitch, "I didn't even *know* it."

Afterwards she complains about her violent brother, nicknamed

The Return

"Fatty." "Was he mad? I guess he was ... My mother kicked my father out and Fatty didn't want anyone near either of us, my mother or me ... I'd get away from it. I'd say 'Go to hell', but my *mother* ... he wouldn't have *anyone* near her, not even buyin' her coffee! He was *nuts!*"

Was this because he loved his mother?

"Love her? No, Fatty was never good to her. He even tried to kill her once, when there was a fellow she was going with. He was stone *crazy*, he'd say you can get money, go and get it, as if he wanted her to hustle for him ... he never pulled any real shit with me, no real violence, he'd come and call me a fucking tramp, things like that, but if he went further I'd call the cops ... This guy was *nothing ... nothing!* I was so grateful when he was dead it was *pathetic!*" (As with many of Maria's family, relatives, and friends—violence was an essential part of their lives. Fatty was shot one night in a bar. Her nephew was shot in a driveway. Her father was killed in a brawl. She herself escaped death several times.)

And did she have any sisters?

"No, only a younger brother, Gerard. I loved him to death, but I blame Fatty for what happened to him. Fatty would put him through the transom or the window of some place that he wanted to rob, and if he whimpered he'd beat him ... He was crazy that boy. Something happened to him. I remember when I was about three my father was beating my mother and Fatty scaled a plate at him, and my father took him and put him against the wall and broke his nose and cracked his skull. . . ." Again her voice rises shrilly: "He would get headaches after that, but I don't think it was anything to do with beating, he was *always* vicious, even when he was *tiny.* . . . Once he put Gerard into a café to rob it, not knowing that the racket guys were in there settling up their money, and Gerard almost got killed. Lucky Leoni, he would have shot him dead if he'd seen him. I was scared to death." She gives a deep exhausted sigh, and the shadows under her eyes against the dark rather unhealthy tone of her skin make her look twice her age. "Of course I was dead wrong with Gerard ... Now there was no dirt in my life, not me myself" (another deep sigh) "but I never stopped Gerard. I'd find him shooting with zip-guns, vandalism, things like that. I'd beat him you know, but I wouldn't say "that's wrong." He was my baby. I just loved him to *death*. Once he turned a gun on a cop and the cop slapped him, but he didn't turn him in for the gun, only for vandalism ... And I turned on the cop like a *tiger* ... just because he slapped him, when he *should* have broke his god-damn neck! That's how I was with Gerard."

This vivid sketch has been delivered in a little under fifteen minutes and, as is usual in such cases, it makes the abstract political scene recede into the distance. As she begins to talk about "jew-boys" again it is easy to see from what narrow brutal and violent lives such prejudices spring. "Oh I don't mind Jews, but they'll always get the better of you."

But aren't there Italian Jews?

"Are you *kidding* . . ." Her voice makes everyone turn to look at her. "Why Toole is teamed up with an Italian Jew-girl right now. You ask her. . . ." Maria leans on her elbows and lights another cigarette. Then she sighs and settles aback into the corner of the booth, lowering tired black eyes. "Oh my life! I tell you I never done anything to anyone but *me* . . . Perhaps if I had, I wouldn't be in this friggin' net I'm in now"!

To alternate one kind of conversation with another, to balance one kind of information against another, is to become depressed by the "inferiority" of democratic participation! The speakers hardly realize that they are on a stage, that they themselves are part of the play. "The system is at fault," a serious-looking girl says firmly (the fact that she is studying domestic science and can hardly be considered an expert does not lessen her solid certainty). "How can we be so *rich* and still have slums?"

But aren't there many reasons for slums?

She dismisses the question impatiently: "Thinking never gets you anywhere anyway, you have to *act*. No justice is possible under capitalism. Period!" She pushes back her hair angrily.

And what does she do for action?

"I put up or shut up!" the girl says proudly. "I strike. I fight. I go places. I join my brothers and sisters." A relaxed joyful expression appears on her face. "It's wonderful."

And are you demonstrating against Vietnam?

"*Am* I!" she says.

(But such joyful demonstrators and "joiners" don't carry the same load of responsibility as do more seasoned intellectuals, journalists, and educators. Now that the internal situation in South Vietnam is tending to deteriorate, and with it the belief that American efforts will force Hanoi to the peace table, there is the fear that if the war—that is, a "decent peace"—is not lost on the ground, it may well be lost on the home front. It is reported that the Vietcong think that "their friends in America" are doing well!)

December 18

And today something is over. A natural fullstop has been given to the visit to Australia. Harold Holt, the Australian Prime Minister, has disappeared on the Cheviot Beach at Portsea in Victoria, and is presumed drowned. Fifty-nine years old and considered an expert skin-diver, Holt was in the habit of swimming every weekend. Yesterday he went for his usual pre-lunch swim in a particularly heavy ebbing surf. His companion, Alan Stewart, thought it rough and turned back; Holt kept swimming and then suddenly he disappeared. Stewart gave the alarm and soon the police boats were searching the area and four helicopters were on their way from Melbourne with police divers and equipment, looking for this man who had been Prime Minister for only two years and had "not been given time to show what he could do." All night long and through today, more than a thousand police, ambulance men, skin divers, soldiers, navy personnel, have been searching the sea, the beach, the reefs.

Holt's political importance has been that he firmly reoriented Australia's foreign policy away from Whitehall and towards the United States and Southeast Asia. If Menzies called himself BRITISH TO THE BOOTSTRAPS, Holt popularized the slogan ALL THE WAY WITH LBJ. His presumed death leaves in question future national policy. Just as Kennedy's sudden and premature assassination emphasized America's vulnerability, so does Holt's death emphasize Australia's. But Kennedy's life was cut short by bullets and Holt's seems completely accidental (although "death by water" is not unknown in the execution of political murders). All the same, if a malevolent force had wanted to do Australia harm (particularly if there had been a desire to cut off abruptly the political will to vigorously execute the Vietnam war) a better way of doing it could hardly have been thought up. For Holt represented the Australian will to victory in the present conflict and his advance into that tremendous surf at Portsea yesterday, and his just as prompt disappearance is a gain to the enemy, and has about it something symbolic. . . . The very beach situation itself suggests isolation: without people, without bodyguards, the Prime Minister swimming in rough sea with no expert swimmer at his side, his only companion having to run a quarter of a mile to his car, and then drive to give an alarm.

There remains now the inescapable thought that the way lies open for Whitlam.

1968

AMERICA WILL
GO DOWN

America will go down
With H. Rap Brown. . . .

January 1968

The old boarding house in New Hampshire has views from all of its windows; onto the peaks of the mountains, onto sharp outlines of pine and fir. If the broad verandas suggest summer and the creak of rocking chairs, the economy of the house is that of the cold; its windows and passages protected, its chimneys deep in the center of the studs, its nearby barn with tiny windows, its tool shed of solid stone. Walking in the woods one hears no sound but the squeak of new snow underfoot, the occasional whirr of a saw in a distant shed, the gurgle of half choked water where it runs capped by a hood of ice.

There is not much political discussion at the boarding house. A rather conservative woman whispers that some of the "hippies" in the village talk as though *"we* were the enemy and not the Vietcong." But her anxieties are more local than those that dominate the larger horizon, where the presentiment is that 1968 will be a bad year. On the whole the United States seems to be withdrawing from world affairs; the *élan* of being the leader of the free world has been eroded by slurs, attacks, and a corresponding reluctance to go on with the established role. This is sadly typified by an irritated congressman who, after some quite minor anti-American demonstration in Saigon, exclaims testily, "If they don't *want* us, then we'll get out!"

The *New York Times* reports that the Vietcong killed 3,820 civilians and kidnapped 5,368 in 1967 (in both cases double the number of 1966). The biggest recent Vietcong attack was on a Montagnard hamlet last December, with the view of demonstrating to the villagers that the Americans couldn't protect them. The 600 VC were armed with Russian-made napalm-filled flamethrowers and they left 252 dead and about fifty wounded. (It is noticeable that such stories from the "other side" do not inaugurate world-wide anti-napalm propaganda campaigns!) In Australia the Labor Party, historically adverse to all overseas military involvement, is gaining support by promising to withdraw the country's token forces from Vietnam. As for Britain (suffering so much economically) she clearly won't be able to wait until the mid-seventies to get out of Southeast Asia. In those waters which command the eastern approaches, the vacuum looms.

In the little world of the boardinghouse, the black situation is dramatized. One of the smaller tables has been "taken over" in the dining room by a trim and energetic black man with a pointed beard and a habit of wearing a forage cap to meals and another man, taller, lighter-skinned, and graceful (the Panther type!).

By means of the technique once used against themselves, these two make a social circle with several token whites! Only once during these last weeks does the conversation become general; that is during coffee after dinner when a certain kind of cohesion gathers. The conversation has something to do with genocide in the army. "But the U.S. army has been fully desegregated since the fifties," protests the woman who had whispered about the Vietcong. "It can't be as bad as that. Three years ago half the army's Negro soldiers re-enlisted."

"Pardon me Madam," the tall, handsome Negro (whose name is Donald and who makes African sculpture for parks and playgrounds) remarks with a charming but somewhat cold smile, "We don't like that term . . ."

"What term?" she seems bewildered.

Elvis, the man with the pointed beard answers for him. "Knee-gro."

He adds again in a tone of contempt, "*Knee-gro.*"

"I'm sorry." She is flustered. "I wasn't thinking. . . ."

"No you weren't," Donald answers, "you certainly *weren't.*"

"But *genocide* . . . ?" she insists miserably.

"Well, I'd like to ask *you,*" Elvis pushes his cap onto the back of his head, immediately losing his commando image, "genocide is a white folks game. I'd like to ask you how many of *us* are being killed in Vietnam?"

The woman recovers confidence. She is a statistician and numbers are easy.

"Well I know that only about 2 percent of the officers killed in Vietnam are Ne—I mean black!"

"Officers?" Elvis looks at the ceiling. "Officers and all that shit? Aren't most of the officers honkies? How would we have a *super*—" he lingers on the word, "*flu—i—tee* of Black officers in a *cracker* army? Only thing is our enemy may not be the same as white folks. *Our* enemy is here in *this* country. Black brothers are being 'used up' over there for Colonial rule."

At some point or other the conversation peters out. Donald is offered coffee and accepts it. Elvis gets so many unwilling laughs with his outrageous rhetoric that he appears mollified. But when the next meal comes they are sitting at the segregated table again.

The alert and child-like Samuel is also at the boardinghouse to, as he puts it, "get his things together." Because of his Jewish heritage he has become extremely disillusioned by SNCC's attacks on Israel. Today he wears a pale blue velour sweater-shirt and his fringe is combed down to give him the look of a rather plain but coy girl. "All the Jews who went to the south, where does this leave them? Theodore Bikel and people like that?"

But is it only SNCC and the Blacks? Isn't it a whole section of the New Left?

"Yes, yes," Samuel is delighted to get support. "It is obscene. The Blacks are kowtowing to Arab chieftains as if they never heard of Arab slave dealers." He looks quickly across at the Black table and lowers his voice. "They even had a black man climb a tower in Baghdad and shout 'Black Power' at the hour of the Muezzin...."

And what about Cuba? (Samuel had formerly been enthusiastic about Cuba.)

"I should hope that *Cuba* isn't anti-Semitic?"

Wasn't it a Cuban officer who said that the Israelis used *Nazis* in their drive through Sinai?

Samuel shuts his eyes as if in pain.

Someone else pressures relentlessly. "And what about Jews on the Left who take part in this?"

Samuel turns pale. "More obscene. More." He looks as if he is going to burst into tears.

January 17

In the South End, the streets which glitter in the piercing rays of sunlight are characterized by the same sad moral vacuum as ever, the same sense of alienation and loss. It is as if Boston had been shaken, and all the human debris had fallen into these deadend streets, the lost, the unwise, the ignorant, and ill—and this in spite of a fairly active Urban Renewal program. The streets seem to proclaim that material aid alone will not obliterate the dark stains of the past. The bells of St. Patrick's are tolling. A long line of men and women, dressed in black, are moving from under the shadow of the El and converging upon the traditional arched doorway. Someone has died, and presumably lies inside in a coffin lined with purple silk. A respectable Catholic citizen perhaps? Or one of the lords of petty crime, who in defiance of what the Cathedral represents, has made the money sweat and pour from the shabby surrounding streets.

. . . In the subway a gang of boys spilling themselves onto the platform, pushing, screaming, wearing bright blue satin-faced jackets, strangely secure in the hydra-headed gang rhythm. Adults watch from across the moat between the tracks, as the group eddies about a boy called Richie who has a yellowish tight-skinned face and a protruding nose and stands with a fixed idiotic smile, while another boy pokes at him with a hockey stick, and then suddenly makes an obscene gesture. The watching boys double up with delight. Richie hops on one leg and does an ungraceful version of the twist. He smiles vacantly but turns his head anxiously from side to side, while the boys intone with a slight threat in their voices; "*Go it* man! *Go! Go! Go!*" And the train comes to receive the whole group into its anonymous interior, to sweep them away like so much trash, to who knows what other part of the city.

And at dusk outside the Settlement House, a loud thump attracts attention; a very large woman is lying flat on her back beside a bench, her face pale and moon-like, her large bare legs stretched out, bluish and stained. An anonymous man appears, and makes statements with the sad objectivity of one born to the neighborhood.

"Wouldn' touch her if I was you." And then "What is it? Drunk is it?" We stand listening to her hoarse but reassuring breathing. "Passed out on the bench n' fell off," states the man knowingly. He has already called the police from the phone across the way. "See the bottle?" (The neck of a whiskey bottle is sticking out from under her skirts.)

A visit to Jasmin (who has been rewarded for her accident by an apartment at the Cathedral Project, which lifts yellowish towers beside the solid bulk of St. Patrick's). Black children are playing in the snow, pushing about a big glo-pink ball.

Jasmin opens the door with her hair pushed up into peaks and her still childish legs emerging from a quilted housecoat. She takes me into the living room where Junior, who now acts like her common-law husband, is spread out on the sofa, his legs outstretched and his gloomy eyes fixed on a TV science fiction movie. His is thinner than when he was in prison so that the elongated bone-structure of his body makes him look like some large jointed model. They live incognito these two, the name on the door is not their name. In the background the usual shadow sits, an anonymous man who seems to be waiting for something, perhaps for a telephone call heralding the arrival of the drug dealer.

Jasmin brings in a tattered issue of *Muhammed Speaks* in which a whole supplement is devoted to the ultimate destruction of the white world. The whites, it seems, are to die a fiery death. She indicates a piece called "Old World Dying, New World Coming" which talks of the powerful rich world of Christianity, seemingly as immovable as mountains but as Elijah Muhammed notes slyly, "mountains can be removed by high explosives."

"We are living in the . . . doom of the white's man's world," Jasmin reads aloud. "The U.S. government is active in its deceitful work of trying to slow the progress of the resurrection of our people . . . America must be taken and destroyed, according to the prophets . . . '*The heavens shall pass away with a great noise, and the comets shall melt with fervent heat, the earth also and the works that are therein shall be burnt up* . . .' " Jasmin is not quite sure that she believes all this, especially since she herself has been brought up a Christian, but it is obvious that it tunes in well with her earlier Evangelical training. "Dig this," she says and spreds out the folder entitled "Universal War," which modernizes the whole apocalyptic vision by setting the United States in an emerald sea and surrounding it with a lurid pink sky. Inside the boundaries of the United States itself, Elijah Muhammed is shown stretching protective arms to gather the black people, while in the sea around the coasts hundreds of warships are being sunk, armadas of airplanes are overhead, and great armies ring the country around (all the soldiers looking recognizably Asiatic and training machine guns on huddling whites).

After some discussion, in which Junior joins from time to time, Jasmin dresses in purple pants, a blue nylon blouse, a fawn-colored leather waistcoat and jacket, and we leave the apartment to walk along the darkening street where already neon lights shine upon the still playing children, and where the signs of HARRY THE GREEK and RED FEZ color the snow. In spite of the liveliness of her eyes, Jasmin's face has a curious pallor as if she had lived indoors since the accident. But having already regained her political interests she only talks about the importance of "unity."

"We can't get our black things together if we're busy falling out with each other," she complains. "We've *got* to get rid of the Toms!"

It is snowing and the warrenlike houses, the dirty pavements, the boarded storefronts crouch under a white blanket.

(In my pocket I carry an edition of Leger: " *It is snowing on the cast-iron gods and on the steelworks lashed by short liturgies; on the slag and the sweepings and the embankment grasses; it is snowing on the fever and the implements of men . . . it is snowing out there, out towards the West, on the silos and ranches and the vast unstoried plains straddled over by pylons; on the layout of unborn cities and on the dead ashes where the camps were . . .*"

1968 / America Will Go Down

January 28

Because of the omnipresence of Vietnam and especially because of the Pueblo crisis (the USS Pueblo proceeding under strict electronic silence off that coast, was seized by Korean warships five days ago), it is hard to concentrate on the South End. It is equally distracting to hear Dr. Martin Luther King, supposedly the High Priest of nonviolence, set up an echo of what may spell the doom of any peace in Vietnam advantageous to Western values. As an essentially peaceful man, his need to retain a hold on the black civil-rights movement is driving him into "going along with" the black extremists. As he moves from the moderate black center, this center is left exposed and vulnerable.

Small escalations increase. Eldridge Cleaver, whose star has risen since his publication in *Ramparts* of an analysis of his career as a rapist, now gives a description of a meeting held in the Bay Area in February last year (it is the kind of material which makes social history). He admits that he "fell in love at first sight" with this startling scene. He details the characters: Jack Trueblood; a girl called Lucky; Marvin Jackmon, the poet who composed *Burn, Baby, Burn;* Willy Sherman, who had been in San Quentin; Bill Sherman, member of the Central Committee of the Black Panther Party of California; Victoria Durant; a "sneaky little fellow Nasser Shabbazz"; and Vincent Lynch as "smooth and black as the ebony statues he brought back from Nigeria." Also a "frightened little mulatto, who didn't open his mouth."

Cleaver describes in true macho style, the "deep female gleam" in the eyes of watching women as four men enter the room, "wearing black berets, powder blue shirts, black leather jackets, black trousers, shiny black shoes, and each carrying a gun." It is the gang made political. In front is Huey Newton. Behind him Bobby Seale with a .45 caliber automatic, next to him Sherwin Forte, an M-1 carbine with a banana clip cradled in his arms. "Where was my mind at? Blown! Racing through time, racing through the fog of a perspective that had just been shattered into a thousand fragments. Who are these cats? I wondered at them, checking them out carefully. They were so cool and it seemed to me not unconscious of the electrifying effect they were having on everybody in the room." Huey explains to the meeting that they are going to "talk about black people arming themselves to . . . exert organized force in the political arena . . ." the only "culture worth talking about is a revolutionary culture . . . we've got to talk about political power growing out of the barrel of a gun." The scene unrolls to the glory of the new black heroes. Sister Betty (Malcolm's wife) is taken away "under black protection," a TV man is pushed out of the way. Huey taunts a policeman: "Oh you big fat racist pig, draw your gun!" Then he slides a clip into his gun chamber and says "I'm *waiting*." Eldrige is thinking, "This nigger is crazy." But Huey literally laughs in the cop's face and "disappears in a blaze of dazzling sunlight." ("*Work out soul-brother! I was shouting to myself! You're the baddest mother-fucker I've ever seen!*")

To admire this new (black) breed of American fascist (striding around in uniform, fingering triggers, taunting authorities, and bullying black moderates) is to confuse psychological imperatives with the truth of history. But the Panther program is more ominous with obvious Neo-Marxist overtones, with the separatism of extreme black nationalism, and the incendiary terrorist stand of the Maoist. Although it might make martyrs of the Panthers, its potential for trouble cannot be dismissed.

Today, talking to blacks in the streets, it seems that Cleaver and his friends are regarded with a mixture of pride and humor. "Those boys is struttin," one old man says as he loads garbage onto a truck. He smiles, showing broken front teeth and broad shining lips. "They *loves* it!" Yet no one in the streets understands Cleaver's stress on the "internationalization" of the struggle (they rather see the whole thing as a demand for 100 percent American Rights).

In New York City there has been a clash between two black leaders, Roy Wilkins and Roy Innis, on the question of "Black Separatism." Roy Innis, thirty-four years old, is now Director of CORE, the Congress of Racial Equality—and he has held a news conference to support Black Power demands for separate Black Studies departments and dormitories on all college campuses. Roy Wilkins, sixty-seven years old, and executive director of the NAACP, is attempting to get a court ruling against such demands. For Wilkins such a retrogression negates what he has been working for all his life—equality and integration. But Innis, confident and aggressive, obviously feels that he spearheads the new wave. He says, "Mr. Wilkins should withdraw from the stage and let younger men take over."

February 3

Black High School students in New York are demanding better lunches, more freedom, more dances, and more holidays. Now even children are making demands, and naturally the demands are childish! There are racial outbreaks in a number of schools. Pupils at the Lee High School in New Haven are arrested for fighting in the cafeterias, for strewing crockery and food all over the floor (a squad of policemen is rushed to the scene). The drive among "Third Worlders" to recruit the young is helped along by LeRoi Jones, sentenced for carrying a gun during last summer's riots in Newark, but still recipient of a job as leader of an "advisory" group at the Robert Treat Elementary School in Newark! His influence on unsophisticated black pupils is not likely to encourage integration, in fact a "moral holiday" has been declared, and black children are discovering that there is considerable pleasure in taunting and needling whites.

February 22

About 600 people, mostly blacks, attended a Memorial Program for Malcolm X in East Harlem yesterday. The speaker Herman B. Ferguson (like LeRoi Jones, a "special adviser," in this case to the board of New York City Intermediate School 201) urged the audience to get "weapons for self defense against whites" and to practice using them so that when the "hunting season" came, they would be ready. This is the same Ferguson who was indicted last year for participating in the RAM plot to murder moderate civil rights leaders! He has not yet come to trial, and it is hard to understand not only how he managed to be appointed as a "special adviser," but also how he happened to get paid for it! (The governing board which cosponsored the Memorial Program, together with the Afro-American Teachers Association and the African-American Students Association, was set up under a Board-of-Education-approved, Ford Foundation-supported experiment, to test community control of local schools.) One new teacher, who happened to enter the school on the day of the program, reported that a play shown (the "World of LeRoi Jones") had this dialogue:

> Who murdered the black man?
> Whitey, whitey.
> Who should we lynch?
> Whitey, whitey.

Speakers and performers also denounced the "white man and his bitch," described the United States as the "Fourth Reich," and urged Negro youths not to "fight colored brothers" in Vietnam. Reporters were not permitted while this was going on, though one black photographer managed to enter by disguising his identity; he noted that there were many high school students and younger students present, and that some of the adult audience wore African costumes and had put pins on their lapels proclaiming The New Order (a slogan curiously reminiscent of Nazi Germany).

1968 / America Will Go Down

February 25

In this time of the flexing of black muscle, LeRoi Jones announces that the Blacks will take over nine cities (he mentions New York, Newark, Baltimore, Detroit, St. Louis, Cleveland, Boston, Washington, and Gary). "No matter what self hypnosis whites engage in ... they (whites) must yield control, unless ... (they) want to waste many lives ...." In Newark he announces, "We will govern Newark, or *no one* will govern Newark ... we are Americans who have no further need for America as it exists in its present state." He goes on to talk of taking power "by any means necessary." And the ultimatums are topped by Ben Stewart, the leader of the Black Student Union at San Francisco State, who advises that "the best thing whites can do for blacks, is *die!*"

(As a footnote only, there come echoes from Britain of troubles there. Duncan Sandys and Enoch Powell express to an uneasy Parliament, fears of a British racial future similar to that of the United States. There is talk about the "horrors of Newark and Detroit," about "swamping birth rates," and about "illegal immigrants being smuggled across the English channel at so much a head, to deserted beaches in the north.")

February 28

Walking along the edge of the Charles River where, as living, panting witnesses to the "interracial" life, black runners in Harvard colors alternate with white runners, and jog along through damp grass and melting snow past the grey river and the factory buildings. Further up along Mount Auburn Street with its pale-stoned cemetery there are reminders that verbal battles, in spite of their potential for death, are still warmer and more alive than the cold residue of the slaugher in Vietnam.

But this slaughter is of various kinds, and in an intellectual center such as Cambridge, it is disappointing to find that certain slaughters are not noted at all. At Hue, where the North Vietnamese broke the Tet ceasefire, an Australian, Brian Mullins, talked with the survivors who described the Communists entering the city on January 29 and occupying it for twenty-four days, while a systematic massacre took place. The Vietcong had been furnished with photographs and dossiers of Hue's anti-Communist leaders and government officials, and these were hunted down—young and old, men and women, Vietnamese and foreigners. The Thervada Buddhist Pagoda and a nearby high school were used as operational headquarters. Since the aim was to destroy the local infrastructure, the net was thrown widely to include government officials, doctors, nurses, religious leaders, students, and officials home on leave. The massacres began after ten days. Three hundred were detained at the Gia-Hoa High School. The victims were forced to dig a huge grave behind the school, had their wrists tied with wire, were made to kneel, and were machine gunned. Many were still alive when the graves were filled. Now it seems that at least 4,000 people were killed in all, but that an extra 1,000 are still missing. Graves have been found in the school grounds, in the grounds of the Tuong-Van Pagoda on the banks of the Da Mai brooklet and in the Bai-Dau cemetery. From one village alone, Phu Xuan, 460 residents were massacred, women, children, teenagers.

From inside a pagoda at Ap Dong Gi—night after night after the beginning of February, a Buddhist monk heard shots and cries. Afterwards sixty-seven bodies were found. There had been a death march from the Redemptorist Church, to which many had fled for refuge, to Ap Lang Xa Con two miles away. Here twenty were buried alive, among them Tran Dien, one of Hue's five senators in the National Assembly. Two hundred disinterred near the tombs of the Emperors Tu Duc and Dong Khanh, among them a number of priests. [The source for this information is the *New York Times*, *Time*, the *U.S. Government White Paper*, and such Catholic-oriented magazines as *News Weekly* and the *Sentinel* which had access to local Hue sources.]

The story of Hue, however, does not seem to be "discussed" at the local cocktail parties.

Brian Mullins interviewed many members of the *Association for the 293 Victims of the Vietcong Offense* and many relatives in rural areas. The victims of crossfire, he stated, could not have been more than several hundred. He was also told that the Communists in their advance often forced civilians to walk in front of them as they entered the city, and some of these civilians told him how fervently they hoped that American bombs would fall and allow them to escape in the confusion. One school teacher said that he *longed* to see American faces. The justification about the deaths from crossfire is publicized because that already noted indefatigable agent and authenticator, Wilfred Burchett claims that most of the deaths in Hue were caused by the Americans! He has apparently not looked into the mass graves. Professor Nguyen Duc Mai, a province official and teacher of English, now Professor of English at Hue University, gives numerous details, and states that the Vietcong were thorough as they advanced through the hamlets, and that all through the area, in the Nam-Hoa and Phu Thu districts, mass graves have been or are being discovered.

Talking casually to students in Cambridge, I find the word "massa cre" still produces automatic reactions about American mistakes, or "dropping napalm," or "crossfire in the streets." Nothing that has happened so far in Vietnam can be compared, in spirit or importance, with the story of Hue—which in essence illustrates the core of that theory of the "annihilation of dissidence" which has been the key factor in victory after victory for the Communists.

February 29

It is pleasant to find that at least one group visiting Vietnam (in this case the United States Inter-Religious Committee on Peace) is willing to proclaim that after so brief a visit they are not prepared to make a statement! Bishop Lord, leader of this group, says that he "accepts the fact that the NLF is 'probably' under the leadership of Hanoi" and adds, "We don't want a Communist takeover." Yet as some sad symbol for the future, this admission is accompanied by the news of thirty-nine missionaries, with their women and children, who have been massacred and multilated by the Vietcong in Ban Me Thuot. (It is also interesting that the admission of Bishop Lord about the makeup of the NLF is publicly clarified at just this time with the publication of photographs and names of important NLF leaders showing the two most powerful and high-ranking North Vietnamese officials, Vo Chi Cong and Tran Nam Trung, both of whom have aliases. Vo Chi Cong's true name is unknown, but he is a founder of the NLF and thought to be the overall field director of the VC insurgency in South Vietnam.

The fact that so large a percentage of Western intellectuals, professors, journalists, opinion makers, favor a withdrawal from Vietnam is partly responsible for key questions remaining unanalyzed. It is more popular to write or talk of the "error" of the American presence than it is to discuss what is actually happening or what might happen in the future. The present case in point is that of "negotiations." Milton Sacks (at Brandeis) says that "negotiating while fighting" is a favored Communist device, and that in Korea this cost 15,000 American lives. He thinks, therefore, that the administration would be wise to insist on an immediate cease-fire rather than to prolong the negotiating so that General Giap's theories of fighting while negotiating can be carried out.

According to a young man at a garage this morning, however, the opposite course might be beneficial (the idea that fellow Americans will be killed does not stand in his way). "There ought to be a *dose* of killing," he insists, "and then the American people would get *really* fed up!"

As he stands there, well dressed, smoking cigarette after cigarette, he seems symbolic of a "fanatical, no-quarter war against a war," during which the problem of communism in Southeast Asia is *not* a problem, and every proposal made by the Vietcong is rejected by the United States for a "bad" reason, and every proposal made by the United States is rejected by Hanoi for a "good" reason.

Later

Thoughts about the persistence of "misinformation." As Fairbairn says, the battle continues to be one of ideas. Nor can one quarrel with the success of Hanoi's world-wide propaganda drive to instill defeatism in the USA (a propaganda drive which is after all supported by the vaster and more generalized military and propaganda drive against the United States carried out not only by Russia and her satellites, but also by China). With regard to this drive it is now admitted by Jonas Radnanyi, former Hungarian *chargé d'affaires*, that in 1966 the Foreign Minister Janos Peter had told Dean Rusk as a diplomatic "hoax" that Johnson's 37-day bombing pause would lead to negotiations with Hanoi. If this *was* a hoax, it was an effective one.

A note from a social worker who asks me to visit P—, who is in prison on a charge of killing the man who had murdered his brother four years ago. I look through the grill at Charles Street at P— whose long lean black frame is not yet in prison blue, but instead is smart in orange corduroy slacks and a yellow dashiki low at the neck, through which a (gold) peace emblem is visible swinging on a leather cord. The features of this young pimp (now murderer) are harmonious—but are unable to hide the soul's discontent which is suggested by the evasive glance of restless burning eyes. He admits that he has sought out and shot the man who—in a quarrel over a sweater—had gunned down his brother (the victim had only been one week out of prison). "If I hadn't, I'd have had no respect," he explains in a tone of finality and regret, his tone accepting the fact that revenge is the law of the street, and the law of the street rules. P— has been brought up since early childhood to a familiarity, and so a contempt, for violence. ("Blood and power intoxicate" Dostoievsky points out, "coarseness and depravity are developed; the mind and the heart are tolerant of the most abnormal things, till at last they come to relish them . . .") In P—'s attitude there is less sorrow for the past loss of his brother with whom he had quarreled violently—than bitter anger at the encroachment upon the clear rights granted to him by the assassin's action.

The peace symbol swinging from his neck is part of fashionable *décor;* it is less a peace symbol than an anti-Vietnam badge. It seems that during former stays in prison and during the immediate days, he has absorbed the idea that he is, in some way or other not guilty; that the killing of his brother and his own revenge killing, is washed away by the slavery of his ancestors; that his whole life of crime is obviated thereby. Moreover he has been politicized by prison-visiting radicals. He speaks of the "white brothers" who are visiting the cells and as he puts it, are "spreading the rap."

At a time of change, politics, supposedly the process by which the irrational is brought under control, become themselves irrational; in fact political turmoil shows by its very existence that the moral order is no longer accepted without challenge. (As Laswell says, "a political difference is the outcome of a moral crisis.") This is where the white activists come in. . . . Two moral orders conflict; it seems necessary to ask which order will triumph? Will the victor in the end be the advocate of a greater criminality?

March 29

Again fear is intensified by the encroachment of crime values into the world of learning. At a coffee shop in Cambridge a freshman student announces in a low voice that for the first time he is scared of blacks.

"I was mugged the other night walking home from the library; the point is that it seemed to have nothing to do with money, but something to do with the hatred in the man . . . I've seen a kind of hatred in riots, but that was more like play acting. This was *real* . . . it was impersonal as if I'd been a rat or something." He is young and thin-skinned looking, and his voice is obsessed. "This guy was dark black and had a cap pulled low over his eyes, and shades on. After I'd pulled out my wallet he still went on beating me; but he didn't even bother to look at me. I could see the lips drawn back from his teeth . . ."

The student hesitates, "There is a black in my freshman Soc-Science class and he keeps a gun in his closet . . ."

Some hours in an apartment with a group of prostitutes and their pimp. The living conditions are bourgeois; this is considered correct. Solid mattresses, spotless white counterpanes, rose-colored lampshades, and "His" and "Her" towels in the bathroom. The walls of the apartment however are stained and streaked, the coffee is served in cups without saucers, the pizzas brought in from outside are eaten straight out of the boxes.

In long conversation it is seen that, although the financial question is paramount and perhaps rules all, a wild and sometimes poetic extravagance often occurs. The satanic aspect of love is emphasized. (One is reminded of how Baudelaire talks of the solemn houses in which his ancestors lived—idiots and maniacs—victims of terrible passions. He [Baudelaire] confused the smell of women with the smell of furs, and found the mixture "of the grotesque and the tragic curiously agreeable to the senses, as are discords to a jaded ear.") These men and women live in a similarly pathological enclave and amuse themselves by spinning tall tales, recounting dreams of vast wealth without lifting a finger, dressing up commercial cruelty in skins, velours, silks, jewelry; yet not ceasing to exalt the name of "love." As far as clients are concerned, these seem also to have given up with pleasure their suburban self control and now recline happily enough in the South End gutters.

Kafka said that psychoanalysis has claimed to uncover many symptoms of disease, but that he looks upon this as a hopeless error. "All these so-called diseases, pitiful as they look, are beliefs, the attempts of a human being in distress to cast his anchor in some mother-soil. . . . Who can hope for a cure here?"

Passing the abandoned houses. The empty lots. The bars and restaurants where dark faces turn as one enters. The day's crime reports merge with the slow cruising of a police car. "Three Girls Stab Rob Man 33." "Killer for Hire Guarded Closely Charles St." "Eight Boys Hunted Two Dollar Killing." "Kids Pay $100 For Fake Licenses." There is also the prostitute's crime sheet which keeps up with street activities and even with pimps' vacations at expensive resorts! (Present issue "Victim Bars Wild Midnight Ride with Crazed Armed Trio.") An empty world, in which papers such as this provide the only literature.

The grey painted staircase of the dingy brick building just off West Newton Street has names and slogans cut into the wall. Of the three young militants who live in the apartment, only Harris (slight and bearded) could actually be called black. José is a muscled light-skinned Puerto Rican who slips a revolver out of his belt as he lets me into the room, and puts it on a shelf. Esteban, also born in Puerto Rico, is shorter and quieter with pale, yellow skin and a soft nasal voice.

José reproves me for speaking Spanish. He says, indicating Harris, "We have a brother here who can't speak Spanish." Then he adds that he himself is a "stone black advocate."

Harris in the meantime has settled himself on the sagging couch and has begun to ruminate about America. "Life in America is an experience . . . If I was in Puerto Rico where they accept every skin color I'd be different; but here its amazing how removed I am . . . All this anti-white shit didn't happen suddenly. Boom! No, it came gradual. White America hides itself."

José, as if not listening to Harris, speaks of candy stores where the kids wouldn't play with him. "All of a sudden it hits you—you're *black*"! He excuses himself abruptly and comes back after a moment carrying a wooden board, a knife, a *Nescafé* bottle filled with marijuana and a small pipe with a yellow bowl and chased silver fittings. "Excuse us—we've got to do our ritual." The ash is scraped out of the pipe, it is filled, lit, and passed around from hand to hand. The smoke blends the faces into a softer pattern. (Suddenly two people at the other end of the room become visible behind a half-drawn curtain. One is a white girl with a round ordinary face. The other is a large Negro dressed in gray slacks and an African dashiki. They remain silent.)

Harris is talking about intermarriage. "I can't have in mind a situation to bring this (intermarriage) about, because I can't see developing a strong black race with a white chick. I gotta be with someone who's gone my route." (This Nazi-like concentration upon pure race is touchingly innocent, especially as he now justifies it by an appeal to the community of suffering.) "It's because of the mental beating a black woman has had."

"I can *imagine* sleeping with a white chick," José admits honestly "but *marry* one—No"! He communes with himself for a moment, "There are exceptions to all things," he says at last, "especially where women and money are concerned." Then he recovers himself. "Women are irrelevant! Politics are more exciting"!

Everybody is laughing. Harris and José are exchanging what seems to be a secret handshake. José explains, "We have our heads together on many issues right now, such as the 'Movement' . . . we have a lot of personal and intimate things to talk about rather than women . . . You better believe it." His tone is suddenly hostile and half turning away from me he gives a short abrupt laugh. "It's off *her*" (to "off" someone is a Mafia term employed when a victim is to be eliminated). "True some chicks are very heavy and knows what's happening, so that a token force of whites are allowed in." He looks pained. "A man does what he wants to in love . . . It's a matter of preservation of the species, of physical and psychological chemistry. I admit you could even *marry* a white chick. . . ."

"Let me rap" Esteban urges. "I hate to see a Puerto Rican come here and get poisoned. I was in the army for three years of my life. They trained me, sure, but you could see the prejudice of the way it was happening." José, seemingly bored, steps over all the extended legs to go out and get a jam jar of ginger ale, which he then doles out into three cups and passes to his brothers. Harris interrupts Esteban to delineate the layout of self-defense. His dark skin glows and his face lights up. "Any whites who tell me to be nonviolent in face of white men don't respect black men. . . . Now after 1965 they respect us, but not before."

Through all this conversation there is a faint somewhat distorted military touch. But what is being *done* for "self-defense"? Harris answers briefly that this is "classified information." Would the blowing up of the State Department be classed as self-defense, for instance? No one answers. Instead Harris begins to discuss a "home force."

José, who has been absent for some time, returns dressed in navy blue tights and a small pair of shorts, explaining that he is an instructor of First Degree Korean-style karate *Tai Kwan Do.* He has been proficient for six years and now he teaches it for a living. "People in history," he maintains squatting on the floor, "couldn't keep adequate security force without educating people. While we educate people, we're aiming to subsidize a group to represent us with arms. Then, if the *man* comes after us, we'll have someone to say 'Hey'."

Might not the majority of the black people actually prefer to be protected by the police, especially since there are a growing number of *black* policemen?

At this Harris gets very angry.

"We're being messed on by some of the black police, as well as the white police. We're being messed on by the very people sent to protect us. Black police will do anything to get money!"

How many of the police would side with the militants in a showdown?

José is objective enough to say, "There's no way of telling." After a moment he adds, "I doubt the black police would support us. . . . Power is at stake you see. Put a 38 Police Chief Special in his belt, and a black man becomes powerful." Harris interrupts tersely, "That's only good for every Uncle Tom over fifty."

But isn't this also a fantasy? How many of those *under* fifty are really with you?

For a moment the atmosphere is tense again, then I suggest that anarchists in the past have robbed banks to get money for political movements. Harris puts back his head and roars with laughter. His red tongue and white teeth are visible in the dark cavern of his mouth.

"You don't know *half* . . . you don't know *half* . . . ! If you're talking about the Oakland, California deal, well, we don't know *nothing* . . . *nothing.*" José is laughing too, but he warns me, "You watch out or you'll be burnt on the bullshit!"

He rises to his feet, his muscles bulging through the blue tights so that he looks rather like Superman. "You were onto fantasy a moment ago, but I gave up all that when I gave up Captain Marvel." Underneath he is irritated, and intent on proving his manhood. "You may quote this for the rest of your life. Remember *this.* The black man who calls himself black will die for his people. He's *proud!*"

Harris is watching with glowing eyes. Now he too springs to his feet and shouts, "Dig it!" The two exchange their handshake again.

"If he sees people taking advantage of his women," José goes on, "if he sees a pig beatin' on one of his women, for instance, he'll be willing to *die*—he'll be willing to *kill!*"

Can a real revolution be provoked, whether black women are interfered with or not?

The doubtful tone irritates José again. He frowns and states bluntly, "In a black Spanish home, the *man* has the say."

Harris for some reason tries to apologize. "We've all been talking very frankly, very *down.*"

Afterthoughts about these militants suggest that their disappointment in America is not profound, although the rather antique air of the conversation exposes the trite aggressive expressions current in Marxist jargon—words like "oppressors" and "oppressed peoples," the "Party," the "Movement," the "vanguard," the "Gestapo police" and "American running dogs." The Black Panther position papers, some of them taken from *The Correct Handling of a Revolution* by Huey Newton, urge "quick execution" as a variant to rioting in the streets. ("When the masses hear that a Gestapo policeman has been executed while sipping coffee at a counter, and the revolutionary executioners fled without being traced, the masses will see the validity of this type of approach to resistance.") Training in revolution is referred to in the same paper as "certain physical activities" (the rumor is that training necessitates setting fires, rioting, hijacking, and stealing for the cause—just as gangland aspirants are required to prove their allegiance by practicing acts of violence). There is much stress on leaders being tested revolutionaries, so as to minimize the opportunities for Uncle Tom informants. ("The party must exist above ground so long as the dog power structure will allow, and hopefully when the party is forced to go underground, the message will already have been put across to the people.")

Yesterday's experience is compounded by conversations with two Negro mothers who confide that their sons are being "indoctrinated" into race hatred by the Black Panther party. So-called Afro-American study groups are being formed and young students are being urged to join, or being "shamed" into joining.

"Seems like it's just they join to be with their friends!" one woman complains in her soft voice. "It's nowhere to go home now, nowhere to be in church. My Bo-Bo's used goin' to church with us an' now it's sneakin' off and bein' with that Panther group. It's Brother this and Brother that—no one's your brother is not a *Panther.*"

1968 / America Will Go Down

(One young black records going to an after-school group and being encouraged to join protests and marches. He went south on a prepaid trip after the shooting of Meredith, and listened to Stokeley Carmichael urging black youths to arm themselves for future conflicts. Now he is planning to go to Cuba with a group of young black students. His mother, feeling that he is being drawn away from his studies and sports into a world far from her, a world she knows nothing about, is vaguely oppressed by this.)

There is reason enough for her fears, since the kind of "people's war" for which her son is presumably being groomed (in spite of its being highly unlikely that it would be seriously undertaken in the United States) has "total" aims in which parents would have no rights over sons. As Crozier points out, "Those who resort to people's revolutionary war aim at a complete destruction of the enemy's administration, the undermining of the society in which both operate, the shattering of the enemy's will to resist . . . these sweeping aims explain why People's Revolutionary War is the most 'total' form of warfare yet devised, transcending the strictly military fields, and impinging on psychology, social organization and politics."

Already this People's War philosophy has left scattered throughout the slums of our big cities strange little admonitions, which come straight from Mao's texts—not stealing from the "people" for instance, helping them with their work in the community, (and presumably giving the children of the "people" breakfast as do the Panthers).

I ask Jasmin why she uses this term Third World Peoples.

"When I say 'Third World' I mean the poor blacks, the poor yellow race, the poor brown race, the Chicanos, the Chinese, the Indians. All those who have been much abused. It's irreparable, the damage done to that *Indian* race."

Can she describe what the damage was?

She takes this personally and says abruptly, "You know any blacks done harm to the Indians?"

She does then think of it in the international sense?

"Yes, now I think of it in an international sense because the people of the Third World are getting together now. Fidel's emissary Ché Guevara . . ." she stumbles over the name, "he was sent on an expedition into Latin American countries to rouse the Third World Peoples, that is the poor, the much maligned peoples, to an awareness of what was going on—to rouse them into one 'fighting' body, one mass of the oppressed."

But isn't this rather artificial? Do the American blacks really see themselves like this?

"We do have blacks that refuse to join the Third World people," she admits, "it's not to be held against them. When you have the slave

248

mentality you know, there's always going to be those bootlickers, the Uncle Toms, always the snake that crawls in your midst and makes like part of you, and can't wait to crawl back again. But always there's those who'll really cling to the masses." (Jasmin talks of work a great deal, although she has done very little of it in her life. At this point in her development she likes to see herself as related to the toiling of the proletariat). "We's niggers, field niggers, all of us," she emphasizes.

But aren't most of the radical leaders middle-class, after all? Ché Guevara, for instance?

She is a little taken aback. "I don't see thinking persons saying that Ché is *middle-class*. . . . I don't think he was marching around in a fancy uniform or livin' in a big white house on a hill. Ché was not *that* ilk."

Later that evening, near a bus stop in the South End, a group of Puerto Ricans are talking. They refer to themselves as "Third Worlders." At one point a young Puerto Rican says he intends to go to Cuba, perhaps this summer; that all Third Worlders should go to Cuba; that only in Cuba do they know how to treat brothers from the Third World. He adds that "oriental" brothers from Vietnam are there to meet with black brothers and that everyone is getting wise to ways to "get even with the Imperialists who live in the belly of the beast."

March 3

Efforts at coordinating New Left and Old Left and Black forces continue at a rural camp outside of Chicago where plans are being made to disrupt the Democratic National Convention, which begins on August 26. The meeting was arranged by MOBE (the National Mobilization Committee to End the War in Vietnam) and most of the radical groups are represented. The press is barred. There are elaborate efforts to keep the meeting site secret (many of the delegates came by train or car to a central depot and were then shuttled to the conference by a fleet of private cars). Among those present: Dave Dellinger, Tom Hayden, William F. Pepper of "napalm" fame, Linda Morse, and Rennie Davis. In this "political" spring, there was another gathering: The Peace and Freedom Party founding convention, held in Richmond, California, at which there was maneuvering for a Negro and Mexican-American coalition, with the Panthers playing a leading role. The gathering ended up with a toast to the "man who lives in the heart of every revolutionary—the incorruptible ever-loving leader, Ché Guevara." The whole convention sprang to its feet with cries of "Viva!"

The ranks of the *lumpenproletariat*, or "lumpen" as they call themselves here in the South End, grow daily. Jasmin has taken to wearing what seems to be a revolutionary uniform of tight blue jeans, a pale blue shirt, and a Guevara-style dark beret.

I ask her whether black activists in the ranks in Vietnam are encouraging resignations or desertions?

"Yes, in the service in Vietnam they doin' just that," she states emphatically. "Encouragin' blacks to get out. Some of them are Communists, because the men come back an' tell us that they (the Communists) join the movements and then they look for the brothers." She adds that the brothers think for themselves too. "We need these brothers here for the knowledge Uncle Sam gives them. Thank God for that. When we took them over there and trained them how to be cold-blooded killers, and so forth, that was good for us. When they got back here with Sam they could use their knowledge." Does she think that Third World activities are closely linked? "There's nothin' that goes on in the Third World now that's sporadic, that's really separated. There's a nationwide hookup. We have had rallies here and others there, for like Angela Davis. It's not isolated. Brothers on the West Coast give their time for us here, and vice versa. It's organized very well."

But is it the Chinese ideology *on the whole?* Are the leaders Maoists?

"Well perhaps that's true . . . but I can't go along with that, due to the fact that I never talked to a Chinese man in my life, nor a Chinese man to me and I got to really say it . . . white America wants to blame it on Communism, on anything but the fact that it's blacks." She stops and says with a final nod; "Blacks is *tired.* Blacks don't really care if it's Communists wake 'em up to some other factor, or whether it's some Asiatics or some Eskimos. If it makes sense to them, they gonna accept it."

And has Junior's brother brought back tales of black organization in the prison?

"He wasn't too hip to that sort of thing, but he's hip to the men inside the prisons being stripped of everything, and deciding to get organized and together. They say 'Man it's no need me and you fightin' each other, when it's whitey who's got his feet in both our mouths, yours and mine.' "

Rhetoric gets the better of her and she runs on about how these prisoners (most of them including Junior's brother, in prison for serious crimes such as murder, rape, aggravated assault) suffer because their manliness is denied them.

And do they rap?

"Are you kidding?" she asks admiringly, "they get together in cells, in the metal shops and the paint shop. They look towards Eldridge and George."

And do they smoke?

"Do they *smoke!*" Jasmin cries. "Why there's everything in God's world to be had in the joints! But not as much as there is in 'Nam." (It is true that more and more reports have been coming out of Vietnam about the GIs killing their officers, wandering across enemy lines, and as at Cam Ranh Bay, crashing their helicopters. Most of this seems to be because of "Maryjane" the soldier's sweetheart, the use of which supposedly increased one hundred percent last year; and which, in Saigon, according to laboratory tests is suprisingly strong, containing four percent resin as opposed to one-half percent in that obtainable in the United States. Because of this the Saigon marijuana has caused, medical reports say, dissociation, screaming convulsions, and flash-back effects previously found only with LSD users. Moreover the easily obtained cigarettes, packaged to look like *Lucky Strikes* or *Camels*, are sometimes dipped in opium tincture.)

March 28

By train from upper New York State to New York City: from the cold country, the chilled oat-colored fields, the frozen lakes, the pines and firs, from the large ornate houses, the out-size barns, towards the megalopolis of Manhattan and its surroundings, towards the core of Grand Central Station. That sensation of giving up rural peace and cleanliness for something closer to reality—the steady shuttle of traffic across the train windows, the assault on eyes and ears. Some of the well-dressed competent people inside the carriage are slightly rigid with worry. A tall willowy teenager is making her way towards the door, wearing a smart but somehow ridiculous blue wool suit. Straight mouse-brown hair; her long legs moving gawkily in high-heeled plastic shoes; purple smeared on her eyelids; a square make-up box in her hand. She looks strangely fatigued. As the train enters the underground to approach the station, we sit in the artificial blue-tinged light in this long tube which burrows straight for the city's heart, the center of *luxe et des lumières* (as Proudhon said of Paris).

On the slow descent from the train, a writer acquaintance is seen ahead, pushing through the crowd, a book under one arm, his intellectual's head bent like that of a bird. He waits to take my suitcase. Apparently he is going to address a group of highschool boys about the Vietnam war.

What does he tell his high school audience?

"Only one thing. I warn them that we have to rid ourselves of the *moderates*, that the moderates are the real enemy."

1968 / America Will Go Down

March 29

New York City forms its usual attractive backdrop for the Easter celebrations. Magnolias are blooming against grey stone. Women are wearing new hats and white gloves, men in decorous black mount the steps of St. Vincent's at Sixty-sixth or dip their heads to go under the arch of St. Patrick's. The plate glass of Fifth Avenue glitters with new clothes, new books, new gadgets (yet the approach of the celebration of a Christian festival doubles on this stage of one of the biggest and most sophisticated cities in the world, with a dramatic, amorphous, and questionable political play).

We travel up Broadway by taxi; the taxi man argues that he is not on the side of Martin Luther King. The taxi is old and redolent of the ghetto and the driver, unshaven and wearing a thick wool scarf around his brown neck, is gently belligerent, his statements softened by a Georgia accent. After several muttered comments, he says that he knows there are some people in charge "shouldn't be alive." He repeats this several times. Finally he says; "There going to be a revolution; something got to happen."

On Amsterdam Avenue we pass a tall man in an orange plastic suit (in this decade of the psychedelic, the Beats and the Hippies, a special liberating effect seems to be a multiplying of personality, a loosening up of those mores which place the human form in a Madison Avenue straitjacket).

The driver has thought of what he wants to say: "We got to get outah bondage—outah bondage."

March 29

A Yip-out is being held in Central Park, and it is a change to be among "white" revolutionaries instead of "black." Many of the diverse noninvolved mingle with crowds of the involved (i.e., those attached one way or another to what is loosely called the "movement"). Most of the former are young and bear distinguishing decor: tattoos, skin designs in day-glo colors, flowers in their hair, fancy dress jackets, decorations of various kinds including antique medallions, image buttons, bandeaus hung with beads, arm bands à la Viking, or belts à la Boadecia. It is a hot day and across the rather wan grass, sometimes lost in that pale glittering light, the bright figures are milling around, seated on the grass, huddled at the foot of the music truck, or giving out "freebies"—free GREGORY-FOR-PRESIDENT posters, free flyers for the just-announced FESTIVAL OF LIFE to be held in Chicago on August 25, free white balloons let loose into the smoggy air.

252

1968 / America Will Go Down

The released balloons seem as ephemeral as the touchingly child-like hopes of some of the YIP-out participants. They drift off across the horizon of the large and unmanageable city. Under a tree a young woman flower child sadly regards a wilted daffodil while she tucks bare feet under a long homespun skirt, and two children (flower children of the flower child?) climb the tree itself. Over the grassy spaces small groups carry out different activities. One collects canned food for Resurrection City; one gives out posters and pamphlets to those who promise to publicize the festival; a hollow-eyed bearded man in a fitted khaki suit hung with Hindu bells (who later admitted when accused of being "hostile" that he had had some "bad trips") stands beside a band and holds out what looks like a wooden begging cup. In a rather dusty hollow another gathering engages in a rite made up of lighting candles, playing on a bamboo pipe, prayers to Krishna (Hare—Hare—Krishna—Hare), and the absorbed dancing of a very plain but exalted girl with a long bedraggled skirt. Finally, at last two Negroes appear, bare-chested, blue-jeaned, wearing mod felt hats in gray and brown, and accompanied by a fat-hipped girl in a Chinese-style pajama outfit (apparently a Third World coalition).

But the tone of the gathering is inactive. Even while the planes drone overhead, while transistors speak of "Chevrolets," "Timex," and "Antacid Gel" and the warmth and pollution of the city weigh upon the crowds, there seems some retrograde impulse in this park picnic, a desire to tear down the mammoth technological gods and replace them with Wordsworthian communion, phallic symbols, and gentle sensual rites. As one starry-eyed couple from Newark, New Jersey, put it: "Trying to have a groovy time."

If one were to ask such a diverse group to "take me to your leader," the answer would be that there *were* no leaders. But the fact remains that a group of "organizers" stands on a small rise where the band is, that several of the committee are addressing the crowd through a bull horn ("would everyone please sit down"), while Abby Hoffman himself, head of the Yippies, dressed in what looks like a Hiawatha jacket, tattered jeans, and a head band, is gazing out over a crowd that forms the perfect united front. YIP (from which the word Yippie is taken) stands for Youth International Party, and there is some indication that the earlier rampage in Grand Central Station when partitions were smashed, signs painted on walls, a glass booth smashed, and the hands ripped off the big clock had been staged in order to swing the Hippie movement towards activism. A Mr. Lampe, organizer of this midnight gathering of more than 5,000 at a public crossroads, had said innocently that they all thought "It was going to be like a spring tonic"! But soon a "Yippie" was being described as a "Hippie who'd had his head bashed in by the police," or a "radicalized Hippie."

And political content certainly permeates the Festival, amorphous as it is. The main point seems to be to stimulate attendance at the

1968 / America Will Go Down

Democratic Convention in Chicago (as Abby Hoffman says, "I know how to stimulate actions, but not to control them").

Later

Brief political conversations are as quickly broken up as patterns on a chess board, but it is still possible to take part in them. One of the most fancily dressed organizers or leaders, whose cap is brown velvet, whose Nehru jacket is of fine embroidered yellow material from India, whose pants are almost white, and whose jewelry is a heavy silver Maltese cross, says emphatically that he does have political ideas: "I'll go further than that. I'm for Revolution. For destroying the whole shooting match . . . . What's the revolutionary aim? Socialism. Like Russia . . . like Cuba. . . . At least they're trying. You say that those societies are more repressive than this one we are complaining about? How do you know?" And then in answer to a hurried analysis of why I thought I knew: "No, I haven't been to Russia or Cuba. No, I don't read. Why don't I read? Because our papers are fakes."

On the way home from the Festival an encounter with a younger friend, Michael Macdonald. Did he agree that the affair in the park was part of a drive to get the Yippies politicized?
"Oh the Yippies? Yeah, I saw that thing in Grand Central station."
Well, what did you see?
"I saw about 6,000 young kids floating balloons. I had just been reading Elias Canetti's *Crowds and Power* in which Canetti describes the formation of so-called 'crowd crystals' when manipulated by demagogues. This was most appropriate, for while the demagogue in question, Jerry Rubin, was to be found far behind the ranks, in fact hovering near the Hotel Biltmore, the kids were confronting the cops. When this crowd whose 'crystallization' was taking place had need of a demagogue, he was off elsewhere. Just as well, because if the crowd had had a demagogue in it—it would *really* have been a disaster."
Mike is tall and thin and exceptionally intelligent. What had he felt?
"I felt that everyone was wanting to have a good time, like in the old panty raid. They were all there to get laid, or to meet their fellow freaks. But I'm trying to make the point that there was *no political point at all—none. . . .*"
So you think the whole thing was spontaneous?
"Well of course the kids got the idea via the media." He thinks it over. "No. Of course it's revolting and disgusting. These kids don't represent any organized economic group, so for that reason they have no power. For the Yippie leaders to get them beat up is very cynical."

254

1968 / America Will Go Down

After thinking further still he adds, "What appalls me about Hoffman and Rubin is that they should have called the Yip-in in the first place; for anyone with common sense or a knowledge of Canetti's 'confined spaces' would assume that this would happen. A crowd like that gets restless, it's bound to happen."

He explains that the Festival I had just attended was held in an open space, the Sheep's Meadow, and that a tolerant attitude was agreed upon by the police; but when you had a milling crowd confined in Grand Central Station, the police were bound in duty to interfere.

So you *don't* think the gathering was spontaneous?

"If you wish to say it was a conspiracy, please indict the AP and the UPI . . . but I'm ready to agree that it was a deliberate act to get those kids involved. However, you must include the New York Police Force for being so slow in closing the place after a few thousand had appeared."

We walk up Fifth Avenue. Mike is elegant in a dark suit and silk shirt, and obviously doesn't consider himself a member of the counter-culture; as a matter of fact, he talks about political unrest in an extremely aloof manner.

On Broadway at 122nd and not far from Columbia University, there is a small storefront plastered with mimeographed flyers, advertisements for student activities, and photographs of the "Movement." This is the office of the Liberation News Services.

Among the teachers tapping by on their high heels, on this, the last day of school before the Easter weekend, an old man stands staring at the storefront. With a severe expression on his face, he asks the dark thin student who seems to be in charge, "Liberation? Liberation from *what?*" and the student seems embarrassed, as if it were, in the end, a question not too easily answered. The storefront appears to be a single room. It has tables and chairs, a telex, two typewriters, pigeonholes, and at the end a large blackboard divided into columns and indicating the type of event or happening reported, the name of the reporter, and the deadline suggested. At the side of the room an electric coffee jug stands on an up-ended wooden box. Two girls enter behind me, wearing short skirts, black stockings, and sloppy jackets. One has shining dark hair and clutches a copy of *Why Children Fail* by John Holt. The other is plain and serious, wears glasses, and has her throat tied up rather clumsily with a Prussian blue scarf.

The young thin dark man who is now typing (and whose name seems to be George) looks up at the girls and asks them: "Can you type?" and adds in a tired voice that he has been on duty for twelve consecutive hours. (From a conversation with George, and from an examination of the literature, it seems that the LNS or Liberation News

Service, attempts to coordinate material for the underground newspapers. It is also allied with various other news services: Student Communications Network, *Presse Estudiante Nationale* in Montreal, Afro-American News Service in SNCC's Atlanta office, and the European News Service in London. Hanoi and Peking are not on this member list, but it is noticeable that they are shown on another list as recipients of news.)

Where do the stories come from? George (editor and student) answers candidly that they come from all over, that there is no check on their authenticity and that they often have to be rewritten. I see a story about Rap Brown which goes something like this: "So Rap Brown was hit on the head and was bleeding. He held his head and it was hit again. The blood poured to the ground, but Rap Brown didn't fall with his blood. . . . After he was taken to the station, they stopped hitting his head. . . . Meanwhile his loving wife and his loving children waited for their Daddy." There was no mention of the fact that Rap Brown had been arrested for possession of a gun. What about this? George looks a bit embarrassed, and folds up the story as if to throw it away. "That's not ours," he says. Outside the door on the storefront window, a photograph clipped from a newspaper shows hero "Rap" looking rather self-satisfied. It has a verse attached to it:

> *American will go down*
> *with H. Rap Brown. . . .*

Whether America is to "go down" in just this way is one thing; but there is also the whole question of a free press. (According to statistics eight countries are listed as having lost their free press between 1966 and 1967.) And now there is the new urge to bar reporters from reportable gatherings. As an example, today at the Diplomat, that rather faded white-and-gold-lobbied hotel which has been adopted by the "new Negro"—we hear that Stokeley Carmichael is going to speak. The speech is to be held in the upstairs ballroom; and outside small groups of black men and women have already gathered, while upstairs a row of smart (and lighter-colored) girls sit at a long table with red rosettes on their lapels and piles of literature in front of them. Husky men are putting up sound equipment. Another white reporter arrives; and as our pale faces appear at the doorway, three young black men advance upon us and ask us to return to our newspapers and tell them to send black reporters instead. We argue vainly for a moment or two, murmuring about "freedom of the press," and cravenly attempting to give assurances that we are not hostile. One of the young guards smiles and is pleasant. The beautiful young ladies at the table look modest and uninvolved. A short and rather dwarf-like man pushes his way forward and with his brief black beard jutting towards the ceiling asks belligerently, "Why don't we *throw them out?*"

1968 / America Will Go Down

At that moment Stokeley Carmichael, wearing a particularly attractive dashiki of black velvet, edged with embroidery, sweeps into the room with his black entourage. In spite of the humor of the situation and the special charms of the "black is beautiful" idea, it is upsetting that not only are whites being kept out of "black" meetings, but that there is a lack of vigorous "black" writing and analysis.

April 4

It is midnight in New York City.

Martin Luther King has been shot. He stood on the balcony of the Lorraine Motel outside Room 306, in sweltering Memphis, where there had been warnings of tornadoes. (It had been hot the summer before too when the city had been filled with rumors of rioting and black/white confrontations, and of a SNCC barn on the outskirts filled with arms.) Apparently Martin Luther King had just shaved and dressed for the evening and had called down gaily from the balcony to a band leader and soloist who was standing in the courtyard, and had asked him to remember to sing a special song for him that evening, "Precious Lord Take my Hand."

A few moments later a shot rang out and King fell to the balcony floor "slowly, slowly, in a dream sequence," as someone testified. He fell in a pool of blood, the right side of his jaw shot away. . . .

In New York streets the ominous feeling of something being about to happen. A coldness and emptiness in the streets. Restless groups of young blacks converge on Times Square, there is the soft murmuring rhythm of police cars. At the mall in Central Park black leaders are going to address the crowd.

April 5

The most militant of those who spoke last night was James Forman of SNCC. He projected the apocalyptic nature of the event. "The end of non violence has come . . . we can go to the streets and take care of business. . . ." He talked about blowing up water plants, power plants, high buildings. But apparently the words rang out without echo against a sea of faces. Listeners seemed stunned: for some reason these were not the words they wanted.

The papers show the front of the Lorraine Motel like a cross-section in a theatre. In the hot colorless light the black figures appear and disappear, emerge onto the balcony and into the courtyard below, their

257

white shirts contrasting with their skin and hair and arms. In the courtyard a maid in a white uniform, a policeman with his badge making a star on his chest. One has to imagine that a street away there is a window of a shabby bathroom where a stranger propped a gun on the sill until he had King caught in his sights.

Police have sent out a call for a white Mustang, with a red and white rear tag. It has been seen in various places. On Highway 78 between Birmingham and Memphis, a few blocks down from a house on South Main Street, in an area of second-hand stores and pawnshops. (Here there is a long hall with yellow-green linoleum, a single fifty watt bulb in the ceiling, a door with the doorknob missing. Inside a tattered shade, a sagging metal bed, a faded greasy red sofa. This is Room 6B, rented and paid for by the assassin.)

Even while Martin Luther King lay on the balcony, the blood flowing from a wound as big as a fist—but *"flowing and banking up on itself, while his eyes turned this way and that and changed color slowly, the lens and the iris merging into each other and fading . . ."*—the news of his murder was already flashing onto millions of TV sets. Not very long afterwards, in fact with little pause for grief, the black nationalists were rounding up their forces, telling them that the old way was "bankrupt," that from now on arson, rioting, shooting, had come into its own. As the news spread along Fourteenth Street and its narrow intersections in Washington D.C. on April 4 and as a crowd gathered around the main office of the Southern Christian Leadership Conference—while President Johnson's voice was sounding over radios and transistors and urging restraint—Stokely Carmichael (who has been in Washington since last year but using it only as a headquarters for his trips to Chicago, Buffalo, Detroit, Hanoi, Havana, etc.) is heard by a colleague in the SCLC to mutter bitterly, "They've taken Dr. King off; it's time to end this non-violence bullshit." And moments later, brushing off some of the moderates who had run after him, he is proceeding down Fourteenth Street with a crowd of young militants at his heels, urging the closing of businesses and schools.

April 6

Constant reports come over the radio. The battle to close the schools of Washington has been won. W. L. Hall, organizer for SNCC, is reported as pressuring one principal: "Close the schools within thirty minutes or *we* will." The papers report a policeman hearing a young black announce, "They're going to burn down the whole town this weekend." Arson and violence have begun in more than forty cities. Taunting blacks surge around cars driven by white motorists. Young boys get drunk on cans of beer found in the rubble. At Howard University black nationalists haul down the American flag to hoist that of the *Members of Ujamma*. Here speaker after speaker stresses genocide. Carmichael has held a news conference at the Headquarters of the New School of Afro-American Thought at 2208 Fourteenth Street, NW. Since early in the year he has been attempting to organize the taking over of local institutions by blacks. Now he says, "When white America killed Dr. King last night she declared war on us. There will be no crying and there will be no funeral. There is no longer need to make intellectual decisions. Black people know that they have to get guns." Someone from the crowd, perhaps a reporter, calls out, "Stokely, what do you see all this leading to? A blood bath in which nobody wins"? To this Stokely answers, "First, my name is Mr. Carmichael, and secondly, black people will survive the bath."

Later. The National Guard has been called out to patrol the burning smoking Washington Streets, where broken glass glitters, where firemen are pelted with stones and tin cans, where police wade through the debris of smashed and trampled goods, where the air is thick with the smell of tear gas and spilled liquor. A fireman records seeing a young black watch looters stream out of Morton's supermarket, then pull a bottle filled with gasoline out of his pocket, light the fuse and hurl it into the building. This same young arsonist repeats his actions on two other occasions. At Morton's afterwards the body of a young black boy of twelve is discovered, burned beyond recognition. Is this Washington, monument to the New World, where today the dome of the Capitol is half hidden by smoke, where cinders drift amongst the pink petals of the cherry blossoms?

Those who take strong positions at crucial moments in history may expect to die violently. If Martin Luther King had been an object of hate to white citizens' organizations in the south, a more complex danger faced him from black militants, so that he was presented with a double jeopardy (in fact the most vocal and aggressive of his own race had rejected him, calling him Uncle Tom and derisively nicknaming him "De Lawd").

But whether black or white prompted this convenient death, they brought about, from the point of view of Marxists, and/or Third World forces, an ideologically correct result. Even if King had been assassinated by the whitest of the white, or the blackest of the black, in death extremists would step over his body to riot and burn; black moderates long subjected to fear of being caught between two forces, of being thought pro-whitey by the militants now find themselves left leaderless. No similar event could have been more calculated to disarm one group, and place weapons in the hands of another.

1968 / America Will Go Down

April 10

While prayers and eulogies were delivered yesterday; while behind the coffin covered with flowers, young black men clasped their hands and sang "We Shall Overcome," while King's widow Coretta, her sorrowful face half-hidden behind her black veil, sat in a pew holding to her youngest child, the police fanned out through the south hunting the assassin, concentrating on Birmingham, Alabama; Chicago, and Mexico. Special squads leafed through passenger lists at Delta and Southern Airlines, visited gun stores, and telephoned Mazatlan on the Mexican Pacific coast, to which an unobtrusive long-nosed man was thought to have obtained a travel card.

... it's time to end this non-violence bull-shit.
Stokely Carmichael,
after the assassination
of Martin Luther King.

The cobbled street near the river glistens under the lights with a peculiar soulless patina, and blocks of buildings cast shadows on the corners—parabolas of black checkered squares, poles and wires with intermittent lights. In the foyer of the New Yorker Theatre on Broadway the legitimate show is over and a group of bearded young men have set up a stall and are giving away free copies of New Left literature—copies of WIN, publicity from the Free School of New York, flyers for the Student Communications Network, and a long laborious, closely reasoned appeal for volunteers for study groups and action committees—asking volunteers to accept a role which might not appeal to their egos but which would have political results (roles as counselors, servers, persuaders, and organizers). The appeal sounds a depressingly manipulative note. It contrasts with, but also somehow compliments, the films being shown to the half-empty house. These have been put out by Camera News, Inc., and are described as "socially committed newsreels" which are "aggressively and unequivocally biased." According to Mr. Robert Kramer, the film director who helped found Camera News ("We aren't interested in presenting a balanced picture."), the documents had been made possible because of the gift of 180,000 feet of free black and white film (the name of the donor is not revealed). Most of them are anti-war, anti-Vietnam, or anti-draft documentaries. (Although appeals against war are legitimate enough these films have been so cut that shots of the faces of white soldiers, taken from below so that the chins are expanded to brutal proportions, are juxtaposed continually with the dead bodies of soldiers with oriental features.)

There is also an aggressively pounding musical accompaniment. The flailing batons of police in demonstrations are isolated from action and vague distorted pictures of rioters are immediately followed by the up-and-down rhythm of the batons and occasional shots of a savage white face, never a black face, so that the continual stress seems to be upon white brutality. The applause is sporadic and unenthusiastic. (Memories of a Candian documentary called *The Mills of the Gods*, produced by Beryl Fox, in which drunken sadistic-looking GIs are shown bawling out the verses of the "Battle Hymn of the Republic" while shots of dead Vietnamese spring out again and again from under the heavy G.I. boots.) In the context of a world movement devoted to identifying the white race with cruelty and murder, such propaganda is becoming more and more common. Tonight the unpleasant impression created by the films is disturbing because of the recent assassination. Leaving the theatre a man in the crowd ahead of me complains to the group in the publicity booth that the films are "racist." "I thought I was coming to see something serious." "Yes," his small but spirited wife says sourly, "Give me back my two bucks"! "*We* think they're serious," one of the young men says slowly, "*we* think . . ." "They're essentially dehumanized," the older man protests. "War *isn't* human." The bearded young organizer looks quickly at his companions and then at the older couple who stand in front of him blocking the exit. "There is no communication between my generation and the people who make wars," he adds with desperate proud finality.

April 18

Last night the showing of the films had seemed a symptom of the white radical turning upon himself. Now it is possible to look at the King assassination and see how whites have reacted. (Because King was *black*, his death had to be due to white racism. This is stated again and again; if not stated openly, it is implied. I. F. Stone went so far as to deny even white sympathy, ". . . the masses they sang were not so much of requiem as of thanksgiving. . .").

On the other hand, if Stone is right, he fails to note how many black militants also give the impression of rejoicing. Now at last there is no longer need for "intellectual discussion." This from Floyd McKissick. Other blacks, for instance Jared Israel, of the jet black hair and the well-developed karate arms, founder of the Harvard PLP saw the assassination as a great advance. "The assassination of Martin Luther King was a great step forward in the liberation struggle of the black people."

And further back still there is Malcolm X's recognition of the restraining power of this inspired preacher. "King was the best weapon that 'the man,' who wants to brutalize Negroes, has."

The truth is that the bullet has struck home deeply, wounding America itself, as did the bullet which killed John Kennedy. Americans, not understanding how important they are, how much their dream has meant to the world at large, can think of nothing to do but apologize. It seems natural to many of them that the assassination of King should be used as yet another reason to attack their values. But it is as if they don't know how it all happens, how in this period of attempted political change, when she has actually made tremendous and pragmatic transformations in her own society, the United States has been designated "the enemy." Does she know that in a thousand secret meetings, under the arc lights of platforms, in village communes in China and Hanoi, in remote rooms in Bagdad, Accra, and Capetown, as well as in slum rooms in Harlem, the word has gone out: "The United States is the common enemy." ("United States imperialism is the root cause of all evils and the common enemy of the people in Asia, Africa, and Latin America," Chou En-lai said in 1956 before the second Bandung Conference in Zanzibar, to a cheering crowd.) And now that the United States has been declared the enemy, not only by "outside" groups, or by those "inside" groups ideologically opposed to her; but as well by some of her establishment and many of her intellectuals and professionals—a sense of guilt is defacing truth. That a concerted effort is directed against her is not easily accepted. As Whittaker Chambers said long ago "it was an invincible ignorance, rooted in what was most generous . . . it was rooted too . . . in what was most singular in the American experience, which because it had prospered so much apart from the rest of the world, could not really realise that there was a crisis in history. . . ." America, the first modern gathering of all nations, like that early democratic Russian gathering, accepts the guilt ("the *Mir* bears all").

This passive American acceptance is one of the symptoms of our time. The stunned confusion which followed the assassination of John F. Kennedy in 1963 seems to have left the nation weak and unable to gauge its own responsibilities; beyond that the immediacy, in fact the torrent of everyday events leaves little space for adjustment.

Now suddenly an irony becomes evident. The young U.S. activists are more interested in "making revolution" than in examining their own values, and because of this are blind to global nuances. In Prague, once capital of the Holy Roman Empire, there have always been strong attachments to the West; and at last this attachment begins to bloom in a modest but unprecedented confrontation with the Soviet Union. Czechoslovakia, coveted by Hitler because of its strategic situation and its arms industry, and taken over by the Russians after World War II for somewhat the same reasons, is now challenging totalitarianism, which, in their wrong headedness, American extremists continue to woo. Therefore even while youthful crowds surge along the streets of

1968 / America Will Go Down

Prague going to rallies for Dubcek in desperate hopes of true liberation, delegates from the American New Left also pass through the city, but to meet with delegates from North Korea, North Vietnam, and China.

Prague is said to be a fairy tale city. (In 1970 I spent a week there, and found this especially true at sunset as seen from any of the seven hills upon which, like Rome, it is built. The Hrad, or Castle, was the birthplace of Bohemian kings, and here courtyards of fitted stone, enclosing churches, chapels, and statues, form an oasis from which one looks down upon the city with its warm complex of pinkish hip-tiled roofs and upon the windings of the Vltava River with its parade of bridges—where once a single stone ford made it possible for wooden carts laden with salt, in that ancient trade which linked the East with the Frankish kingdoms, to cross on their way to Byzantium. In the heart of this romantic place, like some malignant foreign body arbitrarily introduced, a new-looking, no-colored tiled building, rather like an oversized tomb—the Ministry of the Interior, i.e., the Ministry of Fear—rises to emphasize the police powers of the new-style socialist regime. It was called by one Czech, with whom I managed a brief conversation, the "most hated building in Prague.") One of the many episodes which mars the city's tranquility at this moment is the mysterious death last August of Charles Jordan, Vice President of the Joint Distribution Committee (JDC), a leading U.S. Jewish Relief Agency. Jordan had disappeared from his Prague hotel and his body had been found floating in the Vltava River. The Czech authorities had refused to delay the autopsy so that JDC doctors could attend it. They finally declared that Jordan had committed suicide and might have jumped into the river from the First of May Bridge, although friends declared that this was impossible. They said Jordan had been cheerful and healthy, had sent normal postcards, had planned to travel through Europe with his wife. Later, when Ladislav Mnacko, a Czech writer, defected, he told Westerners that the death was almost certainly an example of "homicidal anti-Semitism." (There is a great deal of sympathy towards Israel among the Czechs themselves, but the Communist officials follow the hard anti-Israeli line, and Jordan, who was a particularly energetic organizer, may have triggered the suspicions of the secret police by visiting Jewish communities in Prague and associating with dissidents.) The *London Times* noted on August 26 last year that journalists have been threatened and that one British traveler was searched and dumped across the border. But as a more sinister corollary to the whole Jordan affair, a Swiss pathologist, Professor Ernst Hardmeier (who was retained by the JDC to conduct an autopsy) was found dead three months ago in a snowy forest near Zurich several hundred yards from his locked automobile. The professor was sixty-three years old and had not finished the examination of minor evidence relating to the case.

As if influenced by the new ferment of inquiry in Czechoslovakia, there is now, in April, a demand for the reinvestigation of an older and more burning case of supposed murder (that of Jan Masaryk, son of Thomas Masaryk, founder of the free state of Czechoslovakia). This is partly because the body of Dr. Joseph Brestansky, deputy President of Czechoslovakia's Supreme Court, was found hanging from a tree near Baluce, south of Prague, on the second of this month. Dr. Brestansky had recently been given the task of the rehabilitation of those unjustly tried and sentenced by the Stalinist purges of the fifties. Again, a few weeks ago, another man, Major Bedrich Pokorny, a former Czech intelligence officer who had investigated Masaryk's death, was found hanging in the woods near Brno. His death was also listed as suicide; but dead men tell no tales, and Czechs believe that he was killed to prevent him from testifying.

Some of the Masaryk story is mirrored in the experiences of Marcia Davenport, an American journalist who first saw Prague in 1930, who associated the romantic river with the music of Smetana, who delighted in crossing the Charles Bridge where the Gothic saints are haloed with iron lace, who loved the butter-yellow baroque houses of the Lorentanska, and leaned as have so many enchanted visitors upon the parapet of the Hradni Prikop to look down on the ancient roofs, the gardens, the onion domes, the palaces with their fairy tale facades.

In *Too Strong for Fantasy* she speaks of the years which came later. "... They hide (Prague's) noble architecture with a tribune draped in red banners, surrounded by streamers of lying slogans and bloated lithographs of party satraps; then it is raucous with drilled robots shouting as Hitler's pigs used to do. ... The loveliness I first met half my lifetime ago is gone forever ... I could not know that then; in the wildest of nightmares I could not have dreamt it. ...."

In 1945 when the Germans were surrendering everywhere in Europe, when Patton's army had been forbidden to move further, and when the Russians were occupying the airport and were taking their time in entering the city, Jan Masaryk had a residence on the second floor of the Czernin Palace (referred to as the Cerninsky) up the hill through the old streets of the Mala Strana, that square flanked by superb Baroque palaces on which the old Castle faces. She (Marcia D.) describes the magnificent rooms, the sitting room and library, and finally that long narrow room with very high richly decorated ceilings, with enormous windows looking over the Loreta, and one plain brass bed. Through those days the scene in Prague was that of two opposing processions. There were two Red armies, the European one, which did not act too badly, and that other of Malinovsky, an army of primitives, unshaven, filthy, retreating with their loot, with everything from window curtains to pianos, mattresses and chairs, all loaded onto stolen carts and pulled by thin stolen horses. And as the one procession retreated to the East, another entered, an army of "tortured legions," returning from the Nazi concentration camps, the thin large-eyed relics with their numbers tattooed into their flesh; up the streets past the Gestapo headquarters where in the white-tiled dungeons the torture instruments were still laid out, and where blood still stained the blade of the guillotine.

As Marcia Davenport says, the Communists, wherever they went—in the concentration camps, in the armed forces, in the underground, in the West—used every device to undermine the governments they called "bourgeois." They collaborated with the Nazis, they formed cells in the camps whose purpose was to betray Czech democrats, they laid the groundwork during the war for the entities called National Committees (Narodny Vybor), which mushroomed in every community as the tanks and guns of the Red Army drew closer. During the 1948 takeover, Marcia watched Jan, her lover, crossing the street in his old brown coat, on his last day, his guard beside him. Another shadow fell in behind. A few days later Jan's old friend, John Foster called her and told her that Jan had been found dead in the courtyard below his windows. "I know," she writes, "that there are innumerable entrances to the Cerninsky Palace, other than the main ones. And more cogently there are many ways . . . of entering the rooms that were Jan's without using the principal passages and doors. Jan and I had not failed to explore these features and we used to shudder after we had counted a total of eleven different means of access to his private rooms.

"One man who saw Jan's body that morning says that he lay flat on his back dressed in blue silk pajamas, his legs extended straight and his arms straight also with the palms of his hands flat on the ground. The bones of his heels were shattered (a typical suicide jump would go feet first, the legs and feet are telescoped into the body on impact). The above meant that Jan's body was unconscious before it hit the pavement of the courtyard. There was also plaster in the finger nails, abrasions on the finger tips, the room was in disorder. The autopsy was done in such haste that the physician of Dr. Benes could not attend it. And within a few months the doctor who was present, Dr. Tetly, was dead himself in the Prague Police Headquarters. He was given—or gave himself—an injection of gasoline!"

We live in an age of martyrs, in a century from which pity has been eradicated, in which the struggle for liberty is so intense that all the trappings of humanism fall away. As Bert Wolfe put it in *Das Kapital*—

1968 / America Will Go Down

100 Years in the Life of a Doctrine, "Capitalism, according to Marx came into the world conceived in sin, a congenital blood stain on its cheek, dripping blood and dirt from head to foot, from every pore." Yet Marx had never produced a blueprint of a new society, had only criticized the old, and it was left to his followers to attempt, by ideological pressures, by gun and torture, and by the extension of the old Tzarist police state to bring into being his "new" society. Present-day Czechoslovakia is as good an example as any of the internal struggle created.

After viewing this Czechoslovak reality, the polite ideological wrangling which goes on every day in a normal democratic society, the attrition so to speak of daily political life, approaches frivolity. In this sense the long exchanges of letters one sees in the columns of U.S. journals (for instance those being published in the *New York Review of Books* between Mary McCarthy and Diana Trilling about Vietnam) are distinguished by the fact that they take place in a country where an exchange is at least possible. And one of the curious aspects of this correspondence is Mary McCarthy's expression of solidarity with Pavel Litvinov and Larissa Daniel, and her imagining that they have a future, while being careless of the future of their counterparts in North Vietnam, or implying that in North Vietnam such people don't exist.

Into such blind gulfs as this fall the graduates of our Western knowledge factories, possessed by the mythic possibilities of their personal missions. Just as there is something wrong with Mary McCarthy's easy comparison between herself, a non-captive American, and someone like Pavel Litvinov, so there is something wrong with the comparisons of the New Left delegates who at this time travel to Prague (encouraged and probably paid for by the STB, i.e. the Czech Foreign Intelligence Service, *Statin Tajna Bezpecnost,* in their turn supervised by the "uncles" of the KGB). The New Left delegates see Czechoslavakia and ignore the Czechs themselves; and Mary McCarthy sees Russia but not North Vietnam, forgetting that old reactions of the thirties can be repeated in the sixties, that now as then the real voice is that of those who are afraid to speak. How doubly true this must be, is stressed at the very moment when Ho Chi Minh has announced the death decree for those who engage in "defeatist" talk against the war.

April 28

The house on east Sixty-sixth Street has a small garden at the back. The spring has brought green leaves to the trees below. Looking out from the upper window in this enclave of protected back gardens, a fine tinge of green appears across almost all of the worn brick walls; already tulips bloom in one of the shadowed window boxes, and a cool breeze blows up from the river two or three blocks further east.

The devastating aftermath of Martin Luther King's assassination has been displaced by the turmoil at Columbia University where students, according to a phrase of Hayakawa (President of San Francisco State College) are opposing what they call the "illegitimacy of contemporary authority." Apparently, a student named Mark Rudd, a Columbia junior, has been one of the main sparkplugs behind a stream of demonstrations, leaflets, proselytizing, and obstruction of normal student activities. In January he became president of SDS, and early this week he led 100 radical students in a sit-in strike in Low Library, explaining to newsmen that he was "amazed that it worked." The point seems to be less a question of Columbia itself than an attempt to show that without undue effort a big university can be taken over and its activities brought to a standstill. In other words it is a "radical exercise" sponsored by SDS and echoed and applauded all over the country.

(Maurice L—, a graduate history student at Columbia, explains on the phone that the strategy had been planned at the SDS National Council in Bloomington, Indiana, last December where Communists, he thinks, played an "open" role for the first time. What does he believe the strategy is? "An attempt to draw blood, to polarize the community over the question of bringing in the troops, to pressure against the war, and against military research in the big universities." And what is Rudd himself like? "He's one of those high-keyed types who'd make a good executive! But he's turned his talents towards revolution instead. An authoritarian adolescent underneath. Besides that, he's just back from Cuba, and he's making a big thing about Ché Guevara.")

April 29

Lunch with Sol Sanders who is now an Edward R. Murrow Fellow at the Counsel for Foreign Relations and is about to finish the galleys of his book *A Sense of Asia*. Ostensibly our meeting is to talk about the media and Vietnam, but the immediate situation at Columbia preempts much of the conversation. Mark Rudd and his fellows have hold of one of the deans in Hamilton Hall and are releasing demands ranging from amnesty for themselves to stopping construction on the gym bordering Harlem. Math Hall has been rechristened a "commune." A Karl Marx poster and a red flag have been hoisted. Stairways have been greased. Liberals have been shouted down. Maoists have been invited in to show movies, and the slogan Lenin Won, Fidel Won, We Will Win is scrawled on the walls. Tom Hayden has also appeared, and Stokely Carmichael is supposed to be paying a flying visit.

We sit drinking wine. Sol talks of the nature of the students involved, and of the psychological needs of the activists. "I heard this ardent Trotskyist calling out that the 'new man will know how to live in a society where freedom has replaced necessity.' That reversal of a classic phrase gives away a whole generation!"

Soon we are discussing the old sad mistakes that men make in war, the mistakes which occur whenever vast operations are set in motion. We talk of the inadequacy of the press coverage of the Vietnam war. "In late 1964 I had a luncheon for McNamara in Saigon with a group of correspondents," Sol says, "and I remember thinking that a certain journalistic stupidity was partly responsible for much of what was happening. There was a famous episode in the spring of '63, the Battle of Ac Bac when a South Vietnamese regiment shelled itself—this was written up as a 'horrendous' thing as if it were the first time in history. There were all sorts of unjustified, even some quite irrelevant, accusations. It was said that Diem was 'out of touch with reality,' that 'he never got out of the palace' and so on. Well, people at the luncheon were talking and I was silent, my friend turned and said, 'Sanders, you've been here longer than anyone, what do you think?' And I said, 'Well, you can have 500,000 American troops here, and they will still get ambushed if you don't have intelligence.' I remember the knowing smiles when I said this, as if it were unfashionable just to mention intelligence. Yet actually these journalists were the ones out of tune with their age, scarcely aware of the role intelligence must play in such a war, and especially in this age of nuclear power." He pauses and adds: "The problems of Asia are on a vast scale, and essentially what Americans have to sell is ideas; ideas which are the opposite to that dogmatism in the Communist philosophy which begins with the preaching of a determinist doctrine, and degenerates into a simple necessity of the manipulation of power for power's sake."

From the house on Sixty-sixth Street, a long tangled phone conversation with J—, mostly about Columbia. J—'s quite sharp intelligence does not protect him from an emotional predisposition towards the idea that youthful political activity has a special virtue. Since SDS has assiduously projected the image of spontaneous rebellion, he seems to have the idea that the "uprising" has an authentic ring.

But aren't high-pressure radical salesmen pushing the "revolution" in the same way that Madison Avenue pushes the "man of distinction"?

"Don't be so cynical," he advises. "Go up to Columbia, walk into history"!

1968 / America Will Go Down

"I was there several weeks ago."

"That was before the revolution." (He laughs as he says this.)

"I was at Berkeley in 1964. It's all familiar to me. They used the same strategy."

"The way you use the word *'strategy,'* as if military commandos were out there with their men."

"Lenin used the word. . . ."

At lunch the argument with J— goes on, in the same pervasive half joking but bitter atmosphere in which at this time in America's history so many operate, the atmosphere of a civil war: Jews against Jews, parents against children, friends against friends.

"You're not like Mark Rudd, are you?"

"Mark Rudd?" he sounds surprised. "Why should I be *like* him?"

"First we will make the revolution, and then we will find out what for?"

"Did he say that?"

In spite of his impulsive sympathies, J— has an orderly mind. "So you're saying that he's really down there exploiting these fellow students?"

"Yes. To make the revolution he needs strong young 'front-fighters,' as they call them. The question of exploitation has been decided long ago. It's taken for granted. In fact, he was quite satisfied; he said 'the cop violence is good.' "

Afterwards we walk up from the noisy lively restaurant warm with the smell of seafood towards Fifth Avenue.

"So you think he's a Commie?" J— asks in a sly voice.

"What does the term mean any longer? He's just back from Cuba. He adores Ché Guevara. He's undoubtedly listened, learned, worked on Cuban projects, perhaps had lectures, training, advice. The idea is to 'make' the revolution."

Soon, unaccountably, suddenly against the logic of old friendship, of a pleasant meal, of the stupor of wine in the middle of the day, we are in another angry battle over Vietnam. The question this time is the "domino theory." The domino theory is being caricatured by those who suggest that immediately upon the withdrawal of the U.S. from Vietnam, the whole area will automatically turn towards Communism (rather than agreeing that in such a case the Southeast Asian countries would have to adjust their economic and defense policies to those of Peking rather than to those of Washington). J—'s voice rises, "Don't tell me you've fallen for *that* lousy piece of propaganda? Why you and Dean Rusk, not to mention L.B.J. . . . ." His protests bounce off the strong walls of Manhattan buildings. The surprised, swiftly-moving pedestrians on Fifth Avenue glance sideways at a man and a woman shouting at each other about the "domino theory."

"It's *vanity*!"

"What do you mean *vanity*?"

"It's pure *vanity* to dismiss a realistic danger like that. It means disregard for countries too weak to defend themselves. You can choose *not* to fight in Vietnam—and no one can foresee history—but you can hardly dismiss the possibility that *not* fighting will mean the fall of other countries."

A youngish, very elegantly dressed man, holding the arm of a girl in a smart black dress who clutches a bunch of spring flowers, moves ostentatiously past us. He bends his head towards her and says in an annoyed voice, "The one with the loudest voice will win!"

Just to look at Morningside Park (that symbolic green belt which separates Columbia from Harlem, where the university's plan to build a gynmasium building provided the occasion for the demonstrations that led to the uprising) is to remember the similarities and the differences in the ideologies of those groups which have been trying to take over buildings on the campus. The park is considered hazardous and now it is nicknamed "Muggerside," a fact which should have made the university gym project desirable to Harlem residents as an anti-crime move—and in fact did so, until articulate groups began to foster a movement against it. Today the excavation for the gymnasium (which was to have had a free community swimming pool and other facilities on the ground floor) seems abandoned, and all work halted. Only one or two children loiter around the edges of the half-dynamited site.

If the turmoil at Columbia was to some extent triggered by general SDS policy to exert pressure against the war in Vietnam and against the use of universities for defense research, the purposes of the Black Coalition, in their "pure" enclave in Hamilton Hall (looked down upon by a giant poster of Malcolm X) approached, via nationalism, the same goal. "Negroes hold Hamilton Hall," Rudd had said, and added that this was a question of division of labor. "Now we have *two* strongholds."

The blacks reigned supreme in Hamilton Hall in a litter of documents, broken fixtures, milk cartons, and sandwich papers (with a security officer darting in at one point to rescue a Rembrandt valued at $48,000).

Beyond the irritating sense of the "imposed revolution" is the present linkage of anti-Semitism with the New Left. Even at Columbia, with its high percentage of Jewish students, it is being accepted that there should be identification first of the "White Establishment" as "racist and Nazi-minded," and of the police as the "Gestapo"; secondly, of America itself as Amerika; and thirdly, of "Zionists" and "Israelis" as those who engage in "genocide." The purpose appears to be to draw what free-floating hostility exists in the inhabitants of this whole Columbia-Harlem area into one single channel.

Ever since the Israeli victory last year—and this is what is "new"— there has been a marked expansion of the activities of the Organization of Arab Students (OAS) which has about 10,000 members who pay seven dollars a year to the New York City Headquarters, and about 7,000 more belonging to a hundred U.S. and Canadian chapters. The general aim is to influence public opinion. Now this organization has begun to petition support from all the New Left and black extremist groups, and to draw as many Arab students as possible into contact with them. Last month OAS members began visiting the Arab delegations and embassies in New York and Washington, and the consulates in the U.S. and Canadian cities. There are stories of special pressure being used and of money being collected from Arabs living as far away as Latin America. In fact the OAS—which is supposed to be cultural, educational, and open to all kinds of ideologies—is now heavily bearing down on Israel and identifying with propaganda in the black groups. (*The Black Conscience* for this month, published in Detroit by the Organization for Afro-American Education, denounces Israel and uses material published by the Socialist Workers Party, i.e., the Trotskyist party, which although it would cause Trotsky to turn in his grave, has ranged itself firmly alongside black militant anti-Semitism.) In concrete terms, Al Fatah has moved in to occupy a vacuum. There is the most dramatic support in the New Left/Arab/black coalition for the Palestinian Liberation movements, for Red China ("We salute the great Chinese people"), for East Germany and North Korea. The white Israelis and "white Colonial oppressors" are lumped together and opposed to the third-world anti-colonial, anti-capitalist dark-skinned peoples in that kind of bitter polarization which marks an ominous step forward in negative political campaigns. Every speech, every article, and the whole vocabulary in use are impregnated with visceral references to Israelis who are planning genocide; pro-Israel imperialists who are using napalm; whites who are pro-apartheid and exploiting blacks in South Africa; and black victims of white Zionist Jewish landlords here in U.S. cities. There are even references to gas ovens with the old victims (the Jews) mysteriously turned into operators. All the nations of Africa are brought into this on the whole very primitive propaganda, and it is sometimes broadened until it reaches as far as Fiji and the islands of New Guinea. As a friend in B'nai B'rith notes sardonically, "There seems no one left to condemn Arab genocide against the blacks of the Sudan!"

1968 / America Will Go Down

Friday, May 11

The Connecticut Thruway, going North again. Coffee stop where the food is served cafeteria style; and the pre-fab walls are of imitation walnut paneling. A boisterous argument is going on between a waitress and a young male helper who shouts from the kitchen, "I wuz going to help you bring that butter out that's all. No kiddin'."

The waitress, standing near a case of cartons of chocolate milk, is polishing glasses. "This joker," she comments, "this big-mouth. . . ."

A truck driver leaning on the case suggests, "Give'm a rap on the teeth!" (Good-humored laughter echoes through the room.)

"Well—" the waitress shouts back to the kitchen, "thought you was bringin' me a present for Mother's Day."

After a while the boy shouts in return, "You ever see that movie?"

"What movie?"

From the depths of the kitchen. "That movie, that *war* movie."

"*What* war movie, I said."

"I said the war movie, didn't I?"

The waitress comes into sudden focus. She has orange-colored hair, and a slightly pale face with orange-colored lipstick; yet she is attractive in that inimitable vigorous "All-American" manner.

"Oh *ferget* it," she says with scorn.

Waiting at a garage to have a tire repaired; sitting on a slightly worn patch of grass and reading "The Steps of the Pentagon" by Norman Mailer in the March issue of *Harpers*. The cars rush by on the highway with that same impatience which characterizes Mailer's writing. There is a perfume of early flowers, sun-baked tires, and gasoline—as well-integrated as the prose.

The article is ostensibly about the demonstration of October 21 last year when the New Left and its accompanying retinues tried to march on the Pentagon, but it owes a lot to the novelist's frank revelations about himself ("Mailer was the worst kind of snob," "Mailer hated to spend his time with losers," Mailer was not quite at home with some of the men on the march who were "too nice and too principled," Mailer "felt small in Washington," Mailer was "fatally vulgar," and so on). All ages have their imperatives; in this disarming way the author struggles with the imperatives of his age, too big, too unspeakable to be dealt with easily, with the morass of confusion and anxiety into which Americans are now plunged—with the abandonment of principles in a society which has been great because of them. He celebrates "these mad middle class children with their lobotomies from sin, their nihilistic embezzlement of middle class moral funds, their lust for apocalypse, their unbelievable indifference to waste. . . ."

1968 / America Will Go Down

Reading in the sunshine, a faint tenderness stirs for the author's more open and uncalculating past, for the "ham on the stage," the "staggering Prince of Bourbon with his mug," the "fragile, alert, intelligent Jew." It is even interesting to follow his effort to polish up his "good left hook," his "straight to the jugular"—to see him stop from time to time for the "heartening beef-tea of obscenity . . ."

The article has reservations about everything; about the solemn giving up of draft cards ("he did not even know if he supported the turning in of draft cards"); about the whole course of courage ("If you disapproved of the war too much to shoot Vietcong, then your draft card was for burning"); about the "flint of eye" and the "single-mindedness" of certain chaplains; and of course about himself ("who had seen himself a guerrilla in the hills . . . and now a figurehead"). What remains unclear is whether he marches on the Pentagon to chastize her as a lover, or to play a reporter's role. He has saddled this mysterious "bitch" of an America with all the guilt of having lost her frontiers, of being in the technological vanguard, of having given her greedy citizens air conditioning and microwave ovens, and her children easy and permissive living, even of having produced an extravagant and lying media to which he (by *force majeure*) belongs. (*"One marched on the Pentagon . . . because . . . because . . . and here the reasons became so many and so curious and so vague, so political, so primitive . . . that one could only ruminate over the morning coffee."*)

Perhaps this is because it is easier to "imply" (as a novelist does in a novel), to build up and project, to show this small fallible hero, tiny under the shadowed slab-like Pentagon walls. It is easier, but unsatisfactory, for the hero runs in and out of the police lines, and is arrested without effort or pain; and calls his wife; and worries about getting back to New York City for a party; and revels in his choices; and makes his pronouncements; and all the time in Cuba, from which the New Left (as he says) draws its political aesthestic, there are few choices—the escapees slip into the shark-infested water and try to swim to the Base (where America is) and get into tiny rafts made of inflated tires, and try to make it across the straits (where America is). Just as now in the Czechoslovakian liberalization, the defendants of the Slansky Trial emerge from a long silence to receive decorations and to give brief previews of what happened to them—previews which form a background to scenes from a Czech film not yet shown, the body of Jan Masaryk in the courtyard, the bodies hanging in the forests, the body on the frozen road in Switzerland. And those back from the dead—Loebl and London and the others—telling of the dungeons with wet floors where they couldn't lie down, the eating from bowls with their hands tied behind their backs, the not being allowed to sleep, the thirst, the lights in the eyes, the orders, "Walk . . . Walk . . . Walk . . ." So that in all these Mailer words, so justly chosen, so true to life, there is something missing. One word perhaps about freedom's peril.

Visiting the University of New Hampshire to spend a few hours with a young Palestinian graduate who works in the Sociology Department there, and plays an active role as an editor of OAS publications and a speaker at various rallies and conventions. He looks somewhat as one might expect: rather short with large dark intense eyes and a handle-bar moustache, yet curiously gentle as well (out of keeping with the fiery and rhetorical style with which the Palestinian Liberation Movement is associated). His name is Salem Tamari. He explains that he was born in Jaffa in Palestine in 1945. "My attitude towards my own society began crystallizing on the West Bank," he says. "That was between 1962 and 1964. In 1964 I had an opportunity to come to this country. But living on the West Bank I was always aware of Pan-Arab sentiments. We are homeless in a way, almost like the wandering Jew, rootless. We showed both an antipathy to the Arab regimes which were very oligarchic and detached from the people and felt an identity with other struggling Arab peoples, and increasingly with the Egyptian leadership." Tamari's English is not perfect and now he says, "Nasserism was the most mass movement."

What did he remember of his early childhood? "I remember moving under fire in a car, and I remember living in a tent for a short time. I think this uprootedness contributed more than anything else to a feeling of having a common nationality with the Arabs. I am a Christian," he adds as if to forestall surprise. "Oh, religion is not so important in this case. The Christians who develop national sentiments are even more zealous than Muslims. It is always suspected that they have identified with the West because of their religion, so that they must prove themselves."

How then did he come to identify with Arab nationalism?

"Well, it was gathering arms for the Algerians which influenced me. Arabs had been outside the political arena of all these countries for centuries. Now they looked at the French being forced out of Algeria! What a brilliant achievement! At that time I was trying to write, and existentialism was a major influence on most of the students. I read Sartre and Simone de Beauvoir; it seemed a way out of religious dogmatism. I read the *Wretched of the Earth* by Fanon in Arabic. My home life became unimportant. I began to have violent nationalist reactions. When I went to Jerusalem to school we could see from our windows on the wall the Israeli soldiers patrolling; this was once our country, and now we no longer had access to it."

Tamari, except for his emotional experiences, is beginning to seem like an American radical, reading the same books as they do, committed to what he rejects, clinging to Western advantages. "I used to like

1968 / America Will Go Down

Gorky but he was banned in Jordan . . . even Marxist literature was banned. . . . The anti-Semitic literature was not good. I saw the Protocols in Lebanon, but the Left doesn't encourage this kind of thing." (His view of the Left apparently leaves out Russia, which has been busy turning out blatant anti-Semitic material.) "Anti-Semitism is a short solution," he says, "it wants to put politics on a mystical supernatural base." He goes on to blame Israel for what is happening. "Anti-Semitism and racism were always absent through history until the coming of Zionism."

Can this be true? Surely Zionism itself was necessary *because* of racism?

He says in a calming tone, "We shouldn't associate hostile feelings towards Israel with being against Jews."

But doesn't it really end up this way? Isn't the cause of the Palestinians associated with very lurid propaganda which projects hostility towards Jews in general?

Tamari says stubbornly that he defends the cause of the Palestinians because they need it here in this country where the Jewish propaganda is very clever. But what about these OAS journals, these speeches?

"What can I do?" Tamari asks, misunderstanding the question. "I'm thousands of miles away, the best I can do is write and talk. Yes, I am a member of OAS, and I went to rallies where other Left groups, the Trotskyists were speaking, and where SDS and the black groups also meet and speak. It's generally much easier to influence them than the Young Democrats or the Young Republicans, who always want a share of the pie." As he talks he gets more involved and more intense. "Yes, we managed to forge an organic link with black groups when SNCC began to support the Palestinian Liberation movement last year. Today we are very close, there are *solidarity* links with the Black Panther Party. You ask about Russia. As a Palestinian how do I relate to Russia? Well at first, in the early 60s I was very sympathetic, since Russia supported us in the beginning. But she then rushed quickly towards a cease fire. She favored stability in the Middle East; in reality that means consolidating Israel's position."

But after all hadn't Russia made the war possible in the first place?

"How did she do that?"

Didn't she supply arms? Then through her own propaganda try to persuade the Egyptians that Israel was massing troops on the Syrian border, when there were no such troops?

"Well, even if I'm wrong," Tamari says, "it is inconsequential; it's the intransigence of Israel which started the war, Moscow isn't important."

If Moscow wanted the war and this is part of her strategy in the Middle East, why isn't this important? Didn't she put the Arabs in a situation which is profitable to *her*?

He is flustered. "Well the Soviet Union is the more welcome. You say that the Soviet Union has many advisers in Egypt, and that they have already a somewhat entrenched position. This is true." He gets impatient. "I don't support official armies. I support *Resistance*. I am against the 'Zionist colonial settler' nature of Israel."

Tamari's position as a supporter of the "Resistance" is a delicate one, since he is operating as a reasonably objective teacher in an American university. He now says that he is against the whole idea that you need a homeland for the Jewish people. "You don't need one," he says angrily, "any more than you need one for the gypsies. The Jews are not a nation."

But if this is so, then neither do the Palestinians need a homeland, nor are they a nation. Palestine so-called was once Syria and always called a part of Syria, and the Palestinians sold much of their land to the Jews. Tamari, who had spent a lot of time explaining his Arab nationalism and its emotional base, now finishes the conversation by saying firmly, "The most progressive form of any government is secular".

On the outskirts of Boston a telephone call to Toole, who had sent me a new address in the now-renovated "Combat Zone" (where some of the bars had been swept away and where other houses were being renewed at government expense.) The letter written in her careful script tells about a trip to New York City "for a cup of coffee more or less. I stood there for about three or four hours, then came home again. If I'd known you was there I might of seen you, but the little that I did see doesn't have me yearning to go back. Maria is up at ninety-nine, she'll be home in June. . . ."

Toole has given a telephone number under the new address, but now a strange woman answers and gives me another. The woman adds cautiously, "Are you a friend?"

"Yes, I'm a friend."

"Well, when you call, ask for Jerry."

The familiarity of Harvard Square, the sense of hundreds of students, crisscrossing the streets with books slung over their shoulders in cotton bags; a sense of an intellectual beehive with the indefatigable students secreted in the comb, their young heads and shoulders benignly bathed in light, their brains absorbing the excreta of stores of print.

Dinner with friends at an inexpensive Greek restaurant. "To come back here," A— says, his cheerful tone suggesting a well-adjusted nostalgia, "it's really great. But it also lets you know that you can't come home again"! He has just been to India, to the Philippines, to Ceylon, where he has been setting up research projects in "interpersonal human and business relations." We talk about this all through the shish kebab and the salad. Over coffee it turns out that A— too has been reading *The Steps of the Pentagon.*

And how had it seemed to him?

"Oh great, just great . . . I thought of you because of what he said about Australia." (In his discussion about the reality of leaving China, Mailer had said: ". . . one could laugh at the thought of Australia going Communist. The Hawks were nothing if not humorless. If Communist China had not been able to build a navy to cross the Straits of Formosa and capture Taiwan, one did not see them invading Australia in the next century. No, any decent Asian Communist would probably shudder at the thought of engaging the Anzacs, descendants of the men who fought at Gallipoli. Yes, the Hawks were humorless and Lyndon Johnson was shameless. He even invoked the defense of Australia.")

As an Australian, who not many months ago stood on that empty northern coastline beside the Timor sea; who saw mile after mile of untrodden sand with no airplane shadow thrown across it but those of the few tiny brave Cessnas carrying mail to lonely settlers; who traced the 3,000 mile long ship route from the south to the isolated port of Darwin; who listened to the stories of the northern citizens who in 1943 saw that town leveled by a few Japanese zeros in the space of fifteen minutes or less and joined a subsequent panic-stricken stampede to the south, I found the "defense of Australia" a more urgent question. But like the caricature of the domino theory, the thesis that Australia would have a black-white choice between going Communist and nothing else is simplistic and since it is impossible to transport this little table cluttered with the remains of a cheap Greek dinner and set it down on the somber empty mangrove swamps of the Gulf of Carpentaria, only a stone's throw from New Guinea, Timor, Indonesia, it seems enough to try to persuade A— that it is unwise to prophesy about history, but that it is incautious not to fear it.

Reaching Toole later tonight is as difficult and discreet as making contact with a foreign spy. When "Jerry" is called to the phone, the voice is so husky and blurred that it is hard to be sure that some man has not crept into Toole's large abandoned female body. "I'm like a pigeon on a roof," she (he) affirms, giving the address. "If you run into any fucking broads in the passage, ask for Jerry"; and half an hour later when she opens the door of a little slattern of a wooden penthouse on a building behind the Symphony Hall on Commonwealth Avenue, it is hard to believe that she is *not* "Jerry," since she looks coarser than ever and wears a cap pulled over her eyes and a cavernous coat of grey Irish tweed. Her voice has developed a gravelly tone, which goes with her costume, and the continuous use of the phrase "dear heart." Yet when the door is closed, some of her femininity seems evident—the room is tidy, a pink counterpane is spread carefully over the bed, and a huge poster of Brigitte Bardot covers the wall behind it.

"I tell you, I'll never go to jail, dear heart" she announces, taking the top off a bottle of beer, "They won't put me in ninety-nine. I'm wanted on another count and I'd do a year for that, and five for this."

But why is she hiding out?

She looks sideways under the visor of the cap. Half turned away, the back of her neck where her hair is tucked under the cap, looks curiously vulnerable, "I stabbed Lou-Beth with an icepick. I was drunk and it came within an inch of her heart."

"You *stabbed* her! Is she in the hospital?"

"Yes, she was on the table too. I missed her heart by half an inch." There is undeniable pride in her voice. "I'll never go back to ninety-nine. If I go back, I go in a pine box, dear heart."

Estranged from Primrose, with Maria in prison, Toole had apparently taken up with Lou-Beth, a pale-faced little girl with a lisp. Now she begs, "If you go up to the joint, tell Maria I wanta see her just once. She said she wrote me a letter of about forty pages."

And what does she (Toole) do hiding in this room all day?

"I write and I read, and I drink. And I live in this roomin' house full of broads. They all think I'm a guy. There are about fourteen of them and they think I'm the 'most.' Every time I come in, one of them blondes is knocking on the door. 'Do you want any soup?' 'Can I iron your shirt?' I say: 'Do me a favor, and get to your room.' I can't turn round but there's one of them chippies. . . ."

We sit in silence for a while. Toole looks melancholy. Finally she says: "If anything happens, see Maria and tell her I wouldn't of done it but the guy Lou-Beth was with pointed a gun at my head, and that's when I went crazy. Tell Maria in case I don't see her that he was pointin' this gun at me, and this is when I got pissed off, I'm not gonna argue with a gun."

What happened?

"I went outside and sat in the lounge at the St. Moritz and she had the fucking balls to walk in there, and we fought and she bit my thumb half off. I grabbed this ice pick and stabbed her four or five times." Her voice goes on and on. Outside in the darkness there are random shouts, the sound of cars starting up and roaring off. Steps in the passage outside. Toole seems to have deteriorated; her patina of respectability has vanished. "I was on them black pills—biphetamines; and I was taking nembutal as well." She begins to tell about a murder in the Combat Zone. "Dolly was goin' with a black guy. What man could carry *her* around and get nothing for it? The cops came aroun' . . . some other guy left him propped up against the taillight." The Irish face with the visor pulled down is curiously out of place against the bright backdrop of Brigitte Bardot. She indicates the poster with a wave of her hand. "I got that there because of the broads. It impresses them." She indicates a smaller poster of Joan Baez over the washstand. "If it's a broad from Cambridge I use *that* one. I also got me a Nehru jacket in green!"

She goes on about Maria, who seems to obsess her. "I just wanta walk into that place and say 'Hullo Maria, I'm eatin' my heart out.' I wanta ride up to ninety-nine with you and surprise her. If she weren't in jail she might of found herself shot down." She reverts to a sentimental melancholy. "Here I am cooped up. If only Maria would get herself together and get outa there."

What about Lou-Beth?

With a wave of the hand Lou-Beth is dismissed. "Oh she's all right now. She deserved what she got. She's one of those know alls. She talks about books. Blah . . . blah . . . blah. Then she's talkin' about war and peace—Blah blah blah!"

It is midnight before it is possible to leave for Cape Cod.

It rains on Cape Cod, through which the lilacs blooming beside the old wooden houses shine with their soft lavender. A French friend (Robert) accompanies me to Provincetown to visit the bars, where the summer crowds are dancing under a flash of lights as hot, on a miniature scale, as the flares from riots in the cities. Under the low roofs of the Atlantic House there is the smell of beer and whiskey, as if it had been well scrubbed into the wooden tables. Near the piano a man leans in a suit which is decidedly green. There is also a girl with a dress made of a very stiff violet material; from the inadequate bodice of this dress her brown breasts burst out. (Later in the Ladies Room she claims that the dress will stand up by itself!) She is a "negrito" type (probably Portuguese), has round dark eyes, and two little gold chains which cut into the flesh of her neck.

The dancing crowd includes many young men and women, their skins flushed from the first postwinter sun, all in the extraordinary clothes of the time: a frontier heaviness to boots and sandals, a rather haphazard number of ties or handkerchieves worn around necks, waists, or as headbands, fatigue jackets, soldier's uniforms, long woven skirts, round hats, cloth caps. The clothes of a bygone age, all touched up with a faint deliberate decadence— see-through blouses, the shine of eyelid grease or beads, the extravagance of disordered hair.

Robert agrees that the atmosphere of Provincetown is rather tawdry, more so than during his last visit. "But all the same there is still *'une innocence Américaine'*."

May

In the Cape Cod spring, which covers the dunes with pink-white beachplum blossoms, the Prague spring seems vulnerable and far away. It is symptomatic that the usual groundswell of Western student protest deals with fundamentally unsatisfiable demands. Apart from grievances like those so well advertised at Berkeley (overcrowding, alienation, bureaucratism, etc.), the basic situation in the Western universities is one of penetration of student organizations. In England for instance, the guiding hand is the Radical Students Alliance, an organization only a year old, which is being infiltrated by the Trotsky-ist Socialist Labor League and various anarchist groups (all of which hate each other, but work together all the same). Both the Trotskyists and the anarchists have links with the "Provos" in Holland, who in their turn keep contact with German groups. At least one anarchist group organization has a tie-up with anarchists in Tokyo University. And the big anti-American demonstration in London on March 17, where delegates arrived from Germany, France, Belgium and Sweden, was modeled on Japanese methods. Here the Prague spring with its potential contradictions comes into focus, the Student Committee of the Communist Party in London has tended (according to *News Weekly* May 1) to operate under the orders of the International Union of students in Czechoslovakia. Again the anomaly. While Prague students march for freedom, students in Columbia are using the spring weather to set up a Mao-type device of canceling all "top honors" in the marking system (presumably in support of an egalitarian situation in which those busy with scholarship can't be separated from those busy with revolution); and in Germany the student movement also ignores the problem of "liberty" in favor of free rides on the overhead railway donated by East Germany.

May 23

In Paris an ironic little comedy is being played out. The representatives of Hanoi in sober suits, white shirts, and black "Establishment" ties, argue politely and laboriously about peace terms; while at the Lutelia ballroom the Chinese appear in traditional but well cut Mao tunics and drink champagne at a diplomatic reception with the plump representa-tives of the French Communist Party. All this to the accompaniment of the tangle of students (led by Cohn-Bendit, i.e., Danny the Red, of the flaming hair) who tear up the city paving stones to make their barricades. Red Guard types hob-nob inside the Sorbonne fortress, while the Chinese Reds drink champagne! (In France the syndicalist student movement has been more stimulating than any other single influence; the idea is that the student should separate himself from parents and career in order to take industrial action, i.e., "go on strike" and express solidarity with the proletariat. This movement has been so popular that it has spread to Belgium, Germany, Holland, Canada, Ireland, and Spain.) In Italy the situation seems to hinge upon a more reformist attempt to gain power. Ever since Togliatti's adoption of Khrushchev's exposé, the Italian Communist leader has acted the part of the great revisionist (this in spite of the fact that for years, and with his own brother-in-law Paolo Robotti in prison, he was curiously obedient). Togliatti's challenge to Moscow, known as his "testament" was notable for pushing for free discussions between Communists and non-Communists, and for "understanding" of the religious masses. It is perhaps due to this, and to the liberalization of religious doctrine under Pope John XXIII, that only this month, the Communist party in Italy gained twenty-seven percent of the vote in the elections. This suggests that the idea of the acceptability of Marxism is gaining ground in the church (given special emphasis by the French worker-priest movement—Les Prêtes-Ouvrières—and by similar movements amongst the unwordly religious in Latin America). If it is true that the problem for freedom in the West has ceased to be military and has become political, it is because, in these and similar situations, ambiguity and deception are permitted and even Christians are cynically called upon to help this deception ("dialogue is not an end in itself but a way of spreading the Marxist-Leninist view of the world"—*Voprosyi Filisofi* Nov. 9, 1967).

On Cape Cod such details tend to escape us, although there are few not touched in some way by revolutionary upheavals. Mrs. M— has made the mistake for instance of renting her cottage for the spring months to a group of young activists from New York who are supposedly resting from the fatigues of Columbia and New York University. She deplores the fact that without her knowledge the original rentees had sublet to another group, that the first group had failed to pay for the utilities they used, and that the second group had "liberated" many of her towels and blankets. A psychiatrist who is present remarks that the idea of violence is seductive not only for students but also for authority figures—sometimes parents or professors obtain vicarious satisfaction by watching the young overturn old values. Mrs. M—, helping herself to a rather stiff drink, admits that she probably got vicarious pleasure from renting to this attractive younger group. "I *wanted* to have my house turned into a commune!" (One of her friends warns her that she wouldn't be cured of this romantic idea until something really valuable—at least a refrigerator—was destroyed.)

June 6

Robert Kennedy was shot last night at 10 p.m. at the Ambassador Hotel in Los Angeles. He was shot in the hotel pantry after his speech. There was a stainless steel warming table, and he was standing near it and stretching across to shake hands with one of the kitchen workers. A voice said, "Kennedy—you son of a bitch," and two shots rang out.

In one of the newspapers there is a picture of a hand holding a gun emerging from between two cameramen not a yard from Kennedy's head, and Martin Katrusky the waiter, described it. "The guy looked like he was smiling . . . and he reached over like this . . . and the next thing, I seen Kennedy starting to go down on his knees."

Roosevelt Grier was sobbing, "Oh no! Oh no!" There is another picture hard to look at, in which Kennedy's face seems haloed with light, and yet wavering, already involved with death. The eyes stare, are terrified and surprised, like the eyes of a deer caught by a hunter.

Less than two hours after the shooting a prayer is read in London on the BBC. "We pray for the American people that they may come to their senses." A West German asks an American correspondent, "Has America gone mad?" And a man in a cafe in Brussels questions, "Will anyone want to become President of the United States?"

The assassin has been identified. He is a young Palestinian Arab called Sirhan Sirhan, born in 1944 in Jordan; a zealous, emotional, immature fanatic who so identified with the Arab cause that he was carrying around a schedule of Kennedy's speaking engagements, and a clipping about the candidate's support of arms to Israel. This information came indirectly through his brothers Adel and Munir Sirhan, who came to the police station with a morning paper showing a picture of the slight, intense, dark-skinned, wild-haired young man, photographed as he tried to break away from those who were holding him after the assassination at the hotel. "This is our brother," they said.

Like many assassins, Sirhan had apparently written down his intentions, and with strange carelessness left his bedroom littered with evidence—including several notebooks demonstrating his passionate sympathy with the Arab cause, and his specific intentions towards Kennedy. One of the phrases written in these notebooks is: "RFK must be killed before June 5th."

People gather in the streets in many cities across the nation, and especially outside the entrance of the Good Samaritan Hospital in Los Angeles (where all last night reporters waited hour after hour and television lights fought with the shadows) and where Robert Kennedy still lies unconscious with hemorrhage from the middle brain. Inside

1968 / America Will Go Down

the Cathedral of St. Patrick's in New York City 2,500 people attend a mass performed by Archbishop Terence Cooke, dressed in the red Pentecostal robes. "Let us pray brethren . . . in another experience of monumental national tragedy . . . let us intensify our prayers . . ."

"We pray to the Lord," the congregation responded.

And in those poorer areas, to which Robert Kennedy paid special attention, people gather; especially in Harlem where not long ago he strolled with an entourage of fellow strollers and black children; and even in the bars and parks where the winos hearing the news began to drink a little earlier than usual. "I'll shave tomorrow" one says solemnly.

The protests, the expressions of grief, of horror, are beginning to give place to opinions and ponderous statements, from all sorts of leaders and political figures and heads of countries. Many of the statements have a curious patronage and are based on the immediate assumption that America is responsible for this murder, has asked for it, and is so much worse than other countries because of it. "Violence breeds violence." "We have a violent society." "This violence is part of the violence of Vietnam." "We love it . . . we love violence . . . we love to fight." This from a psychiatrist. And an East European diplomat (from a country notorious for the removal with extreme prejudice of political rivals and dissenters) declares coldly, "How many coincidences . . . and how many inexplicable incidents must occur in your country before you face the fact that there is in the United States . . . an organized violence, that this is no accident" (the journalist who reports it adds, "The fact that the shooting might have been prompted by other than domestic pressures, was not taken into consideration!").

Nor does the talented historian Arthur Schlesinger, Jr. overpowered perhaps by grief at his friend's death, take this other possibility into account, but asks at the City University commencement exercises, "What sort of people are we Americans . . . the answer . . . is that we are today the most frightening people on this planet."

Yet already it seems clear that, in the broadest sense, this is a political murder; and as such, a part of that "dark intolerable tension" which Schlesinger speaks of (but not to be "automatically" dismissed as the mindless violence of the American people). It might, in fact, in political terms be the opposite of this. This assassination, as also the other assassinations, might have occurred not because America is not stable, but because it *is*; not because America is not successful as a society, but because it *is*; not because America is not satisfied with its leaders, but because it *is*; and not indeed because America is violent, but because it is fundamentally devoted to peace and democracy. It is a supposition at least (and one which few declarations seem to consider) that however weakened recently, it is America's inner strength which is at issue here, and which stands like a challenge in the way of forces obsessed with destroying it. The United States (and now increasingly *only* the United States) is capable of challenging the growth of totalitarian governments. . . . This does not mean that R.F.K. was necessarily killed by an agent of the KGB or of the Chinese Secret Service (in one big conspiracy, in tune with the kind of exaggeration which dismisses the "domino theory" as meaning an overnight fall of every Southeast Asian country to communism). But it does suggest the totality, the cohesion of the "war against the West." Warfare is engendered in more ways than one. For as a commentator suggested, at certain times weak and deranged minds flourish, and these, borrowing piecemeal from confused ideologies, take their death cues.

As a dramatic example of what appeals to whom, at this very moment when Robert Kennedy lies dying, it is reported in the *New York Times* (on the other side of that great spread of national grief) that during the trial of Herman Ferguson (indicated last June with Arthur Harris and a group of other black extremists from the Revolutionary Action Movement, for plotting to assassinate moderate Civil Rights leaders and government officials) Edward Lee Howlette, police undercover agent en route to a rifle range for target practice, was asked by Ferguson if he remembered the five names on the list given him by Max Stanford (leader of the National Branch of RAM) as assassination targets. These names were Roy Wilkins, Whitney Young, Robert Kennedy, Larry Neal, and Larry Elliott.

At this evidence the defense lawyer jumped to her feet and cried, "I move for a mistrial—when every American is filled with emotion at the terrible events of this morning . . . we are asking more than is humanly possible of the jury!"

The motion was denied.

June 7

History does not pause in what one poet has called "the lurid flow of horror and insane distress and headlong fate." Robert Kennedy is reported to have said to a reporter on the very night of his death, "I like politicians . . . I like politics . . . It's an honorable profession . . . That was Lord Tweedsmuir." And now while the coffin is flown from Los Angeles to the cathedral and hundreds of men stand vigil beside it; and while people weep; and Mrs. Mary Sirhan sends a telegram to the Kennedy family: "It hurts us very bad what has happened and we express our feelings with them and especially with

1968 / America Will Go Down

the children . . . I want them to know I am really crying for them . . ."; and as the Poor Peoples Campaign broadens the scope of its purpose "to end violence and hatred" at Resurrection City, U.S.A., in the mall of the Lincoln Memorial; the Soviet Union, displeased by the identification of the assassin as an Arab, accuses the United States of unrestrained terrorism and of trying to deflect her guilt onto foreign circles. "The identity of the assailant who was arrested at the scene of the crime," states *Nedelya*, "continues to provoke contradictory rumors . . . Political terror has become a daily reality in the United States . . This reminds us of the dirty and false hints . . . that appeared on the day of the assassination of J. F. Kennedy."

When a dog is large and has strong teeth, you
bow and smile and call him "Mr. Dog."

Chinese proverb

June 8

History does not stand still because of Robert Kennedy's assassination. If Sirhan Sirhan identified with the Palestinians and, as he supposedly has said, with the "poor people and the blacks," that is with the Third World cause—it is quite in order, that parallel with his attack on Kennedy, Black Power slogans are echoing in the Caribbean Islands. Seven or eight black men, part of a roaming band, have been terrorizing the Bahamas, pushing their way in and out of hotels in Freeport, talking about their rights, injuring white tourists and hotel employees, slapping waitresses, breaking windows and mirrors, and stabbing those who try to resist them. Eventually Black Power in the islands is bound to become more organized. In fact it needs no great exercise of the imagination to wonder whether the injustices suffered by minorities will continue to be used (as they are already) to create a "ring of trouble" for the United States: whether the revoluntionary liberation movements stimulated below the border in Mexico will eventually be successful; whether separatist emotion will effectively weaken Canada; whether the Caribbean will be turned in the end into a Soviet Sea.

June 15

SDS has been holding its convention in East Lansing, Michigan, with a strong Communist flavor apparent. There were the red flags of revolution, the black flags of anarchy, the red arm bands of a thousand uprisings, the khakis of the guerrilla, the sayings of Ché, the declarations of national officers (for instance Bernadine Dohrn who said, "I consider myself a revolutionary Communist").

At the same time there is a hardening of secrecy and anti-intellectualism in the American radical movement. It is true that the movement is a combination of many different voices, but undoubtedly because of the concessions made to the Communists by SDS in 1965, a familiar powerful coercion is now operating. Radical censorship was evident at Columbia where no press but the SDS press, that is Liberation News Service, had been allowed inside Mathematics Hall. After the hall had been seized by the students, and according to an article in the New Republic on June 8, one of the self-appointed censors asked Dotson Rader, "Who do you work for motherfucker?" (This made it necessary for Rader to climb into an attic and "liberate" a typewriter so that he could do his work in peace. He was also told that if he didn't use the word "commune" he'd have his head bashed in.)

Now at the present convention, TV and radio coverage has been banned. In fact SDS leaders depend more than they dare to admit upon the looseness with which the U.S. media works. "The ability to manipulate people through violence and mass media," Dave Gilbert of SDS said at Columbia, "has never been greater, and the potential for us radicals has never been more exciting than now."

In Paris the month old strike continues—with little or no gasoline available, numerous people walking to work, the automobile factories still out, and a manifestation (*un manif* as it is called) held every so often, to make the gutter run, not with blood, but with flaming gasoline, and to turn the moon orange from tear gas. DeGaulle, frightened by the business-like alliance of students and Communist-led trade unions, is already dissolving the extreme left groups (amongst them La Voix Ouvrière, Révolte, Le Comité Liaison de Étudiants Révolutionnaires and as proof of the Trotskyist revival the Jeunesse Communiste Révolutionnaire).

June 20

It is not far from the violence of Paris to Sirhan Sirhan, the murderer of Robert Kennedy. Sirhan is now sitting in a windowless twelve-by-twelve-foot cell in Los Angeles County jail, where he is undergoing psychiatric examination by two defense experts. (Russel E. Parsons is to serve as his defense counsel.) And already it is clear that everything impinging on the case has political meaning and is to be used as such. The Secretary General of the Action Committee on American-Arab Relations, Muhammed Mehdi, that expert inspirer of last April's "Genocide Day"—whose job is to encourage contact between Third-

World supporters here and Al Fatah—has been using the United States media to assert that Robert Kennedy was an "indirect victim of Zionism."

Now that three charismatic American leaders have been gunned down, the exact interplay of radical ideologies is of urgent interest. (It is a far cry from the time when McKinley used to dine alone in the White House, and security was so lax that one evening as he was sipping his soup, he looked up to find a curious stranger who had wandered in from the street.) The fact that there has been a startling increase of threats against President Johnson recently suggests that it is worth asking whether a better "ideological" job will be done on Sirhan Sirhan than was done on that other devotee of the Third World—Lee Harvey Oswald.

June 28

Ten days ago the police occupied the Sorbonne, relieving so to speak, a mere 200 tired young men and women, who filed out and disappeared into the streets of Paris. The red flags, all except one too high to reach, were taken down. The police carted away hundreds of clubs, chains, gas masks, plastic helmets, and plastic garbage can lids used as shields. A friend back from Paris remarks that he saw one solitary poster as he walked by in the rain *L'Imagination au Pouvoir*. And nine days ago more than 50,000 Americans marched in Washington to mass around the Reflecting Pool in front of the Washington monument and to emphasize the need for a just share for American minorities. About half of the marchers were white.

In this city swept by arson and rioting last spring, where certain streets are still blackened and charred, there is now a Poor Peoples' plywood town, its streets deep in mud from recent rains. Not far away white hippies and young Negroes splash in the Reflecting Pool and chant peace slogans. As with the breakup of the occupation of the Sorbonne, Resurrection City is due to close on a note of random violence, for the Parks Police estimate that one hundred assaults and violent incidents have occurred since the shacks were set up more than a month ago, and that at least twenty visitors have been robbed, beaten up, or stabbed just outside the encampment fence. And overwhelming for the mere effort as this temporary city is, it does not much impress some of the younger blacks who were putatively "born into a time of violence." As one said scornfully as he loitered on the edge of the crowd around the pool, "We got a brand new bag."

1968 / America Will Go Down

June 30

The ghetto in fact is not going to shed its intensive coloring because of a little attention from the Establishment. Earlier this month a former leader of the Blackstone Rangers (one of those terrifying deep ghetto gangs) testified about the black militant plot to assassinate the non-violent civil-rights leaders—first publicized when leaders of RAM, including the ubiquitous Herman Ferguson, were arrested. The assassination list, according to this youthful gang leader, also included Martin Luther King Jr. among its potential victims. The Reverend John Fry, pastor of the First Presbyterian Church, denied under oath that he had encouraged the gang to extract money from merchants, to hold marijuana parties and initiation orgies in the church, or to murder a certain dope peddler. Although he had gang weapons stored in the church safe, he stated that he was doing this to cooperate with the police. The crux of the matter is that whatever the complicity of the Reverend Fry and his associates, black militants were in touch with the Blackstone Rangers and had given them money, guns, and grenades. (That the Office of Economic Opportunity had granted $927,300 to two Chicago gangs, the Blackstones and the Devil's Disciples, some of whose leaders were paid salaries of $6,500 a year and members $58 a week, as encouragement to attend classes, gives point to the charge of "excessive" liberality on the part of the U.S. government. Now the OEC program is being phased out, and in line with other anti-poverty programs is being investigated by a Senate subcommittee.)

Such democratic correctives seem far removed from the continuation of the Ché Guevara story. In May a key interview with Gunther Maennel was published in the West German weekly, *Welt Am Sonntag*. Maennel is the man who defected from East Germany in 1961 and who now states that Tania, the girl who was with Ché Guevara in Bolivia, was there because she was under orders from the East German Ministry of State Security (MFS). In other words, Tania, who was really Tamara Bunke, was actually assigned by Maennel himself to penetrate the Guevara movement. The story has about it all the required touches of an authentic Iron Curtain spy story—beautiful woman, child member of CP youth movement, patient training in subversion, false passport, phony marriage, and final job in the office of the Bolivian Presidential Press Office. Since another movement hero, Régis Debray, the French intellectual, was so closely associated with Tania as also to run the risk of being victimized, it is not surprising that he reacted furiously when a reporter gave him the above information, and put it down to a conspiracy of the imperialist powers. How true it is that many devotees of the Ché cult, seriously bent upon giving their lives to guerrilla revolution, would find it hard to cut their way through the Cuban-Bolivian-Soviet Communist Party relationship, as easily as they dream of doing through the jungles which form a background for their hero.

June 29

Talks on a Cape Cod beach with Ben, who seems representative of a certain current ambivalence amongst activists. He is short, slight, charming, wears striped dungarees and has a habit of running his hands through his dark hair. Having graduated from Middlebury College, he spent part of a year at Princeton, where he did Chinese studies and made a beginning at mastering Mandarin before he dropped out. Because of his membership in SDS, he was turned down for the Peace Corps in Malaysia. He is now temporarily living in a broken down Coast Guard Building on a sand spit running into the Atlantic ocean. He says that his interest in China began with a nostalgic feeling about travel, with teachers in Asian history, with reading *The Good Earth* and *Fan Shen*, and so on up to Marx, Lenin, Mao, John Fairbanks, Benjamin Schwartz, Chalmers Johnson, etc. ("Ninety percent of those going into Chinese studies are basically alientated from Western culture . . . any value system looks more appealing than your own. . . . When I think of it now, Buddhism was important to me because it was anti- or a- Christian.") Yet isn't he really interested in practical politics? (I've never been able to get excited about politics . . . I'm too much of a snob and don't enjoy day-to-day contact with political people.")

In fact he is fastidious, sensitive, likes isolation, and reacts fiercely to authority.

("I remember reading Conrad. . . . He's principally literary but reverts always to the political idea. *Nostromo*, for instance. . . . It's beautiful. . . . It's spectacular. . . . I went to the March on the Pentagon at the end of 1967. What I hated then was the physical contact . . . the reality of force . . . bayonets in your face and the disgusting psychological reasons for marshals being there. . . . It was then that I decided to work against war.")

These last rather innocent words (suggesting that to form part of the SDS united front was to "work against war") echo as we walk along the beach. At this very moment the xenophobic Peking regime has cut even further its contacts with the outside world. Many of those 150 odd foreigners living in the Friendship Hotel seem to have disappeared. Some are under arrest. The chaos and xenophobia extant, reminiscent of Russia during the purges, was so great that even Edgar Snow was held up in Japan for months and finally had to leave without reaching the mainland. As the last straw, that old warhorse Anna Louise Strong, once in trouble in Moscow for favoring China, was reported in bad favor on the wall posters of Peking! According to Tillman Durdin, more than thirty foreigners have been arrested as spies.

It is obvious that Ben, who reacted so sensitively to a U.S.-type confrontation, would be unlikely to stand up to a similar test in the more rigid environment of China (what would he think of the gloomy record I had read in Australia of Keith McEwen, who during the Stalin regime and at the age of twenty-five, agreed to go to China to study Marxism-Leninism and learned to his cost that "socialism," as Khrushchev is reported to have said to Sukarno, "should mean that every minute is calculated").

Another conversation with Ben. He walks around the room, fingers books, runs his hands through his hair, gives a half humorous look from under his rather long dark lashes. "I never liked the propaganda in the articles. . . . Sometimes I felt embarrassed. . . . I'm really a dubious sort of SDS member." For what then had he been ready to form a front with pro-Peking groups? He admits that there was a sort of insincerity.

"At Princeton radical life was a stylistic thing. There were black students with Eldrige Cleaver beards and dashikis, who'd go off after meetings and step into their Mustangs. As for the white radicals, they wore seersucker suits and carried umbrellas! In Columbia and N.Y.U. it was better, because there was some sort of real content in the life style."

As the historian I. R. Sinai comments, one of the strangest spectacles today is to see a country so conservative as the United States—that is, in terms of social institutions as opposed to technology—trying to line itself up with revolutionary anti-Colonial societies without in any way understanding what is involved in the whole process. He (Ben) has caught onto the streak of fantasy in the U.S. student's devotion to "China," but not onto the political reality of China itself.

July 2

Ramparts has published pages of Ché Guevara's diary, which has just come out in Havana. (Naturally there is the usual *Ramparts* built-in deceit. The edition has been edited to remove reference to the thirteen high-ranking Cuban army officers, including four members of the Central Committee of the Cuban Communist Party, who accompanied Ché. The four members of the Central Committee were Major Juan

1968 / America Will Go Down

Vitalio Acuna, Major Antonio Sanchez Diáz, Major Alberto Fernandez Montes de Oca, and Captain Eliseo Reyes Rodriguez.)

Yet the diary has its sadness. Far away in those hostile Bolivian mountains, a small group of idealistic and mistaken men lived through a series of disasters. Members of the group were drowned, ambushed, or wounded; food and medical supplies were lost; Ché suffered tremendously from asthma; two of the group defected. There was that old revolutionary bugbear as well—ideological rivalry. In his introduction to the diary Castro castigates Mario Monje of the Bolivian Communist Party whom he claims sabotaged Ché's efforts; but fails even to mention the most important reason for failure—which is that while for Castro and Ché the whole Bolivian project was obviously of much importance (it was supposed to trigger off another Vietnam, and cost Cuba a great deal of effort and at least several million dollars)—the peasants not only remained unmotivated by the "Revolution" planned for them, but actively helped the army to hunt Ché down.

There is a strange juxtaposition in the news today. The recent disarmament memorandum addressed to the United States by Mr. Kosygin is being commented upon by that older journalist who first exposed Hitler's ominous intentions, Edgar Ansel Mowrer. He notes that a ban on the use of nuclear weapons simply means that in case of attack by superior Soviet conventional forces, the North Atlantic Treaty Organization would be powerless. Also that measures to end nuclear weapons and limit stockpiles means nothing without "on-site inspection." So also the limitation of nuclear means of delivery means nothing, or the ban on chemical weapons. He suggests that a ban on bomber flights carrying nuclear weapons beyond national frontiers and the limitation of missile carrying submarines would simply put Europe, the Middle East, and the far East at the mercy of the Soviets, and that a ban on underground tests would prevent the United States from catching up with Russia on larger bombs. As for the liquidation of foreign bases, this would free Russia from the fear of U.S. tactical and middle-range nuclear bombs as well.

Nor is the general military drive against the West, Mowrer adds, halted at the Pacific since Australian naval experts are concerned about the Red Navy following new routes into the Indian Ocean (through which passes about seventy-five percent of Australia's imported oil). Similarly the Australians are disturbed by the pushing of a new anti-draft movement. (A pamphlet is circulating in Sydney which suggests sabotaging military equipment, starting fires, wrecking radar, and putting aircraft out of action. It contains the following advice. "At the medical, act simple. Tell the doctor that when you're away from home you wet the bed. If he does not believe you, prove it as soon as you are conscripted. Don't answer any questions on homosexuality, just smile. Learn how to touch the fellow you're talking to suggestively. Be a little pathetic.")

July 14

Attempts to find out more about what is going on in Czechoslovakia are frustrated by the sudden arrival of Toole and Maria. Maria has been paroled, and Toole, now out of hiding, has not only presented her with some inexpensive earrings from Mexico but also persuaded her to take a trip in a hired car, along with a plentiful supply of pills. Naturally they are both "high" on arrival; but by some miracle have managed to make the trip from Boston without accident.

"I like the country," Maria insists. "I like the dawn. I like the light." She seems to have nostalgic childhood memories. "When we were in New Hampshire we went out early every morning mushrooming."

"I was glad to get out of the South End," Toole explains. Her face looks pasty. "I tell you it's like a nut house. . . . There's been three suicide attempts since Friday."

Maria, who is also pale and somewhat shabby in her North-End-style black skirt and white blouse, asks: "Gee, d'you want to cheer me up? Suicide is contagious!"

Toole goes on relentlessly in her flat unemphasized voice. "Poor old Dot thought she was Batwoman. She tried to throw herself down the stairwell at the St. Moritz . . . that was after she'd had her two quarts of vodka . . . She certainly gets her vitamins!"

A photographer friend Dan McS— has also arrived from Boston, and is surprised to find such an extraordinary couple resting in the chairs on the lawn. He immediately becomes interested in a photographic study, but Maria stretched out under the locust shade, shakes her new earrings and says that she can't be photographed, because she doesn't have her hippie costume with her. "Toole bought me some green dungarees to go to hippie meetings on the Common. With a striped jersey and yellow sneakers! What an outfit! It'd stop a five-day clock!" She adds in a sad and rather thoughtful voice, "My daughter is voluptuous, really voluptuous . . . she doesn't know what it means yet." She looks in an interested way at Dan McS— (who is particularly handsome) "I am not beautiful now . . . I am beautiful inside—nobody can say I'm not . . . I'm not immoral." The question of morality hangs in the air for a moment. The beer which the girls are drinking seems to have quieted them down a little; in fact they are getting so lethargic that they show no inclination to go on to Provincetown (nor later as it nears midnight, to go to bed). "Who wants to sleep?" cries Maria. "I only dream bad. If I dreamed good I'd go to sleep."

1968 / America Will Go Down

About two o'clock in the morning when the rest of us are in bed, a loud quarrel breaks out between Toole and Maria. Toole is accusing Maria of telling lies about her and Maria is saying that people are always "putting shit on her." "I'm not satisfied with that" she shouts, "I wait till the whole shithouse comes on me!" There is the sound of crying. A piece of furniture crashes to the floor. Asked from the top of the stairs what is going on, Toole replies that Maria has accused her of "strangling" her. "That's what she's like—she's a nut! You got a *nut* in your house!" "I can show you the bruises," Maria protests tearfully. After a few moments, Toole, who is evidently not used to the silence of the country, complains that she can hear moths. Maria tries to placate her. "Moths are all right. Moths are my guardian angels."

Twelve A.M. Breakfast. A conversation about the growth of drug use in Australia. (This month in Queensland, a radical group called FOCO has moved its headquarters into a disused building in an old market in Brisbane, and joined other groups to sponsor youth meetings and dances. The group shares space with the Communist party youth organization, the Young Socialist Party, and there are rumours that FOCO has become a center for the distribution of drugs). Toole says that she would be glad to go out to Australia and help to wake it up.

"The fuckin' Pacific," she says walking to and fro in the kitchen. Maria's reaction is more feminine. "I'd like to go to Australia. Those hats with one side turned up. I like *them*."

After what must have been close to a sleepless night the shadows under her eyes are darker than ever and again she refuses Dan's request for photographs. "I need sunshine first. I have the jailhouse pallor!"

"I can't be photographed," Toole asserts, "I haven't got my middle denture because Maria threw it away, so I wouldn't smile at other girls."

In the afternoon everyone decides to go to Provincetown.

"I'll take you around the bars," Toole promises, "I'll show you some *real* trouble."

Maria feels that everyone should go to church first, but no one takes this seriously. Toole simply comments that she lights candles and says prayers but isn't interested in anything else.

"I don't like to listen to a lot of shit."

There is a good deal of maneuvering to arrange that Dan should do the driving, and to persuade Toole to leave the pill bottle at home. During the drive she and Maria are affectionate in the back seat—Maria remarking that her husband was not a bad fellow. "He wouldn't say anything. He might shoot me but he wouldn't talk back to me." Toole grunts and remarks that it is safer to let people talk back.

"Yes when you don't fight back, they don't fight," Maria says wisely, "last night when you were choking me I didn't try to resist!" After a few obscenities from Toole, she tries to reassure her, "I love you to death, but you must admit that you are miserable!"

. . . In the Provincetown streets the heat and the smell of the sea.

A miscellaneous drift of people. Strange sweatshirts with slogans and scenes. Fat women in revealing halters and shorts. Blacks with exaggerated Afros and psychedelic clothes. Children eating cotton candy. Artists in open booths doing sidewalk portraits in pastels.

"I always wanted to get my portrait done," Maria says wistfully. She saunters, walking with her stomach thrust forward in a rather insolent way. Toole takes her arm.

"You got some grey hairs," she accuses Toole.

"That's from thinking." Toole excuses herself. After a while she adds, "We'll have to get married . . ." "You wouldn't have the nerve," Maria retorts.

It is relaxing to drink beer in an open-air cafe and to hear the faint sound of the slap of the tide coming through an open screen. Dan and I listen to long descriptions of Ladies Rooms in various Boston bars.

"This one had water laying all over the floor," Toole reports. "I told the manager and he said everybody *else* uses it . . ."

"Once a cat came in the Ladies Room at Cavannas," Maria contributes, "carrying a big rat in its mouth, and . . . on my soul the rat was still moving."

"That's nothing dear heart," Toole consoles her, "at least the rat was in the cat's mouth. . . ."

More beer is ordered and the afternoon grows warmer. Somehow the girls are talking about suicide again. "Once Maria cut her wrists, and took an overdose, and turned on the gas," Toole announces in her new gravelley voice, "and when they asked her if she wanted to commit suicide, she answered 'No'."

"Yes," Maria smiles, her worn once-handsome face in battle with the dark bruises under the eyes, "I cut my wrists, and took twenty-six goof balls, and turned on the gas, and I still didn't kill myself . . ." She pauses and while we all look at her she adds slowly, "It's hard to kill yourself." Later in the afternoon we fill their car with gas, and say goodbye to them on Route 6, while the traffic whizzes past us. "Drive *slowly*," Dan commands.

Toole is still occupied with death and disaster. She climbs into the driver's seat and pushes Maria over. "Move your ass,. . . ." She pauses reflectively, her round face solemn under the man's tweed cap which she has suddenly produced from some inside pocket. "I wonder how many friends have killed theirselves since we been away . . . ?"

July 25

There are other kinds of death wishes. The green summer leaves of the city of Cleveland are scorched where a four-hour shootout against police took place. It was no spontaneous incident—but deliberate shooting to kill. The Reverend DeForest Brown, head of the Hough Development Corporation, confirmed today that the leader of the shootout was one of several militant Negroes who had received funds under a $31,000 summer program. Afterwards Police Chief Michael J. Blackwell said that an agent had assured him that a triple-mounted, belt-fed machine gun was in the possession of the black nationalists in the city and that had the police been sent in, they might have been cut to ribbons.

The leading character was a big gaunt black man with flaring nostrils, called Fred Ahmed Evans (a veteran of the Korean war with a dishonorable discharge for striking an officer), always dressed in a handmade dashiki and a skull cap. He dabbled in astrology and frequently called down retribution on the white man whom he labeled "the beast." ("I am a Swahili subject . . . as for the whites . . . as ye sow must ye reap . . . you can't walk the streets of the ghetto without walking into the beast . . . yeah the *beast*"!) Evans had a group of young followers who met at his headquarters where a sign saying The New Lybia was hung on the door. The disciples, who had names like Malik Ali Bey, Londus, Emir Eban Karab, Nondu Bey, etc., had been trained and disciplined and promised action on the "final" day, and Evans who had a habit of posting lookouts on the roof of his house was informed that police were in the neighborhood. ("They told me the beast was on the scene," he said later.)

After the police had been withdrawn, Ahmed's men came out of the house again, wearing bandoliers, and fanned through the neighborhood, when without warning, two of them attacked a civilian in a police-like uniform, who was attempting to hitch an abandoned 1958 pink Cadillac to a tow-truck. The man was shot in the back. At the same moment a sniper from the opposite side of the street joined in the attack. Police arrived and a street battle followed in which three men were killed and twelve wounded. Ahmed Evans, who says this violence is in the stars, asserted that he only stopped firing because his carbine jammed. As with the Blackstone Rangers in Chicago, the money funnelled into the ghetto has gone to the training of paramilitary groups! When he finally surrendered he was asked what he thought he was accomplishing. "It's only the beginning . . ." he boasted.

1968 / America Will Go Down

July 26

Chilling hints keep being dropped by *Pravda* that the Russians will intervene in Czechoslovakia forcibly if there is any further advance of liberalization.

The Czech past has been opening up. Everyone in Czechoslovakia wants to talk. Everyone has so much to say. The press has carried stories of torture perpetrated by the Soviet police. Dr. Eugene Loebl (president of the Slovak National Bank) has described how he was interrogated after his arrest in 1950, kept awake for days on end, and once for an entire week, during which he was not allowed to sit down. He was accused of being the agent of Tito, then of international Zionism and Israel, and then given narcotic injections to weaken his will. Richard Slansky, brother of the murdered Secretary General of the Communist party, was beaten, had a rubbish tin put over his head, and was exposed to freezing weather for days on end. Every day before interrogation a police official stuck a sharpened pencil into his forehead to establish how much fat he had and how long his resistance might last.

Daily in radio and press, small landlords are telling how they were treated by the state security—beaten, starved, and even placed in special refrigerators until they were ready to talk (shades of Cuba under Castro). Mrs. Svermova, widow of the man called the "Czech Lenin," told of how she tried to protect herself against prison brutality by saying that she personally knew Lenin's friend, the revolutionary leader Clara Zetkin. The guard asked, "Who was that—another Jewish whore?"

July 27

At a cocktail party. In the room of the host's teenage daugher a small photograph of Robert Kennedy on a table near the window catches the last of the golden afternoon sunlight. (It is five weeks since he was shot in Los Angeles.)

Outside a young woman stretches out her hand on the finger of which glitters an enormous blue-stoned ring. She is somewhat of a supporter of the New Left, and seems to feel that she must ask for "faith" in the good intentions of the USSR *vis â vis* Czechoslovakia. Yet it is astonishing to hear her *apologias* at this very moment, when in the country concerned, the horrors of the Slansky trials are being uncovered. A student reminds her that the Communist party came to power there in the first place by violent means. Another young man peers

302

through his glasses. "All the opposition leaders were arrested then—why should they not be arrested now?"

"That was in the *past.* . . ."

"But it's all self evident," the young man says earnestly, "the United States should speak up and warn against any aggression."

"Oh *no!*" The young woman put her hands over her ears for a moment. "Don't you see that that is just what we must *not* do! In this way we ourselves become warmongers. Aren't we doing enough in *Vietnam?*" she wails.

August 11

Maine. Portland—Freeport—Boothbay Harbour—Camden. Large white wooden houses; tremendously cozy hotels with wide floor boards painted dark green and slate grey; solid bath tubs; peppermints in barrels at the cashier's desk in the diningroom.

A strange restrained lily-white climate in which to read in the *Village Voice* about John Hatchett in New York City, who is in danger of losing his job because of a rabid article in which he accuses the Jews of dominating the New York public school system, and spelling "death for the minds and souls of . . . black children." Or to read in the *New York Times* that a Cuyahoga County grand jury charges that the disorders in Cleveland last month were organized and exploited by a small group of trained and disciplined professionals, that the pattern for the fire bombing and destruction was selective, and that "irrefutable" evidence was shown to the effect that (the leaders) pledged reciprocal support to, and with, the Communist Party of Ohio . . . These aberrations exist in the same world as this orderly New England town where we spend the night.

August 14

The island of Monhegan standing off the Maine coast presents towards the Atlantic a rugged barrier of grey precipitous rock. The air, impregnated with salt spray, encourages in the woods a thick growth of moss and lichen which in summer gives off a warm odor of rotting fertility. Tangled vines are thick with red raspberries. On the warmer side of the island, where small stony beaches curve between pale headlands, it is possible to watch from sunwarmed levels of rock the effortless planing and swooping of hundreds of birds. The water icy, even in mid August, takes away the breath of the rare swimmers. About fifteen feet from the shore the heads of small grey seals bob to and fro against the chill stretches of sea.

August 21

Last night's roaring fire is still glowing faintly in the huge stone fireplace at the boarding house. Someone comes in and carelessly throws onto it a great armful of logs. The clang of the breakfast bell comes from the *Trailing Yew*, a restaurant on the headlands, and half the island's visitors begin to walk along the pale sandy path in the fresh morning, between the hedges of wild roses. Afterwards sitting on wooden benches in the sun, the visitors watch the haze lift from the sea, and lobster boats rocking in the water. Down below someone spreads out nets, and there comes the far sound of a hammer.

A man we know is calling us. "Come, come quickly"! He beckons again and again with his arm. We walk over to join the crowd around him, and to listen to his tiny transistor radio which balances on a flat rock. It is the voice of the world intruding upon the peace of the island. Czechoslavakia has been invaded.

At 11 P.M. . . . armies of the Soviet Union, the Polish People's Republic, the German Democratic Republic, the Hungarian People's Republic, and the Bulgarian People's Republic crossed the state borders of the Czechoslovak Socialist Republic. . . ."

Later

There are differences between this takeover and the crushing of the revolt in Hungary, but the memories are the same. In the case of Hungary, the curtain was only torn briefly, little more than long enough to let the West hear the cry for help, a cry that went unanswered. ("Our troops are fighting . . . I notify the people of our country and of the entire world of this fact. . . . Any help? Any help? . . . Quickly . . . quickly . . . quickly. . . . Any help? . . . Any help?")

September

In the forest recesses of the little island, the heat soaks into the sand of the paths, the air is heavy with the perfume of the hardy wild rose, which opens pink or white petals to disclose a frank golden heart. The cries of the radio mingle with the cries of the birds.

1968 / America Will Go Down

The Communist parties of the world are beginning to abandon their Czech comrades, for once it seems the term "running dogs" should be used to describe this group which comes to heel for Moscow. (Even the Australian Party, at first so supportive of the Czechs, is beginning to bury the movement for freedom under heavy Russianized propaganda. The French CP, in spite of a few words disapproving of "military intervention," is saying that a "positive" agreement has been reached. A *Tass* report tells the convenient story that Czech workers have been urging the Soviet troops to remain until the "anti-socialist forces" are defeated.)

Liberals are being quietly removed. The Novotny men are back in the seat of power; the Czechs are fleeing to Switzerland. The number rises to 8,500; 30 and 40 a day are still seeking refuge. From the papers Dubcek's worried face gazes out. It seems that there are 100,000 troops in the country for an indefinite period. ("People accuse us of collaboration—but what other solution do they suggest? I did what I had to do.")

There is a Chinese proverb which says: "When a dog is large and has strong teeth, you bow and smile and call him 'Mr. Dog.'"

... primitive tokens
As absurd as they are savage.

W. H. Auden

The boat which leaves the island two days later provides an opportunity to review those who had chosen to holiday on a patch of land where the coast water is icy, where the only car to be seen is a shaky green truck which collects the trash, and where *The Trailing Yew* meal bell peals out three times a day, as school bells did in villages long-ago!

On the whole the returnees seem rather studious. They sit on the deck boat with their backs against the sun-warmed planks. They read the classics—Thoreau, Hardy, Melville, and they write letters with intent concern. Two teenage boys play checkers. A girl called Cathy sings in a soft not-too-spectacular soprano as she strums a guitar.

In this whole boatload there seems only one fragment of the counter-culture; a copy of an underground paper from Detroit abandoned on the deck near the steering house. This announces that "Unashamed sexuality as a plank in the platform of the New Left, is running on all over the world. . . . Not only is rock and roll a revolutionary force, but so are orgasm and nudity. 'The more I make love the more I make revolution' was a slogan for striking Parisian students. . . ." The writer of the article goes on to urge teenagers to develop their own sexuality, since teenagers are "a narcissistic age-group in which a hot-blooded interest in sex and nudity can be expected." As a windup there is a modest global aim, "We have to establish a situation on this planet, where all people can feel good all the time."

Hamburgers at a drugstore in Oguinquit, newspapers and chocolate bars. G— (who is to ride as far as Boston) is seduced by cigarettes, eau de cologne, and a copy of *Playboy*. In this glittering temple of glass and nickel, with its incredible choice of perfumes, hairsprays, and bright-covered magazines, the island which had had so pleasant an absence of luxury, seems far away and Spartan. Gone the quiet walks over carpets of green moss, gone the sudden cries of birds piercing the silence.

1968 / America Will Go Down

The Democratic convention has come and gone, but the papers are full of its repercussions. Police were accused of brutality and several are to be indicted. The demonstrators were said to have been obscene and profane and to have attacked the police with broken bottles, rocks, and lye. Leaders like Dave Dellinger (Chairman of the National Mobilization Committee to End the War), Tom Hayden of SDS, Abbie Hoffman, Jerry Rubin, and Bobby Seale of the Panthers, are to be tried for conspiracy to incite riots. The National Guard was called up to spell police, exhausted after chasing 2,000 dissidents out of Lincoln Park. Enough tear gas was used to send about 60 demonstrators to first aid stations or hospitals. A number of police who lost their cool when they were pressured by fleeing crowds had pushed demonstrators off the sidewalk and into a plate glass window at the Conrad Hilton. There were numerous other incidents. Rennie Davis, involved with trying to pull down a U.S. flag, got a 3-inch gash on the top of his head. Allen Ginsberg captured a mike and warned demonstrators to chant "OM" all together. ("It helps to quell the fluttering of butterflies.") Jean Genet, in love with the heavy-thighed policemen in their blue uniforms, was the reporter voted "most original." William Burroughs, author of *Naked Lunch*, straight from London and wearing a grey fedora, spoke about "unworkable systems." Norman Mailer said he was "sick about everything" but he had a deadline and "just wanted to salute everyone." Hippies chanted "Pigs must go! Pigs must go," and Yippies brought a pink pig in a burlap bag with the intention of nominating it for President. In the underground press there was the usual sophomoric little comment, "Chicago was the turning point. Before that everything we had done could be absorbed or ignored. But now the salad days are over. History is pointing its finger at us; Hey white boy, are you ready to grow up? Or is it just a game? The Black people, particularly the Black Panthers are interested in coalition .... but can *we* get ourselves together enough for them to bother taking us seriously?"

September 28

Even in Cuba dissidents have been inspired by the Czech affair, and today Castro admitted that rebellious students called in Havana *"los beats"* have been infected by the "Spring." But obviously the ruthless puritanism of The New Cuba has as much general distaste for dissidents as it has for homosexuals, and now it is even taking a long time to admit that Russia really invaded another Communist country. [Some USSR supporters managed to take it in their stride. The famous "agent of influence" Pablo Neruda—who helped Siqueiros to take refuge in 1940 after his murder attempt on Trotsky; who earned the Stalin prize in 1955 by poems of glorification (the Soviet hydrogen bomb is as "grand as the sun") who said that JFK was mentally unbalanced and Tito a traitor "covered with blood," and France a "little country bowing to the cowboys of Washington"—has been one of those who had no trouble. His comment about the invasion was simple, "The Soviet Union is my mother."]

Of crucial interest for the United States is Castro's reaction to the takeover. Last January Raul Castro accused the Soviets of conspiratorial activities. He named numerous KGB officials—Rudolf Shlyapnikov and Mikhail Roy of *Novosti* were two—a number of pro-Soviet Cubans were then sent to prison. This was interpreted as a serious split between Cuba and Russia, but it was apparently smoothed over by various economic concessions. At least after the invasion, even while Communists all over the world were (in their first surprise) denouncing the "unsocialist" takeover, and at the very moment when ardent Cubans were marching in the streets of Havana in support of liberalization, Castro mounted the podium to deliver not one of his impassioned, independent, impromptu spseches but a quiet statement in favor of the Soviets—in other words, a considered capitulation. [According to information brought to the West in 1971 by two officers of the Direccion General de Inteligencia (DGI), Orlando Castro and Gerardo Perazo Amerchazurra, who defected from the Cuban Embassy in London, the following events took place. To control Fidel's independence and to pressure Cuba, the Soviet Union curtailed the flow of oil to the island, so that the economy ground to a halt; Castro was forced to give in. The Soviets promised more oil and other necessities, and exacted a promise that criticism of the USSR should cease. The DGI found itself with a new superchief who supervised proceedings on behalf of the Russians, i.e. the KGB. The Cuban army was reduced in manpower, and the money funelled into clandestine operations.]

It was not only Castro who capitulated after the invasion. Some of our academic optimists were caught off balance and taken to task by Bertram Wolfe at Stanford, not because he so much likes to triumph over his intellectual colleagues but because he was challenged by them, and forced to reply. "I know of more than one political scientist and department chairman who has told his department and his graduate students that the word 'totalitarianism' should be abandoned," Bert Wolfe commented. Towards the end of his long reply he stressed what is consistently evident, in fact a "root defect," not only in academic circles, but in generally informed circles—an "undervaluing of our institutional freedom and pluralism." In fact he brings it back to the intellectuals in the end: "The chief problem is that our political elite is in part made up of loosely generalizing intellectuals; and our ruling officials bewildered by Russia, have taken rather too seriously the succession of illusions coming from their 'brain trusts.' "

Ernest, with his gentle voice and his non-violent exterior, is astonishing about Czechoslovakia. Just back from some peace demonstration on the West Coast, he is strangely tentative about the non-peaceful invasion (in which, after all, high-school boys trying to defend their country's liberty were run down by the advancing Russian tanks and crushed into the pavements). He talks of Russia in the simple familial sense of someone he understands, and in whom he has been slightly disappointed. "Perhaps she (Russia) will have the sense to back down. I have a premonition that she will be persuaded to make some compromise because of the strong world reaction." What is lacking in his attitude is any central idea of the totalitarian imperative—the impossibility of Russia allowing an important satellite to link itself with a democratic tendency.

October 18

The Washington airport. A small white plane comes in to land against a pinkish-grey pollution. From the limousine looking down on the greenish Potomac (no longer a river of romance, where Edgar Allen Poe went canoeing before breakfast). Green signs—North and South. An overpass with tennis courts below and moored yachts on the yellow water of the inlet. A cyclist with a pack on his back. The Promenade L'Enfant. The recognition of buildings such as the Internal Revenue Service Department, and the Department of Commerce. That sense of being in a capital.

Up Pennsylvania Avenue to 112th Street, where at a corner, old Washington seems represented by a few tiny narrow houses propped up irrelevantly in the middle of nowhere. In their doorways lounge two elegant Negroes—a tall man in striped sports shirt and slacks, a girl in red pants and a white blouse and bright green block-soled shoes. They both wear floppy white hats. For some reason, the whistles of the policemen here sound like the whistles of birds. . . . Suddenly there is a glimpse of the White House, unpretentious, reassuring. With this sight some twist of the heart, a sense of danger.

Ahead a long low dull-colored building. The Pentagon. "Here you are," a friend opens the door of his car, "the five-sided Dream Palace." He adds with a grin, "Know what's underneath us? The Athletic Club. I used to play squash there once." Yet inside this great complex of

1968 / America Will Go Down

American military endeavor, an air of pleasant casualness. Light flashes from the shiny badges of the uniformed guards. A row of healthy decent-looking American countenances stare rather woodenly out of big picture frames—Admiral Elmo R. Zumwalt, Junior, General Creighton W. Abrams, the Honorable Howard Callaway. These vie with a series of posters announcing an Army Ball. (Reminders of how a certain Polish spy commented about the ease of spying in America, and of what little expertise it took to collect information in these same Pentagon corridors.)

A secretary from one of the departments takes me along a labyrinth of bluish passages (which she comments crisply have been painted for the "first time in ten years"). We pass a snack bar and look down into the pleasant garden courtyard. "I walk about a mile a day to work," she comments with a sigh. We descend stairs into corridors which are painted a light yellow.

Later, after two interviews, there is another long walk to the Rotunda, from which the visitor emerges through the turnstiles into the world of the "lay" Pentagon, a complex of banks, candy shops, bake shops, newspaper stalls, book shops, drugstores, and clocks that indicate that it is ten of five in Burma, ten of twelve in Chicago, ten of seven in Hawaii, ten of eight in Moscow, and ten of two in Tokyo. When the cab emerges into the sunlight again and crosses the bridge near the Lincoln Memorial, where the graceful gilded statues from Italy flash their light against the sky, the driver tells how he has had L.B.J. in his cab.

"When he was a Senator. And Rosalind Russell *she's* been in this taxi . . . Walter Winchell . . . You *name* it!"

In the train going back to New York. A tall young girl in a lamb wool's coat has thick reddish-gold hair, and big eyes behind purple-tinted glasses (she introduces herself as Sally K—. She says that she has flown out from Berkeley, California and has just been to Washington to visit her grandmother). Had she been in Berkeley in 1964 when the first campus troubles were starting?

"I dropped out and went to Alaska."

Alaska sounds too healthy to be in style! She must have missed a lot of political activity?

She takes off her glasses, looking prettier with her eyes exposed. "I thought it would be real adventurous to go to Alaska."

How had it turned out?

"Well things *did* happen to me."

Like what?

"Like everything." She explains that she had gotten involved with a young man who was flying food and guns to Biafra and was wanted by the FBI. "He was very political. . . . in fact he was a Communist." She says this with considerable pride.

"Yes, I was working in this cocktail lounge, and one day Jerry comes in, and he has long flaxen hair to here," she indicates her shoulders. "Well . . . He could never pass as a hippie . . . but he wore these round glasses, and he had a gun and a knife . . . I thought it was kinda real *nutty*. . . . We were both expatriates from Berkeley. I said 'what are you doing in this crazy place?' and he said, 'I'm working for the International Red Cross, flying food to Biafra . . . want to help?'—Just like that!" She pauses. "You know some men have that special look when they've seen a lot. . . . He had it . . . a *mystical* look."

What was his background?

"His Daddy is a German shrink. You see he's a pilot, he worked for the Bush pilots and got involved in these relief things, these flights. I asked him did he mean it, for me to help? and he said 'Yes,' so I told him I wanted to go. . . . I walked out that evening."

She expects reproof and looks up from under her eyeslashes; but she is obviously puzzled (what had her experience done after all to provide her with any suitable caution)? "Oh yeah . . . yeah . . . I know! But he was just a fascinating person that's all. He was about twenty-seven and I was twenty-two at the time. . . . It all seemed plausible."

And did she know much about politics?

"We—ell . . . I didn't know Biafra was put out of bounds by the U.S. government. . . . You see," her tone is profoundly serious, "I was completely for the humanitarian cause."

What happened then?

"He told me to get a passport and I did. He said he was in trouble in the States because he'd been warned already, and last time he'd gone on a forged passport." She looks embarrassed. "By that time he was my lover, and he was such a *good* lover." She laughs again. "He said he couldn't take me all the way into Biafra but he'd fly the plane to an island off the coast where the IRC had permission to land, and he said I could help there."

Had she helped Jerry with money?

"Oh he had $2,000 on him when I met him . . . no, I *didn't* see it . . . he said he had to go to Fairbanks," she explains, "to get ready to fly, so we traveled by plane, by train, by thumb, by motorcycle, camping on the way, until we got there. No one knew where I was . . . my mother or my father or my family . . . that worried me a bit. And at Fairbanks, he got word to leave with the IRC at five A.M. the next day, and he went to draw $10,000 out of the bank there. He said he'd deposited it some time back. I waited for him, then he phoned and said that two FBI men had caught up with him and arrested him. He said to leave the hotel immediately and go to this place outside Fairbanks where he had some friends and to wait for him. . . . I went, and it was a sort of ranch. . . . You see wherever we went he had friends, sometimes the people were Communists or activists, and they have 'safe' houses. . . . That was on a Friday. . . . Why am I telling you all this . . . to someone who's a stranger?"

Perhaps it's easier to talk to a stranger?

"I suppose so . . . well, he called that night and said he'd been released on his own recognizance, but that his bank account had been frozen. He asked me to phone my mother and tell her to send two air tickets to San Francisco. He came out and picked me up. He said he wasn't going to spend 20 years of his life in jail, and he was going to Cuba; would I like to go with him, that I'd have to renounce my U.S. citizenship?"

And what had she said? "I said 'yep', that as a matter of fact it sounded *fascinating*." There is a short silence. "When we got to San Francisco, we went off to Mexico."

And how was *that* trip made?

"Well we picked up my car, and we drove it to San Diego, and then sold it and went over the border."

She laughs. Her red hair glints in the light from the window. "We stayed in Mexico . . . Oh" (she snaps her fingers). "We were in a bar and the owner of this bar was supposed to get us two forged passports, and then two men came in, and one of them said, "How was Alaska?. . . . So we just *froze*. . . . Jerry was sitting there drinking cognac . . . sometimes he'd seem to have about fifty of those things a night . . ." ("No," she answered in reply to questions "he didn't seem to have any trouble with drugs,—literally—he was on liquor. I'd only drink coffee.") "When these men came in he seemed to go pale. He told me to walk back to the hotel and wait for him."

Did he always send her away when something like this came up?

"Yes," she says, "on the campus at Berkeley when he was talking to Communists or organizers, he'd always say, 'you wait over there'. He said that he didn't want me to get involved."

And who were the men in the bar in Mexico?

She looks confused.

"I don't know . . . I think they were FBI men. I never asked him much, so I still don't understand . . . But he came back to the hotel and said 'We're leaving. We're going back to San Francisco. . . .'"

The route back didn't seem to have been as easy as the route down. . . . She'd begun to hate all that running.

"Friends of his put us up all the time. . . . 'Safe' houses . . . I kept losing weight. . . . I lost twenty pounds. I got down to 100 before I got home." "The FBI followed us everywhere. I called home and they'd been there." She laughs again. "I said to my mother 'Gee, that's fascinating.'" Then her face sobers. "We were hurting for money. I borrowed, and that's why I went back to work this winter, six days a week. Around February Jerry said he was tired of it, and would turn himself in. I was frightened because I felt they might get me for aiding and abetting. He told me to go home and stay there."

The train has stopped at Philadelphia. Down at the service bar in the passage, a melancholy Negro in a red uniform with green epauletes is explaining to two irritated passengers that there is no hot coffee because the water heating unit is out of order. "No sir," he is saying, "Can't get things repaired so easy these days." (There seems something ironic, on this high-speed train with a capability of 150 miles an hour, about having no lunch car, no hot coffee, and as a final straw, only two kinds of sandwiches).

Back in our seat Sally begins to talk about how Jerry had phoned her and said that he had been on his way out of the country with forged documents, and had been shot in the stomach.

"Shot! By whom?"

"I don't know . . . the FBI, I think."

The FBI seems to be playing a large role in this story; but if the FBI had shot him and he was disabled, how had he managed to escape from their custody? If a rival political group, or rival dope dealers had shot him it might make more sense; but whatever had happened, Sally seems unsure about it.

"He flew back to San Francisco and I met him at the airport. He was deathly sick and he had stitches all across his stomach. . . ."

Did she see the stitches?

"Yes, I saw them. He said that he was really going to give himself up now and he told me to drop him off at the Federal Building, so I did."

The conductor comes to check our tickets. She hands hers over with a listless sigh.

Her friend's general activities seem to suggest Third-World politics of some kind. Was he pro-Chinese?

"Oh yes . . . Pro-Mao, Pro-Fidel, and Pro-Arab."

Did he talk much of the Third World?

"Oh yes, we rapped about it for hours!"

And of course, he would be anti-Israel and pro-Black Panther? "Oh, yes. Absolutely. "He's in prison now and I don't see him because I don't want to see him; it's simply not worth it."

Her large eyes stare into space. "I would have gone off to Cuba," she snaps her fingers, "just like that! I would have given up my passport and perhaps not been able to come back. I've seen him on campus. Students who wouldn't even listen to their own professors would gather around him for hours. He just used to *mesmerize* them."

Her tone sounds a little bitter, as if she had been no more astute than those students. Her voice has been growing fainter. Soon she is asleep, curled up in her wool coat. Only the top of her head is visible.

October 25

The story told by the girl in the train is not without an eerie romance, but at the same time it is quite believable. This scenario of one middle class girl falling for a political con man, getting an airplane ticket from her mother, selling her car to go to Mexico, and borrowing "bread" as they run from the FBI, displays the imperatives of the movement—i.e., the constant running, the "safe houses," the uninformed sexual partner. It is probably however a mild version of other stories still extant in the political underworld.

There is always now this sense of unavoidable confrontation. Attacks are being leveled at the United States from all sides, not only from the two communist super states (which at once want to imitate and catch up with the Western democracies and to wage open war against them) but also from the rising Third World powers, which resent the wealth and influence of the West and are affected by the constant hammering of anti-Western and anti-white rhetoric.

The atmosphere is an atmosphere of war. [In a memoir published in the *New York Times* about the 1962 missile crisis, one paragraph grips the reader with a certain dread, with a sense of the essential fallibility and helplessness of human beings.]

R.F.K. notes that as he sat with his brother, in those terrible moments when a decision was being made to risk confrontation with the Soviets, J.F.K. asked what would happen if two Soviet ships at that moment approaching with a submarine towards the blockade barrier, tried to enter the forbidden area? The answer was that the aircraft carrier Essex was to signal the submarine to surface.

And if the submarine failed to surface what would happen? Then came the answer. Depth charges would be used until it did so . . . In the minds of both the brothers there was a terrible doubt. Had a mistake been made? . . . Should something further be done?

"His hand went up to his face" wrote Robert Kennedy," and covered his mouth. He opened and closed his fist. His face seemed drawn, his eyes pained, almost grey. We stared at each other across the table. For a few fleeting seconds, it was almost as though no one else was there and he was no longer the President . . . Inexplicably, I thought of when he was ill and almost died . . . ."

1968 / America Will Go Down

October 26

As a counterpart to the trial of Sirhan Sirhan, certain facts about James Earl Ray have come out (through William Bradford Huie, who has the contract to write Ray's life story). The facts are that ten days after Ray's escape he went to work in a restaurant called The Indian Trail, in suburban Chicago. Here he washed dishes, peeled vegetables, was impeccable in his conduct, graduated to "food server," had his pay raised, got along without friction in the kitchen with twenty-seven Negroes and four Filipinos—and received two telephone calls in two months. One reported episode fits in with a pro-Third World Cuban-connected conspiracy theory, a conspiracy about which Ray himself had not been thoroughly informed. This is that Ray reported a meeting with a blonde Latin called Raoul, who told him to go to Birmingham and wait for a "job" for which he would give him money, and a passport to anywhere in the world.

Apart from this, all the information so far discovered about humble-seeming, long-nosed Ray suggests that he is only a small-time hood, with a tremendous inferiority complex and a wide if non-spectacular criminal experience.

Jasmin has chosen a more effective way to get out of prison than James Earl Ray, and has joined a reformed addicts group, members of whom go out into the streets to try to bring addicts back to headquarters. I find her in a brown-painted house with a battered front, and a broken fence. Inside the house it is warm, clean, orderly. One Negro who has a noticeable limp is preparing some soup in the kitchen, and younger men are "rapping" in an alcove which is labelled OFFICE. Jasmin appears at the top of the stairs, smiling down with that charm she undoubtedly has, like an actress making a first appearance. Her hair is cut to a modified "Afro," her skin is a clear brown. The exaggerated "street" clothes have disappeared. I wait for her—the usual long wait. She has to help with making the "soul food" in the kitchen. There has been some sort of conversation about assignments and shopping allowances; after this she is rather subdued. The man in the office admonishes, "Don't stay out too long."

In the car Jasmin talks of "whites" and of how "whites" have exploited "blacks." (She is obviously in a "black nationalist" phase again.)

"I'm out of that bag of depending on 'whitey.' I'm with the blacks now. You've been a good friend to me—bringing me books and coming to see me when I was down. I could always depend on you. But now it's all changed . . . I mean, I've chosen a black way of life." She is

318

warming up to a speech against "Whitey." It is not personal but rather rhetorical. Bound up perhaps with the early years of her life when she had gone to listen to the "preachers," (and later had practiced at home, standing on a chair with her brothers listening to her).

After a while it is possible to break into her fantasy. "But *I'm* white. You wanted me to come to see you. Shall I go away?" The hypnotized expression fades, a flicker of warmth comes to her eyes. "No," she hangs her head. "You're my friend."

Later that day, walking up Massachusetts Avenue from the South End where the trees still heavy from summer hang over the warmed pavements and the last chrysanthemums are for sale in front of the florist shops, Jasmin stops to point out the nearby alley where she has tried, as she puts it, "to bring her first addict to reason."

In her new evangelistic role, both condemning her own people and condemning whites, she accuses the radicals—black and white—of trying to use the blacks. "There is always a group on the outskirts, agitating for something."

She thinks for a while. "In the drug groups they imagine we're a bunch of animals. They get into some project like Project Renewal and then they try to implicate it by Communist talk. People are there for drugs and they're not able to take care of their health, much less standing any pressure on the brain, with a whole lot of stuff they never heard of before!"

Then she doesn't feel that politics should be mixed up with other things?

"Not when people are trying hard to benefit theirselves!" She becomes very quiet and earnest, forgets her aggressive preaching. "Anyone will make some little jive promise when they're grasping for a straw, and embrace it for a while, but they don't really mean it. Those radicals should understand this, and not take advantage of the fact that people are reaching out."

If Jasmin is temporarily removed from the struggle, this is not because the struggle has in any sense abated. The forces which have attacked the minds and sensibilities of ghetto dwellers are vividly set out in a book published after the King assassination by the *Washington Post* called *Ten Blocks From The White House.* In it young men wearing masks and hoods to hide their identity, speak openly. "I learned how to start fires in the service. Uncle Sam taught me in basic training." "Deaths don't bother me, I look upon them as a sacrifice." "If you dig into [the white's] heart you can see he has done beastly things . . . he walks different . . . smells different. He's a beast, baby." "It's not rioting going on, it's revolution . . . rioting is spontaneous; revolution is planned." "Fire? . . . It's like a cleansing agent . . . fire is a purifier."

1968 / America Will Go Down

In these statements, at once violent and naive, the uninitiated might not note the varied strands of political influence—the Fidelista concept of death as a revolutionary necessity, the Maoist isolation of the white man, the Cuban distortion of José Martí's reflection about the "belly of the beast," the Black Muslim's need for the apocalyptic fire.

And now in 1968 one of the not sought for pieces in the generalized political puzzle is still the key role of Cuba. Cuba is the fulcrum of activity. Just as the blacks are beaten with the racist stick inside Cuba itself, in order to stimulate revolutionary fervor, so race feeling has been manufactured inside the United States by pro-Cuban groups, with the aim of persuading black Americans to join the revolution of the Third World, to travel to Cuba to learn to be professional terrorists, to look for leadership to Havana instead of to Washington. Already the catalog of internal manipulation by Cuba-inspired groups or agents is fairly extensive. Cubans assigned to the United Nations arrested for encouraging sabotage of oil refineries in New Jersey in 1962. Cuban-trained blacks active in a plot to bomb the Statue of Liberty in 1965. (Robert Collier having met and talked with Ché Guevarra at the UN.) Effective links set up between Cuba's DGI and PL base in Harlem, and between U.S. students and Vietcong delegates in Havana; the Cuban UN Mission being the first to bring black power leaders together with Puerto Rican extremists (a task carried out by Mrs. Laura de Meneses de Albizu, long-time member of the Mission, and widow of the extremist once involved in the plot to assassinate Truman, who introduced Carmichael of SNCC and Juan Mari-Bras, Secretary General of PMI, thus setting in motion the coordination of Communist flanking movements in Puerto Rico with the infiltration of Negro communities on the mainland); Stokely on the island in January of this year organizing a march on Fort Brooke with the FUPI (student arm of the PMI) to protest the conscription of Puerto Ricans to Vietnam; Mari Bras (who established the Free Puerto Rican Embassy in Havana and linked the FUPI with the opposite number to the student organization of LASO) traveling with him to Cuba for the OLAS Conference; and Stokely writing to Ché to announce that "Black Power is moving toward urban guerrilla warfare," and Stokely in Paris, where students and others stamp gleefully to his words—*"We — don't — want — peace in Vietnam. We — want the Vietnamese — to — defeat — the U.S."*

These are the manifestations of the subversive war. Arson. Calls for violence. Stimulation of riots. Appeals to black gangs, Black Muslims, black psychotics, to Chicanos, to Chinese, to Puerto Ricans ("to destroy U.S. Imperialism," to "destroy the Beast"). Calls to black and white students, to create a common front, to give money, aid, leadership. Chiming in at suitable moments, the orchestra of broadcasts from the USSR (attempting for instance to arouse rebellion in the ranks of the U.S. armed forces). All this under the banner of the Third World; but also under the supervision of the KGB, since this influence has been powerful in Cuba ever since Castro first associated himself with the Soviet Union; and is especially so now that KGB directors are firmly entrenched in the offices of Cuba's Secret Service.

In spite of the obvious messages of the Tri-Continental Conference. In spite of the relentless takeover of Czechoslovakia (like Cuba an essential part of the current Russian defense system), the role of Cuba comes across without emphasis. Excited U.S. leaders reply to the first minor depredations of the attempt to stir up People's War with demands for "more welfare," and for "understanding." Hubert Humphrey declares: "We will have open violence in every major city and county in America if new welfare programs are not passed." Psychiatrists refer rather loftily to "necessary gestures of rebellion." But what is important here is that the black militant movement is recruited as a tool of the Communist movement, that it bypasses the brilliant earlier period of Civil Rights, and is firmly locked into the Havana-based guerrilla machine.

There are other kinds of black times. Today up at a studio near 117 Street, where there is a rehearsal for a show to be put on at Christmas.

The studio is hung with weapons (big drums are piled in one corner). O— looking rather fatter than when he last visited Boston and definitely more prosperous (he too has benefitted by the Poverty Program) produces some kind of rum drink, and a seat on a tiny ceremonial stool. The room is full of smoke. Two girls wearing Yoruba costumes dance to the drum beat in that small-stepped way, with their dresses bunched at the back, which makes them look like birds coming out of a patch of buffalo grass to case the open ground.

O— wears a woven purple dashiki and a small embroidered purple cap, but his old African innocence has almost gone ("I never get less than $500 a night now"). In spite of this the late afternoon wears away with a kind of magic—the sound of drums, the women's turbans bobbing in the dance, one goldish, one greenish, the sudden fierce chant of a tall, lanky black who leaps up and plants his splayed toes flat on the boards, the haze of smoke and rum—this kind of Black Nationalism is easy on the nerves.

In fact as far as the downfall of 'Amerika' is concerned, it is a question of *"chacun à son gôut!"* Jean Genet, French literary giant, has just published in *Esquire* his reflections about the American scene—including his omniverous appreciation of the police and the blacks. He announces that America has a "magnificent, divine, athletic police force" and he looks at the whole panorama of the Democratic Conven tion through the arches formed by the thighs of these men standing at ease at the top of the steps. He is enraptured by the azure helmets and the black leather vizors and by the top-grade sky-blue cloth and hard rubber of the muscled legs and torsos and bellies. Only on the side, and casually, does he feel that America itself is a "heavy island, too heavy" and that it would be good if it were "demolished and reduced to powder."

December 27

Walking down Eighth Street in Greenwich Village with B—, on the way to an early off-Broadway play. There is a pervasive feeling of the disintegrations which have taken place during the 60's. Past the antique shops, and the walk-ups, the butcher shops and the little Italian market, where silvery fish lie in barrels and outside on the street critical old ladies peer into the baskets of clams.

Further up, where, as B— says, it was once a charming Bohemian but safe neighborhood, the newspaper man at the corner complains of "bums" and "junkies." Well, it's not the bums so much," he confides. "I take 'em every day; it's the junkies and the muggers and the soo-icides." (This is the general area of the Circle in the Square, the Bleeker Street Cinema, the Andy Warhol Theatre, the Village Gate and the Bitter End; an area where once no one ever encountered anyone more dangerous than Joe Gould, the "oral historian.") Now it has become a strange refuge for the new "abandoned love life," the "interracial tryout," and the "bad-trip scene"—an area where some kind of disaster is automatically suspected, where special police squads patrol and a hot line has been set up. (Now the fading of a runaway flower child, and her reappearance on the symbolic garbage dump is as familiar as was once the sight of winos passed out in doorways, with a *cache* of empty bottles).

As B— and I walk along, one clear-cut sentence reaches us from a group of queerly-dressed children. The sentence is: "I'm a drop out from St. Louis High but now I'm into Eastern religions."

In the early morning returning to the scene of the "play," a brief discussion with a sacristan from the Holy Trinity Chapel. "Yes—all the churches around here have been vandalized and almost everything that could be carried off easily has been; seems like the hippies around here furnish their pads with benches and votive candles." He smiles sourly, "The churches have been open and because they are open, they are vulnerable." He pauses dramatically, ". . . apparently many of these pads have no bathroom. . . . "

1968 / America Will Go Down

In the doorway of the very theater we went to last night, snuggled up in a patch of sun, and early as it still is, a youngish man with hollow cheeks and a tattered longish hair line is squatting with a guitar. He wears a rather heavy coat with no shirt visible at the neck and his thin listless fingers sweep against the guitar strings, "I don't want to die in a nuclear war," he is singing. "I want to sail to a distant—sho—ore. And live like an ape-man. . . ."

The song seems curiously appropriate for an era of "drop out" and "do your own thing" and "stop-the-draft." Several passers-by pause to listen so that the guitar player, conscious of his audience, puts on a suitable exaggeration and begins to wail out the words, throwing back his thin bare neck:

> *My only idea of lux-ur-eee*
> *Is to swing up and down on a coco-nnnuuut tree-eee*
> *Living . . . like . . . an . . . aaape-maan!*

Back again at 8th Street to buy a copy of the *New York Times*, I find the verbal justification of the surrounding scenes being provided by all the posturing of the Free Press and by the abundance of crime and erotica being presented to the buyer. Enormous numbers of sex and crime magazines, numerous startling covers showing women being dragged by the hair, cut by knives, threatened by pistols with breasts exposed— other covers show decapitated heads resting on railway lines, or human bodies being rayed by powerful machines, or depict young boys in suggestive positions or women twining towards women. (The ads include numerous possibilities: I am a Caucasian Girl . . . Young couple new to swinging . . . Broadminded Date Club . . . Is there an attractive well-built honest girl in the Palo Alto area willing to live with a handsome executive . . . Uninhibited guys, gals and couples. Middle-aged oriental. Satisfaction guaranteed.) There is another copy of *Rat*, its cover made up entirely of breasts; there is a small poster of a naked subteen girl holding a daffodil and printed with an appeal for attention to "lovely soft aesthetic posters."

For a moment it is interesting to stand in the winter sunshine, reading part of a screed from *The Harbinger* (Middletown, California):

> . . . We checked into the bridal suite of the Holiday Inn . . . had supper in our room and after bathing proceeded to set up shop. Out came the incense, candles, bottles, India prints, mirrors, toys, comics, phonograph, musical instruments, movie camera, fireworks (we had bought about $100 worth a few hours before), magic kit and the drugs. We had everything but grass, the brown rice of drugs. Arnie tried to score some from our colored bell-hop but his mind had been whitewashed. He brought us a bottle of vodka which we duly set in place unopened. We had about 35 caps of beige acid which we hadn't tried yet. We each took a cap. As it came on we saw that it was good

and took a few more. We were feeling great and proceeded to get married. We had bought funny fake marriage licenses which we signed with our other names: Vaxy McKoops, Ring, Hank, and the Cat Paw Print. We kissed, danced, lit roman candles off the balcony and sparklers inside which Arnie photographed in the candlelight. We danced and drew arabesques with them . . . I took some more caps. We were traveling very fast now. The speed of sound . . . at least . . . we took some more caps and now really started to move . . .

December 30

It is a bad way to see in the New Year, but 1968 is running true to form—death, disaster, crime, disintegration, terrorism, racism, reverse racism, anti-Semitism. Not long ago sobbing, shouting Iraquis were demanding death for Israelis and Americans, and several commentators in Baghdad broke down on the radio, mourning for the troops killed in Jordan by Israeli jets. (In Egypt, Nasser vowed to punish Israel if it cost a million casualties. In Amman they watched the sky. Moscow talked of aggression. And in Israel they talked of the shelling of Israel's settlements by Iraqui troops.)

While the Jews who are managing to get out of Eastern Europe report ancient barbarisms such as anonymous calls ("Let the *mosiek* [kikes] go") and the painting of swastikas on the doors of their houses.

1969

We are doing things for Stalin that these poor
people do not understand.
> Jacob Golos to Luis Budenz

January, 1969

This is the month for drawing up balance sheets, and as the burden of Vietnam grows heavier, there come echoes from Southeast Asia of the fear that the United States might decide to withdraw from her self-appointed role. Far away voices begin to be heard: "If America gives up it is the end of us all."; "If America were to withdraw it would be an eternal blemish on her honor."

I am making plans to fly to Mexico again and after that on to Europe and North Africa, but the strength of the protest movement here makes the trip itself, planned to coordinate with work on another book, less attractive. Although there is an irresistible need to see more of what is going on elsewhere, the crux of the world situation is surely in this country; its outcome will be decided here.

Today I am in the South End to say goodbye to Jasmin, who has been in and out of prison since her dramatic role as savior of street addicts, and to Cleopatra, who is in the hospital with hepatitis after the birth of Beetle's child. (As a result of her heroin addiction, the doctor reports, she now has a serious degeneration of the liver.)

Walking down Washington Street after these two brief and gloomy visits, I encounter a little crowd on the pavement where a stocky black man explains that he is trying to persuade the Negro to "go for knowledge." He has planted a large poster which says "Knowledge is Power" in the snow of his front yard. "I think the Negro should stop begging and go for books. Yes, I've been to Philly, to Georgia, to New York City. I go around to Black Power things. I try to hook up to find out what they're offering the Nation." (Perhaps he means the Nation of Islam.)

1969

Soon he is ridiculing the power of the RNA. "If they couldn't get together enough for forty acres down there in the South, how could they get all those states?" He is also scornful of the Black Muslims. "They're no *Negro* group. Why, Muhammed was a white boy, let's face it. And this angel whispers in his ear and says, 'It's all right to enslave anyone so long as he's not a Muslim!' Why, those Arabs were the greatest slavers you ever did see! That Elijah Muhammed is one of the richest dudes in America. Why should *he* break the format? He has all these women going around wearing long dresses to the ground, and working in his Temples, and all these dues comin' in."

The speaker appears to be open to irrationality in spite of his constant appeal to reason. Suddenly, out of the blue, he asserts that it is well known that Israeli soldiers bury Arabs up to their necks in the sand, and then use them for target practice. This affirms the fact that during his "voyages into blackness" he has absorbed some of the violent anti-Semitic material now being funneled from the Arab propaganda machine to the black extremist organizations. He produces some rabid pages from *Muhammed Speaks*. "This comes from Arabic sources. You're not going to get such stuff in the *Boston Globe!*"

Depressed by this encounter, I keep an appointment with George H— in a dark little cafe on Tremont Street, where he recounts the latest information about heroin in Vietnam. "The U.S. armed forces were always targets, but after the Tet offensive last year, and when the city didn't rise up to welcome the liberators, since then, perhaps in retaliation, heroin's been pouring into Saigon."

Does he mean as opposed to marijuana?

"Yes—as opposed to marijuana. Some heroin's always been available, but suddenly it's ninety-five percent pure and at the ridiculous price of eight cents a gram. All this heroin is refined and packaged in the same way. It looks very much like a plan to put the U.S. fighting men out of action."

And he thinks this is organized by the Chinese Communists?

"I think so. I think that considering the experience of Japan and Korea, nothing could be more natural. It's part of the attempt to get us out of Vietnam."

In this seedy atmosphere evil seems more easily recognized. "Conspiracy is a word which brings an immediate hostile reaction," he says with a shrug, "but that doesn't make 'plotting and planning' go away. You can't help noticing that the only sort of conspiracy allowed by the liberals is one of which the United States establishment is accused."

We talk for a while of military dangers. "Psycho-strategy is a keen weapon, but there is also military power. Soviet ships are now in the Indian Ocean as well as the Mediterranean; there are also survey ships which are thinly disguised electronic intelligence vessels; and there are the submarines." His face is sharply furrowed in the dim light. "In

328

1955 the Russians had no foreign bases. Now they have moved into Aden, and have a beachhead in Egypt, and the use of the major Cuban ports. Are we such unregenerate traders that we must transport our technology while the USSR escalates her aid to Vietnam? The trucks on the Ho Chi Minh trail came from the Ford-built and Brandt-built plants, both re-vamped with new American machinery while the war was on." He adds in an angry voice, "It burns me up." Apparently what worries him most is the humiliation the United States underwent with the capture of the USS Pueblo. The news lately has recounted Bucher's story of beating and starving in North Korea, of attempts at suicide, of being taken at midnight to see a supposed spy who had been tortured. George H—'s tone is bitter. "To see our men forced to crawl on their knees. . . . "

New York City

Perhaps is it a compliment to the West to say that its open societies have managed to produce citizens hopelessly inexperienced in certain kinds of political evil. And this conversation with George H— is a reminder of the stubborn refusal of doctrinaire liberals to countenance the reality of political conspiracy. Partly because of this I begin to follow up again the long-ago but forever fascinating Trotsky plot, as it lives in these city streets, squares, restaurants—especially those on the West Side around Times Square, the docks, the Bronx; for it was in this labyrinth that the details of the assassination were worked out; much of the action so compartmentalized that the operatives were not fully aware of what they were doing. (But aware or not, it was an American who played the major role of coordinating the activities of the Communist party members here; an American woman who was courier for the *apparat*; two American girls who took part in the gaining of entry to The Cayoacan house; and an American who actually opened the door to Trotsky's first attackers.)

The question of the motivation for this kind of betrayal must surely have a good deal to do with the motivation of present-day Americans who now turn against their own government to serve others. Then as now such citizens were obsessed with future good. "One reason," the gentle long-lashed Harry Gold reported in his solemnly sincere analysis of why he first provided the Russians with classified information, "was a genuine desire to help the people of the Soviet Union to enjoy the better things of life." And as Mr. Huey Newton suggested later in quite another context, "In the name of love and in the name of freedom, with love as our guide, we'll slit every throat that threatens the people."

1969

Through those days of the organization of Trotsky's murder, Louis Budenz, a member of the American party, was taking orders from a Russian agent, Dr. Gregory Rabinowitz (known to him as "Roberts" and planted at the UN under the guise of representative of the Soviet Red Cross). Budenz was one of those who descended almost daily from the then H.Q. of the Communist party to his appointments with the "fatherly" Roberts in offices, restaurants, and finally in the Bronx.

The old HQ was in a wedge-shaped building on East Thirteenth Street, and it was in this building that a (then) young Communist, Whittaker Chambers, working on the staff of the *Daily Worker*, watched the attacks against Trotsky in the party and the press growing daily bitterer and more violent. Chambers could scarcely foresee how the Russian GPU would move into the local American groups to purge them of Trotskyism, or that scores of agents would be put to cover not only Trotsky himself but all possible sympathizers in and out of the Soviet Union.

Chambers had thought that his growing distaste was not for Moscow or for Comrade Stalin, but for the stupidity of the American party. He had not realized that outside the open party, there existed a concealed party which functioned so smoothly that in seven years of being a Communist he had not suspected it. "I thought at that time of the underground as an underground of the American Communist party," he said. Later, of course, he realized that there were actual members of the Soviet secret police, practically all of them Russian born, operating on American soil. Budenz, who was deeper into the *apparat*, learned earlier of the reasons for the befogging of the minds of the rank and file. It was simply that the American comrades were always securely controlled by the Russian representatives. Budenz described Jacob Golos as a little sandy-haired tiptoeing man whose picture, by order from above, never appeared in the Soviet press and who told him that only foreigners get to be top men (i.e., head of the local Politburo) in America; that an American comrade might be a Comintern man in China, or the Philippines, but not here; that it was Comintern policy to make aliens supervisors of all native Reds. This device discouraged and slowed down the spread of distrust with Stalinist methods among the American operatives. Budenz reported a patronizing remark. "Look," Golos said to him one day as they stood at a window on the ninth floor and stared down at the crowds below, "we are doing things for Stalin that these poor people do not understand."

January 18

A small number of extremists rioted at Tokyo University today, regardless of the fact that the student body is overwhelmingly against strikes. They injured 180 of the police sent against them. Clouds of gas and smoke hung over the buildings making the scene look like that of some great battlefield.

Similarly in London a few months ago a handful of militant leftists occupied part of the London School of Economics, again in defiance of the student body. "There is an odor of psychopathic self-righteousness about them," an English writer said, referring to such small groups of activist intellectuals, " . . . for personal aggrandizement they exploit the slightest political crisis." (Perhaps it was into this kind of error which certain U.S. citizens fell long ago when they decided to suppress a natural loyalty to their country).

The fascination of the city lies partly in its never-ending activity. Seen from a law firm's broad plate glass window, the shaft of the Empire State pierces a winter sky cut across by a streamer advertising the latest computer. From the cavern of Wall Street, the crowds look up to see jet fighters (new ones, just off the assembly lines) speeding silently towards Southeast Asia. At a dinner party someone expatiates about crime detectors such as voice prints and neutron activator analyzers. Against all this the plot to kill Trotsky, put into action long ago, seems out of date. In spite of this its psychological know-how is still beyond many present-day political buffs.

The link between Budenz and "Roberts," his underground contact, was Jacob Golos who ran the front business (World Tourists Incorporated) under the cover name of "Timmy" and was the lover of a young woman called Elizabeth Bentley, a rather idealistic, pretty and proper-looking Vassar graduate, who had been inducted into the *apparat* (and who played an important role both in Operation Trotsky, and in an espionage apparatus operated through Communist cells in Washington). She had fallen in love with Timmy, this modest little man with well-worn brown shoes, red hair, and blue eyes, before she knew that he was really Jacob Golos and one of the three members of the ruthless Central Control Commission, responsible for keeping American Communists in line. Golos arranged for Budenz to meet Roberts in the Bronx. Roberts told Budenz how well Ruby Weil had done her work in Paris. (Ruby had been sent to Europe to introduce Sylvia Agelof, the homely bespectacled Trotskyist social worker from Brooklyn to Ramon de Mercader, the young man chosen by the KGB to be the future assassin of Trotsky). Neither Budenz nor Ruby Weil was told that the purpose of the operation was assassination.

1969

Through the summer of 1939 Elizabeth Bentley, as she testifies later, saw the two Mexicans—the tall, dark, fierce-eyed Luis Arenal and an excessively fat man who was an artist, shuttling to and fro from Mexico. Accompanying Golos she was taken to lunches and dinners with them in New York City. Naively she was proud that Timmy's role (so much more important than she had thought) was to be liaison man for the Party in both Canada *and* Mexico. "What I did not know until later," she adds (this famous preliminary to many confessions) "was that the two of them were not just Mexican Communists, but part of the Russian Secret Service Police hatchet squad . . . Even then they were laying plans to liquidate Trotsky."

So it was that on that day when the news was flashed around the world that the Arenal brothers, Luis and Leopardo, were suspected of being involved in the first attack on Trotsky's life, Elizabeth Bentley read the *Times* and called Timmy to meet her on a park bench in Sheridan Square. He ordered her to keep away from the apartment of Rose Arenal (sister of Luis and Leopardo), which she had been using as a letter drop. "The affair is too hot," he said. A few months later and after the second attack, Sylvia Agelof, who had been living in the Hotel Montejo in Mexico City with her lover, was arrested as an accomplice. Police Chief Salazar described her as a small girl dressed in a sports dress of white piqué and a tan coat, wearing thick glasses with gold rims and sobbing constantly. (And in New York City another girl, Ruby Weil, whose role in the assassination suddenly became clear to her, rushed up in great agitation to talk to Budenz at the *Daily Worker*. Budenz was told by Golos to quiet her down at all costs, but on no account to allow her to renew contact with Party Headquarters. As Chambers later testified the Communist Party allowed no obvious link between the underground and the open party. Ruby Weil's name remained under a cloud, blackened by that association with Trotskyists which the rank and file had seen and condemned.)

It is hard to tell how many present-day activists—drawn into a formal Communist *apparat*—would accept with equanimity the rigid discipline imposed in the late 30s. Since the situation of "Revolutionary Pluralism" encouraged by the Sino-Soviet split is dictating a broader interpretation of the party line, forcing the Kremlin into indirect methods (the supplying of arms, money, drugs, the discreet use of satellites, the creation of front groups and demonstrations, and for special purposes the tolerance of loose alliances with Maoists, Trotskyists, Anarchists). This however does not suggest that in serious matters, the old iron structure does not hold. Nor does the political libido seem to vary (repressions of unpleasant material, compensation, rationalization, and the shallow religiosity seem as evident as ever). "I had been terrifically shielded from the whole thing," Elizabeth Bentley said after breaking with the Russians; "and when he (Golos) died, I was thrown into direct contact with the cheapest types I have ever seen . . . gangster types . . . who made no bones of the fact that they had contempt for American Communists."

She was not the only American agent who was gullible and high-minded. Silverman, for instance, was described by Chambers as a slight nervous little man. "In fact he was a child, and the effort that it cost him to be a man was apparent in the permanently worried expression of his eyes." Such agents tended to feel an organic antipathy towards the Russians who, due to the peculiar cynicism of their training, lacked insight into foreign character. Vasili Zubilin (the "loud-mouth") who operated for more than fifteen years in the United States, with and without Embassy cover, had a great scorn for his U.S. contacts. He is said to have boasted to an agent called Morros, "I am the head of the NKVD and feel free here to do exactly as I want to do." He told Morros to keep away from the Russian functions and on one occasion catching him at a party, he pushed him against the wall, holding him by the lapels of his jacket, and shoved a gun into his stomach saying, "Soon you will be no more use to me you fool!"

Time has changed the world political situation but has not made Americans more astute. A whole new generation of the easily deceived has been bred in the incubators of the country where the worker has the highest standard of living yet experienced in the globe. Affluence and contentment seem to have paralyzed its survival sense. Democratic man is after all a fairly new species upon the earth. It might be said also, and with special emphasis perhaps, of those attracted to, or involved in religious affairs, that they appear too affectionate to be shrewd. Castro has put the power struggle within the Church fairly bluntly: "Compared to the Communists the radical Catholic priests are as far to the left of them as the Communists are from the rest of society."

What is at issue of course is not the "liberalization" of the Church, but its manipulation for political purposes. During the Algerian war, priests were carrying explosives, and today practicing Catholics are supporting terrorism. (Now en route to Mexico there is the memory of Budenz telling long ago of Communist shadows flitting back and forth across the Rio Grande carrying messages harmful to the United States, this at a time when Gerhardt Eisler [Berger] characterized Latin America as the soft-under-belly of the United States.) The terrain of Latin America, and especially Mexico, presents a fertile area for the exploitation of religiosity. But if the current politicalization of the Church has many acceptable manifestations, some of them are also especially impudent. Katakolis, the Patriarch of Georgia, for instance, exhorting the United States and Germany at one of the Moscow-supported Peace Conferences in Prague, asked them eloquently, "For the sake of the all-loving God, take a step towards complete disarmament . . . this would be *true* faith." (In spite of such appeals, many Western clerics who were ready to attend such gatherings have now been frightened off by the invasion of Czechoslovakia.)

There is another side to this coin of American faith, hope, and charity. When—in the West—the reactionary and uncreative cult of Communism is given room to propagandize and subvert, it is the freedom, concern, curiosity, and activism of the West which make this possible. In the case of Trotsky it was American integrity which publicized his civil rights, which paid for books and articles dealing with them, which protected the Trotsky archives, which organized an open trial in Mexico, which subsidized the building of Fortress Cayoacan.

In our schizophrenic times, historical recorders may be grateful that this murder at least, boldly carried out during a decade when thousands of political torturings, kidnappings, and murders took place in quiet, throwing off only sinister and muffled echoes, did finally focus upon itself the spotlight of American publicity and so hit the front pages of the global press.

MEXICO

Live Within Sight of the Volcanoes

February 20

So to Mexico again (with the back of the winter still unbroken, with
New York City quieted by blizzards, with even the airport activities
slowed while industrious snow-removing machines creep over the
tarmac). When we reach Mexico City the wide streets are still filled
with activity; children play by the embankments; lights hang in a haze
of trees—creating a mood as close to twilight as is ever seen in this
southern country. Yet not far away there are all the signs of the
encroachment of the technological paralysis. That *malaise* which is
evident in all the big centers of the world is evident here too (with
more than seven million people in this great Mexican valley, that is
three million more than during my visit in 1965). Not to mention a fog
which spreads to hide the brilliant sun, and is created by half a million
motor vehicles, and more than fifty thousand industrial plants.

Yet in spite of pollution the old charm lingers. An Indian woman
seated on the edge of the pavement is quite obviously in the way of
those who pour out of the big airport doors. Her head leans against one
of the cement uprights; her bare feet are in the gutter. Her pinkish
reboso echoes the burnished glow on her face, as bright as the bunch of
orange and red gladiolas which lies abandoned in her lap. Around her
feet the traffic makes a slight detour. Behind her the sky fades into
violent colors. . . . She is fast asleep!

On the very edge of the city, morning comes with its usual highland
brilliance. A man on a horse passes slowly, accompanied by a boy on
foot who carries a willow branch. The rider slouches, only a dark
hawk-like profile can be seen under the wide *sombrero*. The boy behind
walks with that air of rural innocence which has not yet disappeared

from the capital. Slowly they pass; Mexico of the nineteenth century proceeding across the landscape of the twentieth.

But that scene on the outskirts (where the lava plains still lie half empty, and tracks still wind amongst the houses) is soon forgotten in the heart of the city. Here traffic pours four cars deep along the great avenues. The smell of cheap gasoline hangs over the intersections. Planes fly low over houses and shops. Street markets are so crowded that it is hard to push along the aisles. Hotels are filled with global conventions; *Club de Leones; Wine-growers de Bretagne.*

The poverty seems less omnipresent. The white-clad peon is not so much in evidence; workmen are beginning to dress like small shop-owners. Heavy furniture is more often moved by truck than upon the shoulders of *cargadores;* if one sees anything carted through the streets it is likely to be a spotless white porcelain toilet. Even the respectable eagle-eyed housekeeper in her black dress, clutching her bunch of keys as she is followed by a little servant girl lost in a spotless white apron and carrying a huge basket, is becoming outdated. In fact women are beginning to bleach and dye their hair, to paint their finger-nails, to drive cars. This city, which for so long retained its charming provinciality and was for so long noted for its sparkling mornings, has at last passed the limits of health and safety and is becoming as worldly, as difficult (and soon perhaps will be as "indifferent") as Paris, London, New York.

Politically speaking, Mexico reflects the years we have lived through in the United States. If some revolutionary tactics have spread southward from the Northern borders, others, inspired by the political agitation in Latin America, have leap-frogged from the south, appearing twenty-four hours later in various parts of California.

Passing by the house in the Avenida Viena where in 1965 the figure of Trotsky had been omnipresent, I stop again to pay tribute to the persistence of the Marxist myth; a myth which haunts the campuses and gathering places of students all across the globe; and which is taught as gospel to the naive of the Third World.

In the sunny garden there are few flowers. Trotsky's grave seems severe with its shining grey stone, its firm impression of the hammer and sickle, its writhing cactus. In the street they still sing the plaintive *corrido* made up by the folk musicians of Mexico;

> "Murió Trotski asesinado. . . . de la noche a la mañana
> Porqué habian premeditado . . . venganza tarde o temprano . ."

Past the dress shops and the shoe shops, the patisseries, the silver shops, eventually past the Geneva Hotel, that old haunt of Americans, where groups of unmistakably "Northern" types make themselves at home in padded chairs in the shabby comfortable interior.

At lunch at Bellinghauser's (with the political officer from the American Embassy) there is a more engaging atmosphere; tree orchids decorating the tables, lovebirds from Yucatan (bright green with heads of salmon pink) flying in and out of the exotic garden foliage.

We talk about Cuba. (During my 1965 visit Castro's aggressive role had been driving the intellectuals into open debate, and forcing them to choose sides, to "put up or shut up.")

"Few Mexicans," the officer says, "are knowledgeable about the intricacies of Fidel's relationship with the Soviets. Some, pointing to the defeat of Ché in Bolivia, claim that Castro has overstepped the line, that he must be curbed for lack of discipline. These are the ones who are *pro*-Soviet. The romantic Castroites, on the other hand, tend to see him as independent of his Soviet suppliers, and this in spite of his capitulation last year when he supported the invasion of Czechoslovakia."

Dinner with an interesting Mexican woman and her husband. When we are invited to another house for coffee, there is more direct news of Cuba. Here a European film-maker, who has been making a film for the Cuban government, is just back from Havana. He describes the city as "completely closed up."

"In the social sense it is a disaster. Shops, cafés, everything. Nowhere to go, nowhere to eat. In front of one of the few restaurants in the city there was a queue of 350 people. When we got in at last, the bill was $166—that was for ten people to have a small piece of crabmeat on a lettuce leaf."

Seeing that they were making a film at Cuba's invitation, weren't they fed by the government?

"Yes . . . we had some free meals at various locations. But each one of our team spent more than $200 on extra food during the five days we were there . . . ! As for the *campesinos* they get just enough to keep alive—rice, one gram of meat per day, oil instead of butter, an occasional piece of fruit . . . Hospitals are functional . . . Literacy is functional; I certainly don't think the quality of what is put into the brain is high! . . . As in all communist countries they are breeding a nation of robots."

On further inquiry he affirms that no one talks of the prisons or concentration camps in Cuba for fear of ending up in one of them. Nor is any mention made of the recent attempt to escape to Guantanamo. (Two trucks loaded with 160 would-be escapees had crashed the fences of the American base. Cuban guards had opened fire, killing and wounding so many that only seventy finally made it to free territory.)

Mexico

February 26

Descent from the plateau of Cuernavaca, through the damp clouds which hover perpetually over the heights. That sensation of going down, down, to the warm valley of Morelos, to its tourist town of continually flowering gardens. Still today for those who once knew this town with its charms and despairs, nostalgia hits hard. The flowers hang over the pink and yellow walls in the old way. There is the sound of water. The plazas (now encircled by traffic) hold, as if unchanged, those figures so familiar that they might have been painted on boards and stuck into the ground—the balloon seller, the Indian with pots slung over his shoulder, the *turista* with her grey carefully groomed hair.

Our hired car breaks down in front of the church of *Nuestra Señora del Sagrado Corazon* (this is the Virgin for those with "the most difficult troubles"), J—, his face like that of a sharp-beaked bird, begins to instruct us about the political struggles which have taken place in Cuernavaca. He does not however mention one aspect of the history of this city. This is that through the 50s and early 60s, it was known as a haven for a number of active Communists (who, as a result of the theft of certain atomic secrets, and because of the Smith Act crossed the border to Mexico to escape indictment). In 1960 *U.S. News and World Report* gave an exhaustive account of the atmosphere of those days, when Mexico had the reputation of being a key station on the underground railway which spirited spies and defectors out of the country and sent them on ahead to some other way station. The two U.S. National Security Agency employees, Mitchell and Martin, came here en route to Russia; Alfred and Martha Stern under indictment in the United States for the operation of a spy ring for the Soviets made it on Paraguayan passports to Havana; and many minor but equally useful political figures found refuge as well. Frederick Vanderbilt Field, also under indictment, arranged in Mexico suitable sources of livelihood for these exiles: he set up a chicken farm, an ice cream business, financed small shops and so on and Cuernavaca became a town where those with sympathy for the communist cause were likely to find aid, comfort, and friends.

The point about this sketchy view of past history is that some of the human remnants of this period still live in the walled houses in the flowery streets, still gather in the cafés on the plaza. More importantly several of them are now key figures on the staff of an institution called Centro Intercultural de Documentation (CIDOC).

A chance meeting with a young (exiled) American black at, of all places, a golf club. He seems to be employed as a porter, the kind of menial job which, except for a higher salary, he might as easily have occupied in the United States.

"Why am I here? I'm here because I've been to Cuba."

And if he had risked so much to get to Cuba, why did he leave it and come to Mexico?

"Good question." He is tall and leanish with a rather engaging smile, and he seems undecided as to whether or not to confide in a stranger.

What had it felt like—being a black in Cuba?

"You see, I was on my way out."

Out of what?

"Out of the bad 'ole United States."

And in Cuba?

" . . . Well, in Cuba," he leans over the desk and speaks earnestly, "you see, in Cuba everything is done for a purpose. If newspapers yell about racial unrest in the United States, that is OK, or lynching or police dogs. Even a robbery by blacks is OK because the robbery is always because of Imperialism. Right? But there are a lot of blacks in Cuba no one talks about, a lot of dishwashers, for instance. And a lot are in jail. Haitians and Dominicans are in jail too." Here the conversation is interrupted by a telephone call. But he has made his point. (Even while this particular black American works as a porter in a Mexican club because he has been disillusioned by his pilgrimage to Cuba, his black brothers at a college in Marshall, Texas, and at Rutgers in Newark are expatiating about the brilliant revolutionary example set by Cuba, and carrying in their demonstrations posters of Ché Guevara.)

Another self-named representative of the Third World (Sirhan Sirhan) jumps to his feet today at the trial in Los Angeles and shouts that he would rather plead guilty and go to the gas chamber than have people think that he is "getting a fair trial." Enraged as he is at the failure of this provocation, he is led out of the courtroom to quiet down.

The day ends with the documented evidence that he has written that he favors "the overthrow of the U.S. government" and sympathizes with the Russian and Chinese Communists. "I firmly support the Communist cause and its people—whether Russian, Chinese, Hungarian, Albanian or whoever." Written in that robot-like obsessive disjointed manner by now familiar to all newspaper readers; the idea of hypnosis suggests itself.

Phrases from his notebook of death: "My determination to eliminate RFK is becoming more and more an unshakeable obsession . . . RFK must die . . . RFK must be killed . . . Robert F. Kennedy must be assassinated. . . ."

The question as to whether this fanatical twenty-four-year-old could have been manipulated for the purpose of political assassination re

Mexico

mains open. But it is certain that the falsehoods of Arab leaders, the fantasies of Arab hatred, and above all the vitriolic propaganda directed towards potentially radical Third World and minority groups (whom Sirhan has described as "my people") bear part of the responsibility for his act.

[In 1970 Robert Blair Kaiser points out in his book, *RFK Must Die*, that Sirhan has been influenced by the Rosicrucians *(Ancient Mystical Order of the Rosae Crucis)* and by reading something called *Cyclomancy*. He had been introduced to the study of the occult by Tom Rathke, the groom with whom he had worked. Dr. Diamond, the psychiatrist who had examined Sirhan, suspected that he had been hypnotized frequently; but it also became evident that he had practiced automatic writing sessions and self hypnosis with the aid of a mirror. The question remained—and remains—whether this interest in the occult, and this habit of automatic writing, had been exploited or guided by some other person for the purposes of political assassination. Sirhan himself confided to Kaiser that he was afraid someone had been "playing with his mind"; and that Tom Rathke the groom had "offered" him "mental protection."]

Since my last visit to Mexico there have been numerous riots and disturbances, all of them reactivating the ever-present, always pertinent Mexican question of arbitrary arrest and imprisonment. In the universities the familiar overcrowding has been increasing; and with it the piling up of "dissatisfied intellectuals." But it is deliberate subversion which seems to provide the propulsive element. It was in 1968, for instance, that Valeri Vladimirovich Kostikov was arrested by the Mexican police after he had pulled a gun on two engineers employed in the petroleum industry—an industry which is a prime sabotage target.

[The man concerned was one of those later banished from Britain in September of 1971, on charges relating to espionage and the obtaining of technological secrets.] It was also in 1968 that two Communist couriers, Feliciano Pachon Chocanta and Librada Morena Leal, were intercepted carrying money (more than a million pesos) received from a KGB officer in the Russian Embassy in Mexico City—Nikolai Sergeevich Leonov. The money they admitted was for the use of terrorism in Latin America (especially for the Fuerzas Armadas Revolucionarias (FAR) in Colombia. And it was in the summer of last year when preparations were being made to force the cancellation of the Olympic Games, that Mexican Security agents observed the KGB pass over what turned out to be $30,000 to a Mexican Communist Party representative. Again in Mexico City at this time, a certain KGB officer, Nechiporenko, famous for his ability to get along with students and for his habit of visiting villages dressed in the clothes of a *campesino*, was noticed to be collecting a large group of recruits to whom he gave Moscow scholarships. (By 1968, these were in place, it was said, as effective hard-core agents in schools and universities. It turned out later that of those leaders arrested in the July riots, eight had been recruited by Nechiporenko; some had certainly been recruited on other than academic grounds; several had had only two years of high school.)

The Olympic Games were due to be held in October of 1968. Towards the end of July the Young Communist party staged a rally to demand the release of Demetrio Vallejo (this is the labor leader who was sentenced for eighteen years when he was caught in 1959 accepting eighty thousand dollars from two Russian Embassy officers—Nikolai M. Resinov and Nikolai V. Aksenov; Vallejo later admitted that the money was to be used to initiate strikes). During the rally the police intervened, Molotov cocktails were thrown, classes were boycotted, and the students seized the National University and the Polytechnic Institute (where the combined student body numbers 120,000). Most of the activity was pushed by *brigadas de choque* formed by a National Strike Committee. (One reporter noted that, with an eye to media effect, the student risings in Paris and Mexico both occurred when the capitals concerned were focal points of world news—the Vietnam talks were in progress in Paris and the Olympic Games were scheduled to begin in Mexico.) In late July the student demonstrations spread to Villa Hermosa and Jalapa. (It was in Jalapa in 1971 that evidence was first discovered to show that many students spirited out of Mexico, had been trained for terrorism in North Korea.) The rector of the National University, Javier Barros Sierra, caught between two fires, spoke with sympathy of the students—of alienation, overcrowding, the closing of avenues of dissent, of the question of autonomy of the university. In spite of this conditional autonomy, the university campus was briefly occupied by troops to prevent the students from joining those rioting in the center of the city. There were demands from the students that Louis Cueto, chief of Mexico City's police, be dismissed. Mr. Cueto commented: "These are hardly prep school students leading their fellows. The foreigners arrested include a Chilean, a Puerto Rican, an Algerian, two Spaniards, five Frenchmen, and Mika Satter Seeger, daughter of the U.S. folk singer, Pete Seeger." (It turned out that the five Frenchmen involved had helped to lead the student riots in Paris in the Spring.) On August 4 the Mexican CP denied responsibility in a manifesto, which was signed by Siqueiros, and blamed the disorder on the CIA, also claiming that the seven members of the Party seized during the tumult were innocent, and that the subversive material found was forged. On September 7, the President, Gustav Diaz Ordaz, warned that he would use armed force to put down "systematic

Mexico

provocation" and to ensure that the Olympic Games would take place peacefully. On September 19 the army seized the university to end the seven weeks of agitation, bringing in thousands of troops and trucks. There was an immediate outcry against the violation of university autonomy.

Conversation tonight with an experienced American reporter who had made some specialty of covering Latin America; and who traces the evolution of the use of university autonomy in radical causes. "Yes, I did write a piece on the bogus use of autonomy—in other words, the using of this as a shield for terrorism—pointing out that the autonomy idea was central to Latin American political philosophy and dated back to a time when it was perfectly legitimate. The idea of extra-territoriality was used in Argentina in 1919 when it was a quite justified effort against a dictatorial regime; in fact it saved people's lives on many occasions. But the concept spread to the United States in a completely different context. In 1963 and 1964 I said in the *Reader's Digest* that these outrages would eventually operate on North American campuses . . . where slogans and battle cries and news pictures were being repeated within twenty-four hours in California . . . In Columbia I found university professors afraid to speak up against the terrorists; in fact, speaking out had become a highly lethal business." The journalist shakes his head. "I tell you that none of these professors would give their signature to anything, because the terrorists were not idealistic young students; they were murderous bastards."

"In Caracas in 1963 and 1964," he goes on, "they [the terrorists] were kidnapping people, torturing them, killing them, and selling the corpses to the Medical School all in one economical action. The government finally raided the campus. They found a perfect circuit. The activists had the protection of the Communist professors, and access to the university printing facilities; they were able to forge identity cards right inside the university. On one action they held up a bank and only had to flee about 500 yards into the campus sanctuary, where they could defy the police. The government investigators actually discovered tunnels dug under the fences for easy access, and they found wounded guerrillas being treated at the university hospital." He talks about Mexico. "You have a hell of a time finding things out here. A little leaks out at a time and that's about it. What is clear is that from July 26 to October last year, there were days of terror in the Republic. There were assaults, fires, riots, robberies, assassinations. Police were killed by Commandos driving by in stolen cars. How many were killed? I don't know the exact numbers." (In 1976 according to this same informant, about forty-eight policemen were killed between January and August. On one occasion seven policemen were killed in one day.)

Mexico

The taxi-driver is genial and outgoing. "What happened at Tlatelolco . . . ? Why they killed the boys, that's what . . ."

Had he been there?

"No . . . no . . . I was in my own house that night *gracias a dios!*"

Then how does he know what happened? Have others told him? "Everyone knows what happened. The students did nothing. They shot them down . . . just shot them down." He takes his hands off the wheel and makes the gesture of shooting a machine gun from the hip.

Those who were around towards the end of September and in early October, when the *Noche Triste* (Night of Sorrow) took place, agree in general as to the events. What is at issue is the sequence and intent in the happenings and the numbers killed. Through August and September clashes continued. A policeman was shot, hundreds were injured and arrested. While peace doves were being released at the Olympic Stadium in a dress rehearsal for the ceremony, armored cars were standing guard at the University across the way.

Finally, the most serious of the clashes took place around the vocational school in Tlatelolco. On Wednesday night, October 2, about 6,000 students and others, many carrying banners, gathered at the *Plaza de las Tres Culturas* near the Tlatelolco Housing Project, which has 76,000 tenants . . . The rumors spread that the crowds intended to march, with or without a permit . . . Another reporter, this time a Mexican, says that government security forces had a very good idea of what was planned by the Coalition of Leftists making up the National Strike Committee (which included a number of "professional" students). He points out that although no Cubans were captured in the showdown, there was a strong overlay of Cuban methodology in the operations, and many of the students had also aligned themselves with Maoists . . . For these reasons the request for the march had been denied.

Accounts vary as to the order of events. The police were supposed to have advance notice that the Strike Committee was in possession of two or three apartments in the Housing Project; and after a student leader wanted by the police tried to address the crowd, a flare was dropped from a helicopter, and the army moved up to block the entrances. At this, sniper fire came from the 14th and 15th floors; a general was hit in the back and dropped to the ground. Soldiers opened fire on the upstairs rooms. The activists answered the fire and a number of people were killed, including innocent women and children in the crowd and some members of the Strike Committee who were gathered on a lower floor.

When I try to find out about this gunfire, an American security man with contacts in the Mexican government says, "Hell, the whole operation was planned. Student enthusiasm had been dying down, and the march was scheduled to revive it. What's more, martyrs were needed. The centering of so large a gathering in so well-inhabited a place was in itself a provocation. Then in all, twenty-eight people were killed; but not one was killed with the 7mm bullet used by the army. The .Revolutionary Coalition were spraying Mendoza machine-guns, .22s. The Coalition had taken over three apartments in the housing project and over one hundred of them were there when the shooting started. There was panic, of course. Some of the activists tried to run down the stairs, found their way blocked and were arrested."

[Whatever the exact truth of this matter, in February of 1970 Raya Kiselnikova, a blue-eyed blonde beauty who defected from the Russian Embassy, verified and extended the information about Soviet interference in Mexico's internal affairs. A close friendship had linked this girl with Nechiporenko; and she disclosed that he had recruited some of the leaders in the student riots of 1968, and that she had been with Valentin Loginov, another Soviet officer, at meetings with students during those days. She also had knowledge of Russian bribing of magazines and newspapers.

And still later, in February of 1971, an accidental encounter was to much broaden the implications of Kiselnikova's story. An elderly constable was walking home to a village in the mountains about thirty miles from Jalapa when he encountered some young men in an old shack drawing on a blackboard. On interrogation it became clear that a certain Comrade Antonio had persuaded them to become "guerrilla warriors" and to join the *Movimiento de Acción Revolucionaria*—the drawings on the board were of power lines as sabotage targets. Nechiporenko had been the originator of this project. Originally fourteen male and two female Mexican recruits had been flown to Paris under the leadership of a young militant, Angel Bravo Cisneros, and then to West Germany and so to East Germany, where they had linked up with four North Koreans and flown on to Moscow, and eventually to Pyongyang. It should be noted that the Mexican students had been tricked into this whole relationship by the Soviets, not only by falsification of what was happening in their own country, but by passing them over to the North Koreans without prior knowledge. In Pyongyang, in a bleak valley between two stony mountain ranges, the Mexican students had trained in all aspects of guerrilla warfare. Back in Mexico and with ample funds, the student leaders recruited more cadres; clandestine schools were set up in Zamora, San Miguel de Allende, Querétaro, Puebla, Chapala and Mexico City. Safe houses were established in Acapulco and Jalapa. A program of robberies to collect funds was established, along with a blueprint of bombings, assassinations, and assaults on police. In the mountains small raiding parties were to strike at railway lines, bridges, power lines and factories. The aim? According to the arrested students it had been to create another Vietnam here south of the border.

Mexico

On March 17th the Mexican government expelled Nechiporenko and four of his colleagues from Mexico City; and recalled its Ambassador from Moscow. It should be noted that the use of North Korea as an insurgent training ground had been arranged, presumably, at the OLAS Conference in Havana in 1967. The North Koreans were soon setting up friendship societies, organizing press campaigns, and welcoming envoys. With the death of Ho Chi Minh, Kim il Sung was to be given prominence as the great revolutionary leader.]

On the way down Insurgentes to meet Alfredo, the taxi passes by the murals near Pasadena done by Siqueiros in those harsh yet dead colors which he has often favored—a dark cold brown, black and white, also emphasized by broad double lines of silver-grey. The elongated and somewhat disjointed figures appear unpleasant because the sharpness is accentuated by the metallic effect and exaggerated by the curving shapes of the iron work which fences in the mural. It is easy, though perhaps unfair, to project from Siqueiros's work that deadend to which his politics have driven him, that sad and anti-human tone which is the ultimate end of the Marxist philosophy.

It is a different matter with Alfredo, whose philosophical tendencies veer towards the human rather than the ideological (although he insists that dogma is real to him, it has never hardened into that rigid structure which one sees in Siqueiros). We eat in a kiosk next door to the little shop which sells the paper flowers. He says that his movements are restricted because of the political upheavals; he is persona non grata in certain states. He says that he is being watched.

"I am filled with hate, rage, and pain." (His version of what happened at Tlatelolco is closer to the version which appeared in the U.S. press and very different from the "inside" reports of other informants. He admits to the revolutionary confrontation, but feels it justified.) "They shot them down," he repeats, as the taxi-driver had done.

And how many were killed?

"No one knows." His voice has a touch of panic. "There were perhaps 400. . . ." (This figure is of course many times larger than that admitted by the government or suggested by security agents.)

"Parents are still looking for their children. No one knows whether they were killed or whether they got out of the country or went underground. Then there were many many in prison."

Wasn't it announced in November last year that there were new grounds for the accusation that the National Strike Committee was dominated by a hardcore of leftist agitators determined to avoid agreement with the government? Wasn't it true for instance, that the students of a preparatory school at Coapa were literally prevented from returning to class by an armed gang of the Strike Council?

Alfredo flushes. "How could that be true, how could an armed gang *prevent* students from returning? . . . At least, it seems unlikely." There is a confused look on his face, which gradually gives way to the same gloomy expression. Outside in the little park a shoeshine boy is singing a wailing song. Perhaps some of Alfredo's rage and pain is touched with guilt. The pattern of the protests had suggested that when one maneuver failed, another was tried; that the pressure put by activists upon the student masses was constantly increased; that considering the economic investment in the Olympics—and in view of the President's ultimatum to the radicals—the pushing of a confrontation by the Strike group could only have ended up in some such coup de grace as that at Tlatelolco. Now Alfredo, who (whatever other role he had played) had supported and encouraged the students, might have come to feel that he carried some share of responsibility for the outcome.

A visit from R—, a friend in Cuernavaca, and a conversation about Monsignor Ivan Illich, the controversial priest who runs the CIDOC Center and who a few weeks ago made public the classified documents describing his secret appearance in Rome before the Vatican Congregation for the Doctrine of the Faith (during this investigation Illich was conducted to the subterranean chamber in the Vatican through a set of double doors padded with leather)!

R— explains that now the Vatican has ordered that all Roman Catholic clerics cease from participation in the CIDOC Center. "The Center was simply to train Catholic missionaries in the language and culture of Latin America," he says. "The idea was to change the old method of missionaries blundering in and imposing their views and manners and food and clothes on the poor defenseless natives . . ." (R— himself is an expert on the traditional garments of Latin America and feels particularly frustrated to see these disappearing and being replaced by machine-made modern products.)

But what about other aspects of the Illich question?

Isn't this all part of the liberalization of Catholicism which is legitimate enough, but which is also being used—along with Pope John's belief in "melting the Russian ice—to push Finlandization of the churches of the West? What about the way the Center seems to have for its prime purpose the persuading of students and visiting clerics to support the Latin American Revolution?

R— admits that a number of very innocent American ladies have become enthusiastic about Illich, and that one dowager from Texas had even sold her estate and come to Cuernavaca to be near her spiritual inspiration. But he is sure Illich has no concrete subversive plans; that the Center is just what it pretends to be, a focus of education. "I think he's *marvelous*," R— finishes up with a rapt upturning of his eyes.

At the present moment the Center is still providing courses in Spanish and in Latin American culture (courses such as "The Authoritative Teachings of the Colonial Church," "Current Controversies on the Use of Violence," "Agrarian Reform in Cuba," and "Creative Imagination in Controversies on the Use of Violence"). It has served as an informal meeting ground for a variety of scholars and clergymen and others who are interested in social change—anywhere from about 80 to about 350 of them a month. The conflict that Illich's center has sparked in Cuernavaca and other cities only reflects, however, the painful conflict within the Catholic Church itself (aided by Pope John XXIII's belief that, since there was no true faith outside the Christian religion, the church could coexist with Communism and still maintain its integrity). It is quite natural that R— should see the whole modernizing movement as "blind . . . popular . . . instinctive . . . irresistible." But as usual in this age of professional subversion, it doesn't seem to be the case.

The most influential of the new independent organizations involved in Church liberalization in Rome, known as the International Center of Information and Documentation Concerning the Conciliar Church (IDO-C), which is non-profit, has branches throughout the world, and is set up under Italian law with open membership. Its function is to assemble and distribute documentation on the structure and theological effects of the continuing implementation of the decrees, and the spirit of the Second Vatican Council. Historically, IDO-C itself is an offshoot of DO-C, set up by the extreme progressive section of the Dutch Church in 1963 to publish information bulletins in other languages. (Another bureau called *Centro di Co-ordinazione delle Communicazione del Concillie* [CCCC] was established in Israel in 1972 with the idea of promoting journalistic exchanges. This was finally disbanded.) IDO-C's United Kingdom section consists of fifteen—one a veteran Communist party organizer, Jack Dunman, for more than twenty years a leading party member (although an agricultural specialist). Recently Dunman was assigned by the party to work as one of a team of ecumenists, with the purpose of penetrating the World Council of Churches and the Catholic "left." He operates with the support of a group of Catholic Marxists including the president of the editorial board of Slant, a group that publicly acknowledges its close contact with PAX (the Polish organization condemned as an agency of the Polish Communist secret police and set up to sow disunity among Catholics). The general doubt about IDO-C in brief is that what was originally a small group of off-beat *avant-garde* Dutch theologians may now be committed—via Communist Party penetration—to the destruction of essential Church doctrine.

Although there seem reasons to suppose that Cuernavaca's CIDOC is simply another manifestation of this movement, the real question

Mexico

seems to boil down to whether Monsignor Illich is what he pretends to be, that is, a man whose heart is pained by narrow Church doctrine.

At all events, the avid recruitment of students in Mexico to the radical cause, the unexamined influence of Cuba and of the martyr-hero Ché Guevara, the slow steady penetration of the Latin American Church by forces that are sometimes authentically progressive but more often allied to Communist police-state networks such as PAX; and above all, the reflection here in Mexico of the primitive fanaticism which now grips the world—all these foreshadow more violent con-frontations. It goes without saying too that these factors mean a continuance of the professional defamation of that strong "Capitalist" nation across the border—the United States.

March 1

After all this, is is reassuring to spend some time with the sister of the poet Don Felipe, who with her brother was an old friend of Bertram and Ella Wolfe. The poet's full name was Léon Felipe Camino (as Bertram Wolfe noted, a prophetic name, for *camino* means road and here was a man born to wander unceasingly). How he got to Mexico, where he then lived off and on since 1922, is a long story; but during the Spanish Civil War, he returned to Spain, to put, as he said, his work at the service of his country. Last September the poet—who has made a legend of his pilgrimage—died in Mexico.

His sister is a fiery-looking, handsome, infinitely neat, older woman wearing a turquoise-studded cross on her breast. She had married a general from Russia, who had also been an exile; and she says, as she indicates a picture of an erect man in a Russian army uniform on the wall, "So we were, all of us, a family of exiles."

It is enough to say about this afternoon in a quiet apartment—penetrated only occasionally by the cries of children from the street, while the golden sun moves slowly across the outside walls—that it is easy to understand the life of Don Felipe in his shadowed room, with the crucifix above the narrow bed with its velvet cover, and the worn books in the bookcase. Beyond that it is only necessary to read his poetry. I think especially of a small poem called *Piedra Adventurera*, a poem about a modest stone, not fit to be used for a palace or a church, but "little, and light."

> *por las calzadas y por las veredas*
> *Como tu guijarro humilde de las carreteras*
> . . . .
> *piedra*
> *pequeña*
> *y ligera.*

350

Mexico

At a time when religion is curiously and obliquely mingled with politics—when practicing Catholics for instance are advocating socio-political measures which extend as far as terrorism—here is religion of a purer kind.

To visit the house of the artist and architect Juan O'Gorman in Calle Jeronimo, to penetrate beyond a wall of volcanic stone through an overgrown tangle of creepers, cacti, and tropical plants, is a contrasting experience. It is rather like entering a jungle. The entranceway finally broadens out into a grotto attached to the house lit by mosaics set into the roof through which light streams as it might under water. Various figurines and small idols from different anthropological zones are set into niches in the wall; but further towards the center of the space, modern furniture lightens this effect of an ancient past, and is made comfortable with piled-up cushions covered by embroideries from various villages and lightened by numerous terra cotta pots planted with brilliant yellow lillies.

Juan O'Gorman is a tall man with a clever mobile face and greying hair (yet with that casual and friendly air so natural to the artist). There follows conversation which is a blend of wit and worldly observation, interrupted occasionally by his American wife, or by a tall leggy daughter who has come to join us. "Your wonderful universities!" (Juan O'Gorman had studied at Yale.) "Wonderful of course with that special modern feeling, that super conscious pragmatism which might have been found in the time of Caligula or Nero!"

Soon we are talking about politics. "Of course, of course, everything is political . . . even the movement of a hand takes political consciousness. And the hand knows what it does." He begins to laugh.

"Yes there is a strong student movement here, though it has been temporarily quieted. But what has been happening with the students and the young people is very interesting, since one can contrast it with what happened in *our* time.

"In our time we were idealistic and serious. Now today they are anarchists. Both are wrong"! He begins to laugh again. "Can you imagine it, in Paris a group of them—Maoists—wanted to break into the Louvre and destroy the paintings! Can you imagine a serious political philosophy which motivates a young man just starting in life to feel that he is helping humanity by the destruction of works of art!" (His expression suggests that he is alarmed to think of his own large and still unfinished mural at the Chapultepec Palace.)

"We ourselves believed that we were making a revolution for the good of Mexico, for the good of mankind—and *nothing* was going to stop us from making our contribution! . . . . No nonsense about 'doing our own thing'."

But surely "destruction" is a concept not absent from the whole

Mexico

Marxist way of life! To destroy first and then start again from scratch?

"Indeed yes; though in the old days we didn't think of it like that. Many of us would have thought of ourselves as Marxists, but not without certain serious qualifications. There was a good deal of heavy ideological discussion . . . some of us, myself included, thought of ourselves as Hegelians."

And the destruction of Trotsky?

"Ah—what a story. Now Siqueiros, one of the would be assassins; he was just a typical middle-class Portuguese, not a Mexican! The only Mexican thing he has is *machismo*. . . . He was paid by Stalin's police to act out this farce."

He doesn't then think highly of Siqueiros?

"I do not think that he has any particular talent. His distinction was at least partly because of his political view. . . . Rivera and particularly Orozco were the great talents. . . . What was Siqueiros like in those early days? Why, he was a clown type, the sort of man you find in a ring. In fact they even called him *Cirquiroz*," he begins to laugh, "which means circus man. . . ."

It is four years since my last interview with Mexican students—in 1965—when the discussion centered around revolutionary "theory." Today three students agree to talk, but refuse to give their real names. Two decide to identify themselves by the names of animals or birds (*Zopilote* and *Tigre*), and one (with an agreeable smile) calls himself "Alcohol." Zopilote is slightly plump, slightly bald, and has a long dark walrus-type moustache. He says that he has been active in politics, but only in a general sense. Tigre is intense and brown-skinned. Talking about the Noche Triste, he says that he had only reached the outskirts of the crowd when the shooting began and the word came back to disperse as quickly as possible. Alcohol then says that he had seen more, but had been on the opposite side from the firing.

Zopilote says his view of being political depends upon what "political" means. "I worry about the lack of freedom in Mexico and I am interested in action, but not in making policy. I just want to be part of the action." Tigre interjects to say that he is a libertarian socialist. Zopilote answers that you can't be anything if your view cannot be *expressed*. "Take the lack of newsprint. The government is not exactly monolithic, but expression is limited. There are only two or three TV stations."

"It is better than it used to be," Tigre adds. "However, the situation is grave. Mexico is a heterogeneous country more or less, and there are only two roads—one is for the government in power to reform itself from above (and here they don't believe in two-party democracy or economic democracy) and the other is a violent revolution."

352

Mexico

We are sitting in a little lunch bar where they sell coffee for seventy centavos, coffee with cream for one peso and enchiladas or egg tortas for $2.50. "This is our *office*," Tigre says, "we meet here every morning and every afternoon." With the gaiety of the young they discuss the relationship of Cuba to the 1968 "happenings." "Yes," Alcohol says, Cuba was the hot thing then . . . and still is; there has been a lot of traffic to Cuba."

"For a while there were three 'New China News Agency' men hanging around here, but they've been expelled," Tigre adds.

All agree that one of the main purposes of the disturbances had been to sabotage the Olympics—"For the principal of it," Zopilote says. "José Revueltas who used to be in the Communist party was also a member of the Strike Committee, and he was trying to stir up trouble. Then there was an older man who was arranging for some of the groups to have guerrilla training in certain towns. This was at the last moment because it was too late to send them to Cuba. . . ."

Meet Juan O'Gorman in San Angel; the sun on the cobbled streets, on the old buildings. He has, as usual, a seemingly gay air; but mentions a man who loiters at the corner as someone who may be *shadowing* him. (Thus the suspicions of Mexican life.)

With a certain pedanticism which goes rather well with (and adds to) his charm, he gives a small lesson on Indian place names. We drive to Chapultepec to see his unfinished mural in the castle, and walk through the usual pleasant outdoor scene presented by the park. Juan comments on some modest lovers embracing each other among the roots of the old tree. "It is said to be the only advantage allowed the lower classes, that they can be amorous in public!"

The subject of the painting in the central hall of the Castle is the *Cri de Dolores*, given by a priest called Miguel Hidalgo, who was much influenced by secret reading of the French philosophers, and the panel we are looking at is called *La Nobleza y el Pueblo*. This has a Renaissance-like background of terraced mountain landscape crowned with a huge pink castle surrounded by a number of Indian huts. The nobility is presented by richly dressed, rather foppish looking characters, some holding wine glasses, and attended by parasitic members of the Church. These look on as a dark, shrouded figure of the Inquisition directs the whipping of an Indian tied to a broken column. To one side a weary old peasant leans on a spade, and an Indian father holds the corpse of his child on the ground, where it is sniffed at by pariah dogs.

"I try to paint in representative form," Juan says. "This is calendar art, art easily understood by the people." (The crowd standing around us seem to have no idea that this lean stork-like man is the artist who made the picture they are gazing at so earnestly.) "I try to depict the power of law and government, the reality of government . . . it is not like this any longer in Mexico, but we are still trying to seize and hold onto a tolerable liberty."

Cuernavaca again. The pleasant heat caught in the walled enclosures; especially in one small garden where a thin dark gardener is slowly scooping the pale skeletons of bougainvillea blossoms from the top of the pool.

Memories of the Cuernavaca of the past are not involved only with such architectural and arboreal charm; all is colored as well by that particular expatriate life which, because of the town's mild sunny climate was drawn here as to no other part of Mexico. In these narrow winding streets now so choked with traffic—at the cafés, on the benches under the laurel trees, on the veranda of the Belle Vista, which at that time still enjoyed some of the romantic aura of the 1910 Revolution—the political exiles used to gather. In the very early 50s (when I myself lived there), Cuernavaca had become the chief center for the "Hollywood Ten" as well as other sympathizers of what then, in spite of the Stalinist regime, they tended to call "decent socialism." Yet the lives of most of these exiles were also shadowed by what had taken place on their own side of the political fence—by the Stalinist betrayal of the Republicans in Spain, by the pact with Hitler, the murder of Trotsky, the slave camps of Siberia.

There was in those exiles' conversations, their jokes, their attitudes, something close to bravado; a bravado half for the real dangers some of them ran, and half for the rewriting of history which had been forced upon them and had then become second nature. Memories of the time include their angers, their accusations against one another, even their tears, now made all the more poignant if that word can be used to mitigate historical betrayals of such dimensions—by the sudden and mysterious deaths and calamities which have overtaken so many of them since that time. In Mexico City a few days ago this had been rather obliquely described to me by an old and somewhat disillusioned member of the Mexican "Party," as it had been explained to *him*, he said, by another old and ostensibly "not disillusioned" member of the Mexican Party: "Well, it's what they call the Stalinist cleanup."

A telephone call to Ivan Illich brings at first a welcoming, even a servile response. Within a few moments he is testing out this journalist from the North by attacking the United States. (The United States is "despotic." Her attitude to Latin America is that of a "corrupted, power-mad dictator.") A suggestion from the journalist that such an attack by telephone, to a reporter who is inquiring about the CIDOC

Center and not about the United States, is gratuitous meets with an unfavorable response. With that messianic fervor for which he is noted, Illich says abruptly, "Thank you for *helping*." The interview never takes place.

A visit to Cedric Belfrage in his house in Lomo de Atcingo, which is approached through a dark *barranca* where far below one can see ferns and fertile soil and the gleam of water. Up near the road the grass is brown in the heat.

At the Belfrage house there is fertility again. Sprinklers play on the lawn of coarse emerald; banana trees, palms, and jacaranda feathery with lavender blossoms, lean against house walls and patio columns. Mary Belfrage (obviously at least a second wife) is bright-eyed and brown-skinned. Cedric is in shorts, older than he at first appears, with freckled skin which flushes easily and is tight-drawn over his skull where visible blue veins seem to throb in the heat. His eyes are blue also, intelligent but strained. His whole personality in fact suggests strain; perhaps the strain of his old devotion to unpopular causes, perhaps that of his deportation from the United States, or of that leaning on some abstract ideas of socialism. (Later he tells about his deportation from the United States, rather as described in one of his books, *The Frightened Giant*. "Two FBI men stood on the quay; I had to pay my own way to Amsterdam in order to get decent quarters. It was called 'voluntary departure'.... This was in August of 1955.... In England I got a pretty good reception.... After England I travelled. I used to write for the *Guardian* or the *Literary Gazette* in Moscow. I couldn't stand working for other papers. Then I started my own paper in the U.S.A., *The Guardian*. Dwight MacDonald attacked me in *Politics*. Those were very very emotional and partisan days." He himself looks thin and worn. "Even since I ceased to slave for Lord Beaverbrook I've written what I wanted. That's a fairly good record, that's thirty-three years.")

The atmosphere inside the house is pleasant, as it so often is in Mexico—shining floors, blue tiles, embroidered cushions, bouquets of red roses. "We never had it so good," Mary Belfrage says with honesty.

After dinner Cedric discusses his personal development. "I was strongly influenced by the Honorable Ivan Montagu, the oldest member of the Church of England. He used to go around Cambridge in dirty and rumpled clothes. In another, opposite way, I was strongly influenced by Hitler—I don't know why, but I thought it was the most appalling thing that had ever happened, that systematic savaging of human beings." It doesn't seem logical to have been so appalled by Hitler and so slow to be appalled by Stalin. It is therefore not surprising to hear him say: "I was not particularly disillusioned by the

Mexico

Pact. I couldn't understand why so much was made of it. I thought it necessary. I could see that Russia was the victim of the fantastic game England and France were playing against Russia."

But in spite of the period of appeasement—and reluctant as England and France obviously were to go to war—surely in spite of this, the Stalin-Hitler pact had deeper roots? Hadn't the USSR already shown in what direction it was heading, which was in fact towards the complete control of human beings? Hadn't there been all the killings, all the Great Trials?

Cedric admits that he had been influenced by the fact that the American Ambassador (Joseph Davies) could sit through all the Trials without suspicion. "I regarded it as axiomatic that those who believed in socialism would have a rosy picture. I remember that the Trials seemed peculiar, the confessions fantastic, the spectacle of people grovelling uncomfortable. Yet the Hitler-Stalin pact seemed necessary because of *Spain*. Yes, I admit I was a bit confused. I remember that I was trying to figure things out."

Had he been to Russia? "Yes, I went to Moscow in 1936. I was against fascism and so I was on the side of anyone who was against Hitler. Then I read the Webbs' book. In Moscow Louis Fischer was the superman of the day and everyone went to his flat and sat at his feet. I remember, though, that the cult of Stalin seemed incredible. Everyone had to mention Stalin all the time, and in every conceivable place there was a Stalin bust. All the papers would quote Stalin, and then add 'All rise! Loud applause!' I used to think if Stalin was such a good guy why does he allow this? I don't believe in extremes. Mao is a great man but now we have this absurd Mao cult too. Such extremes appall me."

There seems something extreme however about the present scene as we sit in this alien world of Mexico, gazing at an extravagance of red roses, and talking about Belfrage's unresolved confusions.

Surely Marxism itself, with its belief in "inevitability" and in the "automatic success of the great Communist Revolution" is responsible for making these leaders into demi-gods?

Apparently Cedric does not believe in the potency of the dialectic he has often professed. "I look at it a different way," he answers. "In Moscow during the war the figures of deaths seemed out of this world—just like the advances in China seem now out of this world." His tone has a certain abstract enthusiasm. "And as I was amazed by the advance of the Germans, I was amazed by the recovery of the Russians. . . . You see the name of Stalin helped them behave like heroes."

But surely this is a wasteful method of surviving? The deaths of millions through purging?

Without answering my question he reiterates that he has lost his absolute beliefs. "There were the other trials . . . those in Czschoslovakia in 1950. Zilliacus, the labor MP had been in British Intelligence with Tito; when Tito fell out of favor they brought in a series of Zionist plot trials. Then the Russians chucked out Anna Louise Strong! 'No matter what,' I said, 'if Anna Louise is an Imperialist agent, I'm Napoleon!' . . . ."

He does not seem to feel any embarrassment that he took so long to see the light, and there is something very English and deliberate about him as he sits smoking (his pipe, his ashtray, his pipe cleaner and his tin of *Revelation* tobacco) caught still perhaps in that old influence of the Honorable Ivan Montagu.

Suddenly he says, "Except for having a basic belief in socialism, I have nothing. The only work I can do for the cause," (the cause of socialism) "is journalism. On the whole," he goes on, "the Chinese and the Cuban regimes are relatively humane. The Chinese style is what is politely known in the U.S. as brainwashing . . . I have never raised a banner for it. I do not know of any country now for which I have any enthusiasm—not any in the world. . . ."

In the morning there is a sudden illuminating view of the volcanoes. The old sensation of Cuernavaca comes to life again. The purity of those snowy peaks flushed with morning light. (And the old admonition: "If you must live in the Indies, live within sight of the volcanoes.") Mary Belfrage stands at the garden gate and we discuss Cuba, to which Cedric was invited while he was writing a book.

Cedric appears again. We talk for a moment of the political situation in Mexico. He finally gives a sudden insight into his own situation, a political exile who has been persona grata in Cuba, and is now a guest in this country.

"Last year," he indicates the corner of the street, "during the student disturbances which led up to the Tlatololco affair, they had a guard posted here—watching me—day and night."

It is inevitable to wonder whether Cuernavaca had become so favored a town with these political exiles because of its mildness, its roses, its sunshine; or whether rather such beauty, and the rare sudden vision of the volcanoes, was needed to compensate them for the sad corruption of their political hopes.

ENGLAND

The problem of the Twentieth Century is the color line.

W. E. B. Du Bois

England, July 29, 1969

Rain dampens those British faces staring up as we descend from the plane. That British look: the blonde fine skin, the touch of red in the cheeks, the asymmetrical features. Rain pelts onto high-topped taxis, onto seas of umbrellas, onto the yellow slickers of the bobbies. One hears the gentle concerned tones of the porter gathering together suitcases. "Is this all, Madam? These three 'ere? Very good, Madam." He is putting them onto a trolley and warning against going, outside until he has hailed a cab. "You wouldn't want to get your *feet* wet, Madam." His solicitous face looms, and on the ends of his ragged gingery moustache there tremble two large drops of moisture; while a couple of airport hostesses parade by in pillar-box red dresses, which display fine if rather beefy legs.

Having just come from Mexico where hard facts are difficult to pin down, where vague suggestions of terror are held in static mystery; it is good to be in polite and gentle England, a democracy which contains its own slow corrective. Yet there is at once evident that "straining and rearranging" of the world map that Harold Isaacs talks about. I return to a country as green and pleasant as ever, upon which the rain descends as usual, but which, although it is still hung around with the moral pretensions which accompanied its rise to power, has ceased— except in the familial sense—to be the center of a great Empire.

In the terminal there is a long line of incoming passengers. Most of them are dark-skinned. They are queueing up patiently. West Indians in "sharp" suits and checked shirts, their women in blouses of shocking pink and lime green and tight skirts over flexible hips. Indian gentlemen wearing dark suits and turbans but also carrying dispatch cases. Pakistani families of four or five, with fathers who carry sleeping

England

babies wearing tiny silver bangles that cut into the flesh of plump wrists. Exotic women in shoes with turned-up toes and pantaloons of crushed velvet. This, then, is the other big change in England. Not only has her Empire been materially reduced, but her responsibilities have been increased. Those arms of the Commonwealth, once extended in dignified patronage to indicate *dominion over palm and pine*, are now being asked to close lovingly upon a "family of nations." For these are no fly-by-nights. Most of the dark arrivals are immigrants and the lines move very slowly past the processing desks. The passport-holders have come to England to *live*.

Outside the big doors on the west side of the Terminal, there are more signs of the dark invasion. Two Indians are arguing in the rain. One wears a crimson turban with his navy Bond Street suit, and stands beside a new sports car. The more humbly-dressed other, who seems to be demanding transport, is surprisingly accompanied by a Cockney woman who places her hand warningly on the arm of her dark arguing companion and says, "It's five o'two, luv."

It is possible to guess that this dispute represents "High-Caste Segregation" versus "Low-Caste Integration"; but in any case, it is broken up by a British couple, tweedy and well-groomed, who cleave through the argument, see their indestructible leather luggage into a taxi and drive off. Soon the big blue airport bus moves more slowly into the rain, out of the big gates and along the gleaming grey roads. There is left in the mind that already familiar image of queues of the dispossessed and rejected lined up in the airports of the world.

We move past the signs saying Uxbridge—Staines—London and Feltham—Hayes—London; past fields, past trees that in their heaviness suggest the slow damp island growth; past town houses. There is that faint innocent wonder of the traveler ("This place existed when I was not here"); that awed surprise of the jet traveler ("The world is small").

Inside Liverpool Station a number of black porters stand around; an old West Indian is sweeping the floor of the not yet open bar. The race problem again. (The battle over immigration is partly because of the concentration of newcomers in industrial centers like Birmingham, Wolverhampton, Liverpool, and London and partly because many enter illegally. More than 200 seamen a year are supposed to be walking off their ships in English ports.

In the station at least there seems to be no discrimination. Otherwise the familiarity resolves itself into a centuries-old dinginess. Not the sordid gimcrack modernization which made one writer lament about London, "You can't hurt the poor old cow now," but rather a traditional Victorian gloom; one's pocket book weighted down with copper change; a Ladies Room—"it only costs a penny to go" says the thin lady with the umbrella—which does not encourage vanity; the line in the cafeteria leading inevitably towards a "nice meat pie" with a curious-looking yellow crust.

There is a touch of romance too, that leisured out-of-date air being lost in more prosperous countries but still evident here in this little station world, this island within the island of Britain. A girl, perhaps eight years old, with hair like Goldilocks, buys Cadbury's chocolate at the news agent's. Her hair tumbles childishly as she turns to walk down the platform with sedate dignity (yet as if restraining the desire to run). She stops and stares at two small Indian girls who are being helped to board a train by a porter and their mother. They are surrounded by luggage that includes many bulging string bags. The two little dark girls wear quaint clothes, have pointed coffee-colored faces and enormous eyes with long lashes. In their way they are as beautiful as the little English girl, who at first stares at them imperiously, and then gravely offers them pieces of chocolate.

The first and most immediate impression is the question of the absorption of these dark-skinned passport-holders. But the second is the sensation of England's waning authority. The increasing crime in England (the number of drug addicts rose by more than 60 percent in 1968), the shadow of Ireland in the background (trouble in Belfast, signs of violence rising again, the moderates being driven out of political parties), the fall in British production (along with strikes and riots—and what one Australian journalist describes as "going down on her knees to get into the Common Market")—all these provide the material for a permanent sense of dismay. On the surface these problems remain insoluble, and among the British there is a certain discomfort that they exist at all—rather as if they were essentially infectious. With typical British aplomb it is assumed that panic is bad form. At the same time there is a patient attempt (especially when dealing with the Third World) to reinforce the old British rationality and to stress the fact that Western ideas must be approached through Western disciplines. Does Britain then really retain its old incorruptibility? It is hard to believe that it does. The corruption seems to be encroaching from the outer fringes of the old Empire. A few months ago an article in the *London Evening News* pointed out that Scotland Yard established Mao's China as the origin of heroin confiscated in a raid in the West End—this although official statements from Hong Kong police continue to identify the source of all the heroin in Hong Kong as the golden triangle of Burma, Laos, and Thailand. Is Britain reticent about what goes on in her colony because she no longer feels strong enough to cope with it?

England

The birds, the flowers, the sunshine, the damp green grass, the idle strolling of those who have lived their lives in comparative freedom, the sensation of the moderation which has been one of England's gifts to civilization. Sitting in a park chair to read what the Soviet writer Anatoly Kuznetsov has to say on the occasion of his request to remain in England.

"I was an utterly unknown student at the literary institute in Moscow. The authorities told me that it would be possible to remove some of the gloomy passages from my novel, *The Continuation of a Legend* and to add more cheerful passages. Experienced writers told me that this was the way to do it. . . . Everybody does it, they said. I forced myself to write some additional passages . . . so ridiculously optimistic that no reader was likely to take them seriously. . . . Such work did not satisfy the editors . . . I suffered a great deal. . . . Then one day, quite by chance, I bought a copy of *Yunost*, opened it and couldn't believe my eyes. My novel had been published . . . what I read made my hair stand on end. . . . Someone had done the crudest hatchet job . . . cutting, re-writing and adding. . . . I burst into bitter tears of pain . . . my book was now sent around the world, translated into more than 30 languages, praised by the Soviet press. Then came the great scandal. Louis Aragon sent us from France a copy of an anti-Soviet book, *L'Étoile Dans le Brouillard* which turned out to be a translation of my novel. The translator, Mr. Chaleil had written that, of all the Soviet books he had read, my novel had moved him the most. [He] had simply not bothered to translate those optimistic chapters which had been forced out of me. . . . I sat under lock and key. At last the door opened. . . . 'So you've written an anti-Soviet book? . . . Just sit down and write a complaint. Aragon will print it in his *Lettres Françaises* and he wants you to make a statement to the French courts.' I was handed a blank piece of paper. I was utterly overcome, my hands were shaking. I did not produce my complaint the next day. I wonder if you have ever cut a calf's throat? It is only the first time that it is really horrible to stick the knife in. Later the convulsions of the calf and the blood excite in you the spirit of the slaughterman and you stab fiercely till the animal dies. . . . I was caught and condemned to live as all Soviet writers live—that is, keeping silent. . . . "

In the park people stroll by, the sun shines as before, the literary task seems glorified. . . . I am approached by a benevolent ticket collector asking for fifteen cents. I mention that I only intend to sit for five minutes. He proffers a ticket with a smile, "If everyone only sat down for five minutes we wouldn't be getting *any* money *would* we, Madam?" His reasonable approach is compelling; I am glad to have been born under the protection of British justice!

The point about the war against the intellectuals is that it goes beyond Kuznetsov and any individual steadfastness. It is part of the mopping up process after the Czechoslovakian invasion (most of the pressured writers were those who had been involved in protests), and is part of the general oppression. Again it is part of the war against Israel.

The streets at the lower end of the park are filled with publishing houses. Students walk by on their way to the British Museum; and a tall Bobbie stands at the big gates in his navy blue coat, immobile as a tree. The solemn portals of the Museum itself, stained by time and rain, suggest the sacred cult of research, the battle of wits represented by the endless rows of books (and of course this conflict between the giant of the Soviet state and the defiant pygmy writers). It seems impossible to believe that it is all taking place in the latter half of the twentieth century.

Kuznetsov's civil rights brings up those of Ireland. The English are beginning to talk about Bernadette Devlin, that round-faced, twenty-two-year-old who joined the Irish "movement" as a Belfast student and now (with a seat in Parliament) has her picture in the papers with as much regularity as Princess Anne or Prince Charles. The "Baby of Parliament," the "Swinging M.P.," the "Little Blitz of the Bogside," talks about civil rights stiffly, but in an attractive brogue; She seems to have a gift for sincere rebellion. "I am not a candidate in this election," she stated flatly at the Unity Convention, when all those asked to stand were given five minutes in which to state their cases, "because I don't believe we will get the kind of unity I want—which is the unity of the working class, Catholic and Protestant. The unity being talked about here is Catholic unity. I think politics is basically a dirty job. I am not expert enough to play the dirty job clean, and I'm not prepared to play the dirty job dirty."

At the same time her whole-hearted, possibly naive support of what she calls socialism lands her in the middle of civil rights activities which, since the disorders last year, have virtually been taken over by Communists and Leftist elements. Whatever her private and political evolution, she is a key mover in the trend towards revolutionary pluralism, as it was seen on the West Coast in 1964 and later all through the democratic countries. That is, she is part of that romantic Leftist spectrum which ranges from anarchism through Trotskyism to Maoism, and she has just declared herself for the program which is being approved, and perhaps was originally devised, by extremist interests.

It turns out to be too late to interview this Irish ball of fire (whose feet are so small that she had to take rapid steps to keep up with House protocol on the occasion of her "Maiden speech"); but it would be interesting to try to find out how she sees the Soviet role in Ireland's affairs. She would be correct to claim that this role was not particularly active, until the time of her own recent prominence. (Moscow had greeted the old-time requests of IRA representatives with sceptical amusement; Krivitsky, a GPU defector, described the laughter behind the scenes when rhetorical Irishmen with fancy military titles came to Russia to ask for help. In the 1930's the Russians did recruit Irishmen, but they were to work as espionage agents, because from this period, and all through the early part of the coming war, Dublin was a center both of Communist interest and of Axis influence! After World War II, Czech and East German business firms gathered information in Dublin and imported embargoed goods to the Soviets.) Not until this year have there been signs of renewed stimulus of the Irish Communist party, with the official line running parallel to Bernadette's own (that is, to work for the collapse of both Dublin and Ulster governments, and to attempt to unite all of Ireland under a "socialist" regime). In fact it seems uncertain whether Bernadette sees herself in as clear a historical context as this.

[By October in 1971, according to *KGB* by John Barron, the Dutch authorities in the Amsterdam airport intercepted a shipment of Czech arms destined for the IRA. They came from the state firm Omnipol, controlled by the Czechoslovakian clandestine services, which in turn are controlled by the KGB. The arms were to be consigned not to the official Marxist party, but to the non-Communist Provisional faction. As Barron remarks, the Soviet Union did not care who used the guns provided they were used to the detriment of Britain. By 1972 the Provisionals were using Soviet RPG-7 rocket-launchers; and on March 29 of 1973 the Irish navy captured five tons of Soviet arms and ammunition off the south coast as it was being forwarded to the IRA through *Al Fatah* in the Middle East. Again, after the 1968 showdown, one of the demands made of Cuba by the Russians had been that Cuba should train IRA personnel in terrorist tactics.]

August 6

Areas made romantic by the past suddenly take on a less attractive character; Soho Square seems shabby, the fake Tudor summerhouse is stained by the droppings of pigeons. In the window of a shop selling records and theatrical robes there are names familiarized by the international mass media: Buffy St. Marie, Bob Dylan, Janis Joplin. A man with a dog on a leash stares fixedly at a big notice Summer In Sodom in the window of a pornography shop. Also booklets: Rope and Beds; Savage Sex. They are renovating one of the old houses, and near the corner of Carlisle Street, a legend in faded gilt letters says Adams and Charles Black—Publishers. 1807. A pub, The Nellie Dean, has a painted board swinging in the sun, showing a girl in a yellow dress seated by a water wheel.

Upstairs above the office of the *Left Review*, the *Black Dwarf* has its headquarters. On the wall going up, Smash the State is written in chalk, and Create Third—Many Fourth Internationals. There is also a poster for *Solidaridad Con Cuba*, and another stating that A Worker's Vote Is a Trick—the last word having been crossed out by some dissident passerby.

Tariq Ali is a tall, rather handsome Pakistani with romantic moustachios and large dark melancholy eyes. His voice is caressingly gentle and is not raised all through the discussion. "The main inspiration for the British movement," he murmurs, "is of course the war in Vietnam, the atrocities . . . it is because of Vietnam that we have become more and more radicalized." His hair sticks up in peaks, rather as do his moustachios; and he turns in surprise and gentle amusement as a girl rushes into the office, her coat flying, to grab up a paper and rush out again, saying over her shoulder; "I forgot to send a copy of *West Africa* to someone who's waiting at the pub."

"London is my political base," Mr. Ali goes on. "I visit other Left-wing political parties, but I return here. I did political philosophy and economics at Oxford in 1963. No, I found it all completely unnecessary . . . useless. It seems I only learned from actions in the street." After some desultory comments about politics in general, he adds, "Yes, I think change will come all over the world. It is not confined to one country. You are right that I had an aristocratic background, but this background only made me more, rather than less, politically conscious—the gulf between the rich and the poor is so *immense* in my own country." His serious and melancholy eyes explore the corners of the room, seek out someone on the other side of the open door; he makes a sign with his hand as if to say he will be with them later.

"Our purpose is to raise the level of social consciousness and political awareness" he says, "this is the purpose of the *Black Dwarf*." (Copies of the *Black Dwarf* show that it is a paper more original for its name than its content. It is one of the numerous papers which have recently blossomed in the world of the New Left. It has the same rhetoric, the same serious but scornful and elevated tone, the same notes of "the struggle" collected from other capitals. It also has the same, somewhat loose analysis of revolutionary news. In a recent copy, for instance, a policeman is shown with a gun, pointing—perhaps—into the shrubbery, while a man bottom left is running along the street. The locale is supposed to be Berkeley. The caption reports that the policeman fired and the man fell down howling. In the picture, however, the man is still running. Another item describes a crowd of one hundred fifty in Folkstone and calls it the "Folkstone Insurrection."

The *Black Dwarf* was originally founded in 1817 by a man from

England

Sheffield named Thomas Wooler, who supported revolutionaries in Spain, Latin America, and the West Indies, i.e., at home as well as abroad. According to his manifesto, Wooler believed in unlimited immigration and hated authority. One of the links the present paper has with the original is its emphasis on the word "black" and a stress on immigration at a time when the question is politically current.

"We have contacts with the Black Panthers," Tariq Ali says now. On the wall behind us there is a large poster: U.S. Pigs and Panthers. He adds: "The *Black Dwarf* knew where Eldridge Cleaver was when no one else did. We had money with which we bought ammunition for the Panthers. I will not say where the money came from but from certain very rich people."

Doesn't willingness to include diverse groups under their banner make the *Black Dwarf* responsible for their political actions?

"I am not sure that this is so. . ." Mr. Ali replies. He says he does not support either the Russian or Chinese bureaucracies. Both need a new revolution of their own. He states that he is a Trotskyist and that there is a present world recrudescence of Trotskyism.

"The group I belong to believes in the theory of the permanent revolution . . ., this group would be associated with the Socialist Workers party in the States."

A middle-aged man in a buttoned-up raincoat, looking rather like a clergyman, peeps in through the door.

"Stalin," Mr. Ali is reassuring me, "was a most loathsome and vile leader . . . he made a virtue of his stubbornness."

Doesn't Stalin still rule in a sense. In fact isn't Stalinism in the process of being returned to the throne?

"I think we can deal with that," Mr. Ali says gently.

Is it good to be so optimistic?

"If one is a revolutionary one has to be optimistic."

At this point his dark eyes shine as do the eyes of Trotsky in the big poster on the wall behind him. "I am a member of an international Marxist group. We are linked with workers for the revolution both in Britain and Ireland . . . we are in touch with the Spanish Workers Committee . . .," he says. [Later in the seventies Tariq Ali, who received a salary from a U.S. tax-exempt organization in Washington, TNI, of the Institute for Policy Studies—is to embarrass his comrades by too open a support of the terrorism in Canada and Ireland.]

Downstairs two young men lounge in a low-slung sports car, both wearing bright red shirts, with their hair in Buster Brown cuts. A girl holding a roll of posters perches on the hood. We drive towards Mayfair, where the houses are well kept up, where a swaying woman looks, with her short skirt, half-exposed full bosom and black lace tights, like a modern version of Nell Gwyn. Glimpsed through the window of a high black taxi is another girl in a gleaming brown raincoat. Her short hair falls forward; the twenties style, and she is seen suddenly against an apothecary's window, which holds huge sponges and tall-necked glass bottles full of colored liquids. A summer fog is coming down.

Reading *The New Revolutionaries*, which Tariq Ali has edited. Although he speaks with idealism, and condemns betrayals, degenerations, Stalinism, and—apparently—political murder, it seems impossible to balance this with what he is willing to include. The assumption is that to keep his present special pipeline to the black extremists and to the Arab groups (for instance, via the Socialist Workers Party in the United States) he is being tender with whatever is linked to the revolutionary Third World movement. His attitude to the Cuban revolution is similarly tender, even to the point of stating that there is total cultural freedom in Cuba! *Black Dwarf*, SWP, i.e., Socialist Workers Party, links go hand in hand with extremist Arab groups in the United States and the Middle East, those groups which call relentlessly for the complete obliteration of Israel. The SWP has consistently backed *Al Fatah* in its paper *The Militant*, and whatever subtle difference might exist between the viewpoints of the Arab and the Trotskyist groups, there is irony in the fact that anti-Semitism (for that, in spite of all protests, is what it is) should anywhere in the world be plugged in the name of Trotsky (who during his struggle against Stalin was identified with the hated Zionists, and who once wrote wryly to Bukharin: ". . . is it true, is it possible, that in our party, in Moscow, in *worker's cells* anti-Semitic agitation should be carried on with impunity?")

In the bar at the hotel that night, there is a conversation about authoritarianism and its implication in the revolutionary movement. A sturdy British gentleman, who looks like a businessman, argues with a pacifist couple that the violent activists are just disciplinarians in reverse. "They put seventy bobbies into the hospital, sir," he complains to the pacifist with the tooth-brush moustache, "seventy bobbies. My pal Corporal Jones who used to be here on the corner . . . some pretty good men." He refers to the anti-Vietnam mass demonstration two years ago in October of 1967, which Tariq Ali had described as made up of ten thousand people chanting "Victory to the NLF." (And which, whatever its size, was truly enormous compared to the tiny group which showed up on the same day in front of the Soviet Embassy to protest the take-over of Czechoslovakia.)

The pacifist with the moustache admits that he took part in the procession with his wife. "We were marching for peace," he explains, "not for war . . . for peace in Vietnam and in the world. I was only a child during World War I, but my uncle was one of those conscientious objectors imprisoned for his pacifist views."

England

"That was Uncle Charlie, dear?" inquires his rosy and serious wife.

"Um hum," he answers touching her hand. He addresses the other man, who has announced rather loudly that most of these revolutionaries are too damn ready to take over, that they think they know everything when they don't, that they're the opposite of pacifist, that they're bloody well "little Füehrers."

"I know," the pacifist says, "but we march for peace and 'Together.' That is our little contribution."

"Provided you're not going to attack the bobbies and so get a Mosley back into power," mutters the businessman.

The businessman's point of view may be parochial but for some reason he seems more sympathetic as a person than Ali, who has ended an article in a leftist journal with a remark reflecting belief in his own superior mission. ("Most important of all," Ali wrote, "*we* are not to be bought off by the state. *We* mean business!")

August 7

At Liverpool Station Martin is strolling to and fro with a rolled-up umbrella and a pair of gloves with which he slaps his black suit. His spotless shirt, modest tie, and the horned-rimmed glasses on his black, intelligent face—all make him look like a refined African student, on vacation from the University of Ibadan. Yet he had finished his engineering course at the Polytechnic in London, and now is working as a security guard at the station. Only this morning he had worn a porter's uniform, and later he had taken off his peaked cloth cap and exchanged it for a black felt one which he keeps in his pocket. He suggests some Indian curry, and we walk along the damp streets in the direction of Whitechapel. In the Indian restaurant he leans forward over the not too clean tablecloth to speak earnestly about Nkrumah. "I think he's a sad case." His voice is soft and pleasant. "I don't like to open my vocal chords when I'm talking. In any case, I'm not addressing an audience, I'm talking to a lady."

He smiles, showing a flash of white teeth. "Yes, Nkrumah is a sad case. In the eyes of millions of his people he was a god. But his subjects didn't want to sacrifice for the future. They wanted to adore him. When the economy didn't work out well, he began to put his political opponents in prison. The people wouldn't stand for that for long."

Although he associates with more aggressive Africans, Martin is moderate and gentle. "I have two sisters. One is a barrister and the other is a nurse trained in obstetrics. My father wanted me to do medicine but I don't like to see blood." He thinks for a moment and then says seriously, "Yes, I want to help people but I don't like to see blood, so that work in a hospital would not please me. Yet one day, when my wife gave birth to a child, I stood there and could see the blood coming out and the life coming in. I received that child into my own hands and so I conquered the fear of blood. I am a Christian . . . I am very deep in religion." He leans forward again and adds softly, "I want to find out the secret of being."

The Indian proprietor comes forward and suggests another order of curried vegetables. Martin asks for okra, while two little girls with long tapered trousers under their full organdy skirts lean gravely over the table to watch us, tiny earrings in their soft brown ears, glossy plaits untidy and swinging.

We discuss Tom Mboya, Kenya's Minister for Economic Planning and a member of the Luo tribe, who was assassinated about a month ago in Nairobi, shot at point blank by a black gunman. The murder had touched off violence among Mboya's Luo supporters. Since he had been a possible successor to Jomo Kenyatta and was partly responsible (with British advice) for Kenya's solid economic development—and had also been immensely pro-West—his (Mboya's) death was a setback for the democratic block. Martin looks sad. "He was a friend of mine; he tried to bridge the gap between people.

"He was a pluralist," Martin adds. "He didn't mind if American Negroes wanted to go to Kenya; but he wanted them to know what going means. He used to say that one wasn't an African because one put on a Japanese-made *dashiki*."

We talk about the murder, which had been committed by a Kikuyu called Nahashon Isaac Njenga Njoroge and about the evidence given by the nurse, that Njoroge had told her he intended an assassination. "That fellow Njoroge," Martin says rolling his eyes, "we know *him* . . . that one went to school in Bulgaria. We know what they learn there!" He nods his head resignedly. "The anti-West forces wanted Tom dead."

And how do the Kenyans feel about Communism in general?

"A *sartain* group," (Martin was trained by Scottish missionaries), "a sartain group in Kenya have sympathy for the Communists, but never enough to turn the country towards it."

Tea is brought in, the proprietor assuring us that it comes straight from Darjeeling. "What people want is liberty," Martin says with a serious expression. "Tom has two sons and these sons will follow the light of liberty. I do believe that *never never* will that light be quenched."

And what does Martin himself believe politically?

"Ah," he says in a sonorous voice, "government of the people, by the people, for the people. . . . But hundreds of years will pass before this comes to Africa."

Martin's earnest air, his profound respect for order, work, develop-

England

ment and "helping people" seem to represent the moral effect of a church education. He now asks about life in the United States. "The matrimonial love seems to be very flexible?" he questions curiously. "In our African society we live in bigamy. According to native law and custom, bigamy is not a crime. Yes, I would like to go back to Africa for good, for there it is a less *strict* life. But I have misused my resources and how will my kiddies get a place if I leave too soon?

"I also want to deal in houses in Nigeria. One of my aims in life is to help many refugees." He taps his forehead. "It's all in here . . . as long as they need a shelter I would like to provide it, to wake them early in the morning to go out and look for their bread. I want to extend the hospitality of Africa to this country and to other continents."

I wonder whether these large-sounding schemes are dreams?

"No," Martin says. "I have done this before, I had houses. I brought money, thousands of pounds. I rented old houses and fixed them up." He spreads out his brown hands and looks at them reflectively. "I have been doing this for time immemoria . . . yes, for time immemoria . . . It is *possible*. One man could be, if he wanted to, a *universal United Nations*."

We walk along the street and through Petticoat Lane. The yellow lights shine upon the bare, slightly polished stones of the deserted thoroughfares which in the early morning hours will be alive with the tumult of buying and selling. "Some Africans are very sad," Martin says, as if affected by the city's hugeness and loneliness. "They come to me with their problems. One sees often an African who has come here long ago and not gone home. I know one who has been working for fifty years and now he lives, far from his country, in a single room, a lonely man . . . What was all his working *for*? Where is now the support of his life"?

The streets grow less clean and there are alleys paved with broken brick where solitary lights show the stained walls. This is the heart of London's textile industry; the closed shops and factories bear signs relating to Sportswear, Elastic Wear, Fibre and Felts. A little pub is wedged in the midst of it all; its insignia carried out in tile, is a white swan sailing dreamily among water lilies.

At a closed café in Leman Street the Yemenite worker wearing an apron lets us in, but says that everything is shut up for the night. Here, Martin tells me, workmen gather when they are free: Lebanese, West Indians, Algerian Arabs—men of many nations, but of course no Englishmen. The walls are a dirty grey. There is a huge still-hot coffee urn, shelves full of cheap soft drinks. There is a stocky, intense Arab who calls himself Rahman. Rahman tells me that he hopes "the Yews" will never go. "I hope the Yews will be forever there . . . that they will never go . . . that they will keep up advanced." At first it seems that he is liberal in his views and considers that the Israelis with their technological know-how will influence the Arabs. But as we talk about Nasser his hatred becomes clear.

"Nasser did only one wrong. Nasser's only wrong was that he did not move at once. When they wanted the UN to get out, he should have moved at once." Rahman made a gesture with his finger across his throat. "Nasser said maybe the United States won't like it, maybe the Soviet Union won't like it. So he waited. But what did the Yews do? *They* moved, and that was the end."

"You talk good of Yews" he goes on, "but the Yewman is a sly one. I have one in my house. He had a girl and the girl used to kiss him in the street; and I said to him this is not nice to kiss in the street. This Yewman is very nice—oh yes, his children kiss me and hold my knees." He gestures and pantomimes affection. "Oh yes, the Yewman is very nice to me. But when the Arabs fight the Yews, he is savage, he brushes past me in the passage. He hates me. When the Yews win, then he is happy again. He wants then to embrace me again." He pretends to embrace the man from Nigeria. "The Yewman is a *sly* fellow. When I tell him not to embrace the girl in the street, he calls the police. The policeman come and say, 'Is this a house of prostitution?' I say to the policeman '*Our* people don't do that. What for do I do that? If I have to do that I shoot myself.' I go to the Yewman and I say, 'I kill you. . . . I don't want to even see your face. . . . I kill you.' His own face expresses wild fanaticism. "I tell you that I kill him and cut up his wife and children. . . ."

The dim yellow light shines down upon all of us. Martin asks if the Jews and Arabs mix, and Rahman flings out his arms in disdain. His soiled shirt is damp with sweat and he holds his empty glass in one hand. "The Yews don't want to mix with the Arabs," he declares with resentment. "They think they are the best people, the only people . . . the best race. They think they are God!"

The pubs up the street are filled with Irish and English, and the atmosphere is less intense. Everyone is drinking, swearing and singing and a frieze of jolly reddish faces is seen against the wall. A buxom woman leans over the bar of the King of Prussia. At the Black Horse someone is bawling out the verses of "Killarney." Two women are drinking ginger wine among a crowd of men who lift up large tankards of ale. The streets of Whitechapel at this late hour are almost empty; the silhouettes of men appear in odd corners and in vacant lots. One man urinates against a wall. Another, the faint light shining on the stubble of his face, leans drunkenly to try to sell us a handful of cheap jewelry. As he lurches forward, Martin says, "Now he is no longer a man, he is an animal trying to live."

Here is the old problem of poverty, degradation, and ignorance. However political parties change, those on the bottom are the ones who suffer and are least rewarded. Here is England's Third World. That afternoon I had passed Marble Arch, and Warrington Crescent, the site of the African Houses. There in 1960 a political exile had said to Louis Lomax, "The days of the ragged, hungry freedom fighter are over. If a man is a legitimate representative of the struggle in his country, he can get help. There are three organizations which maintain special funds." (At least one of these was funded by the Communists.) In those days all the politically conscious Africans in the major capitals of the world were waiting to be summoned home by telephone calls. Now the activists have moved up a notch, live well in their liberated countries, or in exile in Algiers, Cairo, Paris (and of course, here in London, as also in Africa, the poor remain).

Down Monthope Street and into Brick Lane where the shadows are deeper and the empty houses gape with broken windows and blackened crumbling walls. A tall lean Negro with a shaven head looks up among the tooth-like iron posts which cross the lane. Under a tiny round hat his face appears like that of some gaunt old warrior. We knock several times at a tiny door and duck our heads to get in when it is opened. The manager, a Mr. Dixon, is dressed in a dark suit and quiet tie, wears a gold watch chain across his front, and has a smiling, charming manner.

After a short conversation in Yoruba, he explains to me, "They're gambling; we keep the light low because of the bobbies." He smiles showing one gold tooth. Then he indicates me with his thumb, and adds with a faint high laugh, "She's curious!"

A gigantic black man lurches in through the door. His bones seem twice as large as those of the average man; he wears a loose sweater under his coat which shows bony knobs at the base of his neck. He stretches out his arms and advances. "*Kiss* me. . . ." His voice comes imploringly out of a cavernous chest. "*Kiss* me . . . !"

Martin and Mr. Dixon reprove him, and he apologizes with that familiar Scotch accent. "When I am in a *tempah* (temper) to kiss, I want to *kiss!*" He smiles in an agonized way showing tremendous teeth. Mr. Dixon accuses the huge black man—who is afterwards said to have come from Sierra Leone—of "swinishness and loose living." The man laughs like a child, and shakes him off, but seems ready all the same to obey his orders.

Downstairs in the gambling room, there are Africans from all parts; from Biafra, Lagos, Ifé, Conakry, Dar es Salaam—there are political refugees, and refugees from poverty and war. There is a constant coming and going. "A fellow came from South Africa today," Mr. Dixon says. "He was a blondish fellow; light, very light; he didn't have to leave the country. But he couldn't stand the restrictions. The restrictions are harsh, very harsh!"

374

We drink a cup of coffee standing up in the small anteroom. Mr. Dixon looks a little cynical and smiles again, his gold tooth flashing in the light cast by a single swaying bulb. "Politics all day," he says. "They talk and talk about politics . . . but all they really care about is the horses and the cards!"

August

Through Notting Hill Gate (that once literal gate which had divided the big estates of Holland Park from the genteel streets of Bayswater). Just before World War II this had been an area where the poor mingled with the rich. The prewar high-class food stores had been beseiged by women from the dingy back streets, pushing their bluish babies in battered perambulators and begging from the affluent housewives. Many of the shops of that time have disappeared or changed their names or their *décor*. There are banks with glass fronts, furniture stores, antique shops, cafés which sell not only fish and chips, but also hamburgers and bacon, lettuce and tomato sandwiches. The old pub is no longer exists here.

Somewhere to the back of this area there lives, or lived, a Trinidadian, Michael DeFreitas—son of a black woman and a Portuguese wine merchant—who had grown up in Port of Spain, taken ship on a freighter, and ended up in England (which, as he records, was "home in the mind of every small boy in the West Indies"). The saga of Michael X, as he came to be called, has many similarities to that of Malcolm X. Michael X also lived in ghettos, also became part of the street life, also gambled, became a pimp, worked in and ran clubs, had white women as mistresses, got involved in the Muslim movement, and graduated to political activities. He became in fact—admittedly because of rather forced publicity—the English version of Malcolm X.

With considerable humor, he (Michael) describes the race riots in Notting Hill Gate; the resultant flood of sociologists and social workers into the area; and later on a party of MPs who wanted to see the natives in their "natural" habitat. He tells of his own restlessness; his disorganized life; his indulgence in gambling, crime, and the subtler forms of exploitation; and finally his meeting with Malcolm X, who came to England to speak at the London School of Economics and was at that time in the process of reevaluating his own political stand (having broken with the Black Muslims and created the Organization of Afro-American Unity).

Malcolm X asked Michael De Freitas what he was going to do about his black brothers in England. He took him to Birmingham and when speaking to the Islam students, referred to him as Brother Michael. ("The Islam student body probably interpreted what he said too literally. They booked me at the Grand Hotel as Michael X and that was how Michael X came into being. When I eventually did become a Muslim, I chose a different name, but the mistake went on.") When Malcolm urged him to help set up an organization of Anglo-African Unity (*"which must be set up on an international basis"*), Michael agreed. As the two men parted and as Malcolm prepared to return to the United States, he talked seriously about the possibility of assassination. "If a white man shot me in the South, it would make me a martyr," he said, "and they wouldn't want that. No, when it happens it will be in the North, at the hands of a black man." A few weeks later news came that Malcolm X had been gunned down in the North—by a black man. Just as he received the news, Michael X was writing a manifesto stressing the unity of black men in Britain.

Where Malcolm X's life impinges upon the life of the London ghetto, we come upon political questions which may affect the world of the future; upon crucial aspects of the rise of the dark-skinned dispossessed. Of the two men, Michael X seems the less stable. He is noted for a certain lack of respect. Once at a meeting a black actor suggested that the Queen should be asked to adopt a black baby. Michael X called out—as an embarrassed hush fell over the audience—"Don't let her adopt one. Let her *have* one!" He openly enjoys irritating the Establishment, and describes the Poetry Festival at Cardiff in 1965 when the beat poets and their followers stole the show: the junkies taking off in hotel bedrooms, the drinkers drunk in the passages, the eaters getting through enormous luxury meals at the sponsor's expense, and someone trying to steal a Vietnamese pig from Cardiff Zoo, so as to slaughter it with a bow and arrow and show the audience what Vietnamese blood looked like!

If one thing is more noticeable than another about this account of the political development of a Trinidadian it is that it is interwoven with attempts to transcend the ghetto boundaries. While the lives of Malcolm X and Michael X are less tragic and in a sense less elevated than those of heroes like Toussaint l'Ouvreture, like his, their lives grow more human as the broader world is opened up for them. The miracle of education, the joys of serious discussion, the importance of practical politics, the merging of racial groups, a sense of the wider role of women and a more civilized treatment of them—all these discoveries are evident in their histories.

Walking along the streets of Notting Hill Gate, buying a copy of Michael X's book (*Michael DeFreitas to Michael X*) and reading part of it sitting in the small café opposite the bus stop. In the evenings the streets behind the café are filled with prostitutes, the proprietor tells me. He adds with a sad shrewd smile, "they walk in pairs, too, you wouldn't believe it! One black, one white—no discrimination here!" He rings up five shillings with an air of determination. "It's the fashion now, this race thing." He smiles again and disappears behind a shiny pine door.

Like his murdered brother Malcolm, Michael now uses black unity as a tool, while actually seeking political links with white radicals. Asking for Jewish money, he still welcomes contacts with Arab militants as a means to what is called Third-World power. In other words it is hard not to believe that the pre-vision of a militant black-radical-Arab deal does not permeate this movement in Britain as it does in the United States.

On my way to get a visa for Egypt at the Consulate of the United Arab Republic (one of the old houses in Kensington Palace Gardens—a house with flowered carpets and chandeliers, Egyptianized by a beautiful sloe-eyed secretary, a gloomy portrait of Nasser, a golden-head of Tutankhamen, and scenes of the tombs at Luxor), I buy the *London Times*; only to be reminded that psychostrategy is winning out. In fact today there is a definite feeling that some corner has been turned in Southeast Asia. Nixon has just announced a further withdrawal of U.S. troops. And there is rote-like publicity about Hanoi releasing American prisoners.

One Englishman at my hotel who seems to be quite absorbed by the political situation remarks re this propaganda war that it is hard to recognize the heritage of Karl Marx in the boring barbarisms thought up by his followers. He repeats the old joke about the ancient librarian in the British Museum who was asked if he remembered the man who spent so much time among the books. "Why yes," he replied "Mr. Marx? Foreign-looking gentleman with a beard? I wonder whatever happened to him."

"He—Marx—has been boiled down and is inside the heads of his followers," the Englishman says in a gloomy manner, "even among our minorities here." He indicates the hotel desk where a gleaming young Jamaican is sorting the mail. "That one over there has a habit of talking about his 'surplus value.' That's no joke when the building is practically in receivership!"

There is a feeling of sadness. The sadness comes not only from the sense of what used to be called, in the genteel manner, Britain's "reduced" circumstances, but from what will eventually be her powerlessness to support traditional values. Those opposed to the "West" must not only neutralize Britain, but also keep her quiet.

Sharing a taxi with three boys who are going to Brixton. Two of them have on shiny pants with pink shirts. Only one has a tie (with fawn

England

stripes). The third is dressed in a tight dove-grey suit. All seem to possess ruddy cheeks, light colored eyes, and thick bangs over their foreheads. They volunteer the information that they don't know why I want to go to Brixton anyway, because it isn't the same these days, it's "full of the colored." They then say that they are "Cockneys" and, where there is a question of sharing the fare, gallantly offer to let me ride free, adding that they suggest I "watch out."

"Ram jam," one of them adds enigmatically.

What does this mean?

"Aw, they play spot the white," says the possessor of the striped tie.

So they don't like whites being in the neighborhood?

"Aw, some of 'em aar like that."

"Some of 'em 'll tap y'on the shoulder," says the one in the dove-grey suit, "and when y'turn aahrand y'get a bottle 'nyr faice."

Is it really as bad as that?

"Aah . . . and they'll tike y'money out o'yr pocket. Thaat's their fav'rite trick."

The three are ready to get out now; and the slight one, bound in his tight suit, works out that they each must pay four bob.

"Aht th' cooner, plees," another tells the driver. "Y' can't stop here, it's traffic-like."

As he pays, the one with the striped tie tells the driver, "See arfter the lidy. She orta go on t'tha market."

The grey English sky lowers over the close houses and the taxi moves slowly along narrowing streets cluttered with open-air stalls. Many of the faces in the hurrying crowds are dark—the olive of India, the black of Africa, the lighter browns of the West Indies. There are notes of color, red shirts, colored head-cloths, African tunics, shimmering *saris*. It is a combination of an Eastern or African fair, and the Saturday market traditional in England where florid barkers cry their wares and little old ladies in voluminous aprons sell farm eggs, whipped cream, and chickens; where one smells almost at once the salty coastal smell of haddock and kippers, and sees winkles for sale (with a dash of vinegar, at a few pennies a plate).

The air is full of the cries of merchants. "This towel is worth a quid!" cries a pink-skinned barker, thrusting a villainous green affair at some woman who has dared to pause. "All right, then—take it for 19/11 . . . 'ere it is . . . 'ere you are . . . . I'm 'arking back to prices before the war. . . . C'mon now. . . . Ow's that? . . . . Two for 30£ . . . see ef y'can do better?" He wipes the sweat off his flushed brow.

Brixton has changed since long-ago visits. As many other London suburbs have changed. (Most of them have little ghettoes now. In Nottingham, it's the "Meadows"; in Manchester it's "North Side"; in Cardiff it's "The Bay"; and in London there is Notting Hill Gate,

378

known as "The Grove"; the East End where I'd been the night before; and, of course, Brixton itself, which certainly seems to be turning slowly but surely "black.")

In one of the shops they are selling big green plantains and yams (boiled, these last, and showing their purple skins with the greyish flesh inside). The shopkeeper cuts the yams into chunks with a huge knife, and watches them cautiously fingered by dark young women in bright sweaters, head handkerchiefs, and sandals.

"We 'ave ter pay for them," one told me with her Cockney accent, "and, for the 'ot sauces too."

"That's four an' six," says the shopkeeper.

"Four an' six!" the woman asks with mock astonishment.

"Orlright, three and nine." There is a tone of disgust in the man's voice.

At another stall, coconuts are for sale, and a glass case holding octopi spread out on ice is weighted down with battered-looking tins of okra. After inquiries about the neighborhood, a pretty soft-voiced girl explains, "I doesn't live here; I lives in Manchester." Her neat English navy suit seems out of place on her tropical sensuous figure. Then, as if this were a subject one does not talk about loudly, she murmurs, "There's good and bad here." (She seems automatically separated, not only from the neighborhood, but from those who dress in bright colors and head scarves.)

Near the entrance to the movie theater a chatty white saleswoman vigorously thrusts the top part of her body (in a bright blue blouse) out of the window, letting her glasses, attached to a gold chain, dangle over her large bosom. "Sure there's going to be trouble. This place is getting too much *theirs*, that's why . . . there's going to be a march against the police . . . or so they threaten. . . ." She has a low voice. "No, we never had any trouble before. There were lots of colored, but we lived in peace." She sniffs a little, though in a kindly fashion. "I lived above one of them for years; she was a real friend. But now there's a different type, an uneducated organizing type. The Universal Coloured People's Association, they call it. They broke into a public meeting at the Lambeth Hall last week, talking about Black Power and all."

What's the trouble, then?

"Wee-ell . . ." her slow voice considers. "They talk about this police brutality. I don't think that the police around here are so brutal—a bit rough at times, you know, but then, there are those that ask for it." She leans forward and screws up her eyes. "Trouble is, some of them have no sense of humor. They're *dour*, like the Scotch!"

A moment later, while taking notes outside a record shop, I see behind the glass a young West Indian boy in long jeans and an orange sweater beginning to dance the Calypso. Beside the door there is the word Soul in big black letters.

England

A sharp-eyed coffee-colored man (in the white pants and white tunic one associates with a doctor or dentist) comes out of the back room and looks at the notebook in my hand. "Will you please leave?"

Why must I leave?

"Because that is my order."

His English is enunciated clearly; his eyes glare with an insane generalized dislike.

"That isn't the reason; a shop is a public place."

"Leave . . ."

Tentatively trying to lighten the atmosphere: "I'm only a writer. I only like the music. Are you serious when you say you want me to leave?"

"I apprehended you," he says, jabbing a finger.

But doing what?

"Because I apprehended you taking notes to different things." (Apparently there have been rumors that spies are being sent out by the authorities to listen to conversations.)

A little English woman on the pavement outside the shop whispers; "E thought you wus from the Town 'All. . . ." But protests do not convince the owner of the shop; his face grows darker and more ominous. The old woman, almost trotting, with her shopping basket over her arm, follows me up the street to murmur again, *"They're* the ones that are prejudiced, not *us."*

A little further on it is a relief to be offered a beer by a coal-black Yoruban veterinarian, who pauses to give directions to Somerleyton Street, and then steers me into the Atlantic Bar to talk about the problems of Brixton.

"A march? Most probably. I see preparations being made." His voice is cultured and he props his briefcase against the polished brass rail on the bar before us. "I see various men with posters waiting on the corner over there. Undoubtedly they imagine this is a necessary protest, but their activities are—I think—misplaced. Many of our people," he smiles and a deep dimple appears in a satiny black cheek, "many of our people, and I include *all* dark people now—have problems of adaptation, not only to their work and their housing, but to this Mother England herself. Truth to tell, they have never been so well treated, and this rouses their hopes!" We are sitting beside a tall battered man who has drooping cynical-looking eyes, and is holding a worn canvas bag thickly plastered with Belfast labels. The Yoruban asks if he is, indeed, an Irishman.

"Yes," the man says rather belligerently, "I'm Irish. I *have* been Irish, and I *will* be Irish until the day I am dead. As for these immigrants, I've found that the rogue in one country is as bad as the rogue in another." He begins to talk about the *folly of high-placed men*. "One rogue is as bad

as another." He is nodding to himself. "Profumo . . . Kennedy . . . Holt
. . . ." It is hard to divert him from his pessimistic certainty. "Birds of a
feather," he murmurs, "not a pin to choose between them."

We revert to the race question. To what extent is it only a problem of
prejudice? The Yoruban looks around the pub, and waves a graceful
hand. "No segregation visible in this pub as far as I can tell." (It is
perfectly true that all colors and all conditions are drawn together here
by the mystical bond of "good ale.") He begins to tell a long story
about how his eight-year-old son was run into by a car when he was
playing in the street. "It was scarcely the fault of the British government, was it?" he asks rhetorically. "My son had been told not to play
in the street, but he is willful. Now, if it had been the son of my black
power neighbors, the case would have been placed at the door of the
government which has given them hospitality. At the hospital he was
given every possible attention." The young father drops his voice and
mentions the cities he has lived in. "Lagos. Cairo. Algiers. Paris . . . I
tell you," he announces loudly to the bar at large, "it would have been
a different case there. British justice is *superb!*"

Outside the march is gathering and various demonstrators are carrying
posters which have a startling familiarity: Death To All Uncle Toms—
Immediate End to Police Brutality—Black Power. A few blocks away a
group of dark-skinned men and women are gathering around a table
where a white man is directing the poster carriers and giving out
literature. There are copies of the *Black Power Newsletter* (voice of the
Universal Colored Peoples Association) adorned with the familiar symbol
of the panther. There are also flyers for the Black Power Mass Rally
(Stop the Pigs) stamped with the image of a pig wearing a policeman's
helmet, labeled underneath, Brixton Racist Pig. Several teenage West
Indian boys in jeans and bright T-shirts, are gazing with serious eyes at
the Pig posters, and one of them even holds a poster of his own: Stalin
Is a Revolutionary, which (seeing his age and origin) seems rather
unsuitable. On the opposite side of the road, three or four Bobbies
stand, calm and splendid-looking, their arms folded, the straps of their
helmets resting on their solid chins. An editorial in the *Brixton Adver-
tiser* states that immigrants might better understand the problems the
police have to face, if more of them applied to join the force. ("Only
two applications have been received this year" the Police Inspector
announces in an admonishing British manner, "and that is not good
enough"!)

The speeches start. The rather shrill voice of a short squarish man in
a suit and a fez, floats across the road in the late afternoon sun. "When
you are brutalized by the police . . . when you find yourself brutalized—when the police have hold of you and you are their racist prey—
then you have the right to defend yourself. . . ."

England

A husky man with a blonde moustache, his shoulders straining under his tweed jacket, moves up under the shade of a nearby tree, digs a shooting stick into the ground, sits on it, and begins to make a few notes. His jacket looks "County," but his shoulders suggest the Secret Service. The short dark impassioned speaker on the other side of the road lets his voice rise freely; his words take on a pulpit rhythm. His Oxford accent is modified until it sounds—if one does not listen too closely to the words—like a voice paying tribute to some water god, risen from the Caribbean, or from the steaming rivers of West Africa. "We are bla-ack—we are bla-ack—we are comely and they—they are *white—they* are the dust of corruption—Yes, they *enslave* us—and *behold* while we came from our own true soil—*they* came from the dust of *corruption*—the worth of a slave who gave them his life was less to them than the weight of—*two—dead—flies—!*"

The smallish figure is now obscured in a growing, though still tiny, crowd. "If they speak of living well," the voice cries, "I will say *I too,* like to live well . . . I will ask *questions*—I will say, where is the *gold* you stole from my *brother* . . . ? Where are the *horses* you stole from my *sister*—giving us only a hut to sleep in and a mule to plough with?— My *brothers*—I speak now of these *thefts.*" His voice begins to rise to a wail. "*Since* the day—*Since* the day I was born, I have *seen* these thefts, these *murders*—I will destroy everything in *sight.* I will *destroy—I tell you,* brothers and sisters, *I will destroy—*" A man in a shocking pink straw hat edges up to the speaker and calls out in a thin wavering tone: "Ah-men"! The declaiming voice rises higher and higher, climbs into its possessed Biblical rhythm, falls again into insane logic. "*If I do not* destroy *you,*" it screams, "if I do not destroy *YOU*—I will destroy *MYSELF!*"

A taximan has stopped to listen, and leans out of the cab window with a slightly astonished look upon his face, his arms folded. "*They* got nothin' to crib about," he says.

"Well," the taxi driver says to me kindly, and his voice is the old tolerant voice of England, "they're here, lady, and we got to make the best of it."

Back at the hotel again to pack—and to linger for fifteen minutes in the grassy park where, strangely enough, city as it is, there comes that sense of tranquility known only to English villages and English meadows. There does not seem enough time to breathe again that soft English air.

EGYPT

We do not talk of *that* war. . . . We talk of the
next. The *Jihad!*

August

I had made an attempt to get to Africa earlier in the year, in order to be in time for the Pan-African Cultural Festival scheduled in Algiers. (Eldridge Cleaver and four other Black Panthers were to be guests of the government). But the attempt was not successful, and London had taken precedence. At the same time there is something stimulating about the reports coming out of Algeria describing the three-storied Panther villa in the suburb of *El Bair* and the shining bronze plaque engraved The Black Panther Party—International Section, which decorates its door. These blacks having crossed the line from one political bloc to another, and now sharing the platform with the followers of Mao, and Ho Chi Minh, and Kim Il Sung of Korea, are openly stressing the fact that they are willing to join the Third World forces. Naturally this is a coup for the Algerian in charge of "Liberation Movements", Dhelil Melaika.

En route to Cairo. To the north, Constanta and Odessa—to the south, the Bosphorus. The plane circling in a landscape of rich sunset-colored clouds. When the single word *Yesilkoy* springs into focus, it is surrounded by greenish lights, like the fey lights found in marshes; but the plane door opens to the terminal at Istanbul. Blonde, Norweigan, mini-skirted hostesses (suntanned from days of leave in Cairo) file down the aisle, and give place to dark-eyed *houris* encased in tight navy-blue.

On saying goodbye to Europe one leaves also a certain familiarity—it is in fact saying goodbye to the *West* and welcoming the *East!* Yet under the rule of technology, crossing the dark Mediterranean means nothing but time to drink a highball; idly to turn the pages of a magazine,

Egypt

to see that it advertises Renaults and Madame Rochas, to look at the clock and note it is 2:00 A.M.; to gaze out at Arabic hieroglyphics sprawled in fire across the dark delta below. And at last an air terminal vast as a soiled temple where the black and white decor reaches to a faraway roof; where porters move languidly, where slow clerks, their white uniforms rumpled, carry out casual duties under lighting which has in it a slight touch of underseas green.

In spite of a minimum of entry delay, there seems the possibility that this *laissez-faire* attitude might turn to hostility.

Underneath the high arc roof, where occasional dogs wander, where small groups of travelers cluster, where dark excited children—who should be in bed—chase each other to and fro, the human element is lessened, as in a mosque. Occasionally, too, there is the glint of light on the Russian submachine guns carried by soldiers on the runway outside. Finally the ragged porter pushes his way past the soldiers with one deferential finger hung in the air; his hooked nose stretched wide in a grin as he places the bags in a battered taxi, holds out his palm, and asserts with a kind of ferocious innocence, "Welcome . . ." And as we drive off, a water tank, the shape of lily leaves, the spires of papyrus— symbolic of that civilization familiarized by reliefs on vessels and tombs, by hieroglyphs on gold, wood, basalt—by the very division of the days into hours.

At the airport where the soldiers had ringed the entrances gripping their Kalashnikovs, the Third World-Arab alliance had seemed real (as had also the Middle Eastern welcome to the Soviet Union). And speeding towards the heart of Cairo in a cab invaded by the African heat, it isn't easy to forget the reaching for power of Marxist liberation movements in this and other parts of the world; especially since it all happens to the familiar tattoo of an anti-establishment diatribe in the United States (The Racist Dog Policeman Must Be Withdrawn From Our Communities or Face the Wrath of the Armed People). But here there is that sense of inevitability, which lifts a little the historical burden from the "white man": with Cairo itself now providing a focus, not as it did in the past for potentates, entrepreneurs and Colonial administrators—but for African and Asian representatives, for African exile groups, for contacts with African and Asian students, for these Panthers and other U.S. blacks on the revolutionary circuit, and for Communist contact with all of them. Here in Cairo was the meeting place for the pro-Russian World Federation of Trade Unions and the Trade Union Committee for Solidarity. Here the pro-Chinese Afro-Asian People's Solidarity Council had its birth. Moreover, here, just to make the situation intricate, the influence of Peking was exerted in its early aggressive adventures; sometimes in concert with that of the

USSR, sometimes in conflict with it, and sometimes via the extremist movements in the other Arab countries.

In fact the ancient city gate, first put up in 1087, where both rich and poor used to hang their crutches and bandages, is supposed, until quite recently, to have had slogans written on its towers curiously appropriate to the current political climate. (On one side To Hell With Unbelievers and on the other Down With Those Who Prevent Progress!)

The city is still awake, in some places still bargaining and selling; there are figures lying with classic anonymity on roads, in doorways, or in the very center of the division between the traffic lanes. A family, a man with a child on his shoulders, a white bundled mouse of a woman running behind. Another woman laughing under a light, her shiny green blouse showing enormous breasts as she leans back quivering with laughter. There is the impression of a vast, shabby, half-sleeping city, accented by dark trees which struggle with shadow, and earth under the black night.

In the hotel lobby three or four disheveled men lounge at the desk or on the stairs, but multiply at the arrival of a solitary guest; bow, line up, seize bags, bustle into the elevator, cry "Welcome!" One unlocks a door, one opens closets, one opens shutters, folds up a Nile-green coverlet, swipes ineffectually at sleepily buzzing flies. One announces with proud affection and possessiveness, "I, room boy." A taller one grins, showing discolored teeth, bringing together shoes loose on brown heels, murmuring, "You Ingleesh, nice, very nice . . . ," and then, pointing to the balcony, cries triumphantly, "Cairo"!

And at dawn (as Kipling said, "Always keep a new city till morning") the city is to be seen from this balcony, stretching sand-colored on and on, picked out by palms and myrtles, elongated by flattened roofs upon which there are already a few tiny black-robed figures; rounded finally by mosques where minarets shimmer in the distance as in a mythical dazzling storm of sand. At that moment Cairo captures the imagination.

It is nine years since Nasser was at the height of his power. Now the man who used to walk unprotected in the streets, who engaged so enthusiastically in everything from diplomacy to nationalization, from dam building to rocket making, is not to be separated from secret-service men who quietly enter buildings before his appearances or from a personality cult which includes humorless salutes in articles and advertisements, and even sometimes on the paper which wraps parcels ("Long Life to Our Beloved President—Gamal Abdul Nasser"). There have been also the shifts in the Third World (with Nehru dead; Ben Bella, Nkrumah, and Sukarno displaced; and the Arab world penetrated by the Soviets). There have been the arrests of "Jews" and "Capitalists"; the costly campaign in the Yemen; continued unemployment and overpopulation along with lowered production and the depletion of the exchequer. Above all there has been the continuance of the unproductive messianic view; a growing dependence upon the USSR; and the disastrous Six-Day War.

It also seems that the war has stopped tourism in its tracks. In the hotel one walks through empty corridors, eats in dining rooms without diners. And although it is the hot month, August, when officials are taking their leaves, or spending long weekends in Alexandria, the sense of *stasis* goes deeper than this. It is the feeling of a vacuum, of a lowering of standards, of a cultural loss.

Up the river there sweeps a cool breeze, a breeze which pushes the dust of the avenues before it and seems like a current of iced air superimposed upon the reality of the hot valley. It is a valley which stretches for many miles. Perennially cultivated, it varies in width from one to fifteen miles, and stops short where human cultivation stops and the desert abruptly takes over; the Arabian desert on one side, the Libyan on the other. The city of Cairo bears witness to the valley's richness and the glittering Nile waters roll by in full flood.

In the street of Abdul Kader Hamza the resuscitated British Turf Club has a neglected look, in spite of spectacular carved wooden doors with huge brass rings, and the interior with drawing rooms and sitting rooms where old copies of *Punch* lie on small tables. Here British social power operated with orderly snobbery (Lord Kitchener ousted Egyptian members). Yellow clippings make references to the past; to meetings, subscription lists (headed by Kitchener), to rules ("no unseemly noise on the premises"). The present Greek manager, a short, bald, and slightly mournful little man, affirms that the club still operates, but whether it is still British is open to question. "In the old days we had more than four hundred members and about one hundred and fifty country members as well. And they were all British, but now . . . ," he shakes his head, "about sixty or less."

The credit for the revolution goes to an amalgamation of social and political forces. To poverty and exploitation. To confusion and the erosion of governmental structure. Into an anti-Western and anti-Israeli framework there fell neatly the natural activities of the paramilitary, anti-infidel Moslem Brotherhood (*Al-Ikhwan al-Muslimum*, famous for its terrorist methods and for having sent a delegation to the Nuremburg Rally in 1936). The Free Officers Corps operated in much the same context: some of its members were pro-Brotherhood, some were influenced by the radical and violent *Mirs al-Fata*; some had been pro-Nazi during World War II. There were also, of course, Communists or Marxists with axes of their own to grind.

According to Dan Kurzman, an American correspondent then stationed in the Middle East, the belief was current in Cairo at the time of the Anti-British riots that the Polish Embassy had cooperated with the fanatically anti-Western Moslem Brotherhood. At all events, the Polish Ambassador was asked to leave the country. Two days afterward, Kurzman interviewed Haj Amin el Husseini, the former Grand Mufti of Jerusalem, who was Hitler's agent in the Middle East during World War II, and who was dressed in a long black robe and a flaring white, turban, and said, as he played with the fringe of his beard, that he himself had not been involved in the riots, but that the Arabs would cooperate with anyone who would help them to throw the British out of the Suez Canal Zone, and the Jews out of Palestine.

An Egyptian historian explains later that after the war the Egyptian Communist party was able to gain a new lease on life and to act as a catalytic force. "Members helped to draft the literature for the Free Officers party, for instance, and played a key role in some of the riots which brought about changes. Most of the intellectuals were somewhat leftist, it was a general climate; yet few of us were devoted to Russian-style Communism. The Brotherhood called for *Jihad*; they attacked every element—the foreigners, the Jews, the government. They worked with the Marxist students at the university. When the government repressed them, they went underground."

To what extent had Nasser himself been influenced by Marxist concepts?

"Well, of course, Nasser had suppressed the Communists, but Khalid Muhieddin, who was an original member of the Free Officers Executive and very much to the left, had been a friend of Nasser's and had supposedly introduced him to various intellectuals who may have influenced his way of thinking; to Dr. Rashed Barawi, for instance, who translated *Das Kapital* into Arabic. (Khalid Muhieddin was the man who had been active at the Tri-Continental Conference in Havana in 1966.) Smiling modestly, the historian suggests: "Any of us might have influenced him. After all, it was in some ways a question of a *tabula rasa*. You have to imagine many political combinations; the use of the energy of all groups to eliminate the West, to defeat the Israelis, to rouse our stagnant country. How much was necessary, how much preordained?" He waves his long narrow hand.

As the hot Egyptian morning progresses, the old way of life seems to emerge like some flowering plant to fill the spaces between the buildings: crowds swell around the food stalls; recumbent figures litter balconies, doorways, parks. A boy rides by on a bicycle laden with

Egypt

sheep's heads, which loll in a great bouquet, pale tongues hanging, drops of blood from the damp black hair spraying the crowds. Voices rise in competition with the cries of those who sell wreaths of jasmine threaded upon cotton. There is the aroma of coffee and the rank odor of sweat. Looking downwards one sees naked feet, small jeweled slippers, flopping cloth shoes, loose sandals bone dry on the dusty pavement. Fruit sellers sitting in the shade of buildings offer grapes, watermelons, and ripe, bursting figs.

Ahead in the street walk several American Negroes, their skin colors blending with those of the people of the host country but their manners and attitudes, their clothes, their prosperous gadgets, watches, transistors, binoculors—strictly alien, strictly American. A girl with an Afro, in a cream-colored nylon suit which hangs smartly on her thin body. Two young men wearing white slacks and dashikis. The smaller man has around his neck a heavy chain hung with ivory teeth. In spite of this apparent return to ancient Africa, it is easy to suppose that they consider themselves strolling in Cairo as in a "center of liberation." (It makes no difference that they are in a country where long before, and later than their European counterparts, Arabs and Berbers and North Africans enslaved their ancestors; and that in this city in the nineteenth century, the market with its naked black merchandise shocked Englishmen and Frenchmen and Wild West Americans alike.)

In any case, how see without emotion the emancipated descendants of slaves return to the African homeland—once the scene of an ancient crime—as shrill-voiced advocates of the end of the white man's rule? A gigantic colored photograph of a Senegalese woman, attached to the walls of one of the old houses serving as embassies, attracts the attention in Garden City's circular tree-shaded streets. The photograph of this woman, whose young but coarse-grained face seems to glisten in the heat (beautiful full mouth, spreading nose, barbaric glinting gold ornaments lying upon her forehead under a lilac-colored turban) rouses some feeling of unsuitability. It seems out of place near these European-inspired buildings which date from a time when Senegal did not send black ambassadors to British strongholds, and when the real business of Cairo was taken care of discreetly in the drawing rooms of the British Consulate up the road. Yet now such generally dark-skinned faces are marked with potential power. In the curve of the Shari Ahmad Ragnib Bey, where the old trees spread broad mottled trunks, and in the Shari Ibrahim Pasha Negib, new Embassies bear glittering brass plates and photographs of entire all-African staffs. There is generally a larger photograph of a smiling dark-skinned ambassador complete with blue ribbons and medals against a formal European suit. (It is easy to imagine it juxtaposed to the portraits of "our own" black dissidents—H. Rap Brown, LeRoi Jones, Stokely Carmichael, Malcolm X, Eldridge Cleaver . . . travelers all; rousing the same sort of interest that Claude McKay did when he went to Russia in the early days of the Russian Revolution and sat on platforms with Zinoviev and Bukharin, and was in demand everywhere, and known as the *Chorny,* i.e., the black.)

Trying to locate an American Negro woman who had married a white radical. This radical had been the leader of a Communist youth group, and then, expressing Third-World sympathies, had joined a Maoist faction. The couple had ended up in Cairo, and taking Arab names, were given jobs in the Palestine Liberation Organization (PLO) propaganda department—thus typifying the use of black rebel exiles in the Middle East, where, acceptable to African audiences, they have been put to work in Cairo as Robert Williams had been in Cuba. English is a *lingua franca* in Africa; and the black propagandists broadcast first south to Africa and then west, chatting through the night hours to their "soul brothers" in the south of the United States. It is fascinating if somewhat chilling to think of them being set up in that radio station which Charles Issawi (*Egypt in Revolution*) said had few equals in the world "for sheer venom, vulgarity and indifference to truth."

After wearying forays into the side streets leading off the *Casr el Ainy,* it seems clear that the two I am looking for have already left the city for Amman—or so the thin-legged porter in a dirty robe says—while another occupant of the house comments that it is thought they went to the Fatah camp where the young revolutionary-prone English and Americans are making their headquarters.

Our taxi approaches Giza via crowded streets, via a highway bordered with new blocks of flats and rather vulgar villas complete with domes and minarets. Odd combinations of color; dull red and mustard, lime green, and ocher. The boys, the women with bare feet, the occasional camel. Here, close to the center of Cairo, where the numerous stalls sell cigarettes, Egyptian sweets, and an aniseed drink, men stretch out on the pavement, in utter abandonment to the brilliant day; they adopt the earth as their home, and they lie at peace in the dust (traditionally the babies of the *fellahin* were not washed until seven days after birth). Past a long line of rickety-looking but often pretentious nightclubs, the taxis slow down, as if in respect: Palais des Pyramides, Salle Dorée, Sahara City, Auberge des Pyramides, Arizona, etc. Later I go to one of these with a sophisticated Egyptian. We are surprised to find ourselves sitting at a small table watching a quintet of English beauties who might have come out of an early 30s music hall in Brighton. They are performing to a swinging version of "I Could Have Danced All Night." "Do you think this importation of talent is a contribution?" the Egyptian asks with a dubious smile. He is sorry we have missed the belly dancer, who after all is indigenous and performs a slightly bastardized version of what was once a premarriage ritual.

Egyptians generally speak of "Ageless Egypt" with a special intonation. Past the nightclubs, "Ageless Egypt" is evident again. The shabby camels stand patiently or sink to the earth with their characteristic, strangely human gesture. A woman passes by, erect as one of the cranes, carrying three or four of the cabbages on her head, her long black dress clinging lovingly to her slender braceleted ankles. Beautiful as she is, her figure has a cadaverous look, that same classic emaciation one gets accustomed to in India. Not far away, in the back streets, many of the houses are the traditional peasant houses made of gray adobe—soil mixed with chopped grass and Nile water. The horizon stretches on and up. The houses thin. And then in the heat ahead, blatantly oppressive at midday, mysterious at evening, and sometimes dreamlike as the haze of sun and sand marries with some fortunate slant of light to bring out their towering dimensions—the Pyramids.

Again the hotel is almost empty. Smiling servants in lavishly-embroidered costumes walk on worn but rosy carpets, doze in the elevator opposite intricately-carved cupboards and screens and tables inlaid with mother-of-pearl, gaze out from the nineteenth-century interior toward the desert sands. Harem-style lamps with red and green glass are slung on elaborate ironwork brackets, and give a sense of fatality to empty rooms. During the day only a few brave souls wander in and out of the tombs at the Pyramids; at night a constant procession of cars sweeps up the road to park under the shadow of the Pharaonic past. Up the long dusty slope to Cheops: that burden of human effort, that monument to sweat, that 746 foot base by 450 foot height of faith and fatalism, that ancient creation which looked, Khrushchev told the Egyptians with sublime peasant tactlessness, when placed by monuments in Moscow's Red Square, like "a heap of manure."

It costs ten piastres to enter the museum of King Farouk's palace; and the price is low for the historical perspective. The building itself is oppressive; the state desk of this Eastern-minded monarch is made of heavy black granite and is as inert as an Aztec statue. Polished pink granite gives little relief; the delicately carved screens inlaid with mother-of-pearl present the motifs of a slave past. There is a staircase of marble and pink alabaster where the rounded railheads are illuminated by interior light. The ceiling is a sky. There are gilt chairs and badly-painted murals of modern daughters of the Nile.

None of this affects the validity of the Revolution, or its natural place in the procession of events. Against the fatal weaknesses of the King—who surrounded himself with foreign hangers-on, who, according to various accounts, appropriated for himself some national treasures, and who regularly looked under his bed for assassins—the real or imagined oppression of colonial rule must be balanced. Squirming under British control, Farouk's bitter humiliation, if less pure than Nasser's, could not have been very different to endure. In a sense, they belong to the same stream of history. It is noticeable that after coming to power, Nasser began to fall more and more into his role of messianic avenger, until on the occasion of the nationalization of the Canal, he addressed the British, who "sucked our blood and stole our rights"; the Americans, "may you choke in your fury"; and his own people, "O citizens—the Suez Canal has been nationalized . . . and it will be run by Egyptians—Egyptians—Egyptians!"

It is enough that, symbolically and actually, when the Revolution began, "Palace Time" stopped short. The calendars in the royal offices, engraved as they were with portraits of King Farouk, remained stationary; torn off on that historic date—June 26, 1952. "Revolution Time" had begun.

August 25

Every morning the paper (generally the *Egyptian Gazette*) is pushed under the doors of hotel rooms. Three or four pages of print, much of it an indulgence in indignation, condemnation, and bizarre distortion. An emergency meeting is being called at the Arab League because of the fire set the Thursday before in Jerusalem's Al Aksa Mosque. There is no stressing of the fact that the arsonist is apparently a religious maniac. President Nasser declares that "real force" must now be used against Israel. Israel is responsible, along with the United States, of course, whose creature she is held to be. King Feisal of Saudi Arabia is calling for a Holy War. An editorial rejects the thought of justice by law.

> Who has any faith in Israeli justice—the Israelis are world experts in judicial murder as the case of Adolf Eichmann demonstrated . . . who . . . was captured . . . tried and executed by his accusers.

El Sayed Soloman el Nabulsy, chairman of the Committee for the Rescue of Jerusalem, says that the arson was only a preliminary "to the Zionist plan to set up Solomon's temple on the site of the blessed Moslem shrine."

Varied messages of sympathy keep coming in from world groups. There is a generalized call for "liberation," for *Jihad*, for "purging the land." In the same paper it is announced rather matter of factly that fifteen more spies will die in Iraq at dawn on the following day. This will be the fourth time this year, it is announced with approval, that spies will be hung in Iraq. There is a horrifying memory of the fourteen Iraqis, including nine Jews, left hanging in the Baghdad square on January 27 of this year.

August 26

King Feisal is calling upon his forces to be ready for *Jihad*. He says, in reply to a cable from Prince Sultan, who informs him that the army is ready for the "Battle of Destiny," that Arab patience is exhausted. All along the Israeli-Lebanon front there are attacks by Arab guerrillas. Almost simultaneously there are explosions in the London office of the Israeli Zim Navigation Company (Arab guerrilla organizations are reported to have sent agents to London). The editorial now speaks of the "brazen impertinence of the Israelis." The writer sounds pained that Abba Eban is accusing the Arab leaders of "reviving medieval incitement to interfaith religious warfare;" and he says "the *bizarrerie* of this statement is breathtaking!" The prime policy of Israel, the editorial says, is to "carry out a Jewsade."

Moslems in Ceylon, Indonesia, Kuala Lumpur rally to the cause. Yugoslavia and Somalia send support, and a day later there are to be more demonstrations in Malaysia, where students, along with their more fanatical elders, are to call for *Jihad*. Now Mr. Mohammed Natsir, a Moslem leader in Indonesia, tells reporters that Israel had "long planned to get rid of the Mosque."

The paper is read faithfully; more fascinating than the inadequate breakfast in this luxury hotel where butter, milk and cream are of such inferior quality, and the eggs are as small as those of pigeons. The "re-arrangement" of the news gives a sense of unreality. Moreover there is the feeling that now at last I am in a truly undeveloped country; where Europe's authority is diminished (with little coming to take its place), where the citizens still bow to feudal authority but at the same time call themselves "socialist."

August 27

There have been attempts on the life of Yigal Allon, and shelling of south Jerusalem. Two big stores in London (Marks and Spencer and Selfridge's, both with Israeli links) are threatened by arsonists. The paper congratulates the country that guerrilla attacks are continuing relentlessly, that rockets are exploding on the Israeli border settlement of Yardena, and that responsibility for the Mosque fire, set by "Jewish fascists and their supporters, notably the U.S.," is being revenged. Someone writes a letter to the paper stressing the fact that "the Koran says an eye for an eye and a tooth for a tooth"; the letter ends with "Long Live the Glory of Islam."

Always interesting in the *Gazette* are those articles which relate to the USSR, the tone sometimes bringing back echoes of Nazi propaganda in the late thirties. To read a small piece rationalizing the Nazi-Soviet pact of 1939 is to remember that Nazi refugees were absorbed into Nasser's propaganda machine and are now among the most active of government journalists. This article leans heavily upon references to *Pravda*. More evidence of Russian/Middle East links is the display of military solidarity. Israeli (or for that matter Western) confidence cannot be increased by the news that on August 26 Transport No. 26 crossed through the Bosphorus, making the sixty-fifth Russian naval unit to enter the Mediterranean since the 1967 war. Russian attitudes to the firing of the Mosque suggest a well-controlled satisfaction; there are constant references to the event, and these references call for more solidarity among the Arab states. Since no single act could have been more calculated to elicit support from the conservative Arab states and to spark a renewed call for a Holy War, it seems not illogical to wonder whether the young Australian, Rohan, had been a leftist or Pan-Arab tool. If there is no evidence of this, the Egyptian press, by continually stressing Israeli guilt, makes the weak-minded reader forget that there is even *less* evidence for the other. Moreover, the constant use of words like blood, fire, revenge, purge, steadily corrupt the sense of proportion.

In spite of this, in contact with the Egyptian people (in whose name these violent pronouncements are made) there is continual surprise at their affectionate simplicity, their gentle and civilized attitude. Two hotel maids—Mena and Zara—black eyes liquid with interest and good will, provide the guests with clean towels, flowers, and attention.

"He is a nice man," Zara declares of Nasser. Her short shiny bob swings forward as she smooths covers and sheets, and arranges roses on the table near the window.

"And a hero." Mena is tall with black hair wound around an oval olive-skinned face. She is the daughter of a peasant who was active in the Revolutionary Council in her village, and because of this, she has work in the hotel as part of a course in hotel management. "Every Egyptian, all the people, they like Nasser very much."

Nasser certainly seems popular with the lower classes, though bureaucrats and government officials are supposed to be appalled at the mess he has gotten them into ("the holy war has gotten us into a

Egypt

holy mess"), and the more intelligent and dissident of these fear further repression. This is indicated by the kinds of statements Nasser made in early summer, all of them smacking of Soviet-style calls to "solidarity against enemies of the people." In a June issue of the *Illustrated London News*, Nasser is quoted as stating that he himself has been at fault for allowing a "new class" to arise, and that "we must be aware of the counterrevolution . . . we cannot give freedom to the enemies of the people." These phrases are almost identical to those which all through the year have been sounded in Czechoslovakia as the political purge continues there. Moreover, the phrases are reminiscent of the Russian request after the Six-Day War (via *Pravda* and *Izvestia*) for "the dismissal of all those who were spreading doubts about the nature of the Soviet-Egyptian relations and calling for a resumption of friendly relations with the USA."

And why do the two maids like Nasser?

"He is good because he guides the people and gives them rights."

They both tell stories of the past; Mena maintains that the *fellahin* used to sell their babies for 5 pounds, and still have nothing but "work . . . work . . . work."

"Now the *fellahin* are rich," Mena maintains. Then she admits more thoughtfully, "Yes, if you searched the village you would find rich and poor."

"If there is milk, the babies get it," Zara says. Then she points out of the window in the direction of Cairo, and says that Cairo is no longer poor. "We make the mini-factory and the High Dam."

Both girls say that they like foreigners, because foreigners are very "democratic." There is a reversion to nationalism, as Mena, her eyes swimming with emotion, asks why America helps the Jews against the Arabs.

But do the papers they read always give them the right impression?

Zara hastily upholds the Egyptian tradition of hospitality. "You are welcome here . . . *welcome* . . ." Then she smiles, wrinkles her nose and measures with her hand. "I like you. I like you so much—as a small chicken or a cat!"

Later she comes with a copy of the paper and asks why we (that is the Americans) set fire to the Holy Mosque?

But neither the Americans nor the Israeli government set fire to the Mosque; it was a deranged Australian!

We talk in confused terms about the UN and about the distinction between individual acts and government acts. Rather unfairly I mention that an Egyptian mob had burned down Shepheard's Hotel; and a mob had also burned down the American library. Were the whole Egyptian people to be blamed for that? Zara shifts ground a little and states that before the Six-Day War Israel had wanted to get all the territory from the Nile to Iraq.

"In 1949," she says, "the British gave the Jewels the right to exploit Palestine, and now America gives the Jewels planes. It is difficult for me to speak in English. But America makes training of how to war with the Egyptian people. . . ."

It is scarcely surprising that Zara should equate the Americans with the Israeli enemy, for hadn't Nasser himself said just before the war, "What is Israel—Israel today is the U.S.," and a day or two later, "We are not facing Israel—we are facing the West."

But had it been so simple? The Jews had bought part of the land; some of Palestine had belonged to Turkey; a number of nations, including Russia, had supported the creation of a Jewish state. Even if the paper she holds says that the Israelis want the territory from the Nile to Iraq, this may not be true. Besides the Israelis in 1947 had been ready to agree to partition; in fact up to the Six-Day War, they had planned their weapons for defense only.

We talk about the history of arms sales in the Middle East, how America had at first tried to sell evenly to both countries; that if the U.S. now helps Israel it is partly because Russia broke the arms balance by helping Egypt; that it is now Russia who trains the Egyptians in arms and warfare. Zara makes a face at this. Though Mena, as the daughter of a revolutionary, is in favor of Russia's presence, Zara supports the more general view that the Russians are getting too much power.

Hadn't Egypt given hospitality to the Nazi scientists who came to live here after the defeat of Hitler, and of whom the Israelis, naturally, are afraid?

Zara listens, wide-eyed. She returns throughout the morning, blushing as she tries to avoid the stern housekeeper, eager to persuade me to visit her village.

Typical of the kind of fantasy served up to the people by the Egyptian press was the headline carried by the *Gazette* on Friday, June 9, during the Six-Day War, which said: Israelis Suffer More on All Fronts. UAR Smashes Back. This was a day after Egypt had agreed to accept a cease fire. It is doubtful whether the Arab masses—even the Menas and Zaras who read well—still understand the extent of Egypt's defeat. A certain vagueness, denial, and indignation accompany discussions of the war. A few days later, standing in the street, I see an Egyptian soldier in a rather worn khaki uniform with his arm in a brace, and also seemingly perched on one foot. The skin of his face has a greenish pallor, and when he sees me watching him, he self-consciously puts both feet on the ground and gives a half smile as if to excuse himself. I try to find out whether he had been wounded in the Six-Day War or more recently, and am reminded of that devastating description in the

Egypt

Churchill book of the aftermath in 1967, when thousands of Egyptian soldiers, the tattered remnants of an army, abandoned by their officers, most of their equipment taken, destroyed, or discarded, made their way, thirsty and often shoeless, toward the Canal. The book describes how Israeli rescue helicopters, flying low over the desert saw many lying where they had fallen, their skin blackened, spread-eagled on the hot sands. The soldier speaks no English, but his pale hook-nosed face constantly breaks into a smile as he points to the brace on his arm. While I am trying to communicate with him, another man—taller and fierce-looking—wearing a tight cotton suit wet with sweat, breaks in angrily: "What are you asking him? What do you say?"

I look astonished. "He doesn't speak English. I was going to ask him how he was wounded."

The second man addresses the first in a flood of Arabic, his arms flailing, his eyes blazing.

"It's got nothing to do with him," I protest. "He said nothing. I was trying to find out. . . ."

"Ah," the second man says, "strangers come to find out what they can. If you know what is good, you will not ask."

Can the man be connected with the Ikhwan (the Brotherhood), one of whose firmest demands of members is that they address each other only in Arabic, and that foreigners seeking to communicate in other languages be ignored?

"The war is over. Can't we talk about it? Is it a secret?"

"Over . . . ?" His face dark with passion, comes closer. "The war is not *over* . . . We do not talk of *that* war. We talk of the next. The *Jihad*."

Nasser himself does not escape fantasies of omnipotence. Zara is astonished to find me reading his *Philosophy of the Revolution*, and remarks enthusiastically: "Americans are students."

> "When I now try to recall the details of our experience in Palestine [Nasser wrote,] I find a curious thing. We were fighting in Palestine, but our dreams were centered in Egypt. Our bullets were aimed at the enemy in his trenches before us, but our hearts hovered over our distant country which we had left to the care of the wolves."

Nasser goes on to say that he felt his comrades and himself "thrust treacherously into a battle for which we were not ready." If his profound attachment to Egypt has been responsible for his power over the *fellahin*, over the Zaras and Menas, in retrospect Nasser's essential lack of perspective weighs against him. He describes how he had often chanted as a child, when an airplane flew overhead: "*Ya' Azzez. Ya' Azzez. Dahiya takhud al-Inglez*" (Oh Almighty God. Disaster overtake the English), and had only afterward learned that his forebears had used a similar cry against the Turks. Perhaps at that time he did not foresee that he himself would soon support the compulsive cry of "Disaster overtake the Israelis." And when he spoke of fighting on distant soil, he did not know that he himself would soon be supporting a messianic Pan-Arab role. Or that when he spoke of his fellow soldiers and himself being "thrust into a battle for which we were not ready," Egyptian soldiers might one day claim that it was under his guidance that they were thrust into a battle—the Six-Day War—for which they were not prepared.

Stories from the Six-Day war express the helplessness of the undeveloped but agitated Third World. One gets the impression of officers, many of them vain and undisciplined, frightened by the Israeli onslaught, and leaving their half-trained peasant soldiers to fend for themselves. Here in Cairo where a Revolution is supposed to have taken place, one feels divorced from traditional values and aware of the superficiality of political change. (As the historian I. R. Sinai points out the only "genuine" form of socialism must stand on the shoulders of capitalist attainment, and can only be implemented in a society which has absorbed into its bloodstream Western values and the disciplines of democracy.) A government statistician insists that the *fellahin* are much better off than before; but he seems to forget that if the peasant is granted five feddans of land, these are generally invested in a large cooperative where his own land is scarcely identifiable, and is worked in areas of cotton or sugar, and by gangs just as in the old days. He now has to pay for fertilizer which was formerly provided by the landlord; and since the crops are bought by the government, he may have to wait for his profits for long months after harvest. Not too long ago there were riots because of these delays.

A professor from the University talks more soberly of production— the old problem of would-be socialist governments. "Consumption is rising every day just as is the birth rate; production is declining. One cannot share what does not exist. The law says that children can go to school, but there is no force behind the law."

What about hunger?

"Many still starve," he says, "many more have an unbalanced diet . . . how can progress be made with continuous military adventures? Small children are still used as servants."

Walking back to the hotel late that night, I see in the garages little boys who might be ten or eleven, changing tires, their faces black with grease, just as in the *souk* pale-faced boys of about the same age are perched on stools in the shops patiently tying threads in brilliant hand-woven carpets.

The next day an American talks of how after the Yemen adventure, when millions were squandered, you couldn't even get rice or onions in Cairo. "They had to be imported. The slogans ceased to work, as slogans do. They're talking about raising the legal age for marriage to eighteen. They'd better hurry, about a million new children are born each year. The population simply can't support itself on this strip of land." (This American is a type met with all over the world: one of those numerous modest and competent men, not only scholarly but with a certain kind of know-how; able to see the difference between what really exists and what exists on paper.) "You can't help seeing the general breakdown," he adds. "Even elevators don't work any longer. They say the postal officials are so irregularly paid that they rip the stamps off parcels. The government is cutting its own throat. Tourism has died." He laughs. "As Kipling said, 'The tourist is a dog, but he comes at least with a bone in his mouth, and a bone that many people pick.' Alas, tourists are not happy with ideologies."

Although there are now more emancipated women in Cairo, although the traditional black *mileyah* and the white *yashmak* are seen less often, the position of lower-class women still seems to remain medieval. Women have custody of children only until they are about ten or eleven. After that, by law, they belong to the father. The mother gets nothing except as "guardian of the child." The Orientalist complains, "You can't really meet the women in this society, or not in my experience. The middle-class wife and daughter are too protected."

The waiter at one of the hotels talks on a slightly different level of women who are *engagé*. He has splendid almond eyes and talks of some women who are important in the new unions for women; and then he declares, out of the blue, as if I might get two kinds of women mixed up, "Sahara City, only third-class women there."

And has the Revolution changed women's lives much?

"Here in this hotel I know many kinds of women and I talk to you like an international," he contributes, "First I like the Italian ... zen the Egyptian ... zen the Greece ..." Earnestly he goes through the list; but as if he realizes that sexual preferences are not everything, he acknowledges that the Egyptian woman still does not have much liberty. "The rich woman has enough. The medium woman sometimes; but the poor family woman no. . . . she cannot to dance. . . . she cannot to drink ... she goes outside with mother or sister." He insists on trying to explain the female role in the life of the Egyptian male. "We must have women. The Egyptian man about sex is very strong. . . . we feel to the woman but not one hundred per cent. If I am married I will feel to my wife, but not the whole feeling." He is trying to suggest that "unfaithfulness" is an institution; and his tone says that this is quite natural, that male sensuality must be served—as per the patriarchal promise in the Koran ("I shall lay on no man a burden greater than he can bear"). There follows a series of stories about clandestine affairs and about lovers hidden in cupboards and women in towers—all sounding as if they might have come out of the Arabian Nights. Near the pyramids, Mena and Zara give *their* version of domestic life. On popular songs Zara says that she "like very much" *Strangers in the Night Exchanging Glances*. On family duty Mena says, "It is forbidden to kiss and if he makes so," she pantomimes the embracing of her own statuesque body, "then my father will beat me, or kill me and put me *under the ground*." Zara explains, "I can't go lonely. . . . if you invite me to the United States I must come with my mother. . . . If I go with boy friend to a birthday party my family must go with me. Because nature prevents that girls go alone. I am weak and must go with my mother, father, brother, friends . . . "Pour la femme c'est défendu de sortir seule."

Outside the hotel, bougainvillea blooms lavishly, but is drained of some of its color in the heat. A strange flower with an elongated yellow cup attracts a strange bird with an orange crest; and the man who cleans the pool regards it passively as he pauses in his task of scooping leaves off the surface of the water. His blackish skin is tight over the bones of his limbs, and enormous fine eyes shine out of a hollow-cheeked face. "I get £15 a month and £6 goes for my board. . . . Yes, I am working here for thirty-five years. Oh it was better before, more money, more people, a better life. Europeans then, British, Dutch, French. Since the Revolution it is worse . . . worse. The government deducts taxes and half of what I have over goes for my mother and children in the village. Yes, we have land, but it is little return and my brother farms it . . . I have nothing." He makes a gesture toward his loose blue cotton garment.

From the roadside the afternoon light shines upon an eternal scene. Shadows are cast like tiny dimples on the sandhills bordering the desert. There are convolutions on the roof of the camel shed, the classic folds in the hanging robes and cloths, a thrustback of shadow from the camels themselves, and the little yellow carriages lined up for business. Closer, the ubiquitous flies, the swaying camel tails, the knots and tangled bark in the massive, dusty eucalypts. There is the rich sickening odor of manure mixed with garbage. Everything here lies under the shadow of the Pyramids as in Mexico it lies under the giant Aztec monuments topped with their sacrificial altars; there is the same faintly oppressive feeling, the same weight of a history which seems too heavy to be adequately balanced by the present. "Camel meat," suggests the old man who calls himself a sheik and who is slapping his chest playfully, "it give the body a good powerful." He takes me to see his son, who is fat, round-faced, dark-eyed, and leans over the counter of a

Egypt

little shop that sells ivories, alabaster, and brilliantly-woven carpets. The son is more firey than his mild father, but he is also less competent. "I think the war will stop," the father says hopefully, "I think it will stop from God." "My father is old and doesn't know much," the son says scornfully. He shakes his fat arms, his chest, and beats his legs under the counter. "My legs for Nasser . . . My arms for Nasser . . . My blood for Nasser!"

Outside the shop the farmers go by in their long robes: as they walk, a continuous stream of messianic language pours from the transistors which they hold against their credulous ears.

August 30

The hot and history-laden streets of Cairo. . . .

In this valley the earth produced three crops a year, and once made possible fabulous gardens where almonds were crossed with apricots, and the branches of trees were sheathed with gilded copper through which ran streams of water. Here one king preferred darkness to light, ordered shops to be open all night and closed all day; had all dogs killed; all the honey tipped into the Nile; and all the women shut up inside the houses with the added precaution of forbidding shoemakers to make them shoes. Another king slept on an air mattress on a lake of mercury, lulled to sleep by the distant songs of slave girls. Here Queen Shaggar ground her pearls in a mortar so that no other woman would inherit them, and was in the end herself beaten to death by the wooden shoes of her servants. It was a city of murders and regicides, of beatings, hangings, and crucifixions. But its ancient life, though different in flavor, was no more intricate than that of the twentieth century. (Here after all, in the Esbekieh Gardens, Donald Maclean, British diplomat—recruited by the Russians in the "idealistic" early 30s—was found barefoot and drunk on a bench and was charitably thought to be suffering from Cairo's "Oriental" influence. Opinions changed later when during July of 1951 he took a channel boat in company with Guy Burgess and disappeared behind the Iron Curtain.)

It is in the area close to the bazaars, where the narrow high-storied buildings jut up like scarred teeth from the crowded matrix of the city, that there is a reminder of the omnipresence of religion. Here one finds the mosques—among them the blue-tiled Ibrahim Aga, the ancient Sultan Hassan, the El Kelaun. Inside the older-than-Gothic Sultan Hassan the midday sun slants through deep embrasures to illuminate odd figures scattered at intervals in the vast pillared space and lying in endless relaxation, praying, perhaps sleeping. *El agela mun esh shaitan* (Haste is from the devil). At the El Kelauñ before and beyond its big bronze doors, the scene is as active as the other is quiescent. Crowded stalls do a brisk business selling holy medals, beads, amulets, candles, spices. There is the muddy orange of turmeric, the red of henna. Inside the crowds are so thick that everyone is caught up in the movements of the pilgrims who carry sticks, rub images, pass their hands over their faces as if to collect the sweat and polish with it the silver-ornamented doors. The ornate *mihrab* is credited with heavenly virtue. I see a woman rub lemon onto the silver and lick up the benign juice with her tongue. At the Holy of Holies women are turned back; the male, at ease in the inner room, utters his patriarchal prayers.

If there are dangerous splits in the life of Egypt—a split, for instance, between hysterical government propaganda and civilized tolerant Egyptian traditions, or, again, between the poor masses and the thin layer of officials at the top—it seems likely that it is here, within the Moslem circle, where faith, emotion, and nationalism meet, that the catalyzing element will be found. The Koran strongly urges the duty of the faithful to make war on infidels ("who votes for death will not die") and this duty is accepted without question by many Egyptians who might ordinarily seem moderate and gentle. It is not far from such a concept to the acceptance of a war of attrition against the Jew. And again in this country where man's destiny is still seen by many in the hands of God, it is easy to understand that an ossified religion can be as easily manipulated by the Left as by the Right.

I hear from several students at the university that communism is "Islam brought up to date" (just as "Communism is twentieth century Americanism" was one of the slogans of the 30s). Perhaps this is not surprising, since a large percentage of the intellectuals, who emerged in the Middle East after World War II, were protégés of Western radicalism; but such phrases are conceived of by others in a manner foreign to those who utter them. For here in Cairo the veneer of progress is thin. Small groups of intellectuals or single vigorous leaders can control those who still live deep in the comfort of ancient patterns (they can easily marshal the masses in the name of historical obedience).

The Orientalist had suggested that communism benefitted from Islam's frankly anti-European attitude. "Naive Arab leaders latched onto the spreading faith. What could be more convenient? Activists from Cairo's Islamic University helped to flavor Islam with socialist concepts. No one can deny that Marxist ideology is spreading southwards and eastwards. Front organizations are staging Soviet Moslem expeditions to Mecca. Visitors are *fêted* by specially prompted front organizations. Did you notice that Malcolm X was much entertained by Communists, not only in Cairo, but in all of West Africa?"

Yet, are not Soviet linkups with Islam ironic in view of the long history of aggression against Moslems in the USSR? When the Czars conquered Central Asia, they found it easiest to rule indirectly . . . but under the Soviets isn't the repression much harsher? Aren't pilgrimages to Mecca allowed only under supervision, for instance?

"Yes, this is all true. If there was any loosening up in Russia, it was only during World War II, this to pacify the restless minorities and to bring back needed leaders from 'God's Icebox,' Siberia."

(It is a moment to remember Nasser's own reflections about the political potential of Islam. "The sixty million Moslems in Indonesia and the fifty million in China, and the million in Malaya, Siam and Burma, the nearly one hundred million in Pakistan, and the more than one hundred million in the Middle East, and the forty million in the Soviet Union . . . I emerge with a sense of tremendous possibilities.")

The political logic is inescapable. In order to provide a motive power as great as any that the world has yet seen, it should only be necessary to relate the fanaticism of communism to the fanaticism of the Islam which it in some way resembles.

Seeing off an American friend at the airport, I happen to stand at the barrier beside a young man, curly-headed and merry, a little on the plump side, who holds his prayer beads as the plane mounts into the air. He turns out to be a Jordanian named Hassan, who had formerly done graduate work at the University of Colorado, and explains that his best friend in Cairo is on the plane en route to London. "He will be safe if Allah wills."

Later over coffee in the city bazaar, he expatiates in his fluent but rather imperfect English: "An Arab is a spiritual . . . it is much learning and history. . . . You see, you can't speak about Arab without speaking about Islam. Islam *locomotes* Arab culture. It *dynamites* it, we might say. Oh yes, Madame," he laughs, "it is the opposite to the Western who have too much faith in technology. We can't explain the whole human nature by technology, Madame. Man is *more* than that. We believe in the *unique* and *complete*. Islam is transcendent, more than the *narrow* of nationalism. The concept of nationalism must be considered as passé."

Hassan puts his beads down on the table. He claims that Israel is capitalist and that Egypt is socialist. "Ah Madame, we see Palestine within the cause of international socialism."

As a Moslem, he surely can't support international socialism—does he consider himself a socialist?

"Ah Madame, one hundred percent."

Then you consider Islam as *socialist*?

"Ah yes, Madame, but here is a problem. In certain epochs of history, Islam was in the hands of people who closed the door of interpretation. So now we must reinterpret."

Even if you reinterpret, do you reinterpret, then, as a Marxist?

Egypt

"Madame, I am a *Moslem,"* explains Hassan. He measures with his small plump hands. "There is a lot of difference between Islam and Marxism. The basic concepts and goals are very *touchy,* Madame. I am a Moslem first; and I have studied in Marx because I liked my professor very much, and I can't deny that the doors of reinterpretation must be reopened."

At this point Hassan goes off at a tangent, talking of his love of the desert, of Bedouins, of Alexandria. "I would love to marry a woman of Alexandria . . . it is a miracle thing . . . I have *beautiful* memories of Alexandria, Madame." He shuts his eyes, folds his hands before his face, and throws back his head. "The Bedouin woman is very *beautiful.* You look to the behavior. She entertains a man very *well.* She *sing* to the man, *dance* to him. I love the *Bedouin.* He came from the desert, he came as Mohammed, Jesus Christ, Moses, our Father Abraham, and Ishmael!"

Finally he explains that Islam demands certain duties. "Most thing in the Islam way of life is to *Dar al Islam* . . . this money is really to charity. Here is the link with socialism." He goes on to say that we must all re-read Marx in a dynamic which will resolve contradictions.

I ask what he thinks of Hitler.

"Oh la la." He laughs. "I can say that the rôle of Hitler was to locomote the Jewish people to conquer; that it was a requisite to the success of Zionism. Zionism perfected its existence on the forces of anti-Semitism." (According to this convenient reversal, common among Arabs and certain New Leftists, Hitler is seen primarily as an instigator of Zionism rather than as an active malevolent force.)

A little later Hassan admits that he is aware of the threat to Islam from the Russian presence. He claims however, that he is optimistic. "I am not afraid because the Egyptians have an absorptive quality. They have been tested through thousands of years of conquerors, Madame. What is Western civilization to that?" His voice takes on a certain pathos. "We don't want to be *Russians* Madame . . . We want to be Arabs and Moslems, and have modernism and put our hand where help is . . ."

As we say goodbye, Hassan's last words are rather martial. "Yes . . . Yes . . . it is good to *deter the enemy* of God. It is good to die for Islam . . . It is good to go to Heaven." He adds rather wistfully, "There are women in heaven."

In the late afternoon more time in the *moushki.* Here cobbled courtyards and alleys where tiny donkeys necklaced with blue good luck beads, wait to be unloaded beside mules with copper-studded harnesses. On the pavements of the square, the mules dropping manure soon to be covered by the spewed out husk of sugar cane chewed by children, by the wrappings of bundles, by the discarded straw from baskets. Women in dirty flowered gowns squat with an artistic swirl of skirts, half-

Egypt

covered breasts shining with necklaces and perspiration, the thin material of their veils only hiding the blue and gold of head scarves. Down the narrow *souks* a panorama of ancient life. But change is also apparent, especially in the squares surrounded by mosques, where booksellers do a brisk trade. Tracts and government propaganda are sold for a few piastres. *Mein Kampf* can be brought in Arabic, and new editions of the *Protocols of the Elders of Zion* (an edition of which was published by Nasser's brother last year). None of the papers from the West seems available; for these you have to go in the direction of Garden City; even there they will often have pieces cut out of them by the censor. Instead there are Holy Scriptures, calls to *Jihad*, booklets about the Jewish-American conspiracy, books which glorify Hitler, and the chief newspapers from the Arab bloc. There are also editions of the Soviet papers, in particular *Pravda* and *Izvestia* (featuring this day inaccurate and provocative accounts of the arson at Al Askar, just as during the prelude to the Six-Day War, they castigated Israel's supposedly hostile intentions, printed false information about Israeli troops massed on the border of Syria, and soft pedaled the Arab war preparation).

There seems no more startling evidence of the current political climate than the way in which the ideologies of Islam and Communism lie together on the pavements of the old city.

Take a taxi and cross the river to Zamalik, the island in the Nile where the Russians are to be found. They have turned an old mansion into a Cultural Institute where they show Russian films and hold concerts, and run a library which employs five or six Russian-trained workers. Although an era of democracy and anti-Communism is being predicted, it seems clear that for now, Soviet power is deeply entrenched with many Russian soldiers, sailors, airmen, engineers, and technicians; with the Russians having the use of Egyptian naval and air bases; with the Egyptian army reorganized upon Russian lines; with an economic penetration which reaches into every phase of industry and defense.

In the streets near the Russian Embassy some of the diplomatic colony walk with their families, their blonde women and children strikingly out of place among the poor Cairo crowds, who in stained and patched garments, wandering and artlessly posing, seem so much more in keeping with the dusty streets and trees and even with the soil-colored Nile itself under skies white with heat. The big blondish men in baggy suits and often with pale stand-up crops of hair, appear so obviously from a colder climate, so obviously Russian, Czechoslovakian, that it is somewhat unclear whether the Cairo masses could consider them "friends." It is as strange to see them here in Cairo, complete with their own servants and their own cars, drinking and talking in their own clubs, as it once must have been to watch the

British dancing their restrained ballroom dances under the dome of the building in Garden City.

There is, however, a difference. It is said on the one hand that the Russians have been warned by their own government to keep to themselves, on the other that the Egyptian government has warned them to keep to themselves. (A diplomat from an Eastern European country refuses to meet in the lobby of any hotel, or to park his car nearby; so that it is necessary to walk blocks in the hot sun before we can find a restaurant to have coffee. In this way, old-time shadowy Levantine intrigue gives place to the blatancy of the police state.)

In the early morning, Egyptian children, dark-haired, golden-skinned, troop to school. From behind the school walls the drum beats which mark the student's day accompany a polemic against Israel which sounds like a war cry, and seems to throw a long echo across the sun-baked streets.

In the afternoon groups of older boys drill in the school yards. The instructor is generally blonde; and the boys wear what looks like pale green uniforms. A British attaché asserts that military and political officers from East Germany are being employed for the training of these paramilitary youth groups. (It is evident that to prevent a repetition of the debacle of the Six-Day War, and to see that the Arab nations become efficient tools of Soviet penetration, more than hardware is needed.)

September 1

In the late afternoon at Mr. R—'s apartment. Mr. R— is a short squarish man with Arabic features, who would not look out of place in a gown and tarbush, but who in fact seems more at home clutching an English-style pipe in his hand, and wearing a shirt and grey slacks. He had wanted to be an actor, had become a political journalist and revolutionary, and is now a Communist functionary in charge of a Russian-sponsored "front" organization. (He has been imprisoned three times—under Farouk, under Nasser, and also after what he calls the "Hungarian affair.") All of us, including eight children and a pretty wife, crowd into a tiny sitting room half filled already with gilt chairs and a marble table. The oldest son is six feet tall with a dark moustache, the youngest is a plump baby. There are two serious-eyed girls. The general impression is of glossy curly heads and bony agile bodies. (Mr. R— admits that he does not seem to be supporting the nationally proclaimed birth limitation program.)

Egypt

One of the girls is introduced as "Ethel." "When I heard of the execution of the Rosenbergs," her father contributes, "I said to myself, if I have a daughter, I will name her Ethel."

Again the subject of conversation is politics. Just as he had spoken of hating concentration camps without any reference to the fact that the Soviet Union he supports had been one of the chief exponents of this way of dealing with political enemies, Mr. R— now refers to the "aggression of Israel" during the Six-Day War as if he had no idea of Russia's and Egypt's role in the outbreak of hostilities. He launches into a brief propaganda speech in favor of appreciating the Soviet Union.

"Be sure that before the Soviet Revolution of 1918, no nation could be liberated .. no nation could be capable of emancipating itself from colonialism. With the birth of that human power all things became possible."

He addresses his brother and his wife, who does not speak English but who stares at him admiringly ("Look at her," he says later, "she is a good woman and manages well, but she knows nothing about ideology"). "Who is helping us now in our struggle against Israel? Who is aiding us?" He adds obliquely, "Whoever is against the Soviet Union must be for someone else's benefit."

It is not encouraging to know that ex-Nazi engineers and scientists are still working in the jet airplane factories at Helwan (these were estimated in the early 60s by Sanche de Gramont at more than 450). Now some of these have left, some are said to have changed their names, but among the group as a whole, sympathies remain unchanged; this gives them a natural link with those who specialize in anti-Zionist feeling. It is the Soviets today who, ever since the Six-Day War, have been playing an agressive role in pushing a renewed anti-Israel campaign. Some of the more trite phrases coming out of Moscow ("New Nazis" . . . "Dayan is Hitler" . . . "Pirates of Tel Aviv" . . . "Obscene batallions of Jews") are typical of what isn't limited to the Russian or Egyptian scene, but extends through many of the Iron Curtain countries (and is noticeable even in Peking).

At the same time, Communist party members in East Germany (of course, technically Communists cannot be anti-Semitic) are said to be very disturbed to find Egyptians at various conferences slapping them on the back and saying, "Hitler *gut*, Hitler *gut!*"

All this is more anti-American than anti-Zionist. For only the Israelis and the Americans stand in the way of Russian domination in the Mediterranean, and a Russian throughway to the Indian Ocean. In the long run, the American nation is identified as the "Big" enemy, an honor hardly appreciated by that great noisy pluralistic society.

Egypt

Today is the anniversary of the proclamation of the Republic of North Vietnam. The heat seems to intensify as sunset fades into a quick nightfall. Lights go on over lawns which never seem to get enough water.

At the entrance to the North Vietnamese Embassy—a big Victorian-looking house hung with flags—the small charming Ambassador to Cairo receives his guests in front of floral cartwheels composed of red and white dahlias. President Nasser has sent his congratulatory message to President Ho Chi Minh and a number of highly placed Egyptian officials in formal dark suits stand around with drinks in their hands. Representatives of the press, the educational offices, the museums, mix with the diplomats from the Third World countries, with military officers in splendid uniforms, and African student representatives whose skins are noticeably darker than those of their hosts. Several things predominate. Males (the only two women present are British). Sobriety (with an air of serious preoccupation, most of the guests seem to be drinking orangeade). Darkness (dark suits, dark skins, dark hair). In fact, a group of three from the Soviet bloc draws the eye, because all are white skinned and wear white uniforms decorated with medals. Two Chinese representatives also stand out, appearing rather isolated, but distinguished by the red stars on their costumes, which glow under the dim fluorescent light.

In spite of language difficulties it is possible to make out the tenor of conversations; talk of the coup which had taken place the day before in Lybia, of the high-level Arab meeting in Cairo at the moment, of the formal charging by the Israelis of the Australian Rohan. (And from time to time, the rather wooden atmosphere is broken by subdued but passionate conversations, which give the impression that some of that fierce unbending dogmatism, supposed to characterize the desert Arab, has now, with the Revolution, been transplanted to the governmental heart of Cairo.)

A Palestinian offers whiskey, and then a plate with small pieces of chicken dipped in hot sauces. "We fight for Palestine, nothing more- . . . . Before anything, before socialism. . . . The Russians depend upon Egypt because Egypt is the first country to bring about socialism in the Middle East. Russia depends upon this, but for us it is different, we only need Palestine back." He asks what I am doing in Egypt? Have you seen the ruins of Luxor? "I don't like ruins," he adds. "Those are for my mother and father." But aren't the mosques impressive? "Mosques! Even in Istanbul I don't visit mosques!"

He announces that he comes from a revolutionary family. "Twenty years ago my father died in Palestine. We had land in Syria near the Israeli border, and my father was accused of helping the terrorists. My mother found herself alone; but she educated us by selling sheep and

Egypt

land. In the first war we lost some of our land and some of our houses; but in this war we lost everything! It is fortunate that we had hidden a little money. In Syria it is said 'You must hide some white money for a black day.' And with this money we went to Damascus."

He affirms that he is associated with *Fatah* and the PLO and talks about the *Fatah* camp in Jordan where some British and American students are living at the moment, the "European" camp as it is called. That conversation is cut short by two young friends who also seem to be associated with *Fatah*. One of them has been robbed at his hotel and in a low voice details his losses. "My radio, three of my ties, and my cologne!" He suddenly claps his hand to his pocket and exclaims with annoyance, "Ah I forgot! They got my pen as well!"

This conversation is followed by an even briefer one with a Leftist poet, who seems to take it for granted that all Americans must agree with him that the assassination of J. F. Kennedy had been hatched deep in the heart of the U.S. establishment. His features are rather haggard and his dark eyes burn with emotion as he clutches at my arm, "Tears were wrung from me on that day," he states ". . . crystal drops of tears. . . ." It seems impossible to explain that his Leftist prejudice wars with his grief!

After the reception is over and waiting for transport back to the hotels, it is surprising to hear one official murmur to another, "How the rich and important countries give confidence to their peoples! So they can walk in and find out everything!" In spite of this unrealistic compliment to the "Free World," an immediate reaction is to remember the North Vietnamese representative of the Afro-Asian People's Solidarity Organization describing Vietcong plans to defeat the Americans. "We dig pits. We fill them with sharp bamboo spikes. We *poison* those spikes." His face was lit up by a fanatic determination, as he made gestures with small agile hands to demonstrate how the American soldiers fall into the pits. Again there is the reminder that here at the revolutionary crossroads of Cairo, it is not really the Israeli who is the "first" enemy.

September 3

It is harder to leave Egypt than it is to enter it. Plane reservations have to be checked daily with Security; when protests are made about this uncertainty, the clerk replies fatalistically, "That is how it is."

A last visit to the museum where a tall man in a clean robe gestures possessively: "This way please. I am the *official* guide to this place. *Please*, this way." His large-eyed, strong face shines as he thrusts a fake

410

manuscript into my hands. "Papyrus." He makes the gesture of writing. "Papyrus."

Forgetting dignity, he then gathers up his robe, abandons the role of guide, and runs after a passing tourist to beg a cigarette. Inside the museum the unnecessary aspect of the fraternal war between Egypt and Israel is emphasized; inscriptions, *steles*, symbolic objects miraculously preserved by the burning sands, demonstrate how much these enemies (twin descendants of Abraham) have in common. Supposedly in one of the museum vaults there is kept, carefully guarded, a manuscript written on papyrus, which relates the psalms of David to the Egyptian poems in praise of the Sun God *Amon-Ra*. No list of battles can rival the interchange demonstrated by such a manuscript!

Standing at the end of the gallery where the heavy sarcophagi of stone guard the bound mummies, there is a view beyond the glass cases to a pattern of dozing guards, sprawled in white uniforms with black belts, their berets shining with the silver symbol of Egypt. The gallery is half heartedly barricaded with sandbags, the cases are half emptied of their treasures, the windows are inadequately crisscrossed with tape. Disaster is not far away in any case; modern Cairo lies involved not only in constant expectation of attack (if one can believe the government spokesmen) but in its own nationalistic deathwish.

September 4

The exit permit comes late; am forced to take an 11 P.M. flight on Algerian Airlines. Over supper with friends in one of those rustic summer houses such as one used to find in French gardens, there is the by now familiar and always overpowering smell of jasmine. And the by now familiar conversation, which gives the sensation of living under water; talk of the deteriorating situation, the pros and cons of another war, the sudden disappearance of someone who had wanted to get out (he had simply gone without saying goodbye). There are guarded references to what "they" (the government, or that part of it which is actively messianic) will do. Again that sense of the exploitation of the mass by ideology (and of the naivete of those in the democratic West who imagine that they can easily influence the undeveloped countries where only a few years after great upheavals, totalitarian forces so easily re-emerge). Reluctance to leave Egypt mingles with relief.

At the terminal the heat seems to swim over tired-looking travelers while boys with trays of lemonade bow politely, "To serve you, Madame." In the air the delicious fragrance of lemons. As passports are checked for the last time the passengers file out into the hot night—

Egypt

and are then checked again, this time with a good deal of confusion, at the plane itself. A number of young Iraquis summoned home by an emergency order are among the passengers and now start pushing from the end of the line, so that a typewriter is knocked over and trampled underfoot. There is a babble of excited rumor that the plane will not accommodate all those with tickets, and the pushing continues. (A hush falls as a woman with a British accent—old-time authority asserting itself—cries out *"Stop pushing!"*) Another officer arrives and quarrels with the first officer, who tries to guard the gangplank to the plane door. They shout and shake their fists.

As we finally sink into seats on the plane, the director of an educational group confesses with appealing humility; "I know our faults . . . we are mad . . . hysterical . . . we Middle Easterners. It is because we are nervous." He himself comes from Lebanon. In a speech which is a strange mixture of love and hate he says that the "Jews are a very clever people" and "ready to develop just relations . . ." but adds that he is first of all an Arab; he can't help wanting to push them all into the sea. He indicates that the Arabs are at present unfit for the tremendous missions they have set themselves. The plane takeoff is precarious; many of the passengers have got to their feet and are milling about in the aisle. The machine lists badly to one side.

What remains of the night is spent in a Beirut hotel near the beach. In the depressing modernity of the foyer the Lebanese room clerk is curiously objective, shrugging away the question of war.

"Your first visit to Beirut? Welcome . . . Welcome . . . Napoleon said that every twenty years it was necessary to have a *'mondial'* war. . . . I haven't a side in the war which comes. For me the two sides are bad. I am a Christian, and I don't like to take sides in such a struggle. . . ." He is cut short by the scream of planes overhead.

"Bombers! Ilyushins!" In the cold light of the foyer a young porter closes the door without emotion. The shrill scream sounds again and again. A whine in the distance, a gathering roar, a nightmare crescendo as the planes fly low in formation over the roof of the exposed little hotel, which seems to tremble on its base.

"They show off how many they have," the clerk says. He smiles sardonically. "Perhaps they show off to the West, perhaps they show off to *us!*"

1969

FRANCE

Liberty. . . .

Paris, September 6th

I. R. Sinai, the historian, has called the Indo-Gangetic plain, where all the well-known Western concepts—liberty, democracy, progress—lose their meaning, the "vampire of geography." It is with this in mind, and in spite of the Egyptians being the most charming people in the world, that goodbye is said to the still undeveloped Nilotic *ambiente,* and to that mixture of passivity and aggression which it represents.

Cyprus (though with troubles of its own) at least hints at the moderation of Europe. (Supper there at an unpretentious restaurant on the coast, about eight miles from Nicosia. Delicious fish; sweet figs; last season's white wine, reinforced by the promise of the immature grapes which hang from trellises above the white tablecloths.) And now there is Paris; not far from the Pont du Concorde, just where the rue de Lille opens into the boulevard Raspail.

They are tearing up the pavements. The September sun intensifies the smell of tar so that one might be in any city in the world; exasperated by the noise of power drills and irritated by the traffic. The familiar solidarity of these grey, slightly ornate, buildings. The streets following the river (chestnut trees, cafés, bookstalls); the span of bridges (Alexandre, de la Concorde, Notre Dame and so on) these radiating avenues, these squares, places, vistas, formal arrangements. Yet no longer so reassuring. There is in fact, a premonition of change. If all this beauty resists the pall of fumes, dust, chemicals, if it stands up to the persistent tremor of traffic, what else follows?

The question drifts with the Tricolor floating above the Assemblée Nationale, and it is not even whether Paris—honored by history and time and love and the affairs of men—is vulgarized. It is not whether this great city of Europe will keep one stone on top of another. It is

415

rather, whether of those three French words (Liberty, Equality, Fraternity) the first will retain its primary importance.

The gendarme is elegant in his uniform and his pillbox hat. He strolls rather than patrols. At the rue Royale a boy in a lavender striped sailor's middy stares from a window set deep in the ponderous building at the corner, a cigarette lolling insolently from his mouth, and an old man walks slowly with a worn book jutting from the pocket of a worn coat. The Place de la Concorde opens out—vast in the daylight, looking "ordinary" with its parked cars, yet holding like a scrawl on a blank page the somber site where Louis XVI lost his head.

Soon there are pictures in the windows of a courtyard gallery, compensating for the faint disillusionment in the heavy heat of the morning,—landscapes by Abrogiani, intense colors and a solid laying on of reddish violet (memories are stimulated of Gauguin's sketches sent from the far Pacific Islands, as these were from the provinces of Spain).

Suddenly a woman appears, talking to a young man. Her voice calls out, clear ringing; *"C'est le plus beau jour de ma vie!"* The young man wears a black sweater, corduroys, and rubber sandals; he catches her hand and holds it for a moment in one of those gestures of sympathy which remind us of such moments of our own. She is not pretty; wears dangling earrings, a black skirt, a black lace see-through blouse and her hair in a fringe like a poodle. But her face is ecstatic. . . . At the end of the rue Royale there is the rue Faubourg St. Honoré: bright shutters— blue, green, orange, and rose-red. Opposite, the dignified pillars of the Madeline. On the street corner, where Dubonnet is advertised, the smell of burning sugar from a copper pot over a brazier in which a man is making peanut candy, and the burnt-sugar smell mingles with the perfumes that drift from the florist's. A little brisk woman, stretching out a watercan with an air of benediction, dampens banks of roses, gladioli, fern.

There are many dark faces in these Parisian crowds, but the crowds are not like those seen in Cairo. In Cairo the whole city—stained by the encroaching dye of Africa—veers towards darkness. But Paris is after all only a "city of refuge" for great men of color. Upon the collage of hot flesh, light suits and dresses, of bright nylon flags which advertize goods in department stores, upon the noisy activities of another roadbuilding gang, men of the past impose themselves—Toussaint l'Ouverture en route to a solitary prison in the Juras; Ho Chi Minh shuttling between libraries, the cafés, the photographic studio; Aimé Césaire, the Communist poet, coiner of the word *négritude*; George Padmore writing about how Britain rules Africa; Léopold Sédar Senghor, finishing poems of exile; Richard Wright, from his expatriate base discussing with Louis Lomax the "dependence mentality" of blacks. All these blend with the intellectual past. Toussaint after he had been tricked on board the frigate which was to take him, as prisoner, to France, is reputed to have spoken yearningly of liberty. It reflects the mesmerizing French influence that, after he had been imprisoned in the Jura mountains in the cold of the European winter, in a cell where the walls ran moisture, with constantly reduced rations of food and wood—a Spartan regime deliberately devised to bring about his death—this ex-slave (who had educated himself with French classics, who had once looked at a French officer and said, "My sons will be like that," who had believed in personal industry, social morality, religious toleration, racial equality, and the brotherhood of men, indeed, in a France he had never seen), still could not do otherwise than imagine himself as part of the Republic, "one and indivisible."

It is natural then in this capital to ponder about the brotherhood of man. The Île de la Cité basks under a perfect sun. The smoke grey stone, the forbidding towers, the squares, the mansard roofs, the Cathedral of Notre Dame with its central window like a flower of light. From the tower of the Cathedral one can look down to the foundations, to the site of Lutelia, the old Roman town which became Paris. Beyond there is the Palais de Justice which includes the Conciergerie, in which in its role as revolutionary prison and in conditions which were afterwards to rouse astonishment in the fallen Girondins and Jacobins who were to inhabit it, the innocent and guilty were packed together as they waited for the blade of the guillotine on the Place de la Révolution. Here Louis XVI was shut up before he bowed his head to that same blade, stating, "I die innocent . . . may my blood consolidate the happiness of France." Here Marie Antoinette spent the eleven weeks before she was finally executed on October 16 of 1793.

Ten minutes later the city appears different (it is so much easier to romanticize the past than the present). The sound of power drills is hard to escape. The few visible skyscrapers encroach upon the ancient grey; perhaps to turn eventually this whole center of Europe into one vast Detroit or Chicago. Walking back to the rue de Lille through that area where the barricades were put up last May ("beneath the paving stones there was only mud," as one disillusioned activist put it), the chief reminder is that those who displaced these stones were not the ignorant and wild inhabitants of 1789, thronging from the Faubourg St. Antoine, but a more pampered class, driving to demonstrations in their father's cars, and then—according to one student—"going home to a late supper"!

Back at the hotel there are the already familiar red damask curtains, the rapid-fire gossip of the girl at the switchboard so that it is impossible to put in a call, the locked bathroom which must be opened by the femme de chambre, the difficulties (as if it had been New York City) of bypassing Nescafe for real *café au lait*. The manager, in his stiff-looking black coat, speaks familiarly about "Pom Pom." (He is a man of culture, this Pompidou, he likes modern painting, he has published a study of Taine, he is supposed to be working on a novel.) "But he is a man of stern business also" the manager says, "like *les Anglo-Saxons!*"

The American woman who runs into me in the passage upstairs asks whether it is true that the students tried to "break into the Louvre last year to do away with the pictures"? Her tone is shocked (rather as if the students at Columbia had not destroyed manuscripts, records, books, laboratories, and glass doors). There is some attempt to explain that this particular kind of destruction is in emulation of Mao's Red Guards, who broke up ancient Roman and Chinese vases, and statues of the Venus de Milo ("demons and monsters of the old ruling class"), in other words, it was not for enjoyment only—although it was evidently enjoyable—but in order to humiliate and bring down the old society, and make room for the new.

"But that's *wrong!*" Her face is a little pink and she clutches her towel and toothbrush fiercely, as if all the world were in support of the students.

Of course it's wrong. . . .

Finally she says, "If they go on acting that way, it sure will destroy the tourist trade"!

The political officer at one of the colonial embassies comments that such student behavior would naturally make little sense to a Middle Western lady who'd come to see the Louvre. He is tall and sandy-haired, and except for his broad accent himself gives somewhat of a "Middle Western" impression.

"On home ground," he drawls, "it's more serious stuff. In the democratic countries, it's part of the theater of the absurd." Then he adds that the characters in the U.S. wearing combat boots and with red hairbands over their foreheads confront a state which is extremely reluctant to use force against them.

About the French students he is more sympathetic. "The alienation and competition here in Paris is more intense than in the huge U.S. degree factories. If you don't do well here, you are thrown out on your tail."

"And of course," the political officer goes on, "to add to this reality, the student must speak for someone other than himself—so he speaks for these Third-World workers, for 'the people' . . You know how Michelet loved 'the people'. For the intellectual it is an old love. Yet who speaks for 'the people,' either of the United States or the Third World, or the USSR, or even of China? In fact, who *are* 'the people' and who *is* the 'worker'? In the Marxian sense a farmer planting his potatoes and looking after his cow is not a worker. The overzealous German students got short shrift when they tried to identify with factory workers. . . ."

And is it true that the Maoists directed the upheaval here, is it true that, as Raymond Aron says in *Encounter*, they had self-criticism sessions on TV? And that one lecturer called Western society rotten, and announced that "the weapon of our salvation is being forged elsewhere, in Sinkiang"?

"Oh yes, indeed . . . it was all very Maoist. There were assemblies where participatory democracy was the thing, where the voting was by a show of hands, with a lot of shouting and bullying from the cadres. Resolutions were pushed through, there was a real attempt to gain control of all the organizations. You ask about outside manipulation. . . . Well, the Trotskyists were very active, surprisingly. Then for the specific pro-Chinese groups, May 1968 was their debut. But who knows when the groundwork had been laid?" (According to police reports, French Communist couriers were arrested at the Swiss border early in the sixties with large bundles of dollars from the Red Chinese Ambassador in Berne; dollars which were to be used for Maoist organization and propaganda in France.)

Later in the afternoon, on the corner of the Boulevard Brune, where the pale facade of the buildings seems to be sunk in some mood of autumn. ("Soon we will plunge into the old shadow," Baudelaire said, "goodbye vivid clearness of our short summers.")

Yet this is no longer the Paris of Baudelaire; understanding as he might have been of the characters of his time, and resistant of the leveling which now tends to flatten all distinction. It is not even the "Babylon" of Scott Fitzgerald, the home of vast hangovers and mad pranks at dawn. Nor indeed is it the Paris of Hemingway's *Moveable Feast*—especially the feast of good wine and good bread for reasonable prices, of incredibly cheap cafés such as La Pêche Miraculeuse. Or even the Paris of sitting for hours in quiet over a single *cafe-crème* without the distraction of hasty waiters and the odor of gasoline. It is another Paris where those in the know speak in Third-World terms, where the flotsam and jetsam of France's disintegrated empire rise to demand retribution for the past; where as in all capitals of the West defectors have told of networks of saboteurs waiting to destroy vital installations; where skillful subversive advantage is taken of the existence of old cultural bonds such as those between Rumania and France, and France and Senegal; where young agents of businesses like Air France have been forced into turning in to the Russians detailed resumes of their compatriots' activities. It is, moreover, a city in which a simple but crooked-minded American sergeant, Robert Lee Johnson, could with astonishing ease manage to penetrate the little concrete vault at Orly, vital fortress holding top secrets relevant to the security of NATO and the United States. (And it is a world in which this same sergeant could make what in these days of the voracious media is an up-to-date suggestion. When accompanied by his prostitute wife he stood in East Germany in front of the KGB and was asked what he could do to help them, this not-too-bright Johnson insisted innocently, "I can make propaganda, give press conferences, go on radio, stuff like that.")

Such reflections dramatize our leveling age, an age in which discrimination gives place to affluence and mediocrity, in which the "international" hopes of the nineteenth century are pushed out of place by the dogmatic thrust of the ideologues of the twentieth, in which the tentative slaughters of the past give place to vast heaps of dead (made of sometimes numbered, but often nameless, victims). And as James Gregor, professor of political science at Berkeley put it, "The twentieth century witnesses the ... appearance of the revolutionary mass-mobilizing totalitarian movement."

Again, in our polarized world, the Western intellectual tends to concentrate upon his or her own middle-class milieu. Bruno Bettelheim, the psychiatrist, writing in *Encounter*, views the student sympathetically. He sees deep-seated psychological reasons for student rebellion, and suggests that the young in America hide what really ails them, that there is a current feeling that youth has no future, that technology has made them obsolete. He asks what dissenting youth has in common all around the globe. In Germany there is no Negro problem, in Japan no Vietnam, in Italy and France no one threatens to make nuclear war—the one thing shared is that "all are against the Americans" (this presumably because of the magnitude of their military establishment, and especially the "Bomb"). "But," Bettelheim states, "the Soviet Union has an even larger standing army, relies just as much on atomic weapons, not only represses small nations, but grants her population, including her young people, considerably less freedom—why then the concerted anger against the United States?" And he deduces that the real reason for this rebellion is psychological; that America has so developed the technology which robs the student of an effective role, that the excess of anger is directed towards America. Although this analysis has truth in it—it also downgrades, as do many other analyses, the intense activism of various left-wing radical establishments, those of the smaller Trotskyist and anarchist movements as well as those of Moscow and Peking—which during the sixties and by and large successfully, attempted to influence global youth. If it is true that the "affluent" are hungry for the "reality" of action, it is all the more true that the less youth is forced to grapple with uninteresting reality, the more it is drawn to the drama of the radical-offered public stage. The greater the desire of both major Communist parties, Russian and Chinese, to drive the United States out of Asia, and the more careful the scenario provided as a background for student radicalism, the more likely it is that the students should perform against this scenario, many of them not aware of who provided it, who paid for it, and to what extent their action in it is directed.

Bettelheim is rather incautious. "As I write," he says, "the presidents of three American universities—Michigan, Brandeis, San Francisco State—agree that if the war in Vietnam were to end tomorrow, it would do little or nothing to end student revolt." (In other words, the revolt is self-motivating, and comes from inner needs? Therefore it will continue when the ostensible cause is removed?) It is too early to claim that this prophecy is unlikely, that once the United States is out of Vietnam, and the Communists have gained their aim, the committed activists will relax and there will be, quite logically, a lull in the unrest and a rearrangement of priorities. There is a good chance that this is how it will go. Neither does Bettelheim allow for the fact that schools and universities (as well as ghettos and minority areas—for instance, the city of Newark) are definite targets for the reactivated political youth groups, and become playgrounds in which militant blacks and minorities, due in any case for revolt, can try out their powers—getting advice and aid first through their contemporaries, then through Cuban and other agents in the United Nations; and afterwards broader aid through trained terrorists.

There is nothing mysterious about all this. It has been a pattern since political internationalism was first defined, and since the Young Communist Leagues first sent their representatives to Moscow to form the Young Communist International. (The Communist student movement today is embodied in the International Union of Students, or the IUS, which has its headquarters in Prague, Czechoslovakia. And from these headquarters have gone out directives over the years, ranging from the order to support Castro in the Missile Crisis to the order to put the Youth Movement behind the Arab confrontation with Israel, and the Black Militant provocation of the 'White' U.S. establishment.)

What is noticeable in the 60s is the priority given by the major Communist powers to recruiting youth in Africa and Asia. The blatant use of race as well as the numbers of scholarships handed out have been the key to a certain success. Trained activists from Patrice Lumumba, for instance, or from the Cuban training schools have been noticeable at all the Youth Congresses—manhandling rival delegates, manipulating the agenda, railroading pro-Russian resolutions through the Conferences, organizing against the opposition (the rare Iron-Curtain refugees, the children of Jewish extermination camps, the young Chinese who have swum the Pearl River), and declaring boldly, as did a Cuban delegate at Helsinki in 1962, "We are here to teach the Africans and Asians how to conduct Revolutions." Among these junior activists—scarcely young in years but brought up in the Youth Movement—the new graduates of the Prague training schools stand out: Sekou Touré of Guinea, Lionel Soto, a Cuban graduate of Prague's Revolutionary Instruction Schools, and the Puerto Rican Communist, Narciso Rabell, permanently in Prague as a member of the IUS Secretariat. Then as a forerunner of the savage hatred being cultivated in Africa, there are such men as a Sudanese who screamed out "Fascist" at a harmless Portuguese observer sitting in the gallery at Helsinki; and when reproved afterwards said, "If you people don't like the way we act, we will have to kill you."

The vehemence of the times is pointed up by public pronouncements—for instance, a Red Guard poster hung onto the gate of the Soviet Embassy in August of 1966 states without equivocation, "When the moment comes, we will tear the skin from you, rip out your guts, burn your bodies, and throw the ashes to the winds."

Rhetoric or not, the Maoist influence among the French students, and in other Western countries, makes Chinese contributions to the technique of human control particularly interesting. These show how quickly the forced cultivation of violence, and familiarity with the corruption of power, distort scarcely formed characters. (If political revolutions tend in many cases to "manipulate" the young, the so-called Cultural Revolution may be without precedence in the coercing of millions of immature human beings.) Refugees in Hong Kong and Taiwan and those few who managed to reach the United States (including a well-known musician interviewed in Philadelphia, alias Sison Ma) give a clear picture of the criticism, violent attack—both verbal and physical, not to mention the outright use of torture—visited upon those who, for the sake of the struggle, were called "old party elements," "revisionists," "conservatives," "class enemies," "capitalist roaders," or "the Black Gang."

Students have described being forced to attack their teachers (to humiliate them by putting dunce caps on their heads, dirty brooms in their hands, hanging pails filled with rocks around their necks, beating them, making them walk barefoot over rocks, glass, and so on). The "activist" gang for this work was generally helped by the school bullies, and when the atmosphere was set up, students were encouraged or coerced into taking part—although there are accounts of the more sensitive students fainting or running away in tears. One student describes nightmare regrets after seeing a favorite teacher beaten to death. He quotes, in a general explanation, the comment of one of the work teams: "It is a small matter to beat someone to death, but it is very important to conduct revolution."

Gradually, students became insensitive, felt proud of themselves, learned to love being "unyielding" and to take pleasure in "subduing." Some began to advocate the use of torture, others were for mental torment, threats, and blackmail; still others were for using a combination of the "strong" and "soft" approaches. (According to Mao, ". . . we must begin by administering a shock and shouting at the patient, 'You are ill,' so that he is frightened into a sweat, and then we tell him gently that he needs treatment.") A young student who at first had been profoundly indignant at his role soon began to theorize on how to obtain responses from the prisoners. In short, he began to see himself as a "specialist," a judge and manipulator of human beings.

In letters from the ex-prisoners of Castro, which are still catching up with me, and in the countless notes taken from interviews, there are also interesting details about Cuba which reflect upon the general question of human subjugation. José Prado explains why submission to Castro's regime had become of such overriding importance. "The main point is to incorporate dissenters into the victorious Communist state," he argues. "Cuba has lost most of her professionals and she needs young talented men. But there is also a compulsive inheritance from earlier Communist regimes, the Russian, the East European, the Chinese. Our treatment during the bad years of the Isle of Pines seemed based on Pavlov's theory of the conditioned reflex (as well as some of Mao's theories). We in Cuba benefitted by coming later. . . . They would start to beat you, or someone near you would be beaten, and you would wonder when your turn would come. Gradually you became fearful; when someone was nice to you, you were inordinately grateful . . . it has often been called the hot and cold treatment. Some corporal would be beating you up and then the political man would appear and say 'What happened, *hermano?* Why are they beating you? . . . What? Well, that's bad. . . . Why don't you arrange to rehabilitate?'"

(This alternation of kindness and brutality is familiar to all students of Communist affairs. George Watts, a British technician imprisoned as a spy in China, recounts being kept on tenterhooks, with punishment continually deferred. He describes his interrogator lunging at him with a knife and wounding his hand, and then saying smilingly "Sorry, so very sorry, it was accident.")

Prado explains that in the Cuban prisons the political prisoners developed their refusal to wear the blue uniform to a fine art. "It had to be the blue uniform or nothing. I was kept naked for seventy-two days in Piñar del Rio and without a shower—and also for ten months naked with a dozen others in a cell in March at Camp Five and a Half. With the chill of winter and the poor food I lost seventy pounds." Gregorio Garcia Huet describes spending seventy-two days naked in a G2 cell in the dark, without plate or spoon to eat his meals, which were thrown in to him as food would be to an animal.

In Cuba, the Directorate General of Penal Establishments, under the control of the Ministry of the Interior, is in charge of all penal facilities and has three subordinate departments. Part of the Directorate itself is the Department of Scientific Application, which is concerned with indoctrination and the possible conversion of counter-revolutionaries. This year it is supposedly under the charge of a psychiatrist who is president of the Medical College of Cuba. A long-time Communist, he had been sent to the Soviet Union for special training in brainwashing techniques. José Arenal, a Cuban journalist, writes that when he himself was being interrogated (May of 1964), a Dr. Montes, a former Austrian and naturalized Cuban who had spent some time in Russia, Poland, and East Germany, played a prominent role in this department, apparently doing experiments on how to produce timidity.

"The sinister thing," Arenal writes, "was that . . . we knew about those who refused to be rehabilitated rotting down there in the solitary, walled-in completely dark cells . . . we knew that before a man could be re-made he must be partially destroyed!"

There is more than one dimension to this altering of man's nature. During the sixties I seem to have been traveling through what Lewis Feuer calls "a neo-Marxist period." While there has been vociferous acclaim for Lenin, Trotsky, Mao, Fidel, Ché, Marcuse, Ho Chi Minh, and now Kim Il Sung, talk of Abraham Lincoln or Robert Owen, or John Stewart Mill or Ralph Waldo Emerson has been correspondingly scarce. While revolutionary morals have regressed, neo-Marxist action and propaganda have spread via technological efficiency, there has been no hesitation on the part of the new ideologues to applaud political terror.

But the picture is deceptive. Behind the screen of action, the extremists present their complex and often tortured personalities. If they are rebels, they are often rebels with sensitivity for the future. Having squeezed every droplet of discontent (to use Lenin's phrase) from their own lives, they have added it to the world's torrent; and this psychological need for change has acted upon them until they themselves are changed. "I came at a time of upheaval," Brecht said, "I ate between battles, I slept among murderers. I was careless in loving, and I looked at nature without patience."

Here in the white-tiled subway riding to Madeleine, Opéra, Gare St. Lazare, Villier, Pt. Clichy, Blanche Anvers, and finally Barbés Roche chouart—the cultivated barbarism of totalitarianism seems far away. But one is close all the same to the Third World; and where the station is built up above the criss-cross of streets, two dessicated-looking Arabs in white gowns are waiting for the next train. This is an area of down-and-outers, where many of the underdogs of Paris hide away, the poor immigrants from Martinique, Haiti, French Guiana; sharing a neighborhood, so to speak, with some of the French-speaking Arabs from Morocco and Algiers.

On one side of the street near the subway there is Le Luxor and Le MiniGrill. On the other, the Société pour l'Extension de l'Artisanat Antillo-Guyanas. "We are French Colonials," the rather pretty executive secretary of the organization tells me. She has warm shiny skin and is elegant in a short blue dress with frills. "Here the people of the West Indies can come with problems of work. We are obliged to help, we have nossing else to do."

She explains that the organization tries to be practical. "We follow lessons in French and English. I am both 'steno' and 'teacher.' We also have a professor of French." She indicates a neatly-dressed, golden-skinned young man who has now appeared.

He does not speak English; she explains that he is there to "control the Association." She translates, "He says that the immigrants always arrive with problems of work and problems of house. Two great problems! We have many Algerians here in Paris and many French-speaking Africans. There are many men living alone . . . also a problem. We are mixed and therefore there is no race complex."

The president disappears for a few moments and the secretary allows herself to become confidential. "I have come here to Paris with my husband who worked for a radio company." She smiles. A deep dimple cuts into her cheek. "Yes—he married me in Martinique and I was obliged to follow him to France. But he has left me eight years ago." She pauses. For a moment one remembers that the problems of *la Politique* are as nothing compared to the problems *de l'être humain.* "There are ten years that I have been in Paris," she goes on wistfully. "Now I am adapted. But during the first years I have many nostalgias. . . ."

The president is back again and gestures with thin brown hands to explain that more and more West Indians, Guyanese, Moroccans, Algerians, and other French-speaking Africans come to Paris; that there is a harking back to a known culture. (There is a quick image of Paris as a center of a one-time empire, reigning over the largest part of North America—Canada and Louisiana, not to mention Antigua, Barbados St Kitts-Nevis, St Lucia and St Vincent—now shrunken to Guadaloupe and Martinique, French Guiana, land of leprosy and *libérés,* this leaving out the nineteenth century acquisitions, Madagascar, Algeria, Morocco and Tunisia.)

Someone turns the dial on the record player. In the background the shadow of a thin man begins to dance in a kind of obsession with movement: the inimitable loose-hipped Negro movement, a head thrown back and tossed forward, the face a mask. "He likes music," the secretary indicates first the president and then the record player. "He founded the Association to receive music." The president bends his head modestly, standing in front of the dancing man—the executive twin of this sensuous shadow. "But he does not only want dancing," the secretary went on. "That is a West Indian problem, that of dancing! He sees that there are many other possibilities we have, many other techniques we must gain."

"*Il n'y a pas de problème de race*," the president declares suddenly. The secretary with an ironic smile upon her lips (she has certainly heard this before) translates. "In France now there are no racial problems. There is *perfect* acceptance." She doubles up with laughter and asks mockingly, "But . . . while they are polite and equal, what goes on behind our backs?"

And another young man looks up from nowhere, his blackish monkey-like face tipped in our direction. He makes the scene a little more complicated. "People of the West Indies," he whispers wisely, "can buy the French with a bottle of rum." Everyone laughs.

Today in the *cité*, cradle of modern revolution, September sunshine illuminates the via dolorosa of history, that route followed by the tumbrils which during the Terror lurched out of the Cour du Mai of the Palais de Justice over the Pont Neuf, across the Quai de Louvre, and into the rue St. Honoré. The carts carried their loads of men and women with hands bound behind their backs, and what was sardonically called '*la toilette*' already performed (that is their collars cut open and their hair clipped at the back of the neck—this to make it easier for the executioner). The Place de la Révolution (the Place de la Concorde) shows the usual traffic, the usual parked cars, the monument and fountain, those physical boundaries which bring back the confusions of the victims. (There is Charlotte Corday, young, beautiful, and unduly influenced by the ideas of "Roman nobility," standing tranquilly in the cart in the red chemise of the murderess; Danton with his great head and scarred face; Camille Desmoulins holding a locket of his wife's hair; and so an unending flood of former aristocrats, former revolutionaries, priests, servants, soldiers, clerks, workmen, prostitutes—until at last Robespierre himself, his jaw broken by a pistol shot, carted off after hours of suffering, only to shriek like a desperate animal as the brutal executioner snatches away the temporary bandage supporting his chin. . . . His head, too, falls under the blade.)

From the haunts of the Third World to the Café de la Rotonde in

Montparnasse, with Julian Gorkin. He is a smallish man, intense, emotional, humorous—his hair greying, his skin ivory-colored (there is a little pulsing scar in his forehead). For all of his life Gorkin has been a writer and activist associated with the Left. He wrote for *Le Monde* long ago under the direction of Henri Barbusse, Romain Rolland, and Maxim Gorky. He translated Gide, Trotsky, and other writers. He published more than fifteen books—novels, history, criticism, political essays. He was, at the age of sixteen, already a "revolutionary."

We sit drinking wine, trying to hear each other above the noise of the traffic and the tattoo of commands from a nearby military school. "The terrible problem for the Communist is to believe in community, and in the ideals of the primitive Christian, and then to find all this incompatible with actuality. I still feel nostalgic about that period of my life—so noble, so romantic! Yet I soon began to understand the reality of Russia, the *centralismo*, the totalitarian power, and my dreams collapsed. . . ."

Does he think that the essential cause of such disillusionment is the certainty of the ideologue; is it this which lies at the root of the failure of countless visionary experiments?

"The root cause is Marxism itself," Gorkin says. "What rigidity here." He quotes Stalin, who imagined that to find the right orientation in any situation it was necessary only to be a Marxist, that Marxism could discern the future trends of all current events. "The Marxist ideologues are overconfident."

We talk for a time about what kinds of men and women the French revolutionaries were. (Marat, the man whom Charlotte Corday killed, was often described as behaving like a man demented. Michelet says of Marat that "the sudden transition from a life of study to 'revolutionary action' affected his brain—he, who was unable to see an insect suffer, alone with his pen and ink would annihilate the earth"; and Michelet adds, "This doctor without a patient would take France for his patient and would 'bleed' her!")

"The problem is exaltation," comments Gorkin.

And do we have this same "exalted radical certainty" in Havana?

"Well, Fidel thought he must make everything new" (Gorkin, because of his Spanish origin, is in touch with Cuban exiles). "Although Cuba's food production diminished for a dozen years after he took over the country. Various groups were paid to come and examine the earth of Cuba. Several agriculturalists advised against the wholesale changes in crops that Fidel suggested, but they weren't listened to. The comment was that 'they give this advice because they are bourgeois. So Fidel continued to make his mistakes, to grow the wrong things in the wrong places. These ideologues want socialism to change the very quality of the *earth!* As for Fidel himself, he was hard to find. René Dumont had to look for him everywhere! *Dia y noche sin contacto con su oficina* . . . better he has no office . . . better to listen to him talk for five hours on TV—that's *democracia directa!"*

He takes several quick swallows of wine and leans back refreshed. "Ah, you see what revolutions are like? Cuba is one big concentration camp! The USSR sets the norms. The workers have to work twelve hours for the wages of eight hours. Plus *los dias voluntarios* . . . Yes I agree, revolutionaries become drunk with words. The Jacobins as well as the Cubans. If you could read the speeches which took place far into the night at the convention, as indeed you have read the speeches of Fidel Castro. Words upon words upon words. It is the great problem of our times, the *mystification* of ideas: the youth are made drunk. There is no end to lies, so there is no boundary to beliefs. Did you read the fantastic declarations of Kuznetsov when you were in England? How he had to write out his *mea culpa* at the order of the Association of Writers. This, then, is the use to which the Russians put the creative imagination."

Before we part we talk of a woman who is living in Paris now, but incognito—Caridad de Mercader, the mother of Roman de Mercader, who was known as Frank Jacson, the final and successful assassin of Trotsky in Mexico. This somber woman (described by a former member of the Central Committee of the Spanish Communist party, Enrique Castro Delgado, who managed to get out of Russia after 1944, as "tremendously attractive")—had played a directive role in the Trotsky murder along with her lover Leonid Eitingon; and after it was clear that her son had been caught inside Trotsky's house, she escaped by car to Vera Cruz and thence to Russia. Enrique Castro Delgado said that she had told him then, as they both waited out their time of reward in Moscow, that there was only one last voyage she wanted to make—and that was out of the socialist paradise. They had forced her, she said, to make a murderer of her son, and they had given her a medal for it!

Back at the hotel. Reading *The Bridge and the Abyss* by Bertram Wolfe, that fascinating double portrait of Gorky and Lenin which analyzes Lenin's attempt to do what never had been done before (i.e., to make the Russian people conform to his will, to use them as material for an experiment, to "plough to its depths and turn upside down the variegated, lumbering, lazy human antheap called Russia.")

"He (Lenin) is almost completely lacking in interest in the individual human being," Gorky points out, "he thinks only in terms of parties and programs." [In Wolfe's portrait Gorky states that more people were killed under Lenin than under Wat Tyler or Garibaldi. He says that a Frenchman once asked him; "Do you not find that Lenin is a guillotine that thinks?" Here was a man, a dedicated revolutionary, set upon professedly humane tasks and speaking of kinship with the oppressed—who emulated Peter the Great (*"our task is to learn state capitalism from the Germans, taking it over with all our might, not sparing dictatorial measures, to hasten its adoption the more completely just as Peter hastened the adoption of Westernism by barbarous Russia, not stopping short of barbarous methods in the struggle. . . .").*]

In the name of a messianic mission, a small band of fanatics had seized power in Russia fifty years earlier. Had it been necessary, because of this vision, for a generation to go through famine, civil war, forced collectivization, forced industrialization, concentration camps, cultural dictatorships and blood purges? This is the question asked by Brian Crozier in his "Conflict Studies", a question which he answers by pointing out that in that half-century great things had been achieved by the Russians, but no more than other nations had achieved without such grandiose crimes. ("They had not abolished unemployment, they had merely not paid unemployment benefits. They had not abolished crime and hooliganism; they had merely proclaimed that such things were not possible in a socialist society. Whenever the economy had run into difficulties, bourgeois and capitalist devices—reluctantly adopted or merely tolerated—had rescued it.")

In the streets of Paris, where the crowds of strangers luxuriate in the late summer warmth, it is hard to remember the mad extremes of which human beings are capable.

The French Revolution had hardly begun before a heavy-handed censorship was introduced. According to historians, all of Molière was banned, and most of Voltaire was altered. Actors and writers were denounced and marched off to prisons. Ducis, when asked to write a tragedy, replied that he didn't know why he should, when he could be up to his ankles in blood simply by stirring out of his house. Only inspired revolutionary music was played at the Opera, and coercive group activities were frequently held where all were expected to fling their arms around each other, and join in songfests. In Russia more than one hundred twenty years later the melancholy story of censorship continued without a break. A tremendous propaganda machine was brought into existence. The classics were censored. There was an unparalleled effort to politicize everybody and everything. Lenin put his wife Krupskaya in charge of the "Removal of Anti-Artistic and Counterrevolutionary Literature from Libraries serving the Mass Reader"—that is, the forbidding of the reading of Plato, Kant, Schopenhauer, Taine, Ruskin, Nietzsche, Tolstoy, and other heretics. As Gorky said, "It stuns the mind!" And the story of course does not end here. An even more potent and total attempt was made under Mao Tse-tung in China, in this case not only to control the content of the citizen's head, but to change it (in other words, to wash out what was in it before and put in something else instead).

Nor is modern revolution safe until religion is control. The militant, anti-Christian movement which issued in the French Terror (at first priests were simply despised, then if they refused to take the oath of allegiance they were butchered, and later many were formally guillotined) has been echoed under the Bolsheviks, under Mao, in Eastern Europe, in Cuba—and is extending itself at this moment with help from Russia in the war against the Christians in parts of Africa, a war considered necessary for the extension of the power of the Moslem (and/or neo-Marxist) regimes.

Day by day interchange in the hotel in the rue de Lille stresses how propaganda proliferates in this twentieth century global mishmash.

In that slightly pitying manner which is sometimes adopted towards Americans these days, various French citizens, including the hotel manager, make references to a book current in Paris *L'Amérique Brûle* (America Burns, called in its English edition *Farewell America*). This book may seem to have little to do with memories of various beheadings on the Place de la Concorde or with that *liberté* which was smothered in the octupuslike embrace of those inspired by dreams of perfection.

It is the European version of "unprincipled" works which flooded the market after John Kennedy's assassination. It presents somewhat the same story—that the whole American power structure was responsible for the assassination, that numerous prominent persons had "guilty knowledge" of the "plot," that the American underworld, the segregationists, the military, the Texas oil interests, the Federal bureaucracy, and naturally the FBI, all had a hand in seeing that popular President Kennedy should be done away with. No new evidence is produced; and the text is heavily dependent upon discredited suppositions already published.

Yet in tune with the times, and as part of that current complex of anti-American feeling, compounded first of Communist propaganda, then of liberal imitation, and finally of general disdain towards the one country in the West that has tried, perhaps mistakenly, to stand in the way of the advance of totalitarianism—the French seem to get considerable satisfaction from the book's mere publication. (All this is a reminder that a good deal more than naiveté goes to feed the diversity of views on the Kennedy assassination. We even find Edmund Wilson, although he was sceptical of Russian propaganda during the thirties and long before many of his colleagues, giving countenance to a writer like Thomas Buchanan.) Some attempt is made to point out to the hotel manager that the book is nothing but a hodgepodge of hints, accusations, suppositions.

"What it says has already been analyzed and dismissed by the Warren Commission, and by distinguished jurists like John Sparrow at Oxford."

"Naturellement," the manager says, throwing up his hands. "It is the *mystere* which concerns us. . . ."

At a time when the United States is still suffering from the assassination of Robert Kennedy, and after a spring during which Sirhan Sirhan's history and motivations have filled the newspapers, there is something particularly repulsive about the kind of readiness shown here in Paris to accept anything at all, provided only that the United States is the target. I try quoting Rivarol ("What is not clear is not French!"), but without effect. Neither the manager, nor the man at the English bookstore, nor a group of students at the Sorbonne wish to countenance the idea of deliberate mystification. (According to the *New York Times,* the book had to be printed in Belgium for a company charted in Liechtenstein, probably created for that very purpose. The secrecy laws and tax exemptions of this little country make it difficult to sue for libel as might happen in other countries, especially in the United States. Again the book was marketed in France by a company that had no other product, and it is being offered in America by a firm in Montreal. French sales have supposedly been high. The point about the whole thing is its phony character. Here is a deliberately "made" book; whether for money or for propaganda is not clear. Again according to the *New York Times,* the author is cited as James Hepburn, and is described in the blurb as an American, born abroad thirty-four years ago, who went to the London School of Economics, was graduated from the "Institute of Political Studies" in Paris, met Jacqueline Bouvier in 1951, first visited the United States in 1960, and twice met Mr. Kennedy that year. In fact, Réné Lamarré, head of *Editions Nouvelles Frontières,* the French Company marketing the book, affirmed in an interview that "James Hepburn" was "actually pretty much a pseudonym" representing a group of European and American researchers.

This is supported by the author's acknowledgments in the book, in which sixteen collaborators in the French edition and eleven in the English are thanked; only first names are given for most of those thanked. These mysterious characters are then listed as living in six countries, including the United States. Mr. Lamarré said the manuscript had been offered to, and rejected by, "practically all" American trade publishers "before it appeared in West Germany and France last summer.)"

Why is this book important? The murder of J.F.K. was the act of a fanatical devotee of the Marxist cause, so fanatical that he followed a pattern not unusual with defectors from Communism (in that they first admire Russia and when that fails them, turn their admiration elsewhere; to China and or Cuba etc.). Before the assassination, Oswald had transferred (or pretended to transfer) his obsession with the Russian Utopia to the Cuban Utopia. This is demonstrated by his concrete actions (listening in faithfully to Radio Havana, subscribing to the

Militant, and trying to start a Fair Play for Cuba committee). He was reading both the *Worker* (Moscow oriented) and the *Militant* (Trotskyist and often critical of Moscow); yet the common denominator of these two papers is their mutual dedication to the cause of Fidel Castro. Unfortunately the Warren Commission did not completely fulfill its task in that it did not assess what effect such reading and listening— actually the only method of absorbing political knowledge open to this "difficult" yet naive "loner"—had upon Oswald's mind. Because of this, and in spite of its thoroughness in other ways, the Commission's report gives little idea of the psychological turmoil which preoccupied the assassin.

The original fear of the U.S. Security services was naturally that Oswald might have been sent on a mission of assassination by the Soviet Union to punish Kennedy for the Bay of Pigs, for the successes of the Missile Crisis, and for his continuing resistance to Castro's fostering of liberation movements in Latin America. (To the discredit of the CIA, the consideration of the assassination of Castro himself by American agents, and the half-hearted attempts made to carry it out, must now be added to this list. At the same time other factors and analyses—the publication of *The Kennedy Assassination* by Albert Newman in 1970; the disclosures in 1975, discrediting to the defector Yuri Ivanovich Nosenko; and other available material in the process of being published—increase the likelihood that Oswald *was* groomed and sent by the KGB for his task.)

This afternoon a typical brief conversation with two students on the river bank about *L'Amérique Brûle.* One clutching an edition of Martin Buber to his worn grey sweater is uncertain of the guilt of the United States in this matter, but is all the same unenthusiastic, especially in his halting English, about defending her: "We know . . . we must cognate . . ." his grey eyes gaze far out over the water, "we are likely to be dubious. . . ."

But since it is very clear that Lee Harvey Oswald was profoundly influenced by the Communist faith, that regardless of some disillusionment with the situation in Russia, he then tended to transfer his allegiance to Cuba. Considering this, and considering the contents of Sirhan Sirhan's notebooks, isn't it logical that these two murders should be put down to the inner ideological situations of the young assassins, rather than to the American "Establishment"?

The other student is gazing at me with sudden interest. His wide dark eyes grow wider and he puts his head on one side. "Ah, so you make a case"? he asks.

Isn't it rather a question of a logical approach?

"Ah, *la logique!* Tell me, are your military so logical? Your mafia, are they logical? Your oil men—is *la logique* for them, too"?

Surely these business-like people are more logical than students who have read *L'Amérique Brûle!*

Like a terrier he is about to spring up from the grass, but thinks better of it. In a tone of some despondency (perhaps he had not been quite so convinced by the book after all) he announces; "I do not make my mind only upon *L'Amérique Brûle,* but on many things."

Here in Paris what takes shadowy form (in juxtaposition to Africa) is not so much the familiar Third-World syndrome as the fact that the peoples' liberation movements in the great continents to the south, the east, the west, represent a type of Communist grouping *other than* the traditional parties. These movements (according to Gregory Almond's sociological study *The Appeals of Communism*) are the more threatening because they can appeal to deep and bitter "Anti-white-Western-imperialism." These parties, Almond thinks, will be particularly susceptible to violence and civil war. There are already signs that the resultant suffering may be immense.

Peoples' revolutionary war, as Crozier has pointed out, may involve guerrilla action, but is essentially political and social, with aims more ambitious than those of partisan war. Guerrilla war, in other words, is *included* in revolutionary war; but revolutionary war aims at the complete destruction of the enemy's administration and the undermining of the society in which both operate. Even in the U.S. slums the quick and shallow growth of Maoist concepts blended with the trappings of black nationalism had not been attractive to watch. And if the kind of attack foreshadowed in all-out revolutionary warfare would certainly not be likely to be decisive in a country as strong as the United States, such warfare still might pay off by playing a psychostrategic role. Moreover, in a country where the population includes so many minorities, a peoples' war, or a variant of such a war, could be used as a political tool, giving ample room for the utilization of neurotic hostility by minority leaders. (A recent letter from Jasmin talks about guerrilla groups forming in U.S. prisons and the training they get, and of how if they don't join the Panthers they go into the underground forces. "... And when the time comes you won't find them on their knees praying ... they're readin' *Das Kapital* an' the little *Red Book*"). At all events problems not forseen face Americans.

On the way to the subway. Women pass by carrying shopping baskets, vivid lipstick outlining the wide mouths in their bony brown faces. "*Oui ... Mais oui ...*" one of them says repeatedly. She pauses with her friend at the window of a shop where there are cheap silks, shawls, gauzy materials in brilliant colors, beaded velvet shoes. In another shop a competent French woman is measuring shocking pink satin against the length of a tall agile black girl who seems ready to break into a dance.

In the rue des Isettes the Arab population seems more pervasive yet, the buildings shabbier. In a dirty doorway of what looks like a rundown hotel two men stand in turbans, long wool coats and sandals; their eyes have a dull clouded look. A boy runs by, furtively, a radio under his arm. There is a gloomy-looking entrance to the Public Baths. And at the corner, men standing around seem perennially idle and ugly with disease. An African appears particularly dark against the yellow and ivory of the others; a dreadful pink scar stretches the swollen black skin of his jaw, extends down his neck to his shoulder, and disappears where his shirtless chest is covered by a jacket. An Arab boy of twelve or so stands near him, occasionally clutching his arm.

Today the wandering journalist can arrive in a foreign country and find repeated with astonishing faithfulness a social situation seen only hours before in his own. A conversation begun in one capital can be continued in another. The concerns of a magazine (read and abandoned in the train in Europe) can be duplicated a few hours later (in another magazine, in another language) in Africa or Asia.

In this telescoped world new ways of warfare loom up before us, as revolutionary in their way as gunpowder once was. Brian Crozier points out in his renowned surveys that the study of conflict is in its infancy, that an insurrection may "throw up a leader" previously unknown; but that in most cases, there would not have been an insurrection unless a rebel had willed, plotted, and planned for years that there should be one.

Is rebellion in some degree a biochemical factor, Crozier asks? Is there an X-factor in rebels? And with this question a whole field of other questions is uncovered, questions having to do with heredity, intelligence, sexuality, energy, emotional predispositions, control mechanisms. These are part of a study field as wide as it is deep. It is seen that personal problems, resentments, ambitions, spur action. "They make me feel injustice," Madame Roland complained of the aristocrats of Versailles, when she visited there as a young girl. "Here I am now at the top of the ladder!" exulted Camille Desmoulins to his father. "At last I began to breathe in the hope of seeing humanity revenged," Marat said on the occasion of the Invocation of the Estates General, "and myself installed in the place which I deserve."

Emotional and physical pains are stimulants. Marat suffered from a kind of eczema, Marx suffered from boils, Mao was beaten by his father, Lenin reflected upon his brother's hanging for taking part in a plot to kill the Czar. If these examples seem out of date, what of Frantz Fanon's cancer, Ché Guevara's death wish, the "poor girl" complex of Bernadette Devlin, the early ghetto careers of Malcolm X and Eldridge Cleaver? "Revolution" has the eternity of "art."

What is important is the extent of the sacrifice to be offered up on the altar of social change. Are more generations of rebels, inflated by the hope of Utopia persuaded by Rousseaus and neo-Rousseaus and

Marxists and neo-Marxists that the poor are "noble" and the rich "evil," that the human condition can be alleviated by those who exalt hatred to form the advance guards of those who would, as Aristotle says, "make the perfect the enemy of the good"?

It is scarcely surprising that hopes simplistically held prove disappointing.

In the Ritz bar, in this ambience once associated with adventurous types, it seems highly suitable that an emaciated blonde girl should announce, "It's terrorism which fascinates me."

Why does it fascinate her? Doesn't it make the cost of "making revolution" go up?

The girl (who later turns out to have come from South Africa and is perhaps unaware of her own "nativist" longings!) bats her extraordinarily long eyelashes with the rapidity of a Charlie Chaplin heroine, and glances up and down the bar. "Because it's so *sporty*."

Robert Williams is returning to the United States at a time when the cost of a revolutionary effort is escalating. (Even more effective than the revolutionary "advertizing," "discrediting," "demoralizing," and "provoking" which has been successful in broadening the movement against the authority of government is the concrete kind of terror tactic to which the United States, because of its developed technology, is extremely vulnerable: a few grains of sand, a tiny escape of fuel, inadequate lubrication, a poorly screwed pin, a short circuit—all those little attentions which Robert Williams, holed up in Cuba, suggested to his supporters in American cities.)

In the past three years there has been a gradual escalation of bomb and sniper attacks in the United States (of which the aim in an extreme situation would be to weaken the central offices of authority, i.e. police, firemen, military, etc.). There have also been further threats against highly sensitive buildings and installations, such as police stations, telephone exchanges, water reservoirs, and nuclear plants; and in special cases there have been deaths for selected victims, such as diplomats or CIA or government officials (this so far—unless it be considered that organized activists killed either of the Kennedys or Martin Luther King—has only taken place in other countries—as in the case of the U.S. Ambassador, John Gordon Mein, gunned down in Guatemala, and Army Captain Charles Chandler, shot in Sao Paolo in Brazil: both last year). All through last year the wave of terror in the United States proceeded nonstop with 237 "actions": i.e., fire bombings, sniper attacks, and attacks on police stations. Already the figures suggest that during this year that count will double . . .

1969 / France

In spite of such minor (military) escalations (and if the Australian Geoffrey Fairbairn is right), the importance in the nuclear age of man's mind as "target" cannot be underestimated. Because of this, the "people's revolutionary war" is forcing North Vietnam to cripple in its own people that spirit of the West which it admires, imitates and fears. As today's North Vietnamese fight their battle against the South, two separate and opposed situations operate. On the one hand, the Northern army has been disciplined into a cult of moral superiority, of which it must convince "the people." On the other hand, there is a widespread use of Vietcong terror against those of "the people" who attempt to resist engulfment. This ambivalence springs from the adaptations inherited from the early years of the Communist movement when it was seen that power could not be held without force, and that propaganda about "suffering humanity" and the "will of the masses" and the "upright revolutionary soldier" was therefore more than ever necessary. (Among extracts from the horrendous publicity put out by the NLF for the manipulation of Vietnamese emotions, Douglas Pike quotes this in *Sparkling Fires in the South* by Che Lan Vien: "You have probably heard about the U.S.-Diem troops indulging in cannibalism, disembowelling a man and eating his liver raw.... A young Diemist officer calmly said that cannibalism was hardly a novelty to him, and that although he had never tasted human flesh, all cadets at the [American type] officer's school had eaten human liver ... Without this kind of exaltation of the moral superiority of the North over the South, and especially over the Americans, the terror of the Vietcong would have been insupportable; without coercion and terror, the regimes concerned would not have retained their hold.

Similarly, without clear understanding of this ambivalence which runs through neo-Marxist attempts to take power, some Western opinion-makers find it impossible to admit to the primary nature of the Hanoi situation. This silences the true debate and discourages consideration of important practical considerations. Norman Barrymaine, the British journalist seized by the Communists last year as he traveled to North Korea on a Polish ship in hopes of getting an exclusive Pueblo story, revealed on his release that the war was nearly over when President Johnson, under pressure on the home front, called off the bombing of North Vietnam (see Hong Kong's *China Morning Post*). Again as Douglas Pike suggests in the preface to his excellent study of the Vietcong, the future of the Vietnamese is not an abstraction, and victory by the Communists would mean consigning thousands of them to death, prison or permanent exile. But now as the talks go on in Paris, there seem few speaking for these potential victims; the whole moral question is lost in dehumanized thinking. [Bernard Levin had this to say in the *London Times* on February 2 of 1977: "Even in a century which has gorged itself on atrocities until it has become almost too replete to swallow more, the horrors which accompanied and have followed the fall of Cambodia to the Communists are exceptional both in their peculiar barbaric nature and in the colossal scale on which they have been carried out . . . the capital was simply emptied at bayonet point, of its entire population. Many thousands were exterminated by the Khmer Rouge—not as 'enemies of the people' but in a campaign of indiscriminate terror. . . . So dreadful, so implaccable and so widespread was the carnage that I believe it has even been mentioned in BBC television programs—though not, of course, very often, or in terms which would suggest that those who dismissed as absurd the 'domino theory' during the Vietnam War might have been wrong, let alone that those who worked so assiduously for a Communist 'liberation' of South Vietnam ought to feel troubled in their conscience."]

The political officer contends that terrorism is simply an extension of old instruments of violence, played out in a suitable modern context. I ask him whether he thinks that the U.S. public is enough aware of how terrorism might affect them in the future.

"No, it is not enough aware. . . . The international Communist movements are obviously deeply involved in the recruiting and training of terrorists and guerrillas; yet the U.S. public does not project this into the future. Cuba is here a key factor—a base for arms and training; a jumping-off place for Latin America, Canada, and the United States itself; and since the submission of Castro last year, other parts of the world as well. The key role of Cuba as far as the United States is concerned is proved by Cuban involvement in many parts of the American continent." He counts them off on his fingers. "In supporting the minority movement in Canada; in the wooing and training of young American radicals; in the motivation and directing of militant blacks. As for Latin America, if Ché Guevara's activities were temporarily halted by his death, the real *denoument* is not yet determined.

"It is clear that even in the States itself, continual unrest pays off," he adds. "It is for this reason that I get so irritated by Americans. Day by day the protest movement weakens any resolve to play a determinant role in the Vietnamese situation . . . to gain ground from which freedom might be strengthened."

Midnight in the hotel. The midwestern woman who had come to Paris to see the Louvre is packing to leave tomorrow. The woman whose son was killed in a recent hijacking is still sitting downstairs in the foyer.

Reading in the small rather stuffy bedroom, the essential conflict within the Communist movement is brought alive by a little book containing a vision as pure as that of the early Christians—Angelica Balabinoff's *Impressions of Lenin*, a copy of which has come from Bertram

Wolfe who wrote a foreword for it. This woman was born in Russia in 1878, abandoned her privileged position and lived the life of a political militant and a poor student, in one furnished room after another, with a spirit stove for tea, a small pan for omelettes, a few cups, a few pictures, her notebooks, her ikons. Bertram Wolfe points out that when he visited her in Rome in the early 1960s, she was working at the Headquarters of the Italian Democratic Socialist Party, and as usual without salary.

Angelica was scrupulous, selfless, principled. She spoke half a dozen languages or more; was active in the Russian, German, (in fact all the European socialist movements) and to a lesser extent in the American movement (when Bert Wolfe saw her in a rundown hotel on the West side of New York City, he found her a little unhappy in a city which did not give her the same opportunity for activity as Rome or Moscow, and a little bewildered by the interest of the American "masses" in the World Series). After the fall of the Czar, Lenin (aware of her value to the movement) made this ethical woman the Secretary of his new Communist International. He sent her abroad with instructions to spend millions "many many millions." ("She," says Wolfe "who did not know how to spend more than tiny modest sums, and could not dream that she was to use those millions to corrupt leaders and destroy those who could not be won."). In a discussion of power, Angelica once asked Lenin why notoriously honest people were accused of dishonesty and Lenin answered that to seize power every means must be used. "Even dishonest ones?" she countered. "Everything that is done in the interest of the proletarian cause is honest," was Lenin's answer.

Watching the cruelties continue under the new regime, Angelica finally went to Lenin. "Comrade, there is nothing worse for the regime and for us than to hear that things have not changed, that people are treated as under Czarism: the same police spies, the same methods. Let me work in the prisons, let me save the prisoners and their relatives from tortures, and you from shame, malediction and responsibility." Lenin listened without a word. Finally he said, "You could not resist even a single day among all that anguish. . . ."

Later Lenin looked at her sadly when she protested the senseless cruelties of the *Checka* (the secret police) in the Ukraine. "Comrade Angelica, what use can life make of you?" he asked.

The street outside the hotel is now quiet, and there is that odd light experienced in cities in the very early hours of the morning, a light compounded of the cold electricity in the streets and the distant magical gleam of the moon. In such a light, and at such an hour, Lenin's pragmatic concepts seem as crude and outdated as the great monster machines of the twentieth century which in the name of necessity destroy the complex ecology of the earth.

438

The Luxembourg Gardens spread their subtle charm over the thinning groups in the canvas chairs. The sun is no longer hot: as a corrective there advances the nostalgia of summer's departure.

A couple of young men sitting near by ask to borrow an issue of *Time* magazine, and are glad to accept it as a gift.

"Ah, thank you, Madame."

I ask as I have asked so many students during this visit, "Was the May revolt spontaneous?"

"Ah no, Madame, how can you say it in English? *Le mouvement* takes over."

And was the Chinese model the most popular?

One looks at the other. There is a noticeable hesitation. "For *me*," the older one proclaims, "it was the need for 'breaking up' of stagnation. . . ."

"And there is Cuba," the other student explains in a voice still fresh and eager as if unaffected by all the disappointments since the days of the *enragés*. "We believe that Ché lives!" ("Do the revolutionaries really expect," Professor Aron had asked in *Encounter*, "the bourgeois state to finance a university *à la Cubaine?*")

So Ché lives? Yet it is noticeable, as it had been in Mexico a few months ago, that the image of *Ché* in his uniform and beret, with his eyes on the horizon, appears only on walls in certain cities—in Mexico City itself, in Paris, Berlin, New York, Rio de Janeiro—in other words, in the cities lacking a countryside suitable for guerrilla operations, in the countries pertinent to the struggle against the democratic West. It is not *de rigeur*, for instance, to display the posters of Ché in certain parts of the Communist world, i.e., Moscow, Peking, Warsaw, East Berlin, where he might be a secondary figure, or even viewed, as Peking would say, as "adventurist." (In the *Little Red Book* it is clearly stated, "If we tried to go on the offensive when the masses are not yet awakened that would be 'adventurism.' If we insisted on leading the masses to do anything against their will, we should certainly fail . . .")

According to conversations in Mexico with Daniel James, who is writing Ché's biography, this leader of guerrilla operations had more in common with Trotsky than with Lenin, and was more an idealist than a politician. Here in Paris he seems immensely far from the French students with their European tradition of radicalism. But this is where the contradiction lies; it is easier to dream of fighting in the mountains if you are studying inside the Sorbonne walls or in the once restrained atmosphere of the London School of Economics, or at Columbia surrounded by New York City traffic, than if you are skirmishing on slender rations in hot valleys and on steep ranges. Today youthful indeterminates call themselves 'Maoists' or 'Guevaristas' with equal ease.

1969 / France

The real point is that the image making of *Ché* is mostly for the West; for those innocents who live according to the "unreal media." It is only one more example of churning out "special material" for generous Westerners, who gaze out like would-be adventurers from the still safe fortresses of their libertarian lands.

I am sent a copy of *My Testimony* by Anatoli Marchenko, a book recently smuggled to the West, which gives accounts of Siberian prison life. Nothing in the *Gulag* seems to have changed, not even the horrors of transportation in one of those interminably slow trains with the prisoners sealed into suffocating apartments! One of the interesting things about the book is that Marchenko has a chapter called "The Looney Bin," a description of that section of the camp where those sentenced to long-term psychiatric confinement are kept; and here Marchenko not only meets a friend who had been sent to the looney bin—but on remarking upon the quiet and good behavior of all the prisoners, Marchenko is told by an orderly: "These people are not mad . . . the Serbsky Institute can proclaim as mad almost anyone with even the slightest abnormalities in his psychology—or even completely normal, if that is what the KGB wants." (Special KGB hospitals have been located by Western services in Leningrad, Kazan, Chermyak-hovsk, Minsk, Dnepropetrovsk, Orel, Poltava, and Kiev. Fifteen psychiatric hospitals also maintain a special section for "political" patients.) Marchenko's book (revealing as to the survival of Stalinist methods) acts as a supplement to the other material now surfacing about how the Russians confine their dissidents in special wards for politicals, feed them mind destroying drugs, analyze their behavior, and grope for "scientific controls" subtler, more thorough, and above all "quieter" than those already used. A mad man after all puts himself out of the running. As Pushkin said long ago: "God forbid that I should lose my mind . . . "

The efforts on the part of the state to render intellectual enemies harmless have produced an original use of medical language. According to bureaucratic lingo, intellectual diversity becomes a "split personality," sensitivity to injustice become a "poor adaption to the social environment." Victor Fainberg who was arrested for protesting against the Soviet invasion of Czechoslovakia last year, was attacked by the secret police, had his teeth knocked out, and was put into solitary. When he asked the doctors what "illness he was accused of, he was told, "Your ailment is your dissident way of thinking." Apparently the drugs most often used on dissidents are aminazin, sulfazin, and reserpine. A Canadian psychiatrist, Dr. Norman Hirt, studying the treatment of political prisoners in the Soviet Union, feels that the kinds of drugs given are in their quantity often the equivalent of a chemical lobotomy. Reserpine in big doses causes atrophy of the brain. Dr. Hirt's information comes from eight former Soviet patients and three former Soviet psychiatrists—one of whom had worked for the police and now lives in Israel. Lately it seems that ritalin is being used, which in very large doses causes destruction of the supporting cells in the brain tissue, so that the patient gets the equivalent of a senile dementia.

Although the use of chemical lobotomies against political dissidents is perhaps the final aggression, it should be noted that the system of brainwashing used in China during the Cultural Revolution and before, has also a tremendously penetrative force. [In 1973 a book published here in France threw more light on Red Chinese methods of intellectual control than most of the material so far available. This is a fascinating account of prison life written by Jean Pasqualini under the title *Prisoner of Mao*. Jean Pasqualini whose Chinese name is Bao Ruo-wang, was the son of a Corsican father and a Chinese mother; and he spent seven years in the state labor camp system before he was released in 1964 as a gesture of magnanimity to the French government (in that year recognized by the People's Republic). In the camps a sixteen hour day was not uncommon, and as in the Siberian camps "across the way," the food rations were determined by the work accomplished. Moreover the numbers in the prisons, as estimated by those experts encountered by Pasqualini, were at least as many as sixteen million and perhaps as many as thirty-two million. From these camps, especially those in the far Northwest where the attempt to subdue and bring under cultivation the Manchurian steppes goes on eternally—no one returns. It is a permanent one-way sentence. There are many accounts of "struggle" (that is the process by which Red Chinese dissenters are brought under control) in this book. One such description is that of "struggling" a middle-aged prisoner who sat on a mat with bowed head in the middle of the frozen earth of the courtyard, surrounded by screaming, roaring prisoners; "Down with the obstinate prisoner!" "Confess or face the consequences," "Liar!", "Scum!" "Every time he raised his head to say anything—truth or falsehood, that wasn't our concern—we drowned him with roaring cries." "Is he telling the truth?" howled the cadre. . . . "No!" We all hooted in derisive unison. The struggle continued for three more hours like this and with every minute that passed we grew colder, hungrier and meaner. A strange animal frenzy built within us. I almost think we would have been capable of tearing him to pieces to get what we wanted . . . Our victim finally reached a point where he couldn't bear it any longer. He raised his head and cried out directly at the guards; "Don't waste their time any longer. Punish me according to the regulations." . . . The guards came forward . . . In front of us they hammered home the rivets to his fetters and irons. . . ."

During these last days in Paris, the thought of the United States returns again and again with a certain grateful nostalgia. There is a growing conviction that Western values are the truly revolutionary values based as they are upon a broad and tolerant view of human behavior. If democratic societies have tremendous problems to solve, they at least give breathing space to human beings. This afternoon a final visit to Barbés-Rochechouart. A group of young Americans are giving out literature in the street, most of it in Arabic. One approaches, and gazes with dazzlingly blue eyes. He explains that he belongs to a Christian group composed of three Americans and two Frenchmen. "We believe what is written in the Bible, and we call ourselves *Christians*." He also mentions the Taroe Islands off the north of Scotland, where it seems they hope eventually to make their headquarters. "It is three years since I became a Christian," he says in a far-away voice. "Then I was in school in Indiana, and trying to study philosophy. But soon I found that it was only so many words to me . . . I wanted something better."

The copy of *Decision* which he thrusts forward is in English, and has an article by Billy Graham ("Lost and Refound") and a cover picture of a radiant evangelist holding onto the arm of a timid young convert. "Modern Man," asks the article inside, "does he differ from his ancestors?"

"Are his needs so different?" inquires the tall blue-eyed American pointing to the article.

Perhaps not very different, I agree.

"Man needs health," the voice is gentle and a little clumsy, a backwoods touch in the heart of Paris. "A *well* person does not need a doctor." (It is obvious that he is one of a long line of practical workers, that he is at home here this moment, hopefully cultivating the vine-yards of Barbés-Rochechouart. In spite of the fact that I appear more prosperous than others in this sordid street, and perhaps too willful to be a candidate for his message, he is still wise enough not to assume that I am a hopeless case.)

"God is almighty," he assures, "he opens doors."

It is like a warning. Perhaps the chief error of the rigid political view is that it is so narrow that it cannot fail to be scientifically incorrect. Without opening doors nothing can enter in, and the possibility of the human being remains unknown. "Spiritual need" creates its own politics—as well as its blue-eyed evangelists such as this.

A farewell drink with the officer from the "colonial" embassy, who in deference to several conversational walks around the city has today put on white slacks, a dark jacket, and spotless white sneakers. We cross the bridge near the hotel, walk along the river on the Right Bank, and cross it again further up near Notre Dame. We are discussing the anti-American campaign which permeates the radical movement.

The political officer ruffles his sandy hair. "Since World War II the most skillful Russian and Chinese thought and organization has gone into the radicalization of students, schools for subversion have multiplied and are operating in almost all of the continents (and because of built-in resistance—what Brian Crozier calls a *'pudeur'*—Western intellectuals won't admit to anything that suggests any kind of conspiracy on the part of any Communist powers—even if such conspiracy in its intrinsic form is part and parcel of Leninist theory, and even if conspiracy itself has been an essential element of political maneuvering since long before the Holy Roman Empire).

"For instance," he adds, "here in France both Left and Right have been demanding an end to the American connection. De Gaulle was basically interested in French leadership for Europe. The Communist party was calling for France to withdraw from NATO. The two elements combined to bring about a situation which neither might have supported separately—so that it has been, I think, the same with the great anti-U.S. cry—*à bas les Américains . . . L'Amérique brûle*—and so on . . ."

"But this isn't new," he goes on in a soothing voice. "Certain Americans don't mind, of course; it stimulates their sense of individual worth to find themselves 'accepted' among their country's detractors. I don't think that they realize what a compliment it is that it is considered worthwhile to feed the anti-U.S. bonfire."

It is slightly misty. The reflections in the Seine reproduce the stones of the Cathedral, shifting and dazzling as in an expressionist painting. Two children in dark formal school uniforms pass gravely by, rather as if they are small replicas of priests belonging to a monastic order. We walk over the Pont Neuf. "No, it makes it no better for those who care about America." He recites Mao's *Little Red Book*: ". . . the ultimate target is the United States, stronghold of Imperialism." And Ché Guevara, ". . . the greatest enemy of the human species is the United States of America. . . ." And Chou En-lai: ". . . U.S. Imperialism is the root cause of evils."

Can this kind of campaign along with its appropriate political action go on without eventually being successful? He is slapping his pockets and finds that he is out of cigarettes.

"The thing is that there is an 'inescapable' conflict."

(This word sets up an unpleasant echo in the September evening where along the vista of the street ahead, everything else is pleasant—the brilliance of flowers over a park wall, the rounded corner of a stone house, the lights of a *café* with welcoming tables.) "Yes, *inescapable*," he adds, "it is the great confrontation of our time. It is not simply the West against the East as I see it; but the confrontation between those who support libertarianism as against those who oppose it. Simpleminded Westerners see the necessity for self-determination for the undeveloped countries but do not understand the dialectic of revolution—and heaven knows why they don't understand it by this time. They oscillate between focusing on their own values and on sympathy for the 'oppressed masses.' You can't do that without the power balance shifting. The Communists have developed stern and harsh dictatorships. Both Russia and China are experimenting with human subjugation; who knows what they may turn up in the end?" He shrugs his shoulders. "Will the democracies tend to win out? I don't know. . . ."

The café tables are under a huge chestnut tree. In the twilight the lights hanging in the branches shine onto the green of absinthe in a tiny glass held in the pretty plump ringed hand of a woman in a grey dress. The political officer goes off to buy his cigarettes.

When he returns he says that he is afraid he has been depressing and suggests a movie. But neither of us makes an effort to move. (What film could be more dramatic than what we are talking about?)

It is sunny again. The plane goes in the afternoon. The morning is quite hot. In one of the crowded cafés, a very "American" family is seated—surely the kind of family most to be scorned by adherents of the New Left: a father, a mother, and two children, all of them making their steady way through hamburgers, potato chips, and large ice creams. The mother wears a bright blue linen dress and a blue sweater, with a little blue beanie cap perched on the back of her head. The family looks contented, encircled by a glitter of light, which dances upon the nickel of the chairs, the glasses of golden beer, and the blonde heads of the children.

Around us the grey buildings of the beautiful and balanced city seem to fade into a charmless twentieth century anonymity. Pushing crowds bump into knees of those seated in cafés, gasoline fumes mingle with the aroma of coffee. At once a sensation of sameness, of *dejâ vu*; the hand of technology heavy upon impressionable human beings. Telex brings about an automatic response in the media; the "big business" of revolution produces robot-like political reactions. A well-rehearsed chorus swells from the so-called Underground press (which lies in full view on the stands along with *Life Magazine*, the *London Times*, and *Le Monde*).

"Yes . . . we hate . . . that is we like . . . we love everything which is against America," one student tells me as we chat on the sidewalk.

"We are *anti-American*," a bearded older man explains with the earnestness of discovery. "You are English? No?"

"I am an American; a naturalized citizen."

"Well . . . forgive me . . . we are in general against America."

His qualification suggests that some Americans may be excluded.

"Is he then against Americans, as some might be against Negroes?"

A gleam of doubt touches the eye of the frankest and youngest student. *"Touché,"* he murmurs.

"But we are not against the *blacks*. We are only against the *Americans*. We especially like the Black Panthers."

"Because they are *most* against the Americans?"

"Yes, Yes, because they are *most* against."

EPILOGUE

A record may begin as this one did, simply as the journal of an onlooker caught up in the immediacy of the times. Now more than a decade later, it becomes important, in a sense even imperative, to ask what has happened since 1969, when the last entry was made.

If some of those who speak here have died—John Desmond Bernal, Waldo Frank, Edmund Wilson, Bertram Wolfe—so also have those more celebrated ones who addressed the world in the "collective"— Nasser, and De Gaulle, and Ho Chi Minh, and Mao, and Chou En-Lai. Nor, during a decade which has seen, as no other has, the speed of mass mobilizing communication, and the consolidation of mass urban audiences, can the rest be forgotten: the anonymous ones, broadcasting their views, imposing their emotions, drawing with them a host of those modest men who, as Reck-Malleczewen said, "cling like grapes to the trolleys morning and evening."

To remember the U.S. West Coast in 1964 is to see what effective use has been made of "revolutionary pluralism," and to realize that in 1975 the Americans withdrew from Vietnam more because of dissent and chaos on the home front than because of sheer military inability. When this withdrawal took place it was as if the floodgates had opened. Genghis Khan came not only "with the telegraph," but with troops so trained that they could kill without emotion or doubt. Totalitarianism began seriously to extend its powers and conflicts down through Southeast Asia, consolidating that great swath from Siberia through China and North Vietnam to the rice deltas of the South.

Such a takeover, if thought of at all, had seemed far away during my trip to Mexico in 1965. What had an Asian "People's War" to do with this country south of the border? Yet in Mexico something else, the training and nurturing of terrorists by the Russians, had already begun, and with it the campaign, now so obvious, to forge a "ring of trouble"

Epilogue

for the United States. This Russian-sponsored engendering of terrorism was of course part of the gigantic rivalry, amounting to an undeclared war, which was already extant between the Soviet Union (with its satellites) and the United States. Because unconventional war is the least expensive kind of action to undertake and because, as the Australian Fairbairn explained, the only suitable target in the nuclear age is men's minds, one can see two anti-Western wars being fought side by side—the pragmatic one in which practical gains are made, and in which Cuba and Eastern Europe are catalysts; and the psychological onslaught (i.e. psychostrategy), which seeks to underplay Western doubts about the West's survival.

This strategy has not been found everywhere suitable, of course, nor has it been evenly applied. In Australia, my native land, no overt plans for terrorism were obvious, yet dramas of allegiance were being acted out. When Whitlam came to power there followed the promised turning-away from pro-U.S. dependence toward the Third World. With his government in financial trouble, Whitlam conspired with left-leaning ministers to raise four billion dollars from Iraqi sources. In the ensuing scandal he was dismissed by the Governor General in 1975 for attempted violation of the constitution. But during his tenure, as a horrible example of concessions made to the powerful Soviet Union, a young would-be defector, a Russian violinist called Georgi Ermolenko, was turned over to the KGB.

This was not the only concession to Communist power made by a democracy, for such yielding was taking place all through the West: in the case of the United States, the Pueblo affair, and the agreement to the Soviet ultimatum in the Yom Kippur War. (Although he was not alive to see the Communists opting for heavier stakes, Whittaker Chambers had noted in his book *Witness* that eventually the crucial battle would no longer be fought out between countries, but rather *inside* them.) And the war inside the democratic countries has manifested itself in many ways: in the sharp polarization of opinion, in the escalation of political infighting, in the escalation of terrorist activities, kidnappings, assassinations, bombings, in an absence of balance in the Western media, in an upgrading of espionage against the West, in a constant trade union battle and attempt to sharpen class war, and, finally, in a certain separation from reality.

These in-battles have been accompanied by all the confusion of history in the making. To revisit the agitated North America of the sixties is to see how mysteriously and rapidly that continent reverted to passivity. If, as Andrew Kopkind once admitted in an issue of the *Real Paper*, it had been all "rock and dope and sex and Ho Chi Minh," the euphoric activists at last came to term with their pasts. Joan Baez and Daniel Elsberg made a rather late gesture of even-handedness by visiting the U.N. to protest to the Vietnamese Mission about the postwar treatment of the citizens of the south; but (symbolically) found the door of the Mission locked. Others, too, returned to the unsatisfactory real world. Jane Alpert accepted male chauvinism in, as well as out of, the "square" life. Dave Dellinger began to teach at Yale. Bob Dylan enjoyed his $2 million Malibu neocastle. Black leaders gave up Third-World haunts. Robert Williams surrendered. Eldridge Cleaver returned to the evangelical faith of his forefathers.

But for more than a decade a rip-tide had moved under the surface of fashionable dissent. The social fabric had been weakened and frayed. It was not only that ideologues like Diana Oughton and Ted Gold, had risked and lost their lives; or that Ralph Featherstone had been blown up in a car which carried a bomb. Thousands of other Americans had fled into uncertain exile. The cult of drugs had spread. Normal defense mechanisms were put to sleep. A generation was wounded. "The West," mourned Solzhenitsyn, "suffers from the spirit of Munich . . . a sickness of the will of successful people."

Solzhenitsyn is a man whose fears are not vague, who has felt the future in his skin. In precise practical terms he sees the antidemocratic war move steadily forward. It is clear that in Vietnam where all the devices of "unconventional" war were used, a conventional army eventually invaded from the north—five excellently armed divisions—to deliver the *coup de grâce*. Now as reliable reports come of the weakness of the U.S. defense, the USSR builds up *both* its military and naval might, and its armies of secret cadres. In France last year terrorist acts doubled; and we see the "terror tool" refining itself. Judicial and court dignitaries and ambassadors are kidnapped, as well as business tycoons and bankers. "Pinpoint coercion" demonstrates its possibilities (this may be defined as pressure for specific purposes, the sadistic long-drawn-out bargaining for the life of Aldo Moro in Italy for instance, or the assassination of effective intellectuals). Terrorism upsets the balance in Europe, further weakens Israel, is reaching an apogee as Cuban troops penetrate country after country in Africa to lend weapons and expertise to local liberation groups. Moscow, whose *apparat* has made it possible to use Czechs and Cubans and Arabs to arm and train both wings of the IRA and to master-mind a coup in Afghanistan, has demonstrated her preparedness by massive airlifts into Angola and Ethiopia.

As we enter an era in which, for the first time, the physical security of the United States is placed at risk, our spokesmen seem curiously tentative. Presidents and ministers, members of Congress, religious leaders, intellectuals of all kinds, editors and television announcers, all combine to produce unsuitable statements. Just as Robert Kennedy told C. L. Sulzberger before his assassination that Castro was "very dead" and "getting nowhere," and as President Ford stated that Moscow did "not control Eastern Europe," Javits and Pell, viewing Cuban schools

Epilogue

and hotels built with slave labor, talked of "frank and warm exchanges" and Henry Kissinger thought that the Cubans had acted on "their own initiative" in Angola. Soon Andrew Young was to suggest that the Cubans were "stabilizing" Africa; and after Zaire President Carter asked, with the charm of a child, whether *détente* was not being damaged? (As Santamaria pointed out with regard to Zaire, most of the 3,000 white Westerners fled from that country, which is the source of so many metals necessary to the democracies—in other words, the USSR got what it wanted.)

Recently there has been a U.S. effort to communicate more clearly and decisively with the Soviet Union (and to rally possible allies, including China), but this may be too late. Not only does the West lag in military matters, but the importance of the information war remains unclarified. Was it really necessary for so long a period to go by—in fact, for the Vietnam war to end—before the links between antiwar groups such as the Coalition for Peace and Justice in America and the United States Communist Party, the Soviet-directed World Peace Coalition, and the Hanoi-controlled Central Office for South Vietnam were clearly spoken of? As Denis Warner claims in *Not By Guns Alone*, captured COSVN documents show that military operations in Vietnam were closely coordinated with antiwar operations in the United States, and such activities were supported by the Soviet Union through Swedish and Swiss banks. Where were the investigative journalists then? Was it considered old fashioned to look for the long-familiar use of Communist fronts?

Western reporters in Vietnam tended to relax into what they seem to have felt was an easy task. Among the hundreds who had been in Cambodia during the hostilities, for instance, only a handful went to the refugee camps on the Thai border, where serious information about the new Cambodian society could be obtained. (For that matter, how many reporters went to refugees who had escaped Stalin in the thirties and forties?) How many went to the World Council of Churches to inquire why it was sending aid to guerrillas who kidnapped Rhodesian school-children—the boys for soldiers, the girls for concubines and porters? I myself remember being met with "astonished" liberal protests during the sixties when I argued that the truth about Cuba lay with the Cubans who had escaped Castro. Similarly, in 1969, attempts to find out the truth about China's export of heroin to the United States met with pro-Maoist scorn, counter-accusations against Taiwan or the CIA, and official opposition. I tried to pressure admissions from the Department of Narcotics in Hong Kong that opium and its derivatives were reaching the British colony. The denials were as firm as they were in Washington in 1970. One year later, in 1971, an admission came at last from China itself. The Egyptian editor Mohammed Hassanein Heykal, in his biography of Nasser, described a conversation which took place between Nasser and Chou En-lai. Talking of Vietnam, Chou among other things spoke of the inevitable demoralization of the American soldier: "Their flesh will . . . be close to our claws. . . . Some of them are trying opium. And we are helping them. We are planting the best kinds of opium especially for the American soldiers in Vietnam." (As if the State Department had decided to "go public" at last, a report also issued in 1971, came from Representative Robert Steel detailing the story of 800 U.S. deserters, some of whom were militantly pro-Commuist, making their living as drug distributors in the Saigon underworld.)

There are those among us who would put down these disasters to our overall lack of morality: if the United States had not tried to interfere in Asia . . . if we were not such an affluent and wasteful society . . . if there were jobs for the unemployed. . . . Yet the truth is that global leadership belongs to the Western democracies not because they are perfect, but because they are practised in self-government—more flexible, more just, more balanced—than the regressive totalitarian movements which sweep the world.

In Cambodia the carnage—which Bernard Levin described in the *London Times* as "so dreadful, so implacable, so widespread—has even now not ended. It continues while the capital, according to Yugoslavian journalists, has become a ghost-like city of abandoned schools, pagodas without monks, empty houses. The killing persists in the countryside and flows over the borders of Thailand so that villages are the scenes of raids where the Khmer Rouge take no rice, no cattle, but only lives—for instance, at Khong Khor as reported in 1977 by John McBeth, the lives of five children from one family, cutting their throats with jagged knives and flinging them to the ground like rag dolls. As in pre-Christian times, the "horde" rides. Similarly it rides in Africa, with tribal fervor and Marxist encouragement, making the "Colonial" era seem like a Golden Age.

With reason, critics of North America have castigated the materialism here, the vulagrity, the crime, the indulgence, the pornography and lassitude which entraps the young. Yet in 1976 journalists saw another kind of entrapment, when pathetic orphaned children, only nine or ten years old, were being educated by the Khmer Rouge to aid in killing the "enemies of the people" heaving onto the gallows rope from which dangled their unfortunate teacher, and chanting aloud, "Unfit teacher! Unfit teacher!"

Can we say then that the global outlook is so much better now than that which saw the misbegotten countenance of Hitler (in which, as Count Reck-Malleczewen says "two melancholy eyes were set like raisins"). Or that the flight into civilization is not still more comfortable than remaining at the dangerous outpost?

The Communist regimes (and it is too early to rejoice in the Sino-

Epilogue

Soviet split) had set their hopes on converting the West, but since this had not and now seems will not, occur, short of war, there remains only subversion, that "discreet and pitiless" weapon which the democracies do not completely understand, and to which they are curiously vulnerable. Already new coordinated Soviet-inspired campaigns, similar to those extant during the Vietnam war, pull the strings for an extended antinuclear and antiuranium-mining movement in the West—this while Russia herself has increased her nuclear activities five-fold. And we continue in our disastrous inability to combat KGB aggressions. As Brian Crozier has said, it is a very naive nation which exposes all its governmental mistakes under TV lights, and passes on secret knowledge to its adversaries. In the face of "unconventional warfare" it seems necessary to cease to deny that conspiracy which Babeuf developed and of which Lenin approved, and of which the 60s and 70s have seen so much evidence. It seems necessary not only for the West to hope for peace, but to be armed with scepticism and vigilance, and to prepare for a many-sided war.

In November of 1977, a Buddhist monk Thich Man Giac, who—ironically—belonged to the famous temple of An Quang which helped to topple three governments in South Vietnam, escaped by sea to tell the world about the plight of his country. After his long grim testimony in Washington he was asked whether the present system in his country was more repressive than those before it, including those during the unsuccessful war being waged with the help of the Americans? "Yes," Man Giac answered in a low voice and with what seemed an air of shame, "yes, yes, this system is worse."